T0385053

# Jaguar XJ6
# Service and Repair Manual

## Mike Stubblefield

### Models covered

*(3261-248-9AG2)*

Jaguar XJ6 models with 3.2 litre (3239 cc), 3.6 litre (3590 cc) & 4.0 litre (3980 cc) six-cylinder in-line dohc petrol engines and automatic transmission

*Covers most features of Daimler 3.6 and 4.0 litre models*
*Does not cover 2.9 litre (2919 cc) sohc engine or manual transmission*
*Does not cover XJR models or revised Jaguar/Daimler model ranges introduced September 1994*

© Haynes Group Limited 2003

A book in the **Haynes Service and Repair Manual Series**

ISBN **978 1 78521 360 1**

**British Library Cataloguing in Publication Data**
A catalogue record for this book is available from the British Library.

**Haynes Group Limited**
**Haynes North America, Inc**

**www.haynes.com**

## Disclaimer

There are risks associated with automotive repairs. The ability to make repairs depends on the individual's skill, experience and proper tools. Individuals should act with due care and acknowledge and assume the risk of performing automotive repairs.

The purpose of this manual is to provide comprehensive, useful and accessible automotive repair information, to help you get the best value from your vehicle. However, this manual is not a substitute for a professional certified technician or mechanic.

This repair manual is produced by a third party and is not associated with an individual vehicle manufacturer. If there is any doubt or discrepancy between this manual and the owner's manual or the factory service manual, please refer to the factory service manual or seek assistance from a professional certified technician or mechanic.

Even though we have prepared this manual with extreme care and every attempt is made to ensure that the information in this manual is correct, neither the publisher nor the author can accept responsibility for loss, damage or injury caused by any errors in, or omissions from, the information given.

# Contents

## LIVING WITH YOUR JAGUAR XJ6

## Roadside repairs

## Weekly checks

## MAINTENANCE

## Routine maintenance and servicing

# Contents

These models are equipped with dual overhead cam in-line six-cylinder engines. The engines feature a computer-controlled ignition system and electronic fuel injection. Transmissions are a four-speed automatic equipped with a lock-up torque converter. The transmission is mounted to the back of the engine, and power is transmitted to the fully independent rear axle through a two-piece propshaft. The differential is bolted solidly to a frame crossmember and drives the wheels through driveshafts equipped with inner and outer U-joints.

The front suspension is fitted with upper and lower control arms, coil springs and shock absorbers. The rear suspension is an independent type suspension which also have coil spring/shock absorber assemblies and a lower control arm. The rear driveshaft acts as the upper control arm.

Power-assisted Anti-lock Brake Systems (ABS) with four-wheel disc brakes are standard equipment on all Jaguar XJ6 models covered in this manual. Power rack-and-pinion steering is also standard equipment.

### Your Jaguar manual

The aim of this manual is to help you get the best value from your vehicle. It can do so in several ways. It can help you decide what work must be done (even should you choose to get it done by a garage). It will also provide information on routine maintenance and servicing, and give a logical course of action and diagnosis when random faults occur. However, it is hoped that you will use the manual by tackling the work yourself. On simpler jobs it may even be quicker than booking the car into a garage and going there twice, to leave and collect it. Perhaps most important, a lot of money can be saved by avoiding the costs a garage must charge to cover its labour and overheads.

The manual has drawings and descriptions to show the function of the various components so that their layout can be understood. Tasks are described and photographed in a clear step-by-step sequence.

### Notes for UK readers

Because this manual was originally written in the US, its layout differs from our UK-originated manuals. The preliminary and reference sections have been re-written specifically for the UK market, and the maintenance schedule has been amended to suit UK vehicles. However, it will be noticed that some references to components remain in the US style; the UK equivalent of US components and various other US words is given in the Section headed "*Use of English*". It should be remembered that the project vehicle used in the main Chapters of this manual was a left-hand drive US model; therefore, the position of the steering wheel, steering column and pedals, etc. will be on the opposite side of the vehicle on UK models. References to "right" and "left" will need to be considered carefully to decide which applies to UK models (eg the headlight dipped beams should be adjusted to dip to the left of the headlight vertical line described in Chapter 12, instead of to the right on US models). In other instances, no reference is made to the location of a particular item, but that item may be located on the opposite side of the vehicle on UK models. Reference to the underbonnet photos at the start of Chapter 1 will give the reader the location of the engine compartment components on UK models.

All specifications in the main Chapters of the manual appear in Imperial form; the equivalent metric values can be calculated using the "*Conversion factors*" page.

The only other major difference between UK and US models is in the level of emission control equipment fitted to the vehicle. To meet the strict emission standards present in the US, all vehicles for that market are fitted with various emission control systems (see Chapter 6), most of which are not fitted to the corresponding UK model, especially so on early models. Therefore, a lot of the information contained in Chapter 6 is not applicable to UK models.

### Acknowledgements

Thanks are due to Jean Preis, Rich Wilson and Ray Marcuse of Silver Star Jaguar (Thousand Oaks, CA), Rick Calaci of Conejo Imports (Newbury Park, CA) and Jim Strohmeier and Jonathan Lund of British Motor Cars (Thousand Oaks, CA), for providing valuable technical information. Technical writers who contributed to this project include Jeff Kibler, Robert Maddox and Jay Storer.

**We take great pride in the accuracy of information given in this manual, but vehicle manufacturers make alterations and design changes during the production run of a particular vehicle of which they do not inform us. No liability can be accepted by the authors or publishers for loss, damage or injury caused by any errors in, or omissions from, the information given.**

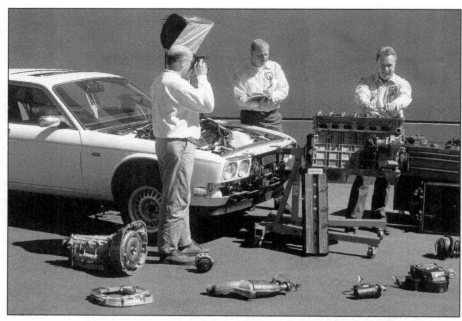

**Haynes mechanic, author and photographer with 1989 Jaguar XJ6**

Working on your car can be dangerous. This page shows just some of the potential risks and hazards, with the aim of creating a safety-conscious attitude.

# General hazards

### Scalding

• Don't remove the radiator or expansion tank cap while the engine is hot.
• Engine oil, automatic transmission fluid or power steering fluid may also be dangerously hot if the engine has recently been running.

### Burning

• Beware of burns from the exhaust system and from any part of the engine. Brake discs and drums can also be extremely hot immediately after use.

### Crushing

• When working under or near a raised vehicle, always supplement the jack with axle stands, or use drive-on ramps. *Never venture under a car which is only supported by a jack.*
• Take care if loosening or tightening high-torque nuts when the vehicle is on stands. Initial loosening and final tightening should be done with the wheels on the ground.

### Fire

• Fuel is highly flammable; fuel vapour is explosive.
• Don't let fuel spill onto a hot engine.
• Do not smoke or allow naked lights (including pilot lights) anywhere near a vehicle being worked on. Also beware of creating sparks (electrically or by use of tools).
• Fuel vapour is heavier than air, so don't work on the fuel system with the vehicle over an inspection pit.
• Another cause of fire is an electrical overload or short-circuit. Take care when repairing or modifying the vehicle wiring.
• Keep a fire extinguisher handy, of a type suitable for use on fuel and electrical fires.

### Electric shock

• Ignition HT voltage can be dangerous, especially to people with heart problems or a pacemaker. Don't work on or near the ignition system with the engine running or the ignition switched on.

• Mains voltage is also dangerous. Make sure that any mains-operated equipment is correctly earthed. Mains power points should be protected by a residual current device (RCD) circuit breaker.

### Fume or gas intoxication

• Exhaust fumes are poisonous; they often contain carbon monoxide, which is rapidly fatal if inhaled. Never run the engine in a confined space such as a garage with the doors shut.
• Fuel vapour is also poisonous, as are the vapours from some cleaning solvents and paint thinners.

### Poisonous or irritant substances

• Avoid skin contact with battery acid and with any fuel, fluid or lubricant, especially antifreeze, brake hydraulic fluid and Diesel fuel. Don't syphon them by mouth. If such a substance is swallowed or gets into the eyes, seek medical advice.
• Prolonged contact with used engine oil can cause skin cancer. Wear gloves or use a barrier cream if necessary. Change out of oil-soaked clothes and do not keep oily rags in your pocket.
• Air conditioning refrigerant forms a poisonous gas if exposed to a naked flame (including a cigarette). It can also cause skin burns on contact.

### Asbestos

• Asbestos dust can cause cancer if inhaled or swallowed. Asbestos may be found in gaskets and in brake and clutch linings. When dealing with such components it is safest to assume that they contain asbestos.

# Special hazards

### Hydrofluoric acid

• This extremely corrosive acid is formed when certain types of synthetic rubber, found in some O-rings, oil seals, fuel hoses etc, are exposed to temperatures above 400°C. The rubber changes into a charred or sticky substance containing the acid. *Once formed, the acid remains dangerous for years. If it gets onto the skin, it may be necessary to amputate the limb concerned.*
• When dealing with a vehicle which has suffered a fire, or with components salvaged from such a vehicle, wear protective gloves and discard them after use.

### The battery

• Batteries contain sulphuric acid, which attacks clothing, eyes and skin. Take care when topping-up or carrying the battery.
• The hydrogen gas given off by the battery is highly explosive. Never cause a spark or allow a naked light nearby. Be careful when connecting and disconnecting battery chargers or jump leads.

### Air bags

• Air bags can cause injury if they go off accidentally. Take care when removing the steering wheel and/or facia. Special storage instructions may apply.

### Diesel injection equipment

• Diesel injection pumps supply fuel at very high pressure. Take care when working on the fuel injectors and fuel pipes.

⚠️ *Warning: Never expose the hands, face or any other part of the body to injector spray; the fuel can penetrate the skin with potentially fatal results.*

---

# Remember...

### DO

• Do use eye protection when using power tools, and when working under the vehicle.

• Do wear gloves or use barrier cream to protect your hands when necessary.

• Do get someone to check periodically that all is well when working alone on the vehicle.

• Do keep loose clothing and long hair well out of the way of moving mechanical parts.

• Do remove rings, wristwatch etc, before working on the vehicle – especially the electrical system.

• Do ensure that any lifting or jacking equipment has a safe working load rating adequate for the job.

### DON'T

• Don't attempt to lift a heavy component which may be beyond your capability – get assistance.

• Don't rush to finish a job, or take unverified short cuts.

• Don't use ill-fitting tools which may slip and cause injury.

• Don't leave tools or parts lying around where someone can trip over them. Mop up oil and fuel spills at once.

• Don't allow children or pets to play in or near a vehicle being worked on.

The following pages are intended to help in dealing with common roadside emergencies and breakdowns. You will find more detailed fault finding information at the back of the manual, and repair information in the main chapters.

# If your car won't start and the starter motor doesn't turn

- ☐ If it's a model with automatic transmission, make sure the selector is in 'P' or 'N'.
- ☐ Open the bonnet and make sure that the battery terminals are clean and tight.
- ☐ Switch on the headlights and try to start the engine. If the headlights go very dim when you're trying to start, the battery is probably flat. Get out of trouble by jump starting (see next page) using a friend's car.

# If your car won't start even though the starter motor turns as normal

- ☐ Is there fuel in the tank?
- ☐ Is there moisture on electrical components under the bonnet? Switch off the ignition, then wipe off any obvious dampness with a dry cloth. Spray a water-repellent aerosol product (WD-40 or equivalent) on ignition and fuel system electrical connectors like those shown in the photos. Pay special attention to the ignition coil wiring connector and HT leads.

A Check the condition and security of the battery connections.

B Check that the spark plug HT leads are securely connected by pushing them onto the plugs and distributorery connections.

C Check that the HT leads and wiring connectors are securely connected to the ignition coil.

D Check that the wiring connectors are securely connected to the injectors and various fuel system sensors and switches.

Check that electrical connections are secure (with the ignition switched off) and spray them with a water dispersant spray like WD40 if you suspect a problem due to damp

# Jump starting

When jump-starting a car using a booster battery, observe the following precautions:

✔ Before connecting the booster battery, make sure that the ignition is switched off.

✔ Ensure that all electrical equipment (lights, heater, wipers, etc) is switched off.

✔ Take note of any special precautions printed on the battery case.

✔ Make sure that the booster battery is the same voltage as the discharged one in the vehicle.

✔ If the battery is being jump-started from the battery in another vehicle, the two vehicles MUST NOT TOUCH each other.

✔ Make sure that the transmission is in neutral (or PARK, in the case of automatic transmission).

**1** Connect one end of the red jump lead to the positive (+) terminal of the flat battery

**2** Connect the other end of the red lead to the positive (+) terminal of the booster battery.

**3** Connect one end of the black jump lead to the negative (-) terminal of the booster battery

**4** Connect the other end of the black jump lead to a bolt or bracket on the engine block, well away from the battery, on the vehicle to be started.

**5** Make sure that the jump leads will not come into contact with the fan, drive-belts or other moving parts of the engine.

**6** Start the engine using the booster battery and run it at idle speed. Switch on the lights, rear window demister and heater blower motor, then disconnect the jump leads in the reverse order of connection. Turn off the lights etc.

# Wheel changing

Some of the details shown here will vary according to model. For instance, the location of the spare wheel and jack is not the same on all cars. However, the basic principles apply to all vehicles.

 *Warning: Do not change a wheel in a situation where you risk being hit by other traffic. On busy roads, try to stop in a lay-by or a gateway. Be wary of passing traffic while changing the wheel – it is easy to become distracted by the job in hand.*

## Preparation

☐ When a puncture occurs, stop as soon as it is safe to do so.
☐ Park on firm level ground, if possible, and well out of the way of other traffic.
☐ Use hazard warning lights if necessary.

☐ If you have one, use a warning triangle to alert other drivers of your presence.
☐ Apply the handbrake and engage first or reverse gear (or Park on models with automatic transmission.

☐ Chock the wheel diagonally opposite the one being removed – a couple of large stones will do for this.
☐ If the ground is soft, use a flat piece of wood to spread the load under the jack.

## Changing the wheel

**1** The spare wheel and tools are stored in the boot. Remove the carpet cover then unscrew the retainer and lift out the spare wheel from the boot.

**2** Remove the jack and wheelbrace its holder which is located behind the spare wheel.

**3** With the vehicle on the ground, remove the trim cap (where fitted) and slacken each wheel nut by half a turn.

**4** Remove the plastic cover from the end of the vehicle jack lifting point tube, nearest to the wheel that is being changed.

**5** Slide the lifting bracket of the jack fully into the lifting point tube. Make sure the jack is located on firm ground.

**6** Raise the jack until the wheel is raised clear of the ground. Unscrew the wheel nuts and remove the wheel. Fit the spare wheel and screw on the nuts. Lightly tighten the nuts then lower the vehicle to the ground.

**7** Securely tighten the wheel nuts in a diagonal sequence then (where necessary) refit the wheel trim cap. Stow the tolls and punctured wheel and back in the luggage compartment and secure them in position. Note that the wheel nuts should be slackened and retightened to the specified torque at the earliest possible opportunity.

## Finally...

☐ Remove the wheel chocks.
☐ Check the tyre pressure on the wheel just fitted. If it is low, or if you don't have a pressure gauge with you, drive slowly to the nearest garage and inflate the tyre to the right pressure.
☐ Have the damaged tyre or wheel repaired as soon as possible.

Puddles on the garage floor or drive, or obvious wetness under the bonnet or underneath the car, suggest a leak that needs investigating. It can sometimes be difficult to decide where the leak is coming from, especially if the engine bay is very dirty already. Leaking oil or fluid can also be blown rearwards by the passage of air under the car, giving a false impression of where the problem lies.

 *Warning: Most automotive oils and fluids are poisonous. Wash them off skin, and change out of contaminated clothing, without delay.*

 *The smell of a fluid leaking from the car may provide a clue to what's leaking. Some fluids are distinctively coloured. It may help to clean the car and to park it over some clean paper as an aid to locating the source of the leak. Remember that some leaks may only occur while the engine is running.*

## Sump oil

Engine oil may leak from the drain plug...

## Oil from filter

...or from the base of the oil filter.

## Gearbox oil

Gearbox oil can leak from the seals at the inboard ends of the driveshafts.

## Antifreeze

Leaking antifreeze often leaves a crystalline deposit like this.

## Brake fluid

A leak occurring at a wheel is almost certainly brake fluid.

## Power steering fluid

Power steering fluid may leak from the pipe connectors on the steering rack.

# Towing

When all else fails, you may find yourself having to get a tow home – or of course you may be helping somebody else. Long-distance recovery should only be done by a garage or breakdown service. For shorter distances, DIY towing using another car is easy enough, but observe the following points:

☐ Use a proper tow-rope – they are not expensive. The vehicle being towed must display an 'ON TOW' sign in its rear window.

☐ Always turn the ignition key to the 'on' position when the vehicle is being towed, so that the steering lock is released, and that the direction indicator and brake lights will work.

☐ Only attach the tow-rope to the towing eyes provided. On some models with energy-absorbing bumpers there are no front towing eyes; on these vehicles the tow-rope should be attached around the rear arm of the lower control arm so that the rope passes on the inside of the coil spring.

☐ Before being towed, release the handbrake and select neutral on the transmission.

☐ Note that greater-than-usual pedal pressure will be required to operate the brakes, since the vacuum servo unit is only operational with the engine running.

☐ On models with power steering, greater-than-usual steering effort will also be required.

☐ The driver of the car being towed must keep the tow-rope taut at all times to avoid snatching.

☐ Make sure that both drivers know the route before setting off.

☐ Only drive at moderate speeds and keep the distance towed to a minimum. Drive smoothly and allow plenty of time for slowing down at junctions.

☐ On models with automatic transmission, special precautions apply. If in doubt, do not tow, or transmission damage may result.

*Caution: On models with automatic transmission, if the vehicle is to be towed with its rear wheels on the ground, and extra 1.7 litres of fluid should be added to the transmission, prior to towing (this extra fluid must be drained before driving the vehicle). Even with the extra fluid added to the transmission, do not tow the vehicle at speeds in excess of 30 mph (50 kmh) or for a distance of greater than 15 miles (25 km). If towing speed/distance are to exceed these limits, then the vehicle must be towed with its rear wheels off the ground.*

## Introduction

There are some very simple checks which need only take a few minutes to carry out, but which could save you a lot of inconvenience and expense.

These "Weekly checks" require no great skill or special tools, and the small amount of time they take to perform could prove to be very well spent, for example;

☐ Keeping an eye on tyre condition and pressures, will not only help to stop them wearing out prematurely, but could also save your life.

☐ Many breakdowns are caused by electrical problems. Battery-related faults are particularly common, and a quick check on a regular basis will often prevent the majority of these.

☐ If your car develops a brake fluid leak, the first time you might know about it is when your brakes don't work properly. Checking the level regularly will give advance warning of this kind of problem.

☐ If the oil or coolant levels run low, the cost of repairing any engine damage will be far greater than fixing the leak, for example.

## Underbonnet check points

◄ **3.6 litre engine (others similar)**

*Viewed from right-hand side*

**A** *Engine oil level dipstick*
**B** *Engine oil filler cap*
**C** *Coolant expansion tank*
**D** *Brake fluid reservoir*
**E** *Screen washer fluid reservoir*
**F** *Battery*
**G** *Power steering fluid reservoir*

# Engine oil level

## Before you start

✔ Make sure that your car is on level ground.
✔ Check the oil level before the car is driven, or at least 5 minutes after the engine has been switched off.

 **HAYNES HINT** *If the oil level is checked immediately after driving the vehicle, some of the oil will remain in the upper engine components, resulting in an inaccurate reading on the dipstick!*

## The correct oil

*Modern engines place great demands on their oil. It is very important that the correct oil for your car is used (See "Lubricants, fluids and tyre pressures").*

## Car care

● If you have to add oil frequently, you should check whether you have any oil leaks. Place some clean paper under the car overnight, and check for stains in the morning. If there are no leaks, the engine may be burning oil.

● Always maintain the level between the upper and lower dipstick marks (see photo 3). If the level is too low severe engine damage may occur. Oil seal failure may result if the engine is overfilled by adding too much oil.

**1** The dipstick is located at the rear of the engine on the left-hand side (see "Under-bonnet check points" on page 0•10 for exact location). Withdraw the dipstick.

**2** Using a clean rag or paper towel remove all oil from the dipstick. Insert the clean dipstick into the tube as far as it will go, then withdraw it again.

**3** Note the oil level on the end of the dipstick which should be between the upper and lower marks. The "M" mark is for use when checking the oil level after the vehicle has been standing overnight; in this case the oil level should be between the "M" and upper level markings.

**4** Oil is added through the filler cap. Unscrew the cap and top-up the level; a funnel may help to reduce spillage. Add the oil slowly, checking the level on the dipstick often. Don't overfill (see *Car care* left).

# Coolant level

 *Warning: DO NOT attempt to remove the expansion tank pressure cap when the engine is hot, as there is a very great risk of scalding. Do not leave open containers of coolant about, as it is poisonous.*

## Car care

● Adding coolant should not be necessary on a regular basis. If frequent topping-up is required, it is likely there is a leak. Check the radiator, all hoses and joint faces for signs of staining or wetness, and rectify as necessary.
● It is important that antifreeze is used in the cooling system all year round, not just during the winter months. Don't top-up with water alone, as the antifreeze will become too diluted.

**1** The coolant level should be checked only with the engine cold. The level is checked in the expansion tank on the left-hand side of the engine compartment. Remove the expansion tank pressure cap and check that the coolant level is upto the base of filler neck.

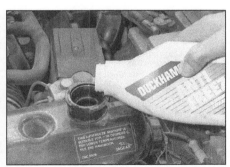

**2** If topping up is necessary, add a mixture of water and antifreeze to the expansion tank until the coolant level is upto the base of the filler neck. Once the level is correct, securely refit the pressure cap.

# Brake fluid level

**Warning:**
● *Brake fluid can harm your eyes and will damage painted surfaces, so use extreme caution when handling and pouring it.*
● *Do not use fluid that has been standing open for some time, as it absorbs moisture from the air, which can cause a dangerous loss of braking effectiveness.*

• *Make sure that your car is on level ground.*
• *The fluid level in the reservoir will drop slightly as the brake pads wear down, but the fluid level must never be allowed to drop below the "MIN" mark.*

## Safety first!

● If the reservoir requires repeated topping-up this is an indication of a fluid leak somewhere in the system, which should be investigated immediately.

● If a leak is suspected, the car should not be driven until the braking system has been checked. Never take any risks where brakes are concerned.

1 The brake fluid reservoir is located on the right-hand rear corner of the engine compartment, on top of the master cylinder.

2 The upper (MAX) and lower (MIN) fluid level markings are on the side of the brake fluid reservoir. The fluid level must always be kept between these two marks.

3 If topping up is necessary, first wipe clean the area around the filler cap with a clean cloth then unscrew the cap and position it clear of the reservoir.

4 Carefully add fluid, avoiding spilling it on the surrounding paintwork. Use only the specified hydraulic fluid. After filling the correct level, refit the cap and tighten it securely. Wipe off any spilt fluid.

# Screen washer fluid level

Screenwash additives not only keep the winscreen clean during foul weather, they also prevent the washer system freezing in cold weather - which is when you are likely to need it most. Don't top up using plain water as the screenwash will become too diluted, and will freeze during cold weather. *On no account use coolant antifreeze in the washer system - this could discolour or damage paintwork.*

1 The screen washer fluid reservoir is located in the front, right-hand corner of the engine compartment. The level is visible through the reservoir body.

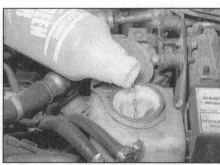

2 If topping up is necessary, add water and a screenwash additive in the quantities recommended on the bottle.

# Power steering fluid level

## Before you start:
✔ Park the vehicle on level ground.
✔ Set the steering wheel straight-ahead.
✔ The engine should be turned off.

 **HAYNES HiNT** *For the check to be accurate, the steering must not be turned once the engine has been stopped.*

## Safety first!
● The need for frequent topping-up indicates a leak, which should be investigated immediately.

 *Warning:*
*● This check applies only to vehicles fitted with a separate power steering system. For vehicles fitted with power steering where the fluid reservoir is part of the power hydraulic system, this weekly check is not applicable.*
*● It is essential to use the correct power steering fluid, this being dependent on the year of manufacture and type of system fitted. A label attached to the fluid reservoir will indicate the specification of fluid. However, if necessary refer to the driver's handbook supplied with the vehicle or to your local Jaguar dealer.*

**1** Wipe clean the area around the reservoir cap then remove the cap noting that it unscrews in a clockwise direction (see arrow on cap).

**2** Wipe clean the cap dipstick then insert it fully into the reservoir and withdraw it.

**3** Note the fluid level on the end of the dipstick. If the fluid is cold (vehicle not having been used) the fluid level should be upto the COLD level marking (1). If the vehicle has been driven and the fluid is hot then the fluid level should be upto the upper (HOT) level marking (2).

**4** If necessary, top-up the reservoir with the specified type of fluid (note that the type of fluid differs according to model - see *"Lubricants, fluids and tyre pressures"* on page 0•16). Once the level is correct, securely refit the reservoir cap. Do not overfill the reservoir.

# Wiper blades

**1** Check the condition of the wiper blades: if they are cracked or show signs of deterioration, or if the glass swept area is smeared, renew them. For maximum clarity of vision, wiper blades should be renewed annually.

**2** To remove a wiper blade, pull the arm fully away from the screen until it locks. Swivel the blade then depress the locking clip at the base of the mounting block and slide the blade off the arm.

# Tyre condition and pressure

It is very important that tyres are in good condition, and at the correct pressure - having a tyre failure at any speed is highly dangerous. Tyre wear is influenced by driving style - harsh braking and acceleration, or fast cornering, will all produce more rapid tyre wear. As a general rule, the front tyres wear out faster than the rears. Interchanging the tyres from front to rear ("rotating" the tyres) may result in more even wear. However, if this is completely effective, you may have the expense of replacing all four tyres at once! Remove any nails or stones embedded in the tread before they penetrate the tyre to cause deflation. If removal of a nail does reveal that the tyre has been punctured, refit the nail so that its point of penetration is marked. Then immediately change the wheel, and have the tyre repaired by a tyre dealer.

Regularly check the tyres for damage in the form of cuts or bulges, especially in the sidewalls. Periodically remove the wheels, and clean any dirt or mud from the inside and outside surfaces. Examine the wheel rims for signs of rusting, corrosion or other damage. Light alloy wheels are easily damaged by "kerbing" whilst parking; steel wheels may also become dented or buckled. A new wheel is very often the only way to overcome severe damage.

New tyres should be balanced when they are fitted, but it may become necessary to re-balance them as they wear, or if the balance weights fitted to the wheel rim should fall off. Unbalanced tyres will wear more quickly, as will the steering and suspension components. Wheel imbalance is normally signified by vibration, particularly at a certain speed (typically around 50 mph). If this vibration is felt only through the steering, then it is likely that just the front wheels need balancing. If, however, the vibration is felt through the whole car, the rear wheels could be out of balance. Wheel balancing should be carried out by a tyre dealer or garage.

**1** *Tread Depth - visual check*
The original tyres have tread wear safety bands (B), which will appear when the tread depth reaches approximately 1.6 mm. The band positions are indicated by a triangular mark on the tyre sidewall (A).

**2** *Tread Depth - manual check*
Alternatively, tread wear can be monitored with a simple, inexpensive device known as a tread depth indicator gauge.

**3** *Tyre Pressure Check*
Check the tyre pressures regularly with the tyres cold. Do not adjust the tyre pressures immediately after the vehicle has been used, or an inaccurate setting will result.

# Tyre tread wear patterns

### Shoulder Wear

**Underinflation (wear on both sides)**
Under-inflation will cause overheating of the tyre, because the tyre will flex too much, and the tread will not sit correctly on the road surface. This will cause a loss of grip and excessive wear, not to mention the danger of sudden tyre failure due to heat build-up.
*Check and adjust pressures*
**Incorrect wheel camber (wear on one side)**
*Repair or renew suspension parts*
**Hard cornering**
*Reduce speed!*

### Centre Wear

**Overinflation**
Over-inflation will cause rapid wear of the centre part of the tyre tread, coupled with reduced grip, harsher ride, and the danger of shock damage occurring in the tyre casing.
*Check and adjust pressures*

*If you sometimes have to inflate your car's tyres to the higher pressures specified for maximum load or sustained high speed, don't forget to reduce the pressures to normal afterwards.*

### Uneven Wear

Front tyres may wear unevenly as a result of wheel misalignment. Most tyre dealers and garages can check and adjust the wheel alignment (or "tracking") for a modest charge.
**Incorrect camber or castor**
*Repair or renew suspension parts*
**Malfunctioning suspension**
*Repair or renew suspension parts*
**Unbalanced wheel**
*Balance tyres*
**Incorrect toe setting**
*Adjust front wheel alignment*
**Note:** *The feathered edge of the tread which typifies toe wear is best checked by feel.*

# Battery

**Caution:** *Before carrying out any work on the vehicle battery, read the precautions given in "Safety first" at the start of this manual.*

✔ Make sure that the battery tray is in good condition, and that the clamp is tight. Corrosion on the tray, retaining clamp and the battery itself can be removed with a solution of water and baking soda. Thoroughly rinse all cleaned areas with water. Any metal parts damaged by corrosion should be covered with a zinc-based primer, then painted.

✔ Periodically (approximately every three months), check the charge condition of the battery as described in Chapter 5.

✔ If the battery is flat, and you need to jump start your vehicle, see *Roadside Repairs*.

**HAYNES HINT**

*Battery corrosion can be kept to a minimum by applying a layer of petroleum jelly to the clamps and terminals after they are reconnected.*

**1** The battery is located in the left-hand, rear corner of the engine compartment. Check the battery terminals for signs of corrosion and examine the battery leads closely for signs of damage.

**3** If corrosion (white, fluffy deposits) is evident, remove the cables from the battery terminals, clean them with a small wire brush, then refit them. Automotive stores sell a tool for cleaning the battery post . . .

**2** Check the battery lead clamps for tightness to ensure good electrical connections.

**4** . . . as well as the battery cable clamps

---

# Bulbs and fuses

✔ Check all external lights and the horn. Refer to the appropriate Sections of Chapter 12 for details if any of the circuits are found to be inoperative.

✔ Visually check all accessible wiring connectors, harnesses and retaining clips for security, and for signs of chafing or damage.

**HAYNES HINT**

*If you need to check your brake lights and indicators unaided, back up to a wall or garage door and operate the lights. The reflected light should show if they are working properly.*

**1** If a single indicator light, stop light or headlight has failed, it is likely that a bulb has blown and will need to be replaced. Refer to Chapter 12 for details. If both stop lights have failed, it is possible that the switch has failed (see Chapter 9).

**2** If more than one indicator light or tail light has failed it is likely that either a fuse has blown or that there is a fault in the circuit. The fuseboxes are located behind the left and right side kick panels and in the centre console glove box (see Chapter 12).

**3** To replace a blown fuse, simply pull it out and fit a new fuse of the correct rating (see Chapter 12). If the fuse blows again, it is important that you find out why - a complete checking procedure is given in Chapter 12.

## Lubricants and fluids

| | |
|---|---|
| **Engine** | Multigrade engine oil to API SG or higher |
| **Cooling system** | Ethylene glycol based (phosphate free) antifreeze |
| **Automatic transmission** | Dexron type II automatic transmission fluid (ATF) |
| **Differential:** | |
| Standard differential | SAE EP90 to API GL5 |
| Powr-lok differential | SAE 90 to API GL5 |
| **Braking system** | Hydraulic fluid to DOT 4 |
| **Power steering (with separate reservoir)** | *dependent on year of manufacture and system fitted - refer to your Jaguar dealer* |
| **Power hydraulic system** | Castrol or Jaguar hydraulic system mineral oil (HSMO) *Refer to your Jaguar dealer* |

## Choosing your engine oil

Engines need oil, not only to lubricate moving parts and minimise wear, but also to maximise power output and to improve fuel economy.

### HOW ENGINE OIL WORKS

#### • *Beating friction*

Without oil, the moving surfaces inside your engine will rub together, heat up and melt, quickly causing the engine to seize. Engine oil creates a film which separates these moving parts, preventing wear and heat build-up.

#### • *Cooling hot-spots*

Temperatures inside the engine can exceed 1000º C. The engine oil circulates and acts as a coolant, transferring heat from the hot-spots to the sump.

#### • *Cleaning the engine internally*

Good quality engine oils clean the inside of your engine, collecting and dispersing combustion deposits and controlling them until they are trapped by the oil filter or flushed out at oil change.

### OIL CARE - FOLLOW THE CODE

To handle and dispose of used engine oil safely, always:

- *Avoid skin contact with used engine oil. Repeated or prolonged contact can be harmful.*
- *Dispose of used oil and empty packs in a responsible manner in an authorised disposal site. Call 0800 663366 to find the one nearest to you. Never tip oil down drains or onto the ground.*

## Tyre pressures

**Note:** *Tyre pressures must always be checked with the tyres cold to ensure accuracy.*

| | |
|---|---|
| **Front** | 34 psi (2.3 bar) |
| **Rear** | 34 psi (2.3 bar) |

**Note:** *Jaguar state that the tyre pressures maybe reduced by up to 8 psi (0.6 bar) on the front tyres and 6 psi (0.4 bar) on the rear tyres to increase the ride comfort. This is only allowable if the vehicle is not to be driven at speeds in excess of 100 mph (160 kmh); if speeds are to exceed this, the tyres must be run at the specified pressures.*

# Chapter 1
# Routine maintenance and servicing

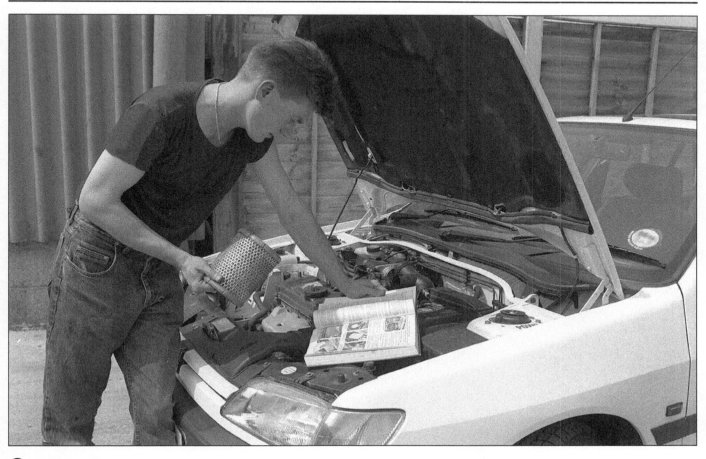

# Contents

# Degrees of difficulty

| | | | | |
|---|---|---|---|---|
| **Easy,** suitable for novice with little experience  | **Fairly easy,** suitable for beginner with some experience  | **Fairly difficult,** suitable for competent DIY mechanic  | **Difficult,** suitable for experienced DIY mechanic  | **Very difficult,** suitable for expert DIY or professional |

## Lubricants and fluids

Refer to *"Weekly checks"*

## Capacities

### Engine oil
Including oil filter . . . . . . . . . . . . . . . . . . . . . . . . . . . . . . . . . . . . . . . . . .  8.0 litres

### Cooling system
All models (approximate):
  From dry . . . . . . . . . . . . . . . . . . . . . . . . . . . . . . . . . . . . . . . . . . . . . .  12.8 litres
  Drain and refill . . . . . . . . . . . . . . . . . . . . . . . . . . . . . . . . . . . . . . . . . .  9.2 litres

### Transmission
Automatic transmission (approximate):
  From dry:
    3.2 litre model . . . . . . . . . . . . . . . . . . . . . . . . . . . . . . . . . . . . . . . .  7.4 litres
    3.6 and 4.0 litre models  . . . . . . . . . . . . . . . . . . . . . . . . . . . . . . .  8.0 litres
  Drain and refill . . . . . . . . . . . . . . . . . . . . . . . . . . . . . . . . . . . . . . . . . .  3.0 litres

### Differential
All models (approximate) . . . . . . . . . . . . . . . . . . . . . . . . . . . . . . . . . . .  2.1 litres

## Cooling system

Antifreeze mixture:
  50% antifreeze . . . . . . . . . . . . . . . . . . . . . . . . . . . . . . . . . . . . . . . . . .  Protection down to -37°C (5°F)
  55% antifreeze . . . . . . . . . . . . . . . . . . . . . . . . . . . . . . . . . . . . . . . . . .  Protection down to -45°C (-22°F)
**Note:** *Refer to antifreeze manufacturer for latest recommendations.*

## Ignition system

Spark plugs:
  Type:
    All models . . . . . . . . . . . . . . . . . . . . . . . . . . . . . . . . . . . . . . . . . . .  Bosch FR 7 D+
  Electrode gap . . . . . . . . . . . . . . . . . . . . . . . . . . . . . . . . . . . . . . . . . . .  0.9 mm
Engine firing order  . . . . . . . . . . . . . . . . . . . . . . . . . . . . . . . . . . . . . . . .  1-5-3-6-2-4
Distributor rotation . . . . . . . . . . . . . . . . . . . . . . . . . . . . . . . . . . . . . . . .  Clockwise
Ignition timing . . . . . . . . . . . . . . . . . . . . . . . . . . . . . . . . . . . . . . . . . . . .  See Chapter 5

1-5-3-6-2-4

**FRONT**

49011-1-00SPECS

**Cylinder location and distributor rotation**

## Brakes

Disc brake pad friction material minimum thickness:
  Front . . . . . . . . . . . . . . . . . . . . . . . . . . . . . . . . . . . . . . . . . . . . . . . . . . .  4.0 mm
  Rear . . . . . . . . . . . . . . . . . . . . . . . . . . . . . . . . . . . . . . . . . . . . . . . . . . .  3.0 mm
Handbrake shoe friction material minimum thickness . . . . . . . . . . . . .  1.5 mm
Handbrake adjustment . . . . . . . . . . . . . . . . . . . . . . . . . . . . . . . . . . . . .  3 to 5 clicks

## Torque wrench settings

| | Nm | lbf ft |
|---|---|---|
| Automatic transmission sump pan bolts . . . . . . . . . . . . . . . . . . . . . . . . | 8 | 6 |
| Automatic transmission dipstick tube nut . . . . . . . . . . . . . . . . . . . . . . . | 20 | 15 |
| Spark plugs . . . . . . . . . . . . . . . . . . . . . . . . . . . . . . . . . . . . . . . . . . . . . . . | 23 to 28 | 17 to 21 |
| Wheel nuts . . . . . . . . . . . . . . . . . . . . . . . . . . . . . . . . . . . . . . . . . . . . . . . | 102 | 75 |

The maintenance intervals in this manual are provided with the assumption that you, not the dealer, will be carrying out the work. These are the minimum maintenance intervals recommended by us for vehicles driven daily. If you wish to keep your vehicle in peak condition at all times, you may wish to perform some of these procedures more often. We encourage frequent maintenance, because it enhances the efficiency, performance and resale value of your vehicle.

When the vehicle is new, it should be serviced by a factory-authorised dealer service department, in order to preserve the factory warranty.

## Weekly, or every 250 miles (400 km)

☐ Carry out all the operations given in *"Weekly checks"* at the start of this manual.

## Every 7500 miles (12 000 km) or 6 months, whichever comes first

*In addition to the operations listed previously, carry out the following:*

☐ Renew the engine oil and filter (Section 3)
☐ Check the spark plugs (Section 4)
☐ Check the power hydraulics fluid level (Section 5)
☐ Check the battery (Section 6)
☐ Check all pipes and hoses for signs of damage or leakage (Section 7)
☐ Check the automatic transmission fluid level (Section 8)
☐ Check the differential oil level (Section 9)
☐ Check the condition of the exhaust system (Section 10)
☐ Check the brake pads and discs for wear and adjust the handbrake (Section 11)
☐ Check the steering and suspension components for wear or damage and check the wheel nuts are tightened to the correct torque (Section 12)
☐ Check the condition of the seat belts (Section 13)
☐ Lubricate all locks and hinges, and exposed cables (Section 14)
☐ Carry out a road test (Section 15)

## Every 15 000 miles (24 000 km) or 12 months, whichever comes first

*In addition to the operations listed previously, carry out the following:*

☐ Renew the spark plugs (Section 16)
☐ Renew the air cleaner element (Section 17)

☐ Renew the fuel filter (Section 18)
☐ Check the ignition system components (Section 19)
☐ Check the crankcase ventilation system (Section 20)
☐ Check the condition and tension of the drivebelt(s) (Section 21)
☐ Check the front wheel bearing adjustment and repack with grease (Section 22)
☐ Check the propshaft fasteners are tightened to the specified torque (Section 23)
☐ Check the front wheel alignment (Section 24)
☐ Check the headlight beam alignment (Section 25)

## Every 30 000 miles (48 000 km) or 2 years, whichever comes first

*In addition to the operations listed previously, carry out the following:*

☐ Renew the automatic transmission fluid and filter (Section 26)
☐ Renew the differential oil (Section 27)
☐ Renew the brake fluid (Section 28)

## Every 60 000 miles (96 000 km)

*In addition to the operations listed previously, carry out the following:*

☐ Check the handbrake shoes for wear (Section 29)

## Every 2 years, regardless of mileage

☐ Renew the coolant (Section 30)

## Underbonnet view from the right-hand side of the vehicle

1 Battery
2 Oil filler cap
3 Engine oil dipstick (not visible)
4 Automatic transmission dipstick (not visible)
5 Brake fluid reservoir
6 Coolant reservoir (expansion tank)
7 Air cleaner housing
8 Upper radiator hose
9 Spark plugs
10 Distributor
11 Windscreen washer fluid reservoir
12 Power hydraulic system fluid reservoir
13 Power steering fluid reservoir

## Underbonnet view from the left-hand side of the vehicle

1 Battery
2 Oil filler cap
3 Engine oil dipstick (not visible)
4 Automatic transmission dipstick (not visible)
5 Brake fluid reservoir
6 Coolant reservoir (expansion tank)
7 Air cleaner housing
8 Upper radiator hose
9 Spark plugs
10 Distributor
11 Windscreen washer fluid reservoir
12 Power hydraulic system fluid reservoir
13 Power steering fluid reservoir

## Front underbody view

1  Air conditioning compressor
2  Drivebelts
3  Anti-roll bar
4  Alternator
5  Lower radiator hose
6  Lower control arm
7  Steering gear boot
8  Steering gear
9  Engine sump drain plug
10 Exhaust system
11 Outer tie-rod end

## Rear underbody view (typical)

1  Rear suspension control arms
2  Differential drain plug
3  Differential filler plug
   (not visible)
4  Exhaust pipe
5  Driveshaft
6  Silencers
7  Handbrake cable
8  Fuel filter

## 1 General information

1 This Chapter is designed to help the home mechanic maintain his/her vehicle for safety, economy, long life and peak performance.

2 The Chapter contains a master maintenance schedule, followed by Sections dealing specifically with each task in the schedule. Visual checks, adjustments, component renewal and other helpful items are included. Refer to the accompanying illustrations of the engine compartment and the underside of the vehicle for the locations of the various components.

3 Servicing your vehicle in accordance with the mileage/time maintenance schedule and the following Sections will provide a planned maintenance programme, which should result in a long and reliable service life. This is a comprehensive plan, so maintaining some items but not others at the specified service intervals, will not produce the same results.

4 As you service your vehicle, you will discover that many of the procedures can - and should - be grouped together, because of the particular procedure being performed, or because of the proximity of two otherwise-unrelated components to one another. For example, if the vehicle is raised for any reason, the exhaust can be inspected at the same time as the suspension and steering components.

5 The first step in this maintenance programme is to prepare yourself before the actual work begins. Read through all the Sections relevant to the work to be carried out, then make a list and gather all the parts and tools required. If a problem is encountered, seek advice from a parts specialist, or a dealer service department.

## 2 Intensive maintenance

1 If, from the time the vehicle is new, the routine maintenance schedule is followed closely, and frequent checks are made of fluid levels and high-wear items, as suggested throughout this manual, the engine will be kept in relatively good running condition, and the need for additional work will be minimised.

2 It is possible that there will be times when the engine is running poorly due to the lack of regular maintenance. This is even more likely if a used vehicle, which has not received regular and frequent maintenance checks, is purchased. In such cases, additional work may need to be carried out, outside of the regular maintenance intervals.

3 If engine wear is suspected, a compression test (refer to Chapter 2) will provide valuable information regarding the overall performance of the main internal components. Such a test can be used as a basis to decide on the extent of the work to be carried out. If, for example, a compression test indicates serious internal engine wear, conventional maintenance as described in this Chapter will not greatly improve the performance of the engine, and may prove a waste of time and money, unless extensive overhaul work is carried out first.

4 The following series of operations are those which are most often required to improve the performance of a generally poor-running engine:

### Primary operations

a) Clean, inspect and test the battery (Section 6).
b) Check all the engine-related fluids (refer to "Weekly checks").
c) Check the condition and tension of the auxiliary drivebelt (Section 21).
d) Renew the spark plugs (Section 16).
e) Inspect the distributor cap and rotor arm (Section 19).
f) Check the condition of the air filter, and renew if necessary (Section 17).
g) Renew the fuel filter (Section 18).
h) Check the condition of all hoses, and check for fluid leaks (Section 7).
i) Check the exhaust gas emissions (see Chapter 6).

5 If the above operations do not prove fully effective, carry out the following secondary operations:

### Secondary operations

All items listed under "Primary operations", plus the following:

a) Check the charging system (refer to Chapter 5).
b) Check the ignition system (refer to Chapter 5).
c) Check the fuel system (refer to Chapter 4).
d) Renew the distributor cap and rotor arm (Section 19).
e) Renew the ignition HT leads (Section 19).

# Every 7500 miles (12 000 km) or 6 months

## 3 Engine oil and filter renewal

1 Frequent oil changes are the best preventive maintenance the home mechanic can give the engine, because ageing oil becomes diluted and contaminated, which leads to premature engine wear.

2 Make sure that you have all the necessary tools before you begin this procedure (see illustration). You should also have plenty of rags or newspapers handy for mopping up any spills.

3 Access to the underside of the vehicle is greatly improved if the vehicle can be lifted on a hoist, driven onto ramps or supported by axle stands.

4 If this is your first oil change, get under the vehicle and familiarise yourself with the location of the oil drain plug. The engine and

### 3.2 These tools are required when changing the engine oil and filter

1 Drain pan - It should be fairly shallow in depth, but wide in order to prevent spills
2 Rubber gloves - When removing the drain plug and filter, it is inevitable that you will get oil on your hands (the gloves will prevent burns)
3 Breaker bar - Sometimes the oil drain plug is pretty tight and a long breaker bar is needed to loosen it
4 Socket – To be used with the breaker bar or a ratchet (must be the correct size to fit the drain plug)
5 Filter wrench - This is a metal band-type wrench, which requires clearance around the filter to be effective
6 Filter wrench - This type fits on the bottom of the filter and can be turned with a ratchet or breaker bar (different size spanners are available for different types of filters)

**3.7 The oil drain plug (arrowed) is located at the rear of the sump - use a ring spanner or socket to remove it**

**3.13 The oil filter is located on the left side of the engine - use a filter wrench for removal (tighten the new filter by hand)**

**3.15 Lubricate the oil filter gasket with clean engine oil before refitting the filter**

exhaust components will be warm during the actual work, so try to anticipate any potential problems before the engine and accessories are hot.

**5** Park the vehicle on a level spot. Start the engine and allow it to reach its normal operating temperature (the needle on the temperature gauge should be at least above the bottom mark). Warm oil and contaminates will flow out more easily. Turn off the engine when it's warmed up. Remove the oil filler cap located next to the valve cover.

**6** Raise the vehicle and support it on axle stands.

 *Warning: To avoid personal injury, never get beneath the vehicle when it is supported by only by a jack. The jack provided with your vehicle is designed solely for raising the vehicle to remove and replace the wheels. Always use axle stands to support the vehicle when it becomes necessary to place your body underneath the vehicle.*

**7** Being careful not to touch the hot exhaust components, place the drain pan under the drain plug in the bottom of the pan and remove the plug **(see illustration)**. You may want to wear gloves while unscrewing the plug the final few turns if the engine is really hot.

**8** Allow the old oil to drain into the pan. It may be necessary to move the pan farther under the engine as the oil flow slows to a trickle. Inspect the old oil for the presence of metal shavings and chips.

**9** After all the oil has drained, wipe off the drain plug with a clean rag. Even minute metal particles clinging to the plug would immediately contaminate the new oil.

**10** Clean the area around the drain plug opening, refit the plug and tighten it securely, but do not strip the threads.

**11** Move the drain pan into position under the oil filter.

**12** Remove all tools, rags, etc. from under the vehicle, being careful not to spill the oil in the drain pan, then lower the vehicle.

**13** Loosen the oil filter **(see illustration)** by turning it anti-clockwise with the filter wrench. Any standard filter wrench should work. Once

the filter is loose, use your hands to unscrew it from the block. Just as the filter comes away from the block, immediately tilt the open end up to prevent the oil inside the filter from spilling out.

 *Warning: The engine exhaust pipes may still be hot, so be careful.*

**14** With a clean rag, wipe off the mounting surface on the block. If a residue of old oil is allowed to remain, it will smoke when the block is heated up. It will also prevent the new filter from seating properly. Also make sure that the none of the old gasket remains stuck to the mounting surface. It can be removed with a scraper if necessary.

**15** Compare the old filter with the new one to make sure they are the same type. Smear some engine oil on the rubber gasket of the new filter and screw it into place **(see illustration)**. Because over-tightening the filter will damage the gasket, do not use a filter wrench to tighten the filter. Tighten it by hand until the gasket contacts the seating surface. Then seat the filter by giving it an additional 3/4-turn.

**16** Add new oil to the engine through the oil filler cap next to the valve cover. Use a spout or funnel to prevent oil from spilling onto the top of the engine. Pour three litres of fresh oil into the engine. Wait a few minutes to allow the oil to drain into the pan, then check the level on the oil dipstick (see *"Weekly checks"*). If the oil level is at or near the H mark, refit the filler cap hand tight, start the engine and allow the new oil to circulate.

**17** Allow the engine to run for about a minute. While the engine is running, look under the vehicle and check for leaks at the sump drain plug and around the oil filter. If either is

leaking, stop the engine and tighten the plug or filter slightly.

**18** Wait a few minutes to allow the oil to trickle down into the pan, then recheck the level on the dipstick and, if necessary, add enough oil to bring the level to the H mark.

**19** During the first few trips after an oil change, make it a point to check frequently for leaks and proper oil level.

**20** The old oil drained from the engine cannot be reused in its present state and should be disposed of. Check with your local authority, or with a local garage to see whether they will accept the oil for recycling. **Don't** pour used oil into drains or onto the ground. After the oil has cooled, it can be drained into a suitable container (capped plastic jugs, topped bottles, etc.) for transport to an approved disposal site.

## 4  Spark plug check

**1** Spark plug renewal requires a spark plug socket which fits onto a ratchet spanner. This socket is lined with a rubber grommet to protect the porcelain insulator of the spark plug and to hold the plug while you insert it into the spark plug hole. You will also need a wire-type feeler gauge to check and adjust the spark plug gap and a torque wrench to tighten the new plugs to the specified torque **(see illustration)**.

**2** If you are replacing the plugs, purchase the new plugs, adjust them to the proper gap and then replace each plug one at a time. **Note:** *When buying new spark plugs, it's essential that you obtain the correct plugs for your specific vehicle. This information can be found in the Specifications Section at the beginning of this Chapter, on the Vehicle Emissions Control Information (VECI) label located on the underside of the bonnet (where fitted)or in the owner's manual. If these sources specify different plugs, purchase the spark plug type specified on the VECI label because that information is provided specifically for your engine.*

**OIL CARE**
FOLLOW THE CODE

OIL BANK LINE
**0800 66 33 66**
www.oilbankline.org.uk

*Note: It is antisocial and illegal to dump oil down the drain. To find the location of your local oil recycling bank, call this number free.*

**4.1 Tools required for changing spark plugs**

1 Spark plug socket - This will have special padding inside to protect the spark plug porcelain insulator
2 Torque wrench - Although not mandatory, use of this tool is the best way to ensure that the plugs are tightened properly
3 Ratchet - to fit the plug socket
4 Extension - Depending on model and accessories, you may need special extensions and universal joints to reach one or more of the plugs
5 Spark plug gap gauge - This gauge for checking the gap comes in a variety of styles. Make sure the gap for your engine is included

**3** Inspect each of the new plugs for defects. If there are any signs of cracks in the porcelain insulator of a plug, don't use it.
**4** Check the electrode gaps of the new plugs. Check the gap by inserting the wire gauge of the proper thickness between the electrodes at the tip of the plug **(see illustration)**. The gap between the electrodes should be identical to that listed in this Chapter's Specifications or on the VECI label (as applicable). If the gap is incorrect, use the notched adjuster on the feeler gauge body to bend the curved side electrode slightly **(see illustration)**.
**5** If the side electrode is not exactly over the centre electrode, use the notched adjuster to align them.

*Caution: If the gap of a new plug must be adjusted, bend only the base of the earth electrode - do not touch the tip.*

## Removal

**6** To prevent the possibility of mixing up spark plug leads, work on one spark plug at a time. Remove the lead and boot from one spark plug. Grasp the boot - not the lead - as shown, give it a half twisting motion and pull straight up **(see illustration)**.
**7** If compressed air is available, blow any dirt or foreign material away from the spark plug area before proceeding (a common bicycle pump will also work).
**8** Remove the spark plug **(see illustration)**.

**9** Whether you are replacing the plugs at this time or intend to re-use the old plugs, compare each old spark plug with the chart shown on the inside back cover of this manual to determine the overall running condition of the engine.

### Refitting

**10** Prior to refitting, apply a coat of anti-seize compound to the plug threads **(see illustration)**. It's often difficult to insert spark plugs into their holes without cross-threading them. To avoid this possibility, fit a short piece of 3/8-inch internal diameter (ID) rubber hose over the end of the spark plug **(see Haynes Hint)**. The flexible hose acts as a universal joint to help align the plug with the plug hole. Should the plug begin to cross-thread, the hose will slip on the spark plug, preventing thread damage. Tighten the plug to the torque listed in this Chapter's Specifications. In the absence of a torque wrench, tighten each plug until you feel it seat, and then by a further quarter-turn only. Do not overtighten the spark plugs.
**11** Attach the plug lead to the new spark plug, again using a twisting motion on the boot until it is firmly seated on the end of the spark plug.
**12** Follow the above procedure for the remaining spark plugs, replacing them one at a time to prevent mixing up the spark plug leads.

**4.4a Spark plug manufacturers recommend using a wire-type gauge when checking the gap - if the wire does not slide between the electrodes with a slight drag, adjustment is required**

**4.4b To change the gap, bend the side electrode only, as indicated by the arrows, and be very careful not to crack or chip the porcelain insulator surrounding the centre electrode**

**4.6 When removing the spark plug leads, grasp only the boot and use a twisting/pulling motion**

**4.8 Use a spark plug socket with a long extension to unscrew the spark plugs**

**4.10 Apply a coat of anti-seize compound to the spark plug threads**

**HAYNES HiNT**

*A length of 3/8-inch ID rubber hose will save time and prevent damaged threads when refitting the spark plugs*

**5.2 The power hydraulic system reservoir is located on the right-hand inner wing - to check the fluid level on 1988 and 1989 models simply look through the sight glass and note the colour of the indicator**

GREEN (OK)

RED INDICATOR (FLUID REQUIRED)

**5.3 To add fluid, remove the filler hole dust cap (arrowed)**

**5.7 On 1990 and later models remove the cap and check the fluid level on the dipstick**

## 5 Power hydraulic system fluid level check

*Caution: Use only Castrol or Jaguar hydraulic system mineral oil (HSMO) in the power hydraulic system (available at Jaguar dealer service departments).*

1 The power hydraulic system controls the ride levelling and the brake servo systems. **The fluid reservoir also supplies the power steering system on some models.** The level of the fluid should be carefully maintained. Low fluid levels can adversely affect the riding and braking capabilities of your vehicle. The power hydraulic system fluid reservoir is located on the right inner wing of the engine compartment.

### *1988 and 1989 models*

2 The fluid level can easily be checked by viewing the reservoir sight glass. A green indicator in the sight glass indicates an OK condition, while a red indicator in the sight glass requires fluid to be added **(see illustration)**.
3 If additional fluid is required, pop open the plastic tab located on top of the reservoir cap **(see illustration)**.
4 Insert the mineral oil dispensing tube into the reservoir filler hole. Push down and turn until the dispensing tube is locked in place.
5 Add fluid until the green indicator in the sight glass appears, then release the dispensing tube by pushing downward and turning the opposite direction of refitting.

### *1990 to 1994 models*

6 The fluid level can be checked by removing the cap and observing the level of fluid on the dipstick.
7 Wipe off the fluid with a clean rag, reinsert it, then withdraw it and read the fluid level **(see illustration)**. The dipstick is marked so the fluid can be checked either cold or hot. The level should be at the HOT mark if the fluid was hot to the touch. It should be at the COLD mark if the fluid was cool to the touch. At no time should the fluid level drop below the add mark.

8 If additional fluid is required, pour the specified type directly into the reservoir, using a funnel to prevent spills.

## 6 Battery check and general information

⚠ *Warning: Certain precautions must be followed when working with the battery. Hydrogen gas, which is highly flammable, is always present in the battery cells, so don't smoke, and keep naked flames and sparks away from the battery. The electrolyte in the battery is actually dilute sulphuric acid, which will cause injury if splashed on your skin or in your eyes. It will also ruin clothes and painted surfaces. When removing the battery cables, always detach the negative cable first and hook it up last!*

**6.1 Tools and materials required for battery maintenance**

1 A routine preventive maintenance program for the battery in your vehicle is the only way to ensure quick and reliable starts. But before performing any battery maintenance, make sure that you have the proper equipment necessary to work safely around the battery **(see illustration)**.
2 There are also several precautions that should be taken whenever battery maintenance is performed. Before servicing the battery, always turn the engine and all accessories off and disconnect the cable from the negative terminal of the battery.
3 The battery produces hydrogen gas, which is both flammable and explosive. Never create a spark, smoke or light a match around the battery. Always charge the battery in a ventilated area.
4 Electrolyte contains poisonous and corrosive sulphuric acid. Do not allow it to get in your eyes, on your skin or on your clothes, and

1 *Face shield/safety goggles - When removing corrosion with a brush, the acidic particles can fly up into your eyes*
2 *Baking soda - A solution of baking soda and water can be used to neutralise corrosion*
3 *Petroleum jelly - A layer of this on the battery posts will help prevent corrosion*
4 *Battery post/cable cleaner - This wire brush cleaning tool will remove all traces of corrosion from the battery posts and cable clamps*
5 *Treated felt washers - Placing one of these on each post, directly under the cable clamps, will help prevent corrosion*
6 *Puller - Sometimes the cable clamps are difficult to pull off the posts, even after the nut/bolt has been completely loosened. This tool pulls the clamp straight up and off the post without damage*
7 *Battery post/cable cleaner - Here is another cleaning tool which is a slightly different version of number 4 above, but it does the same thing*
8 *Rubber gloves - Another safety item to consider when servicing the battery; remember that's acid inside the battery!*

**6.6a Battery terminal corrosion usually appears as light, fluffy powder**

**6.6b Removing a cable from the battery post with a spanner - sometimes special battery pliers are required for this if corrosion has damaged the nut hex**

**6.7a Remove all the corrosion from the cable clamps (the inside of the clamp is tapered to match the taper on the post, so don't remove too much material)**

**6.7b Regardless of the type of tool used to clean the battery posts, a clean, shiny surface should be the result**

never ingest it. Wear protective safety glasses when working near the battery. Keep children away from the battery.

5 Note the external condition of the battery. If the positive terminal and cable clamp on your vehicle's battery is equipped with a rubber protector, make sure it isn't torn or damaged. It should completely cover the terminal. Look for any corroded or loose connections, cracks in the case or cover or loose hold-down clamps. Also check the entire length of each cable for cracks and frayed conductors.

6 If corrosion, which looks like white, fluffy deposits **(see illustration)** is evident, particularly around the terminals, the battery should be removed for cleaning. Loosen the cable clamp bolts, being careful to remove the ground cable first, and slide them off the terminals **(see illustration)**. Then disconnect the hold-down clamp bolt and nut, remove the clamp and lift the battery from the engine compartment.

7 Clean the cable clamps thoroughly with a battery brush or a terminal cleaner and a solution of warm water and baking soda **(see illustration)**. Wash the terminals and the top of the battery case with the same solution but make sure that the solution doesn't get into the battery. When cleaning the cables, terminals and battery top, wear safety goggles and rubber gloves to prevent any solution from coming in contact with your eyes or hands. Wear old clothes too - even

diluted, sulphuric acid splashed onto clothes will burn holes in them. If the terminals have been extensively corroded, clean them up with a terminal cleaner **(see illustration)**. Thoroughly wash all cleaned areas with plain water.

8 Make sure the battery tray is in good condition and the hold-down clamp bolt or nut is tight. If the battery is removed from the tray, make sure no parts remain in the bottom of the tray when the battery is reinstalled. When reinstalling the hold-down clamp bolt or nut, do not over-tighten it.

9 Information on removing and refitting the battery can be found in Chapter 5. Information on jump starting can be found at the front of this manual.

### Cleaning

10 Corrosion on the hold-down components, battery case and surrounding areas can be removed with a solution of water and baking soda. Thoroughly rinse all cleaned areas with plain water.

11 Any metal parts of the vehicle damaged by corrosion should be covered with a zinc-based primer, then painted.

### Charging

*Warning: When batteries are being charged, hydrogen gas, which is very explosive and flammable, is produced. Do not*

smoke or allow open flames near a charging or a recently charged battery. Wear eye protection when near the battery during charging. Also, make sure the charger is unplugged before connecting or disconnecting the battery from the charger.*

12 Slow-rate charging is the best way to restore a battery that's discharged to the point where it will not start the engine. It's also a good way to maintain the battery charge in a vehicle that's only driven a few miles between starts. Maintaining the battery charge is particularly important in the winter when the battery must work harder to start the engine and electrical accessories that drain the battery are in greater use.

13 It's best to use a one or two-amp battery charger (sometimes called a "trickle" charger). They are the safest and put the least strain on the battery. They are also the least expensive. For a faster charge, you can use a higher amperage charger, but don't use one rated more than 1/10th the amp/hour rating of the battery. Rapid boost charges that claim to restore the power of the battery in one to two hours are hardest on the battery and can damage batteries not in good condition. This type of charging should only be used in emergency situations.

14 The average time necessary to charge a battery should be listed in the instructions that come with the charger. As a general rule, a trickle charger will charge a battery in 12 to 16 hours.

### 7 Hose and fluid leak check

1 Visually inspect the engine joint faces, gaskets and seals for any signs of water or oil leaks. Pay particular attention to the areas around the camshaft cover, cylinder head, oil filter and sump joint faces. Bear in mind that, over a period of time, some very slight seepage from these areas is to be expected - what you are really looking for is any indication of a serious leak **(see Haynes Hint)**. Should a

*A leak in the cooling system will usually show up as white - or rust-coloured - deposits on the area adjoining the leak*

leak be found, renew the offending gasket or oil seal by referring to the appropriate Chapters in this manual.

2 Also check the security and condition of all the engine-related pipes and hoses. Ensure that all cable ties or securing clips are in place and in good condition. Clips which are broken or missing can lead to chafing of the hoses, pipes or wiring, which could cause more serious problems in the future.

3 Carefully check the radiator hoses and heater hoses along their entire length. Renew any hose which is cracked, swollen or deteriorated. Cracks will show up better if the hose is squeezed. Pay close attention to the hose clips that secure the hoses to the cooling system components. Hose clips can pinch and puncture hoses, resulting in cooling system leaks.

4 Inspect all the cooling system components (hoses, joint faces etc.) for leaks. A leak in the cooling system will usually show up as white- or rust-coloured deposits on the area adjoining the leak. Where any problems of this nature are found on system components, renew the component or gasket with reference to Chapter 3.

5 From within the engine compartment, check the security of all fuel hose attachments and pipe unions, and inspect the fuel hoses and vacuum hoses for kinks, chafing and deterioration.

6 Also check the condition of the power steering fluid hoses and pipes.

## 8 Automatic transmission fluid level check

1 The level of the automatic transmission fluid should be carefully maintained. Low fluid level can lead to slipping or loss of drive, while overfilling can cause foaming, loss of fluid and transmission damage.

2 The transmission fluid level should only be checked when the transmission is at its normal operating temperature.

*Caution: If the vehicle has just been driven for a long time at high speed or in city traffic in hot weather, or if it has been pulling a trailer, an accurate fluid level reading cannot be obtained. Allow the fluid to cool down for about 30 minutes.*

3 If the vehicle has not been driven, park the vehicle on level ground, set the handbrake, then start the engine and bring it to operating temperature. While the engine is idling, depress the brake pedal and move the selector lever through all the gear ranges, beginning and ending in Park.

4 With the engine still idling, remove the dipstick from its tube **(see illustration)**. Check the level of the fluid on the dipstick **(see illustration)** and note its condition.

5 Wipe the fluid from the dipstick with a clean rag and reinsert it back into the filler tube until the cap seats.

**8.4a The automatic transmission dipstick (arrowed) is located in a tube which extends forward from the transmission**

6 Pull the dipstick out again and note the fluid level. If the transmission is cold, the level should be in the COLD or COOL range on the dipstick. If it is hot, the fluid level should be in the HOT range. If the level is at the low side of either range, add the specified transmission fluid through the dipstick tube with a funnel.

7 Add just enough of the recommended fluid to fill the transmission to the proper level. It takes about one pint to raise the level from the low mark to the high mark when the fluid is hot, so add the fluid a little at a time and keep checking the level until it is correct.

8 The condition of the fluid should also be checked along with the level. If the fluid at the end of the dipstick is black or a dark reddish brown colour, or if it emits a burned smell, the fluid should be changed (see Section 26). If you are in doubt about the condition of the fluid, purchase some new fluid and compare the two for colour and smell.

## 9 Differential oil level check

1 The differential has a check/fill plug which must be removed to check the lubricant level. If the vehicle is raised to gain access to the plug, be sure to support it safely on axle stands - DO NOT crawl under the vehicle when it's supported only by the jack!

**9.2 The differential check/fill plug is located on the rear of the differential housing - place your finger in the filler plug hole to make sure the lubricant level is even with the bottom of the hole**

**8.4b Check the automatic transmission fluid with the engine idling at operating temperature and the gear selector in Park, then add fluid to bring the level to the upper mark**

2 Remove the lubricant check/fill plug from the differential **(see illustration)**. Use a 3/8-inch drive ratchet and a short extension to unscrew the plug.

3 Use your little finger as a dipstick to make sure the lubricant level is even with the bottom of the plug hole. If not, use a syringe or squeeze bottle to add the recommended lubricant until it just starts to run out of the opening.

4 Refit the plug and tighten it securely.

## 10 Exhaust system check

1 With the engine cold (at least three hours after the vehicle has been driven), check the complete exhaust system from its starting point at the engine to the end of the tailpipe. This should be done on a hoist where unrestricted access is available.

2 Check the pipes and connections for evidence of leaks, severe corrosion or damage. Make sure that all brackets and hangers are in good condition and tight **(see illustration)**.

3 At the same time, inspect the underside of the body for holes, corrosion, open seams, etc. which may allow exhaust gases to enter the passenger compartment. Seal all body openings with silicone or body putty.

4 Rattles and other noises can often be traced to the exhaust system, especially the mounts and hangers. Try to move the pipes,

**10.2 Check the exhaust system hangers (arrowed) for damage and cracks**

silencer and catalytic converter. If the components can come in contact with the body or suspension parts, secure the exhaust system with new mounts.

5 Check the running condition of the engine by inspecting inside the end of the tailpipe. The exhaust deposits here are an indication of engine state-of-tune. If the pipe is black and sooty or coated with white deposits, the engine is in need of a tune-up, including a thorough fuel system inspection.

### 11 Braking system - general check and adjustment

 **Warning: The dust created by the brake system may contain asbestos, which is harmful to your health. Never blow it out with compressed air and don't inhale any of it. An approved filtering mask should be worn when working on the brakes. Do not, under any circumstances, use petroleum-based solvents to clean brake parts. Use brake system cleaner only! Try to use non-asbestos replacement parts whenever possible.**

**Note:** *For detailed photographs of the brake system, refer to Chapter 9.*

1 In addition to the specified intervals, the brakes should be inspected every time the wheels are removed or whenever a defect is suspected. Any of the following symptoms could indicate a potential brake system defect: The vehicle pulls to one side when the brake pedal is depressed; the brakes make squealing or dragging noises when applied; brake pedal travel is excessive; the pedal pulsates; brake fluid leaks, usually onto the inside of the tyre or wheel.

2 The disc brakes have built-in electrical wear indicators which cause a warning lamp to illuminate on the instrument panel when they're worn to the renewal point. When the warning light comes on, replace the pads immediately or expensive damage to the discs can result.

3 Loosen the wheel nuts.

4 Raise the vehicle and place it securely on axle stands.

5 Remove the wheels.

### Disc brakes

6 There are two pads (an outer and an inner) in each caliper. The pads are visible through inspection holes in each caliper (**see Haynes Hint**).

7 Check the pad thickness by looking at each end of the caliper and through the inspection hole in the caliper body. If the lining material is less than the thickness listed in this Chapter's Specifications, replace the pads. **Note:** *Keep in mind that the lining material is riveted or bonded to a metal backing plate and the metal portion is not included in this measurement.*

*You will find an inspection hole like this in each caliper - placing a ruler across the hole should enable you to determine the thickness of remaining pad material for both inner and outer pads*

8 If it is difficult to determine the exact thickness of the remaining pad material by the above method, or if you are at all concerned about the condition of the pads, remove the caliper(s), then remove the pads from the calipers for further inspection (see Chapter 9).

9 Once the pads are removed from the calipers, clean them with brake cleaner and re-measure them with a ruler or a vernier caliper.

10 Measure the disc thickness with a micrometer to make sure that it still has service life remaining. If any disc is thinner than the specified minimum thickness, replace it (refer to Chapter 9). Even if the disc has service life remaining, check its condition. Look for scoring, gouging and burned spots. If these conditions exist, remove the disc and have it resurfaced (see Chapter 9).

11 Before refitting the wheels, check all brake lines and hoses for damage, wear, deformation, cracks, corrosion, leakage, bends and twists, particularly in the vicinity of the rubber hoses at the calipers (**see illustration**). Check the clamps for tightness and the connections for leakage. Make sure that all hoses and lines are clear of sharp edges, moving parts and the exhaust system. If any of the above conditions are noted, repair, reroute or replace the lines and/or fittings as necessary (see Chapter 9).

**11.11 Check along the brake hoses and at each fitting (arrowed) for deterioration and cracks**

### Hydraulic brake servo check

12 Sit in the driver's seat and perform the following sequence of tests.

13 Start the engine, run it for about a minute and turn it off. Then firmly depress the brake several times - the pedal travel should decrease with each application.

14 With the brake fully depressed, start the engine - the pedal should move down a little when the engine starts.

15 Depress the brake, stop the engine and hold the pedal in for about 30 seconds - the pedal should neither sink nor rise.

16 If your brakes do not operate as described above when the preceding tests are performed, the brake servo is either in need of repair or has failed. Refer to Chapter 9 for the removal procedure.

### Handbrake

17 Slowly pull up on the handbrake and count the number of clicks you hear until the handle is up as far as it will go. The adjustment should be within the specified number of clicks listed in this Chapter's Specifications. If you hear more or fewer clicks, it's time to adjust the handbrake (refer to Chapter 9).

18 An alternative method of checking the handbrake is to park the vehicle on a steep hill with the handbrake set and the transmission in Neutral (be sure to stay in the vehicle during this check!). If the handbrake cannot prevent the vehicle from rolling, it is in need of adjustment (see Chapter 9). Whenever a fault is suspected, the brake discs should be removed and the handbrake assemblies themselves should be visually inspected.

### 12 Steering and suspension check

**Note:** *The steering linkage and suspension components should be checked periodically. Worn or damaged suspension and steering linkage components can result in excessive and abnormal tyre wear, poor ride quality and vehicle handling and reduced fuel economy. For detailed illustrations of the steering and suspension components, refer to Chapter 10.*

### With the wheels on the ground

1 Park the vehicle on level ground, turn the engine off and set the handbrake. Check the tyre pressures and check that the wheel nuts are tightened to the specified torque.

2 Push down at one corner of the vehicle, then release it while noting the movement of the body. It should stop moving and come to rest in a level position with one or two bounces. When bouncing the vehicle up and down, listen for squeaks and noises from the suspension components.

3 If the vehicle continues to move up-and-down or if it fails to return to its original

**12.8a Check the steering gear dust boots for cracks and leaking steering fluid**

**12.8b Check the anti-roll bar bushings (arrowed) for deterioration at the front and the rear of the vehicle**

**12.10 Inspect the balljoint and tie-rod end boots for tears - tears or damage in either boot will allow contamination of the grease which will lead to premature failure**

position, a worn or weak shock absorber is probably the reason.

4 Repeat the above check at each of the three remaining corners of the vehicle.

### Under the vehicle

5 Raise the vehicle with a trolley jack and support it securely on axle stands. See *"Jacking and towing"* for proper jacking points.

6 Check the shock absorbers for evidence of fluid leakage. Make sure that any fluid noted is from the shocks and not from any other source. Also check the rubber mounts at each end for deterioration If the shock absorbers fail any of the tests above replace the shocks as a set.

7 Check the tyres for irregular wear patterns and proper inflation. See *"Weekly checks"* for information regarding tyre wear.

8 Inspect the universal joint between the steering shaft and the steering gear housing. Check the steering gear housing for grease leakage. Make sure that the dust seals and boots are not damaged and that the boot clamps are not loose **(see illustration)**. Check the steering linkage for looseness or damage. Look for loose bolts, broken or disconnected parts and deteriorated rubber bushings on all suspension and steering components **(see illustration)**. While an assistant turns the steering wheel from side to side, check the steering components for free movement, chafing and binding. If the steering components do not seem to be reacting with the movement of the steering wheel, try to determine where the slack is located.

9 Check the balljoints moving each lower arm up and down with a crowbar to ensure that its balljoint has no play. If any balljoint does have play, replace it. See Chapter 10 for the front balljoint renewal procedure. Check the tie-rod ends for excessive play.

10 Inspect the balljoint and tie-rod end boots for damage and leaking grease **(see illustration**. Replace the balljoints and tie-rod ends with new ones if they are damaged (see Chapter 10).

### 13 Seat belt check

1 Check the seat belts, buckles, latch plates and guide loops for any obvious damage or signs of wear.

2 Make sure the seat belt reminder light comes on when the key is turned on.

3 The seat belts are designed to lock up during a sudden stop or impact, yet allow free movement during normal driving. The retractors should hold the belt against your chest while driving and rewind the belt when the buckle is unlatched.

4 If any of the above checks reveal problems with the seat-belt system, replace parts as necessary. **Note:** *Check with your local dealer service department; the seat belt system should be covered under the factory warranty.*

### 14 General lubrication

1 Obtain a good quality, multi-purpose lithium-base grease. You'll also need a grease gun and other materials to properly lubricate the chassis **(see illustration)**. Occasionally

plugs will be installed rather than grease fittings. If so, grease fittings will have to be purchased and installed.

2 Look under the car and see if grease fittings or plugs are installed. If there are plugs, remove them and buy grease fittings, which will thread into the component. A dealer or motor factors will be able to supply the correct fittings. Straight, as well as angled, fittings are available.

3 For easier access under the car, raise it with a jack and place axle stands under the chassis. Make sure it's safely supported by the stands. If the wheels are to be removed at this interval for tyre rotation or brake inspection, loosen the wheel nuts slightly while the car is still on the ground.

4 Before beginning, force a little grease out of the nozzle to remove any dirt from the end of the gun. Wipe the nozzle clean with a rag.

5 With the grease gun and plenty of clean rags, crawl under the car and begin lubricating all the front suspension parts that are equipped with a grease fitting.

6 Lubricate the rear driveshafts **(see illustration)**. Wipe each fitting clean and push the nozzle firmly over it. Pump the gun until grease is expelled from the U-joint cap seal.

7 Wipe away any excess grease from the components and the grease fitting. Repeat the procedure for the remaining fittings.

**14.1 Materials required for chassis and body lubrication**

1 *Engine oil - Light engine oil in a can like this can be used for door and bonnet hinges*
2 *Graphite spray - Used to lubricate lock cylinders*
3 *Grease - Grease, in a variety of types and weights, is available for use in a grease gun.*
4 *Grease gun - A common grease gun, shown here with a detachable hose and nozzle, is needed for chassis lubrication. After use, clean it thoroughly*

**14.6 Grease fittings for the rear driveshafts are located in the centre on each U-joint**

8 Clean and lubricate the handbrake cable, along with the cable guides and levers. This can be done by smearing some of the chassis grease onto the cable and its related parts with your fingers.

9 Open the bonnet and smear a little chassis grease on the bonnet latch mechanism. Have an assistant pull the bonnet release lever from inside the car as you lubricate the cable at the latch.

10 Lubricate all the hinges (door, bonnet, etc.) with engine oil to keep them in proper working order.

11 The key lock cylinders can be lubricated with spray graphite or silicone lubricant, which is available at motor factors.

12 Lubricate the door weather-stripping with silicone spray. This will reduce chafing and retard wear.

## 15 Road test

### Instruments and electrical equipment

1 Check the operation of all instruments and electrical equipment.

2 Make sure that all instruments read correctly, and switch on all electrical equipment in turn, to check that it functions properly.

### Steering and suspension

3 Check for any abnormalities in the steering, suspension, handling or road "feel".

4 Drive the car, and check that there are no unusual vibrations or noises.

5 Check that the steering feels positive, with no excessive "sloppiness", or roughness, and check for any suspension noises when cornering and driving over bumps.

### Drivetrain

6 Check the performance of the engine and transmission, listening for any unusual noises.

7 Make sure that the engine runs smoothly when idling, and that there is no hesitation when accelerating.

8 Check that the gear changing action of the transmission is smooth and progressive and that the drive is taken up smoothly from a standing start.

### Braking system

9 Make sure that the car does not pull to one side when braking, and that the wheels do not lock prematurely when braking hard.

10 Check that there is no vibration through the steering when braking.

11 Check that the handbrake operates correctly without excessive movement of the lever, and that it holds the car stationary on a slope.

12 Test the operation of the brake servo unit as follows. With the engine off, depress the footbrake four or five times to exhaust the vacuum. Hold the brake pedal depressed, then start the engine. As the engine starts, there should be a noticeable "give" in the brake pedal as vacuum builds up. Allow the engine to run for at least two minutes, and then switch it off. If the brake pedal is depressed now, it should be possible to detect a hiss from the servo as the pedal is depressed. After about four or five depressions, no further hissing should be heard, and the pedal should feel considerably harder.

# Every 15 000 miles (24 000 km) or 12 months

## 16 Spark plug renewal

Refer to Section 4, renewing the plugs regardless of their apparent condition.

## 17 Air cleaner element renewal

1 The air filter is located inside a housing at the left side of the engine compartment. To remove the air filter, release the four spring clips that secure the two halves of the air cleaner housing together, then lift the cover up and remove the air filter element **(see illustration)**.

*Caution: Never drive the car with the air cleaner removed. Excessive engine wear could result and backfiring could even cause a fire under the bonnet.*

2 Wipe out the inside of the air cleaner housing.

3 Place the new filter into the air cleaner housing, making sure it seats properly.

4 Refitting the cover is the reverse of removal.

## 18 Fuel filter renewal

⚠ *Warning: Petrol is extremely flammable, so take extra precautions when you work on any part of the fuel system. Don't smoke or allow open flames or bare light bulbs near the work area, and don't work in a garage where a natural gas-type*

**17.1 Detach the clips and separate the cover, then slide the filter element out of the housing**

*appliance (such as a water heater or clothes dryer) with a pilot light is present. Since petrol is carcinogenic, wear latex gloves when there's a possibility of being exposed to fuel, and, if you spill any fuel on your skin, rinse it off immediately with soap and water. Mop up any spills immediately and do not store fuel-soaked rags where they could ignite. The fuel system is under constant pressure, so, if any fuel lines are to be disconnected, the fuel pressure in the system must be relieved first (see Chapter 4 for more information). When you perform any kind of work on the fuel system, wear safety glasses and have a Class B type fire extinguisher on hand.*

1 The canister type filter is mounted underneath the car on the passenger's side frame rail just in front of the left rear tyre.

2 Depressurise the fuel system (refer to Chapter 4), then disconnect the cable from the negative terminal of the battery.

3 On 1988 to 1990 models, detach the banjo bolt from the outlet side of the filter then remove the union from the inlet side of the filter. Unscrew the filter mounting bolt and remove the filter **(see illustration)**.

4 On 1991 to 1994 models, the fuel filter has quick-disconnect fittings that do not require

**18.3 Remove the banjo bolt from the outlet side (B), detach the fitting from the inlet side (A) and unscrew the filter mounting bolt (C)**

**18.4 On 1991 to 1994 models, slide back the locking collars and remove the inlet and outlet fuel lines**

**19.11a Unsnap the distributor cap retaining clips - pull the cap up and away to access the rotor**

hand tools to remove. Simply slide back the locking collars and remove the inlet and outlet fuel lines **(see illustration)**. Detach the filter mounting bracket and discard the old filter in a proper container.

5 Note the direction of the arrow on the outside of the filter; it should be pointed towards the front of the car. Make sure the new filter is installed so that it's facing the proper direction. **Note:** *Always refit new copper washers where equipped.*

6 Refit the inlet and outlet fittings then tighten the filter mounting bracket. Reconnect the battery cable, start the engine and check for leaks.

## 19 Ignition system check

1 The spark plug leads should be checked whenever new spark plugs are installed.

2 Begin this procedure by making a visual check of the spark plug leads while the engine is running. In a darkened garage (make sure there is adequate ventilation) start the engine and observe each plug lead. Be careful not to come into contact with any moving engine parts. If there is a break in the lead, you will see arcing or a small spark at the damaged area. If arcing is noticed, make a note to obtain new leads, then allow the engine to cool and check the distributor cap and rotor.

3 The spark plug leads should be inspected one at a time to prevent mixing up the order, which is essential for proper engine operation. Each original plug lead should be numbered to help identify its location. If the number is illegible, a piece of tape can be marked with the correct number and wrapped around the plug lead.

4 Disconnect the plug lead from the spark plug. A removal tool can be used for this purpose or you can grasp the rubber boot, twist the boot half a turn and pull the boot free. Do not pull on the lead itself.

5 Check inside the boot for corrosion, which will look like a white crusty powder.

6 Push the lead and boot back onto the end of the spark plug. It should fit tightly onto the end of the plug. If it doesn't, remove the lead and use pliers to carefully crimp the metal connector inside the lead boot until the fit is snug.

7 Using a clean rag, wipe the entire length of the lead to remove built-up dirt and grease. Once the lead is clean, check for burns, cracks and other damage. Do not bend the lead sharply, because the conductor might break.

8 Disconnect the spark plug lead from the distributor cap. Again, pull only on the rubber boot. Check for corrosion and a tight fit. Reinsert the lead in the distributor cap.

9 Inspect the remaining spark plug leads, making sure that each one is securely fastened at the distributor and spark plug when the check is complete.

10 If new spark plug leads are required, purchase a set for your specific engine model. Remove and replace the leads one at a time to avoid mix-ups in the firing order.

11 Detach the distributor cap by unsnapping the cap retaining clips. Look inside it for cracks, carbon tracks and worn, burned or loose contacts **(see illustrations)**.

12 Pull the rotor off the distributor shaft and examine it for cracks and carbon tracks **(see illustrations)**. Replace the cap and rotor if any damage or defects are noted.

13 It is common practice to refit a new cap and rotor whenever new spark plug leads are installed. When refitting a new cap, remove the leads from the old cap one at a time and attach them to the new cap in the exact same location **Note:** *If an accidental mix-up occurs, refer to the firing order Specifications at the beginning of this Chapter.*

**19.11b Shown here are some of the common defects to look for when inspecting the distributor cap (typical cap shown). If in doubt about its condition, fit a new one**

**19.12a Pull off the rotor (arrowed) and inspect it thoroughly**

**19.12b Check the ignition rotor for wear and corrosion as indicated here (if in doubt about its condition, buy a new one)**

**20 Crankcase ventilation system check**

Refer to Chapter 6.

**21 Drivebelt check and renewal**

## Check

**1** The drivebelts, or V-belts as they are sometimes called, are located at the front of the engine and play an important role in the overall operation of the vehicle and its components. Due to their function and material make-up, the belts are prone to failure after a period of time and should be inspected and adjusted periodically to prevent major engine damage.

**2** The number of belts used on a particular vehicle depends on the accessories installed. The main belt transmits power from the crankshaft to the water pump, alternator and the power steering pump. The second belt transmits power from the crankshaft to the air conditioning compressor.

**3** With the engine off, open the bonnet and locate the drivebelts. With a flashlight, check each belt for separation of the adhesive rubber on both sides of the core, core separation from the belt side, a severed core, separation of the ribs from the adhesive rubber, cracking or separation of the ribs, and torn or worn ribs or cracks in the inner ridges of the ribs (see illustrations). Also check for fraying and glazing, which gives the belt a shiny appearance. Both sides of the belt should be inspected, which means you will have to twist the belt to check the underside. Use your fingers to feel the belt where you can't see it. If any of the above conditions are evident, replace the belt (go to paragraph 7).

**4** Check the belt tension by pushing firmly on the belt with your thumb at a distance halfway between the pulleys and note how far the belt

21.3a **Small cracks in the underside of a serpentine belt are acceptable - lengthwise cracks, or missing pieces, are cause for replacement**

can be pushed (deflected). Measure this deflection with a ruler (see illustration). As a rule of thumb, if the distance from pulley centre-to- pulley centre is between 7 and 11 inches, the belt should deflect 1/4-inch. If the belt travels between pulleys spaced 12 to 16 inches apart, the belt should deflect 1/2-inch for a V-belt or 1/4-inch for a serpentine belt.

## Adjustment

**5** There are two belt tensioning mechanisms. The first one adjusts the air conditioning compressor belt, which is accessible from underneath the car. The second tensioning mechanism is above the alternator - it adjusts the tension on the main belt (the water pump, alternator and power steering pump belt).

**6** The air conditioning compressor and the alternator each have a belt tensioning mechanism and pivot bolt(s) which must be loosened slightly to enable you to move the component (see illustrations).

**7** After the bolts have been loosened, belt tension can be adjusted by either loosening or tightening the locknuts on the belt tensioning adjustment rod (see illustration 21.6a and b). Move the component away from the engine to

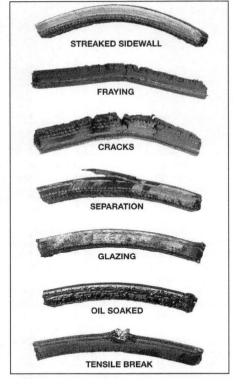

21.3b **Here are some of the more common problems associated with V-belts (check the belts very carefully to prevent an untimely breakdown)**

tighten the belt or toward the engine to loosen the belt.

**8** Measure the belt tension using the method described in paragraph 4. Repeat this procedure until the drivebelt is adjusted properly.

## Renewal

**9** To replace a belt, loosen the drivebelt adjustment rod and pivot bolt as described above, slip the belt off the crankshaft pulley and remove it. If you are replacing the alternator/power steering pump belt, you'll have to remove the air conditioning

21.4 **Measuring drivebelt deflection with a straightedge and ruler**

21.6a **To adjust the alternator/power steering drivebelt, loosen the outer locknut (arrowed) and the alternator pivot bolt - turn the inner locknut anti-clockwise to loosen or clockwise to tighten the belt**

21.6b **To adjust the air conditioning compressor drivebelt, loosen the outer locknut (arrowed) and the compressor pivot bolts - turn the inner locknut anti-clockwise to loosen or clockwise to tighten the belt**

**21.11 When refitting ribbed (serpentine) drivebelts, make sure the belt is centred between the pulley edges (arrowed) - it must not overlap either edge of the pulley**

compressor belt first because of the way they are arranged on the crankshaft pulley. Because of this and because belts tend to wear out more or less together, it is a good idea to replace both belts at the same time. Mark each belt and its appropriate pulley groove so the new belts can be installed in their proper positions.

**10** Take the old belts to the parts store in order to make a direct comparison for length, width and design.

**11** After replacing a ribbed drivebelt, make sure that it fits properly in the ribbed grooves in the pulleys **(see illustration)**. It is essential that the belt be properly centred.

**12** Adjust the belt(s) in accordance with the procedure outlined above.

## 22 Front wheel bearing check and adjustment

### Check and repack

**1** In most cases the front wheel bearings will not need servicing until the brake pads are changed. However, the bearings should be checked whenever the front of the vehicle is raised for any reason. Several items, including a torque wrench and special grease, are required for this procedure **(see illustration)**.

**22.1 Tools and materials needed for front wheel bearing maintenance**

1  Hammer
2  Grease - High-temperature grease that is formulated specially for front wheel bearings should be used
3  Wood block - If you have a scrap piece of 2x4, it can be used to drive the new seal into the hub
4  Needle-nose pliers - Used to straighten and remove the cotter pin in the spindle
5  Torque wrench - This is very important in this procedure; if the bearing is too tight, the wheel won't turn freely - if it's too loose, the wheel will "wobble" on the spindle. Either way, it could mean extensive damage
6  Screwdriver - Used to remove the seal from the hub (a long screwdriver is preferred)
7  Socket/breaker bar - Needed to loosen the nut on the spindle if it's extremely tight
8  Brush - Together with some clean solvent, this will be used to remove old grease from the hub and spindle

**2** With the vehicle securely supported on axle stands, spin each wheel and check for noise, rolling resistance and freeplay.

**3** Grasp the top of each tyre with one hand and the bottom with the other. Move the wheel in-and-out on the spindle. If there's any noticeable movement, the bearings should be checked and then repacked with grease or renewed if necessary.

**4** Remove the wheel.

**5** Remove the brake caliper (see Chapter 9) and hang it out of the way on a piece of wire. A wood block of the appropriate width can be slid between the brake pads to keep them separated, if necessary. Also remove the brake disc.

**6** Pry the dust cap out of the hub using a screwdriver or a hammer and chisel **(see illustration)**.

**7** Straighten the bent ends of the cotter pin, then pull the cotter pin out of the nut lock **(see illustration)**. Discard the cotter pin and use a new one during reassembly.

**8** Remove the locknut, nut and washer from the end of the spindle.

**9** Pull the hub out slightly, then push it back into its original position. This should force the

outer bearing off the spindle enough so it can be removed **(see illustration)**.

**10** Pull the hub off the spindle. **Note:** *Sometimes the inner wheel bearing and grease seal remain attached to the spindle. Grasp the back of the seal with both hands and pull forward to remove them.*

**11** If the grease seal is not already detached from the hub, use a screwdriver to pry the seal out of the rear of the hub. As this is done, note how the seal is installed.

**12** If the inner wheel bearing is not already detached from the hub, remove it at this time.

**13** Use solvent to remove all traces of the old grease from the bearings, hub and spindle. A small brush may prove helpful; however make sure no bristles from the brush embed themselves inside the bearing rollers. Allow the parts to air dry.

**14** Carefully inspect the bearings for cracks, heat discoloration, worn rollers, etc. Check the bearing races inside the hub for wear and damage. If the bearing races are defective, the hubs should be taken to a machine workshop with the facilities to remove the old races and press new ones in. Note that the bearings and races come as matched sets

**22.6 Dislodge the dust cap by working around the outer circumference with a hammer and chisel**

**22.7 Remove the cotter pin and discard it - use a new one when the hub is reinstalled**

**22.9 Pull the hub assembly forward slightly - then push it back into position to dislodge the outer wheel bearing**

**22.15 Work the grease completely into the bearing rollers**

**22.17 Apply a thin layer of grease to the inner and outer bearing races**

**22.19 After refitting the inner wheel bearing into the hub - press the grease seal into place**

**22.20 Refit the hub assembly onto the spindle - then push the grease-packed outer bearing into position**

**22.23 Position the nut lock on the spindle nut so that it lines up with the cotter pin hole - DO NOT loosen the spindle nut from its snug position**

and old bearings should never be installed on new races.

**15** Use high-temperature front wheel bearing grease to pack the bearings. Work the grease completely into the bearings, forcing it between the rollers, cone and cage from the back side **(see illustration)**.

**16** Apply a thin coat of grease to the spindle at the outer bearing seat, inner bearing seat, shoulder and seal seat.

**17** Put a small quantity of grease inboard of each bearing race inside the hub. Using your finger, form a dam at these points to provide extra grease availability and to keep thinned grease from flowing out of the bearing **(see illustration)**.

**18** Place the grease-packed inner bearing into the rear of the hub and put a little more grease outboard of the bearing.

**19** Place a new seal over the inner bearing and tap the seal evenly into place until it's flush with the hub **(see illustration)**.

**20** Carefully place the hub assembly onto the spindle and push the grease-packed outer bearing into position **(see illustration)**.

### Adjustment

**21** Refit the washer and spindle nut. Tighten the nut only slightly (no more than 16Nm/12 lbf ft of torque).

**22** Rotate the hub slowly in a forward direction while tightening the spindle nut to

approximately 27Nm (20 lbf ft) to seat the bearings. Remove any grease or burrs which could cause excessive bearing play later.

**23** Loosen the spindle nut 1/4-turn, then using your hand (not a spanner of any kind), tighten the nut until it's snug. Refit the nut lock and a new cotter pin through the hole in the spindle and the slots in the nut lock. If the nut lock slots don't line up, remove the nut lock and turn it slightly until they do **(see illustration)**.

**24** Bend the ends of the cotter pin until they're flat against the nut. Cut off any extra length which could interfere with the dust cap.

**25** Refit the dust cap, tapping it into place with a hammer.

**26** Refit the brake disc and caliper in the reverse order of removal (see Chapter 9).

**27** Refit the wheel on the hub and tighten the wheel nuts.

**28** Grasp the top and bottom of the tyre and check the bearings in the manner described earlier in this Section.

**29** Lower the vehicle and tighten the wheel nuts to the torque listed in this Chapter's Specifications.

### 23 Propshaft check

**1** Referring to Chapter 8, check the propshaft centre bearing, universal joint and flexible coupling for signs of wear or damage and check that the propshaft fixings are tightened to the specified torque.

### 24 Front wheel alignment check

**1** Accurate wheel alignment requires access to specialised test equipment and as such should be entrusted to a suitably equipped Jaguar dealer or a tyre specialist (refer to Chapter 10).

### 25 Headlight beam check

**1** Accurate adjustment of the headlight beam is only possible using optical beam-setting equipment, and this work should therefore be carried out by a Jaguar dealer or garage with the necessary facilities (see Chapter 12).

26.5 Using an Allen spanner remove the drain plug located in the bottom of the transmission sump pan

26.6a Unscrew the dipstick tube collar

26.6b Detach the tube and let the remaining fluid drain

# Every 30 000 miles (48 000 km) or 2 years

## 26 Automatic transmission fluid and filter renewal

1 At the specified time intervals, the transmission fluid should be drained and renewed. Since the fluid will remain hot long after driving, perform this procedure only after the engine has cooled down completely.
2 Before beginning work, purchase the specified transmission fluid and a new filter.
3 Other tools necessary for this job include axle stands to support the vehicle in a raised position, a drain pan capable of holding at least eight pints, newspapers and clean rags.

4 Raise the vehicle and support it securely on axle stands.
5 Place the drain pan under the drain plug in the bottom of the transmission sump pan. Remove the plug and allow the fluid to drain (see illustration).
6 Refit the drain plug, then move the drain pan underneath the dipstick tube. Loosen the dipstick tube collar and let the remaining fluid drain (see illustrations).
7 Remove the sump pan mounting bolts and brackets (see illustration).
8 Detach the sump pan from the transmission and lower it, keeping it as horizontal as possible in order not to spill too much of the remaining fluid (see illustration).

9 Drain the remaining fluid from the transmission sump pan, clean it with solvent and dry it with compressed air. Be sure to clean the metal filings from the magnet, if equipped.
10 Remove the screws and detach the filter from the valve body (see illustrations).
11 Refit the new O-ring and filter, being sure to tighten the bolts securely.
12 Carefully clean the fluid pan-to-transmission sealing surface.
13 Make sure the gasket surface on the transmission sump pan is completely clean, then refit the gasket. Put the sump pan in place against the transmission and refit the brackets and bolts. working around the sump pan, tighten each bolt a little at a time until the torque listed in this Chapter's Specifications is reached. Don't overtighten the bolts! Connect the dipstick tube and tighten the collar securely.
14 Lower the vehicle and add the specified amount of fluid through the filler tube (see Section 8).
15 With the transmission in Park and the handbrake set, run the engine at fast idle, but don't race it.
16 Move the gear selector through each position, and then back to Park. Check the fluid level.
17 Be sure to check underneath the car for any leaks after the first few miles of driving.

26.7 Use a socket and extension to remove the transmission sump pan bolts and brackets

26.8 Lower the sump pan from the transmission

26.10a Use a Torx-head driver to remove the filter bolts (arrowed) . . .

26.10b . . . then remove the fluid filter from the transmission

26.10c Be sure to remove the old O-ring from the transmission - always use a new O-ring when replacing the filter

### 27 Differential oil renewal

**1** Drive the car for several miles to warm up the differential lubricant, then raise the car and support it securely on axle stands.

**2** Move a drain pan, rags, newspapers and the required tools under the car.

**3** Remove the check/fill plug from the differential. If necessary refer to Section 9 for the check/fill plug location.

**4** With the drain pan under the differential, use a ratchet and socket to loosen the drain plug **(see illustration)**. **Note:** *A special pipe plug socket may be required to complete this procedure.*

**5** Once loosened, carefully unscrew it with your fingers until you can remove it from the case. Since the lubricant will be hot, wear a rubber glove to prevent burns.

**6** Allow all of the oil to drain into the pan, then replace the drain plug and tighten it securely.

**7** Refer to Section 9 and fill the differential with lubricant.

**8** Refit the fill plug and tighten it securely.

**9** Lower the vehicle. Check for leaks at the drain plug after the first few miles of driving.

**27.4 The differential drain plug (arrowed) is accessible through a hole located in the middle of the differential support brace**

### 28 Brake fluid renewal

⚠️ *Warning: Brake fluid can harm your eyes and damage painted surfaces, so use extreme caution when handling or pouring it. Do not use brake fluid that has been standing open or is more than one year old. Brake fluid absorbs moisture from the air. Excess moisture can cause a dangerous loss of braking effectiveness.*

**1** At the specified time intervals, the brake fluid should be drained and renewed. Since the brake fluid may drip or splash when pouring it, place plenty of rags around the master cylinder to protect any surrounding painted surfaces.

**2** Before beginning work, purchase the specified type of brake fluid.

**3** Remove the cap from the master cylinder reservoir.

**4** Using a hand suction pump or similar device, withdraw the fluid from the master cylinder reservoir.

**5** Add new fluid to the master cylinder until it rises to the base of the filler neck.

**6** Bleed the brake system as described in Chapter 9 at all four brakes until new and uncontaminated fluid flows from the bleed screw.

**7** Refill the master cylinder with fluid and check the operation of the brakes. The pedal should feel solid when depressed, with no sponginess.

⚠️ *Warning: Do not drive the car if you are in any doubt about the braking system.*

## Every 60 000 miles (96 000 km)

### 29 Handbrake shoes check

**1** Remove the rear discs and inspect the handbrake shoes as described in Chapter 9. If the shoes are worn or damaged they must be renewed.

⚠️ *Warning: The dust created by the brake system may contain asbestos, which is harmful to your health. Never blow it out with compressed air and don't inhale any of it. An approved filtering mask should be worn when working on the brakes. Do not, under any circumstances, use petroleum-based solvents to clean brake parts. Use brake system cleaner only! Try to use non-asbestos replacement parts whenever possible.*

## Every 2 years, regardless of mileage

### 30 Coolant renewal

⚠️ *Warning: Do not allow engine coolant (antifreeze) to come in contact with your skin or painted surfaces of the vehicle. Rinse off spills immediately with plenty of water. Antifreeze is highly toxic if ingested. Never leave antifreeze laying around in an open container or in puddles on the floor; children and pets are attracted by it's sweet smell and may drink it. Check with local authorities about disposing of used antifreeze. Your local authority may have collection centres which will see that antifreeze is disposed of safely.*

**1** Periodically, the cooling system should be drained, flushed and refilled to replenish the antifreeze mixture and prevent formation of rust and corrosion, which can impair the performance of the cooling system and cause engine damage. When the cooling system is serviced, all hoses and the radiator cap should be checked and renewed if necessary.

#### Draining

**2** Apply the handbrake and block the wheels. If the vehicle has just been driven, wait several hours to allow the engine to cool down before beginning this procedure.

**3** Remove the expansion tank pressure cap **(see illustration)**.

**4** Move a large container under the radiator drain to catch the coolant. Then using a large screwdriver, open the radiator drain plug and direct the coolant into the container **(see illustration)**.

**30.3 Push the expansion tank pressure cap downward and rotate anti-clockwise - never remove it when the engine is hot!**

**30.4 The radiator drain fitting (arrowed) located at the bottom of the radiator**

**5** After the coolant stops flowing out of the radiator, move the container under the engine block drain plug. Remove the plug and let the coolant in the block to drain **(see illustration)**.
**6** While the coolant is draining from the engine block, check the condition of the radiator hoses, heater hoses and clamps (refer to Section 7 if necessary).
**7** Replace any damaged clamps or hoses (see Chapter 3).

## Flushing

**8** Once the system is completely drained, flush the radiator with fresh water from a garden hose until water runs clear at the drain. The flushing action of the water will remove sediments from the radiator but will not remove more serious rust and scale from the engine and cooling tube surfaces.
**9** These deposits can be removed by using proprietary chemical cleaners. It should be stressed, however, that these should only need to be used if the system has been neglected. Follow the procedure outlined in their manufacturer's instructions. If the radiator is severely corroded, damaged or leaking, it should be removed (see Chapter 3) and taken to a radiator repair workshop.

**30.5 The block drain plug (arrowed) is located on the right side of the block**

**10** On 1988 and 1989 models remove the overflow hose from the coolant recovery reservoir. Drain the reservoir and flush it with clean water, then reconnect the hose (see Chapter 3).

## Refilling

**11** Close and tighten the radiator drain. Refit and tighten the engine block drain plugs.
**12** Make sure the heater temperature control is in the maximum heat position.
**13** Slowly refill the expansion tank with a mixture of antifreeze and water until the coolant reaches the base of the filler neck.
**14** Leave the expansion tank pressure cap off and run the engine in a well-ventilated area until the thermostat opens (coolant will begin flowing through the radiator and the upper radiator hose will become hot). Race the engine two or three times under no load.
**15** Turn the engine off and let it cool. Add more coolant mixture to bring the level back up to the base of the filler neck.
**16** Squeeze the upper radiator hose to expel air, then add more coolant mixture if necessary. Refit the expansion tank pressure cap.
**17** Start the engine, allow it to reach normal operating temperature and check for leaks.

# Notes

# Chapter 2  Part A
## Engine in-car repair procedures

## Contents

## Degrees of difficulty

| **Easy,** suitable for novice with little experience |  | **Fairly easy,** suitable for beginner with some experience |  | **Fairly difficult,** suitable for competent DIY mechanic |  | **Difficult,** suitable for experienced DIY mechanic |  | **Very difficult,** suitable for expert DIY or professional |

## Specifications

### General
| | |
|---|---|
| Cylinder numbers (front to rear) ............................. | 1-2-3-4-5-6 |
| Firing order ............................................... | 1-5-3-6-2-4 |
| Displacement: | |
|     3.2 litre engine ..................................... | 3239 cc |
|     3.6 litre engine ..................................... | 3590 cc |
|     4.0 litre engine ..................................... | 3980 cc |
| Bore ..................................................... | 91.0 mm (3.583 inches) |
| Stroke: | |
|     3.2 litre engine ..................................... | 83.0 mm (3.268 inches) |
|     3.6 litre engine ..................................... | 92.0 mm (3.622 inches) |
|     4.0 litre engine ..................................... | 102.0 mm (4.016 inches) |

### Camshafts and lifters
| | |
|---|---|
| Journal diameter .......................................... | 26.9370 to 26.9494 mm (1.0605 to 1.0610 inches) |
| Bearing oil clearance ...................................... | 0.037 to 0.063 mm (0.0014 to 0.0024 inch) |
| Runout limit .............................................. | 0.0406 mm (0.0016 inch) |
| Lobe lift (maximum variation between lobes) .................. | 0.0127 mm (0.005 inch) |
| Valve lifter | |
|     Diameter ......................................... | 33.34 to 33.35 mm (1.3126 to 1.3130 inches) |
|     Oil clearance ...................................... | 0.020 to 0.050 mm (0.0008 to 0.0020 inch) |
| Valve clearances .......................................... | 0.30 to 0.36 mm (0.012 to 0.014 inch) |

### Oil pump
| | |
|---|---|
| Outer rotor to body clearance, maximum ...................... | 0.2 mm (0.0079 inch) |
| Outer rotor OD ........................................... | 69.774 to 69.825 mm (2.7470 to 2.7490 inches) |
| Rotor thickness, inner and outer ............................ | 27.962 to 27.975 mm (1.1008 to 1.1013 inches) |
| Clearance over rotors, maximum ............................ | 0.1 mm (0.0039 inch) |

## Torque wrench settings*

| | Nm | lbf ft |
|---|---|---|
| Camshaft bearing cap bolts | 23 to 27 | 16 to 20 |
| Camshaft sprocket bolts | 23 to 27 | 16 to 20 |
| Crankshaft damper-to-crankshaft bolt | | |
|   3.2 and 3.6 litre | 204 | 151 |
|   4.0 litre | 180 to 220 | 133 to 162 |
| Crankshaft pulley to damper bolts | 23 to 27 | 16 to 20 |
| Crankshaft rear oil seal retainer bolts | 23 to 27 | 16 to 20 |
| Crankshaft sensor bolts | 23 to 27 | 16 to 20 |
| Cylinder head bolts | | |
|   Step 1 | 60 | 44 |
|   Step 2 | Tighten an additional 90° (1/4 turn) | |
| Driveplate bolts | 123 to 149 | 91 to 110 |
| Engine mounts | | |
|   To engine block | 49 to 66 | 36 to 39 |
|   To chassis | 22 to 24 | 16 to 18 |
| Exhaust manifold heat shield fasteners | 23 to 27 | 16 to 20 |
| Exhaust manifold nuts | 23 to 27 | 16 to 20 |
| Intake manifold nuts | 23 to 27 | 16 to 20 |
| Oil pump bolts | 23 to 27 | 16 to 20 |
| Sump bolts | 23 to 27 | 16 to 20 |
| Sump bolts, adapter to pan | 49 to 54 | 36 to 40 |
| Timing chain cover | 23 to 27 | 16 to 20 |
| Valve cover screws | 10 to 12 | 7 to 9 |

***Note:** Refer to Part B for additional specifications*

## 1  General information

This Part of Chapter 2 is devoted to in-car repair procedures for the in-line six-cylinder engines. All information concerning engine removal and refitting and engine block and cylinder head overhaul can be found in Part B of this Chapter.

The following repair procedures are based on the assumption that the engine is installed in the car. If the engine has been removed from the car and mounted on a stand, many of the steps outlined in this Part of Chapter 2 will not apply. We have photographed some in-car engine procedures with the engine on a stand for photographic purposes.

The Specifications included in this Part of Chapter 2 apply only to the procedures contained in this Part. Part B of Chapter 2 includes the Specifications necessary for cylinder head and engine block rebuilding.

## 2  Repair operations possible with the engine in the car

Many repair operations can be accomplished without removing the engine from the car.

Clean the engine compartment and the exterior of the engine with some type of degreaser before any work is done. It will make the job easier and help keep dirt out of the internal areas of the engine.

Depending on the components involved, it may be helpful to remove the bonnet to improve access to the engine as repairs are performed (refer to Chapter 11 if necessary). Cover the wings to prevent damage to the paint. Special pads are available, but an old bedspread or blanket will also work.

If vacuum, exhaust, oil or coolant leaks develop, indicating a need for gasket or seal renewal, the repairs can generally be made with the engine in the car. The intake and exhaust manifold gaskets, crankshaft oil seals and cylinder head gasket are all accessible with the engine in place (although rear oil seal renewal involves removal of the transmission). The sump is difficult for a home mechanic to replace without a hoist and other specialised equipment, since the front suspension, steering and crossmember must be lowered to allow enough clearance for sump removal. If such equipment is not available, the alternative would be to remove the engine for renewal of the sump or oil pump. **Note:** *We assume that the home mechanic does not have access to the specialised equipment, and have photographed our subject engine out of the car for some procedures.*

Exterior engine components, such as the intake and exhaust manifolds, the water pump, the starter motor, the alternator, the distributor and the fuel system components can be removed for repair with the engine in place.

Since the cylinder head can be removed with the engine in-car, camshaft and valve component servicing can also be accomplished. Renewal of the timing chains and sprockets is also possible with the engine in-car.

## 3  Top Dead Centre (TDC) for number one piston - locating

**Note:** *The following procedure is based on the assumption that the distributor is correctly installed. If you are trying to locate TDC to refit the distributor correctly, piston position must be determined by feeling for compression at the number one spark plug hole, then aligning the ignition timing marks (see paragraph 8).*

1  Top Dead Centre (TDC) is the highest point in the cylinder that each piston reaches as it travels up the cylinder bore. Each piston reaches TDC on the compression stroke and again on the exhaust stroke, but TDC generally refers to piston position on the compression stroke.

2  Positioning the piston(s) at TDC is an essential part of many procedures such as camshaft and timing chain/sprocket removal and distributor removal.

3  Before beginning this procedure, be sure to place the transmission in Neutral and apply the handbrake or block the rear wheels. Also, disable the ignition system by detaching the coil wire from the centre terminal of the distributor cap and grounding it on the engine block with a jumper wire. Remove the spark plugs (see Chapter 1).

4  In order to bring any piston to TDC, the crankshaft must be turned using one of the methods outlined below. When looking at the timing chain end of the engine, normal crankshaft rotation is clockwise.

*a) The preferred method is to turn the crankshaft with a socket and ratchet*

**3.8 Align the mark on the crankshaft sensor ring (arrowed) with the bottom edge of the pointer on the front cover**

**4.2 Disconnect the PCV hose (arrowed) from the valve cover, then pull the spark plug leads out by their boots, not the leads**

attached to the bolt threaded into the front of the crankshaft. Apply pressure on the bolt in a clockwise direction only. Never turn the bolt anti-clockwise.
b) A remote starter switch, which may save some time, can also be used. Follow the instructions included with the switch. Once the piston is close to TDC, use a socket and ratchet as described in the previous paragraph.
c) If an assistant is available to turn the ignition switch to the Start position in short bursts, you can get the piston close to TDC without a remote starter switch. Make sure your assistant is out of the car, away from the ignition switch, then use a socket and ratchet as described in Paragraph a) to complete the procedure.

**5** Note the position of the terminal for the number one spark plug lead on the distributor cap. If the terminal isn't marked, follow the plug lead from the number one cylinder spark plug to the cap.
**6** Use a felt-tip pen or chalk to make a mark on the distributor body directly under the number one terminal (see Chapter 5).
**7** Detach the cap from the distributor and set it aside (see Chapter 1 if necessary).
**8** Turn the crankshaft until the small triangle cast into the front edge of the crankshaft sensor ring is aligned with the bottom edge of the timing pointer located at the front of the engine **(see illustration)**.
**9** Look at the distributor rotor - it should be pointing directly at the mark you made on the distributor body. If so, you are at TDC for number 1 cylinder.
**10** If the rotor is 180° off, the number one piston is at TDC on the exhaust stroke.
**11** To get the piston to TDC on the compression stroke, turn the crankshaft one complete revolution (360°) clockwise. The rotor should now be pointing at the mark on the distributor. When the rotor is pointing at the number one spark plug lead terminal in the distributor cap and the ignition timing marks are aligned, the number one piston is at

TDC on the compression stroke. **Note:** *If it's impossible to align the ignition timing marks when the rotor is pointing at the mark on the distributor body, the timing chain may have jumped the teeth on the pulleys or may have been installed incorrectly.*
**12** After the number one piston has been positioned at TDC on the compression stroke, TDC for any of the remaining cylinders can be located by turning the crankshaft and following the firing order. Mark the remaining spark plug lead terminal locations on the distributor body just like you did for the number one terminal, then number the marks to correspond with the cylinder numbers. As you turn the crankshaft, the rotor will also turn. When it's pointing directly at one of the marks on the distributor, the piston for that particular cylinder is at TDC on the compression stroke.

---

**4  Valve cover -**
removal and refitting

## Removal

**1** Disconnect the battery negative cable.
*Caution: If the stereo in your vehicle is equipped with an anti-theft system, make*

**4.6 Apply RTV sealant to the half-circle plugs and insert them into the cylinder head before refitting the valve cover**

*sure you have the correct activation code before disconnecting the battery.*
**2** Detach the PCV hose from the valve cover **(see illustration)**.
**3** Remove the spark plug leads from the spark plugs, handling them by the boots and not pulling on the wires.
**4** Remove the valve cover mounting screws, then detach the valve cover and gasket from the cylinder head. If the valve cover is stuck to the cylinder head, bump the end with a wood block and a hammer to jar it loose. If that doesn't work, try to slip a flexible putty knife between the cylinder head and valve cover to break the seal.
*Caution: Don't pry at the valve cover-to-cylinder head joint or damage to the sealing surfaces may occur, leading to oil leaks after the valve cover is reinstalled.*

## Refitting

**5** The mating surfaces of the cylinder head and valve cover must be clean when the valve cover is installed. If there's residue or oil on the mating surfaces when the valve cover is installed, oil leaks may develop.
**6** Apply RTV sealant around the two half-circle rubber plugs at the rear of the cylinder head **(see illustration)**.
**7** Using a new gasket and spark plug tube seals, refit the valve cover **(see illustration)**.

**4.7 Press the valve cover gasket into the groove around the valve cover and fit a new set of spark plug tube seals (arrowed)**

5.3  The various hoses should be marked to ensure correct refitting

5.6a  Remove the oil filler tube bracket nuts (arrowed) . . .

5.6b  . . . pull the tube up to dislodge it from the housing - it won't come out, but can be removed with the intake manifold

5.7a  Remove the ground strap from the front stud (arrowed), and the engine wiring harness clips from the other studs

5.7b  Remove the intake manifold bolts/nuts and remove the intake manifold - the upper fasteners are studs/nuts, while the lower row are bolts (two arrowed)

5.9  Refit the new intake manifold gasket over the studs (arrowed) refit the manifold

**8** Tighten the screws to the torque listed in this Chapter's Specifications in three or four equal steps.

**9** Refit the remaining components, start the engine and check for oil leaks.

## 5  Intake manifold - removal and refitting

### *Removal*

**1** Disconnect the negative cable from the battery.

*Caution: If the stereo in your vehicle is equipped with an anti-theft system, make sure you have the correct activation code before disconnecting the battery.*

**2** Refer to Chapter 4 to remove the accelerator and cruise-control linkage, safely relieve the fuel system pressure, and disconnect the fuel supply lines.

**3** Label or mark and detach the PCV and vacuum hoses connected to the intake manifold, **(see illustration)**.

**4** The intake manifold can be removed with the injectors and fuel rail still in place. Disconnect the electrical connectors at each injector (label them first for reassembly). If the injectors are to be removed from the intake manifold, refer to Chapter 4.

**5** Refer to Chapter 4 and remove the throttle body.

**6** Remove the three nuts retaining the oil filler tube bracket, then pull the tube up as far as possible **(see illustrations)**.

**7** Remove the ground strap and intake manifold mounting nuts/bolts, then detach the intake manifold from the engine **(see illustrations)**.

### *Refitting*

**8** Clean the mating surfaces of the intake manifold and the cylinder head mounting surface with lacquer thinner or acetone. If the gasket shows signs of leaking, have the manifold checked for warpage at an automotive machine workshop and resurfaced if necessary.

**9** Refit a new gasket, then position the intake manifold on the cylinder head and refit the nuts/bolts **(see illustration)**.

**10** Tighten the nuts/bolts in three or four equal steps to the torque listed in this Chapter's Specifications. Work from the centre out towards the ends to avoid warping the manifold.

**11** Refit the remaining parts in the reverse order of removal.

**12** Before starting the engine, check the throttle linkage for smooth operation.

**13** Run the engine and check for coolant and vacuum leaks.

**14** Road test the car and check for proper operation of all accessories, including cruise control system.

## 6  Exhaust manifolds - removal and refitting

> *Warning: The engine must be completely cool before beginning this procedure.*

### *Removal*

**1** Disconnect the negative cable from the battery.

*Caution: If the stereo in your vehicle is equipped with an anti-theft system, make sure you have the correct activation code before disconnecting the battery.*

**2** On 1990 and later models, disconnect the EGR pipe and remove the EGR valve from the top of the exhaust manifold (see Chapter 6).

**3** Apply penetrating oil to the exhaust manifold mounting nuts/bolts, and the nuts retaining the exhaust pipes to the manifolds. After the nuts have soaked, remove the nuts retaining the exhaust pipes to the manifolds and the lower bolt from the heat shield **(see illustration)**.

**4** Remove the heat shield from the exhaust manifolds **(see illustration)**.

**5** Disconnect the electrical connector to the oxygen sensor. Unless the oxygen sensor is being renewed, leave the sensor in place.

**6** Remove the nuts/bolts and detach the manifolds and gaskets **(see illustration)**.

**6.3 Remove nuts (small arrows) retaining the exhaust pipe to the manifold flanges; two for each pipe - larger arrow indicates one heat shield bolt accessible from below**

**6.4 Remove the upper heat shield bolts (arrowed)**

**6.6 Remove the bolts and nuts and remove the front and rear exhaust manifolds**

**6.8 Refit new gaskets in position over the studs with the markings facing out**

**7.4 Use a large breaker bar and the appropriate size socket to remove the crankshaft pulley bolt**

**7.5 After removing the centre bolt, remove the crankshaft damper with a two-bolt puller - be careful not to damage the sensor ring**

### *Refitting*

**7** Use a scraper to remove all traces of old gasket material and carbon deposits from the manifold and cylinder head mating surfaces. If the gasket was leaking, have the manifold checked for warpage at an automotive machine workshop and resurfaced if necessary.

**8** Position new gaskets over the cylinder head studs **(see illustration)**. **Note:** *The marks on the gasket should face out (away from the cylinder head) and the arrow should point toward the rear of the engine.*

**9** Refit the manifolds and thread the mounting nuts/bolts into place.

**10** Working from the centre out, tighten the nuts/bolts to the torque listed in this Chapter's Specifications in three or four equal steps.

**11** Refit the remaining parts in the reverse order of removal.

**12** Run the engine and check for exhaust leaks.

### 7  Crankshaft front oil seal - renewal

**1** Disconnect the negative cable from the battery.
*Caution: If the stereo in your vehicle is*

*equipped with an anti-theft system, make sure you have the correct activation code before disconnecting the battery.*

**2** Refer to Chapter 1 and remove the accessory drive belts.

**3** Refer to Chapter 3 and remove the fan shroud and fan clutch assembly.

**4** Remove the crankshaft damper bolt with a socket and large breaker bar **(see illustration)**. To hold the crankshaft stationary, remove the flywheel inspection cover (see Chapter 8) and wedge a large screwdriver into the flywheel ring gear teeth.

**7.7 Carefully tap one end the Woodruff key up and out from the crankshaft keyway, then grasp it with a pair of locking pliers and pull it the rest of the way out - be careful not to damage the key or keyway**

⚠ *Warning: The damper bolt is under considerable torque, so be sure the socket is firmly in place and that your hands are not in danger of hitting anything sharp.*

**5** Use a bolt-type damper puller (available at most car accessory outlets) to remove the crankshaft damper **(see illustration)**.

**7** Remove the Woodruff key from the crankshaft keyway **(see illustration)**.

**8** Carefully pry the seal out of the front cover with a screwdriver or seal-removal tool **(see illustration)**. Don't scratch the bore or

**7.8 Remove the crankshaft seal with a screwdriver or seal puller - there are two slots (arrowed) in the cover which allow you to pry behind the seal**

**7.9 Remove the spacer from the end of the crankshaft and clean it thoroughly**

**7.11 Drive the new seal squarely into the front cover with a large socket or section of pipe - do not remove the plastic refitting guide (arrowed) until the seal is installed**

damage the crankshaft in the process (if the crankshaft is damaged, the new seal will end up leaking).

**9** The crankshaft seal rides on a spacer that slips over the front of the crankshaft. Slip the spacer off and clean the varnish off the seal surface **(see illustration)**.

**10** Clean the bore in the cover and coat the outer edge of the new seal with engine oil or multi-purpose grease. Apply moly-base grease to the seal lip.

**11** Lubricate the spacer with clean engine oil and refit it onto the crankshaft. Using a socket with an outside diameter slightly smaller than the outside diameter of the seal, carefully drive the new seal into place with a hammer **(see illustration)**. Make sure it's installed squarely and driven in to the same depth as the original. If a socket isn't available, a short section of large-diameter pipe will also work. **Note:** *The new seal comes with a plastic installer guide. Do not remove this guide until refitting is completed. The guide keeps the seal lip properly oriented over the crankshaft.*

**12** Refit the Woodruff key, then refit the damper. Tighten the damper bolt to the torque listed in this Chapter's Specifications. **Note:** *The damper bolt can be used to pull the damper back onto the crankshaft, but make sure the damper is perfectly aligned with the Woodruff key.*

**13** The rest of the assembly is the reverse of the removal procedure.

**14** Run the engine and check for oil leaks at the front seal.

---

**8  Timing chains and sprockets** - removal, inspection and refitting

**Caution: If the timing chain broke during engine operation, the valves may have come in contact with the pistons, causing**

*damage. Check the valve clearance (see Section 10) before removal of the cylinder head - bent valves usually will have excessive clearance, indicating damage that will require machine workshop work to repair.*

**Note 1:** *This procedure requires that the sump be removed (see Section 12). In a professional workshop, this would be performed as an in-car procedure with specialised tools to remove the front suspension. Given the equipment available to the average home mechanic, this alternate procedure requires removal of the engine from the car.*

**Note 2:** *If your engine is a 4.0 litre, built after serial number 9J160552, and you're experiencing an engine rattle on cold starts that disappears after the engine is warmed up, the problem could be a defective upper tensioner. A newly designed replacement upper tensioner is available from the dealer and should solve the problem. It can be installed easily without pulling the cylinder head or front cover, or can be installed during a chain removal procedure.*

### Removal

**1** Disconnect the negative cable from the battery.

*Caution: If the stereo in your vehicle is equipped with an anti-theft system, make sure you have the correct activation code before disconnecting the battery.*

**2** Block the rear wheels and set the handbrake.

**3** Refer to Part B of this Chapter for engine removal procedures.

**4** Refer to Section 4 and remove the valve cover.

**5** Refer to Section 3 and position the engine at TDC for cylinder number 1, then mark and remove the distributor (see Chapter 5).

**6** Refer to Section 11 and remove the cylinder head. After cylinder head removal, the upper

timing chain will be loosely retained by the two upper chain guides, which are retained by refitting a large rubber band (see Section 10). *Caution: Do not rotate the crankshaft with the upper timing chain disconnected and the cylinder head and camshafts in place, or damage could result from piston-to-valve contact.*

**7** Some models may be equipped with a hydraulic pump used for the brake servo/hydraulic self-levelling suspension system. If equipped, it will be mounted to the front cover. Models not equipped with this option will have a flat block-off plate over the hole. If equipped with the pump, refer to Chapters 9 and 10 for procedures to reduce the high pressure in the brake servo system and to depressurise the self-levelling system. Before removing the engine, unbolt the pump from the front cover and set it aside without disconnecting the hoses **(see illustration)**.

**8** Refer to Section 7 and remove the crankshaft pulley and damper. Refer to Section 12 for removal of the sump.

**9** If equipped with the hydraulic pump, remove the coupling disc and unbolt the drive coupling from the intermediate shaft **(see illustrations)**.

**8.7 Unbolt the hydraulic pump (arrowed) from the front cover, without disconnecting the hoses**

**8.9a Pull the hydraulic pump coupling disc (arrowed) off the drive coupling . . .**

**8.9b . . . and unbolt the drive coupling (arrowed) from the intermediate shaft**

**8.10 Remove the front cover-to-engine block and the sump-to-cover bolts (arrowed)**

**8.11 Remove the upper timing chain from the intermediate sprocket (arrowed)**

**8.12 Unbolt and remove the upper chain guide (right arrow) and the upper chain tensioner guide (left arrow)**

**8.13 Remove the two bolts and remove the lower timing chain tensioner (arrowed)**

**8.15 Remove the lower timing chain from the intermediate sprocket (A), the auxiliary shaft sprocket (B) and the crankshaft sprocket (C)**

**8.16 Apply paint marks on the crankshaft, crankshaft sprocket and the engine block (arrowed) to indicate TDC position**

**10** Remove the front cover-to-engine block bolts **(see illustration)**. **Note:** *Two of the front cover bolts are water pump assembly bolts. Refer to Chapter 3 for water pump removal, although only the two bolts that attach to the engine block need be removed.*

**11** Release the rubber band from the upper tensioners and remove the upper timing chain **(see illustration)**.

**12** Remove the upper chain guides **(see illustration)**.

**13** Unbolt and remove the lower timing chain tensioner **(see illustration)**.

**14** Refer to Section 13 for removal of the oil pump sprocket and drive chain.

**15** Remove the lower timing chain from the intermediate sprocket, auxiliary shaft sprocket and the crankshaft sprocket **(see illustration)**.

**16** Before proceeding any further, apply timing marks on the crankshaft and the engine block, allowing you to locate TDC position without the crankshaft pulley in place **(see illustration)**.

### Inspection

**17** Examine the sprockets for signs of wear or damage. Renew the timing chain if obvious wear or damage is noted or if it is the least bit questionable. **Note:** *If there is wear or damage noticed in any of the sprockets or chains, the entire set must be renewed, i.e. new chains and new sprockets.*

**18** Correct any problems which contributed to chain failure prior to refitting of a new chain.

**19** Check the chain guides for grooves, chips or wear in the contact surface. Clean and inspect the upper and lower tensioners.

### Refitting

**20** Remove all dirt, oil and grease from the timing chain area at the front of the engine.

**21** Recheck the crankshaft timing marks to be sure they are properly aligned **(see illustration 8.16)**.

**22** Refit the lower timing chain on the crankshaft, intermediate-shaft and auxiliary-shaft sprockets. The chain should be lubricated with engine oil.

**8.23a Add oil to the reservoir in the lower tensioner . . .**

**8.23b . . . and refit the tensioner against the guide -
after it's installed, push the tensioner guide back and forth
a few times to prime the tensioner**

**23** Clean and lubricate the lower tensioner. Fill the lower tensioner oil reservoir with engine oil and refit it on the engine block, aligning the notch in the tensioner with the lug on the back of the guide **(see illustrations)**. This should remove all slack from the lower timing chain. If not, push the lower tensioner guide back and forth a few times to prime the tensioner.

**24** Refit the upper chain tensioner guide and mounting bracket to the engine block.

*Caution: Before fully tightening the mounting bracket to the engine block, make sure the mount and chain guide are clear of the lower chain, auxiliary sprocket and intermediate sprocket. If necessary, position the mount for clearance before tightening the mounting bolts.*

**25** Refit the oil pump drive chain and sprocket to the crankshaft (see Section 13).

**26** Refit the upper chain fixed guide to the engine block and place the upper timing chain over the intermediate sprocket and auxiliary shaft sprocket, draping the excess chain over the top of the fixed guide. Lubricate the chain and sprockets with clean engine oil.

**27** Gather the loose portion of the upper timing chain and place it between the upper guides. Use a large rubber band to hold the two guides snugly around the chain **(see Section 11)**.

**28** If necessary, renew the intermediate shaft seal **(see illustrations)**.

**29** Apply a thin coat of RTV sealant to the engine side of the front cover and RTV sealant to the oil-pan mating surface (bottom of the front cover), then refit the front cover. **Note:** *Make sure the top surface of the cover aligns with the top surface of the engine block, by checking with a straightedge* **(see illustration)**.

**30** Refer to Section 11 for refitting of the cylinder head and Section 10 for refitting of the camshafts and connection of the upper timing chain to the two camshaft sprockets.

**31** The remainder of the refitting is the reverse of the removal procedure. If your car is equipped with the hydraulic/self-levelling suspension, refit the drive coupling and coupling disc to the intermediate shaft **(see illustrations 8.9a and 8.9b)**. Coat the mounting surface of the pump with RTV

sealant and make sure the tang on the pump aligns with the slot in the intermediate shaft before bolting the pump to the front cover. Refer to Section 7 for refitting of the crankshaft spacer, damper and puller.

*Caution: DO NOT start the engine until you're absolutely certain that the timing chains are installed correctly. Serious and costly engine damage could occur if the chains are installed wrong.*

**32** Run the engine and check for proper operation.

## 9 Auxiliary shaft - renewal

*Caution: If the stereo in your vehicle is equipped with an anti-theft system, make sure you have the correct activation code before disconnecting the battery.*

**1** Refer to Chapter 10 and remove the power steering pump, without disconnecting the hoses. Remove the plastic power steering pump drive coupling disc.

**8.28a Drill a small hole in the intermediate shaft seal, thread a sheet metal screw into it and use a small slide-hammer pull the seal out of the cover**

**8.28b Drive the new seal in with a seal-driver or socket, to the same depth as the original seal**

**8.29 Bolt the front cover on hand tight, use a straightedge to make sure the cover's top surface is level with the top of the engine block, then tighten the cover bolts**

**9.3  Use a screwdriver to hold the drive coupling (arrowed) stationary while removing the bolt**

**9.4  Remove the auxiliary shaft seal with a small slide-hammer puller**

**9.5  Use snap-ring pliers to remove the snap ring (arrowed) from the shaft - note the three internal hex-head bolts retaining the housing to the engine block**

**9.8  Inspect these areas of the auxiliary shaft for wear**

A  *Oil seal surface*   C  *Sprocket*
B  *Bearing journal*   D  *Distributor drive*

**9.9  Refit the auxiliary shaft rear housing with a new gasket, aligning the oil slot (arrowed) with the housing**

**9.10  Refit the washer before replacing the snap-ring**

2  Refer to Section 8 and remove the front cover and upper and lower timing chains.
3  Remove the power steering drive coupling from the auxiliary shaft **(see illustration)**.
4  Use a small drill to drill holes in the oil seal, then use a slide-hammer puller to remove the seal from the rear of the auxiliary shaft housing **(see illustration)**.
*Caution: Drill straight and carefully to avoid damaging the auxiliary shaft.*
5  Use a pair of snap-ring pliers to remove the snap ring from the rear of the auxiliary shaft **(see illustration)**.
6  Pull the auxiliary shaft out toward the front of the engine.
7  Remove the three internal hex-head bolts and the auxiliary shaft housing.
8  Examine the surface of the auxiliary shaft, it's sprocket, and the distributor drive-gear. If there is noticeable wear or damage, replace the auxiliary shaft assembly with a new one **(see illustration)**.
9  If the auxiliary shaft housing has been removed, clean it, scrape away the old gasket material from the housing and the engine block and refit the housing with a new gasket **(see illustration)**.
10  Clean the auxiliary shaft, lubricate it with engine oil and refit it through the front of the block, then refit the washer **(see illustration)**. Refit the snap-ring **(refer to illustration 9.4)**.

11  The new oil seal for the rear of the auxiliary shaft comes with a plastic refitting sleeve that keeps the seal lip from folding back during refitting. Keep this sleeve in place until the seal is fully installed. Tap the new seal into the housing with a hammer and appropriate-size socket until the seal is flush, then remove the plastic sleeve **(see illustration)**.
12  The remainder of the refitting is the reverse of removal. **Note:** *When refitting the distributor* (see Chapter 5), *use a new O-ring to prevent oil leaks at the distributor.*
13  Run the engine and check for oil leaks at the power steering pump-to-housing interface.

**9.11  Tap the seal squarely into the bore with a socket until the seal is flush with the housing, then remove the plastic fitting sleeve**

**10  Camshafts and valve lifters - removal, inspection and refitting**

### Removal

**Note:** *The renewal of the camshafts requires the use of several special tools. Read through the procedure and acquire the special tools, or their equivalent, before beginning work.*
1  Remove the valve cover (see Section 4).
2  Refer to Section 3 and position the engine at TDC for number 1 cylinder.
3  Refer to Chapter 5 and remove the distributor cap and set it aside along with the spark plug leads. Mark the positions of the distributor body and rotor.
4  Using a feeler gauge, measure and record the clearance between the intake and exhaust camshaft lobes and the lifters for cylinder number 1 **(see illustration)**. Rotate the crankshaft until the next cylinder in the firing order is at TDC and check and record the valve clearance for that cylinder. Following the firing order, check and record the valve clearance for the remaining valves with the appropriate cylinder at TDC.
5  Return the engine to TDC for cylinder number 1. Using the special tool (Jaguar tool no. 18G 1433), check the position of each

10.4 Measure the valve clearance with a feeler gauge inserted between the heel of the camshaft lobe and the lifter

10.5 Position the camshaft alignment tool over each camshaft - the projection on the tool only fits into the slot on the camshafts when they are at TDC - flip the tool over to check the other camshaft

10.7 Loosen this bolt (arrowed) and swing the clamp away from the tensioner, then use pliers to pull the valve out

10.10a As each cap is removed . . .

10.10b . . . replace it with the special spacer block (arrowed) and tighten the cylinder head bolt to 53 Nm (39 lbf ft)

10.11a Each of the camshaft bearing caps are stamped with I (intake) or E (exhaust) and a number (arrowed)

10.11b After cap no. 2 is replaced with a spacer, repeat the procedure for the other caps in the sequence shown - after cap 5, loosen caps 6 and 7 alternately until valve spring pressure is relieved

camshaft to ensure that they are truly at TDC (see illustration). It may be necessary to rotate the crankshaft slightly, to allow the tool to fit into the slot. Once the camshafts are positioned, DO NOT rotate the crankshaft further.

6 Check the TDC marks made on the distributor body and refer to Chapter 5 for removal of the distributor. Note: Plug the distributor hole with a rag to keep out dirt.

7 Locate the upper timing chain tensioner on the right front of the cylinder head. Loosen the bolt on the clamp and swing the clamp away from the tensioner return valve, then remove the valve (see illustration).

8 Remove the tensioner bolts and pull out the tensioner.

9 The camshaft bearing caps are each retained by three bolts (the two front caps on each camshaft have only two bolts), of which one is a cylinder head bolt that threads into the engine block. If the camshafts are being removed as a step in cylinder head removal, the following steps involving spacer blocks are not required, just remove the bolts and caps, then remove the camshafts. If the procedure is being used for camshaft removal or adjustment of the lifter shims, the procedure must be followed exactly to maintain the cylinder head gasket seal.

10 To maintain a good seal on the cylinder head gasket, if the cylinder head is not being removed, a spacer block (Jaguar tool no. 18G 1435) is used to replace each camshaft bearing cap as it is removed. Begin by unbolting and removing intake cap no. 2. Remove the large cylinder head bolt first, then the cap bolts. Without delay, refit a spacer block, with the cylinder head bolt, and tighten it to 53 Nm (39 lbf ft) (see illustrations).

11 Repeat paragraph 10 with the remainder of the intake camshaft caps in sequence. After cap 5 in the sequence, loosen the front and rear caps alternately until valve spring pressure is relieved from the camshaft (see illustrations). Note: No spacer blocks are required with the number 1 camshaft caps.

**10.12  Bend back the locking tabs (arrowed) and remove the camshaft sprocket bolts**

**10.13  Remove the two bolts and the upper timing chain guide (arrowed)**

**10.14  Pull the inner sprocket from the outer sprocket of each camshaft**

**10.17  A magnet can be used to remove the lifters (arrowed)**

**10.18  The valve adjustment shims (arrowed) fit into a pocket in the valve spring retainer - use a magnet to remove the shims and keep them with their respective lifters**

**10.20  Measure the bearing journals with a micrometer to check diameter - measure at several places around the journal to check for taper or out-of-round**

**12** Remove the four bolts in each camshaft inner sprocket **(see illustration)**. The bolts are secured by sheetmetal "washer" plates. Bend down the locking tabs with a hammer and screwdriver tip to remove the bolts.
*Caution: Stuff rags below the sprockets while removing the bolts to prevent a bolt from falling down into the front cover.*
**13** Remove the two bolts retaining the upper chain guide to the cylinder head **(see illustration)**.
**14** Pull the inner sprockets from each camshaft **(see illustration)**. Each camshaft sprocket is comprised of an inner and outer, each with a set of fine splines that lock them together. The outer sprockets, with the teeth, can rotate on the camshafts until the inner sprocket bolts are tightened.
**15** Pull the outer sprockets from the camshafts and allow the chain slacken.
**16** At this point the camshafts can be carefully lifted straight up and off the cylinder head. Take care not to nick any of the lobes or journals during removal.
**17** Use a magnet to remove the lifters, keeping them in order in a divided, numbered box **(see illustration)**. They **must** be returned to their original location if reusing the original camshafts!
**18** Removing the lifters exposes the adjusting shims, sitting in a pocket in each

valve spring retainer **(see illustration)**. Keep the shims with their matching lifters. Measure the thickness of each shim with a micrometer and record the measurements.

### Inspection

**19** After the camshaft has been removed from the engine, cleaned with solvent and dried, inspect the bearing journals for uneven wear, pitting and evidence of seizure. If the journals are damaged, the bearing surfaces in the cylinder head and caps may be damaged as well, requiring renewal of the cylinder head.
**20** Measure the bearing journals with a micrometer to determine if they are excessively

worn or out-of-round **(see illustration)**. Compare the measurements to Specifications.
**21** Check the camshaft lobes for heat discolouration, score marks, chipped areas, pitting and uneven wear. Measure the lobe heights with a micrometer and record the measurements **(see illustrations)**. If there is variance of more than 0.005-inch, the camshaft and lifters must be renewed. If the lobes are in good condition, the camshaft can be reused.
**22** Inspect the top, bottom and side surfaces of the lifters for wear, grooving or scoring. If the lifters are damaged, the camshaft and its lifters must be renewed as a set.

**10.21a  Measure the camshaft lobe at its greatest dimension . . .**

**10.21b  . . . and subtract the camshaft lobe diameter at its smallest dimension to obtain the lobe lift**

10.27a Each camshaft sprocket is comprised of two sections, an inner (A) and outer (B) that are splined together

10.27b Push the outer sprocket over the intake camshaft until it locks in place - then turn the sprocket left to remove chain slack at the right

### Refitting

**23** If the valve clearance for any valve is incorrect, as measured in paragraph 4, refit a thicker or thinner shim on that valve. For example, if the clearance had been too large by 0.004-inch (compared to the recommended clearance in the Specifications), replace the existing shim there with a new one that is 0.004-inch thicker. If the clearance was too small, use a shim that is smaller than the original. Shims are identified alphabetically, in sizes from 0.085-inch (designated size A, the smallest) to 0.108-inch (designated size X, the thickest).

**24** Lubricate the lifters with a thin coat of moly-based lubricant on the top, bottom and sides and refit them in their original positions.

**25** Lubricate the camshafts with moly-based grease on the journals and lobes and lay them carefully in their bearing saddles.

**26** Using NEW cylinder head bolts, replace the spacers, one at a time, with the bearing caps and bolts. Tighten the cap bolts, then the cylinder head bolts to the torque listed in this Chapter's Specifications. The front cap should be installed first, then cap number 7, then alternately tighten the first and last caps to bring the camshaft down evenly. Next refit caps 4, 2, 3, 5, and 6.

**27** Align the intake camshaft with the special camshaft positioning tool as described in paragraph 5. Engage the outer sprocket with the chain, slip the sprocket over the end of the camshaft, then turn it until there is no slack in the chain to the right of the camshaft sprocket (facing the front of the engine). Now align the inner sprocket with the camshaft until the bolt holes align and mesh the splines between the two sprocket halves **(see illustrations)**. Tighten the inner sprocket bolts to the camshaft and bend the locking sheetmetal tabs over the bolts.

**28** Keeping the slack in the chain to the left of the exhaust camshaft, refit the exhaust camshaft outer sprocket, meshed with the chain, over the end of the exhaust camshaft. Insert the timing chain tensioner tool (Jaguar tool no. 18G 1436) at the upper tensioner mounting point **(see illustration)**. **Note:** The chain tensioner tool applies pressure to the upper timing chain to simulate the effect of the tensioner, which is operated by engine oil pressure when the engine is running.

**29** Align the exhaust camshaft to TDC with the special timing gauge tool. Tighten the centre bolt in the tensioner tool to 4 to 6 Nm. When the chain is tensioned, align the inner exhaust sprocket with the bolt holes in the camshaft, engage the splines between the two sprocket halves and secure the sprocket with the bolts and locking tabs. Refit the clip to secure the two sprocket halves together.

**30** Clean the tensioner gasket surface, fit a new gasket and O-rings, push the ratchet down and twist it to maintain the fully retracted position, and refit the tensioner in place of the tensioning tool **(see illustration)**. **Note:** Align the slot in the end of the tensioner straight up and down to fit over the tang on the back of the chain tensioner guide.

**31** Rotate the engine and recheck that all valve clearance measurements are now correct (see paragraph 4).

**32** The remainder of refitting is the reverse of the removal procedure. **Note:** When refitting the distributor, use a new O-ring where it fits into the engine block.

10.28 The special tensioning tool simulates the operation of the oil-driven tensioner - apply 4 to 6 Nm (36 to 48 inch-pounds) pressure on the centre bolt (arrowed)

10.30 Upper timing chain tension components

A  Notch (to align with tang on guide)
B  Tensioner ratchet
C  O-ring
D  Gasket
E  valve (with O-rings)

**11.10  Disconnect the hoses and remove the bolts to separate the coolant housing (arrowed) from the cylinder head**

**11.11  Remove the bolts (arrowed) securing the cylinder head to the front cover**

## 11 Cylinder head -
removal and refitting

**Note:** *The engine must be completely cool before beginning this procedure.*

### Removal

**1**  Disconnect the battery negative cable.
*Caution: If the stereo in your vehicle is equipped with an anti-theft system, make sure you have the correct activation code before disconnecting the battery.*
**2**  Drain the coolant from the engine block and radiator (see Chapter 1).
**3**  Drain the engine oil and remove the oil filter (see Chapter 1).
**4**  Remove the bonnet for easier access, if necessary (see Chapter 11).
**5**  Remove the intake manifold (see Section 5).
**6**  Remove the exhaust manifolds (Section 6).
**7**  Remove the valve cover (see Section 4).
**8**  Refer to Section 3 and Position the engine at TDC for cylinder number 1. Remove the distributor (see Chapter 5).
**9**  Remove the camshafts and sprockets (see Section 10). Place the upper chain between the two upper chain guides and wrap a large rubber band around the two guides, retaining the chain and guides.
**10**  Remove the coolant housing from the cylinder head **(see illustration)**.
**11**  Remove the cylinder head-to-front cover bolts **(see illustration)**.
**12**  Using a socket and breaker bar, loosen the cylinder head bolts in quarter-turn increments until they can be removed by hand. Loosen the cylinder head bolts using the opposite of the recommended tightening sequence **(see illustration 11.23)** to avoid warping or cracking the cylinder head.
**13**  Lift the cylinder head off the engine block. If it's stuck, very carefully pry up at the transmission end, beyond the gasket surface.
*Caution: Though the cylinder head is aluminium, it is still heavy, large and*
awkward to handle. To avoid damaging the body during removal, use an engine hoist to lift the cylinder head out of the engine compartment, or have an assistant help you.*
**14**  With the cylinder head on a workbench, remove all external components from the cylinder head to allow for thorough cleaning and inspection. See Chapter 2, Part B, for cylinder head servicing procedures.

### Refitting

**15**  The mating surfaces of the cylinder head and engine block must be perfectly clean when the cylinder head is installed.
**16**  Use a gasket scraper to remove all traces of carbon and old gasket material, then clean the mating surfaces with lacquer thinner or acetone. If there's oil on the mating surfaces when the cylinder head is installed, the gasket may not seal correctly and leaks could develop. When working on the engine block, stuff the cylinders with clean workshop rags to keep out debris. Use a vacuum cleaner to remove material that falls into the cylinders.
*Caution: Use care when cleaning the cylinder head gasket surface. The cylinder head and engine block are aluminium and can be easily damaged by using sharp*
scraping tools. Gasket removal solvents are available from car accessory outlets and may be useful for safe removal of gasket material.*
**17**  Check the engine block and cylinder head mating surface for nicks, deep scratches and damage from coolant corrosion. If damage is slight, it can be removed with a file; if it's excessive, machining may be the only alternative. See Part B of this Chapter for procedures and criteria concerning the repair of corrosion damage.
**18**  Use a tap of the correct size to chase the threads in the cylinder head bolt holes, then clean the holes with compressed air - make sure that nothing remains in the holes.

⚠ *Warning: Wear eye protection when using compressed air!*

**19**  Remove the rear cover from the cylinder head. Clean the gasket surface and refit the cover with a new gasket **(see illustration)**. Place the side of the gasket with the sealer bead against the cylinder head, do not use sealant on this gasket.
**20**  Fabricate two alignment studs from the old head bolts. Cut off the heads, then slot the ends with a hacksaw **(see illustration)**. New cylinder head bolts must be used when refitting the head.

**11.19  Remove the rear cover from the cylinder head, clean the gasket surfaces and refit the cover with a new gasket (arrowed) - note that the printed-on sealer bead is placed against the cylinder head**

**11.20  Fabricate two alignment studs from old cylinder head bolts and refit them in the engine block - after the cylinder head is installed, remove the two studs**

**11.21a Only use a head gasket with the improved oil transfer seal (right arrow) - the older style (left arrow) is prone to oil leaks**

**11.21b Place the new head gasket over the dowels in the engine block - note the markings for UP or TOP printed on the gasket**

**11.23 Cylinder head bolt TIGHTENING sequence**

**12.3 Remove the sump bolts (arrowed)**

**21** There are variations in cooling holes in some models. Before refitting the cylinder head gasket, carefully check all of the passages and bolt holes in the new cylinder head gasket to be sure it matches your engine block. Also make sure the new cylinder head gasket you're using is equipped with the improved oil transfer hole seal **(see illustration)**. Position the cylinder head gasket over the dowel pins in the engine block, make sure TOP is facing up **(see illustration)**.

**22** Carefully place the cylinder head on the engine block without disturbing the gasket.

**23** Refit NEW cylinder head bolts and following the recommended sequence, tighten the bolts in two steps to the torque listed in this Chapter's Specifications **(see illustration)**. Step 2 of the tightening sequence requires the bolts to be tightened and additional 90°. An angle-torque attachment for your torque wrench is available at car accessory outlets. This tool provides precision when the angle-torque method is required and its use is highly recommended. If the tool is not available, paint a mark on the edge of each cylinder head bolt and tighten the bolt until the mark is 90¡ from the starting

point. After the cylinder head bolts are tightened, tighten the cylinder head-to-timing-cover bolts.

**24** The remaining refitting steps are the reverse of removal. Refer to Section 10 for replacing the camshaft sprockets and adjusting the timing chain and tensioner. Refill the cooling system (see Chapter 1).

**25** Run the engine and check for oil or coolant leaks. Adjust the ignition timing (see Chapter 5) and road test the car.

**12 Sump** - removal and refitting

### Removal

**1 Note:** *The sump cannot be removed with the engine in the chassis without lowering the front suspension and crossmember. This is a difficult procedure for the home mechanic without a vehicle hoist and some other specialised tools. The other alternative requires the engine be removed from the car and mounted on a stand, as we have*

*illustrated here. Refer to Part B of this Chapter for engine removal procedures.*

**2** Drain the engine oil and remove the oil filter (see Chapter 1).

**3** Remove the bolts and detach the sump **(see illustration)**.

**4** If it's stuck, pry it loose very carefully with a small screwdriver or putty knife **(see illustration)**. Don't damage the mating surfaces of the pan and engine block or oil leaks could develop.

**12.4 Pry at the recess in the front of the sump to break the gasket seal - insert a putty knife, if necessary, between the sump and engine block**

**12.8 Remove the bolts (arrowed) and the sheetmetal baffle plate - clean the sump area of the sump with the baffle removed**

**12.9 Lubrication system components**

A  Oil pump  C  Transfer housing
B  Transfer tubes  D  Oil pump pickup

**12.10 Apply a bead of RTV sealant around the perimeter of the sump mounting flange, be sure to run the bead around the outside all bolt the holes**

### Refitting

**5** Remove all traces of old gasket material and sealant from the engine block and sump. Clean the mating surface with lacquer thinner or acetone.
*Caution: Do not use a sharp scraping tool. Both the sump and the engine block are aluminium and could be easily damaged.*
**6** Make sure the threaded bolt holes in the engine block and bellhousing are clean.
**7** Inspect the flange of the sump for any cracks, pits or scratches that could cause an oil leak.
**8** Remove the baffle plate at the rear of the sump **(see illustration)**. Clean the sump area and the baffle, then refit the baffle.
**9** Inspect the oil pump pickup tube for cracks, or foreign material blocking the screen **(see illustration)**.
**10** Apply a bead of RTV sealant to the sump flange **(see illustration)**. **Note:** *The sump must be installed within 5 minutes of sealer application.*
**11** Carefully position the sump on the engine block and push it toward the transmission adapter plate as you press it against the engine block. Loosely refit four bolts, two on each side of the sump. Tighten the four bolts in a criss-cross pattern to the torque listed in this Chapter's Specifications, then loosen each bolt 90°.
**12** Refit the two engine adapter-to-sump bolts. Tighten the two bolts to the torque listed in this Chapter's Specifications, then loosen each one 180°.
**13** Refit the remainder of the sump-to-engine block bolts hand tight until all are installed, then tighten them to the torque listed in this Chapter's Specifications. Lastly, tighten the two adapter-to-sump bolts to the torque listed in this Chapter's Specifications.
*Caution: Failure to follow this tightening procedure could stress or possibly crack the adapter plate.*
**14** The remainder of refitting is the reverse of removal. Be sure to add oil and refit a new oil filter.
**15** Run the engine and check for oil pressure and leaks.

### 13 Oil pump - removal, inspection and refitting

### Removal

**1** Remove the sump (see Section 12).
**2** Unbolt the oil pickup tube and oil transfer housing from the engine block **(see illustration)**. **Note:** *Have a drain pan under the transfer housing, as oil may drip out when the housing is loosened from the engine block.*
**3** Carefully pull the transfer housing and transfer tubes to the rear to separate them from the oil pump body.
**4** Bend back the locking tabs and remove the

three bolts retaining the oil pump drive sprocket to the oil pump **(see illustration)**. Pull the chain and sprocket from the front of the pump. **Note:** *There are shims between the sprocket and the pump. Collect them while pulling off the sprocket.*
**5** Remove the bolts and detach the oil pump from the engine.
**6** Remove all traces of sealant and old gasket material from the oil pump body and engine block, then clean the mating surfaces with lacquer thinner or acetone.
**7** Remove the screws and separate the front and rear pump covers from the body. Lift out the drive and driven rotors **(see illustrations)**. **Note:** *Mark the front face of each rotor before removing them.*

**13.2 Unbolt the oil pump pickup (A) and the bolts (B) retaining the transfer assembly (C) to the engine block**

**13.4 Pry back the locking tabs and remove the three bolts retaining the oil pump drive sprocket to the pump**

**13.7a Remove the bolts and separate the front and rear pump covers**

**13.7b Remove the outer rotor (A) and inner rotor (B)**

**13.9 Measure the outer rotor-to-body clearance with feeler gauges (arrowed)**

**13.10 With a straightedge held tight to the pump surface, measure the clearance over the rotors with feeler gauges**

**13.11 Oil pressure relief valve components**

A  *Relief valve cap*  C  *Spring*
B  *Tube*             D  *Valve*

### Inspection

**8** Clean and dry the pump body and both rotors. Measure the outside diameter of the outer rotor and thickness of both rotors.
**9** Place the outer rotor into the pump body and use feeler gauges to measure the clearance between the outer rotor and the body **(see illustration)**.
**10** Place a straightedge across the pump body and measure between the straightedge and the rotors to check the over-the-rotor clearance **(see illustration)**. Compare your measurements to this Chapter's Specifications and renew the oil pump if any are beyond the maximum allowable.
**11** Remove the oil pressure relief valve cap. Remove and clean the relief valve components **(see illustration)**.
**12** Clean all components with solvent and inspect them for wear and damage. If excessive wear, damage or if any clearance is beyond the Specifications, renew the entire pump as an assembly.
**13** Check the oil pressure relief valve piston sliding surface and valve spring. If either the spring or the valve is damaged, they must be renewed as a set.

### Refitting

**14** Lubricate the drive and driven rotors with clean engine oil and place them in the case with the marks facing out. Apply a thin coat of anaerobic sealant (Loctite 510 or 518) to the gasket flange and refit the cover **(see illustration)**.
**15** Lubricate the oil pressure relief valve piston with clean engine oil and refit the valve components into the oil pump body **(see illustration 13.11)**.
**16** Apply a thin coat of anaerobic sealant (Loctite 510 or 518) to the oil pump-to-engine block-mounting surface, position the oil pump body against the engine block and refit the mounting bolts, tightening the bolts to the torque listed in this Chapter's Specifications. Follow a criss-cross pattern when tightening the bolts to avoid warping the oil pump body.
**17** If using the original oil pump, refit the original sprocket shim pack **(see illustration)**. If a new pump is installed, start off with a 0.38 mm (0.015-inch) thick shim pack, refit the drive sprocket and align the sprocket as follows.
**18** Use a straightedge to check the alignment of the oil pump sprocket with the crankshaft sprocket **(see illustration)**. If they are not aligned, increase or decrease the shim pack at the oil pump sprocket until alignment is correct, then secure the oil pump sprocket bolts by bending up the sheetmetal tabs. **Note:** *You may be able to use all or part of the original shim pack from the original oil pump (if a new pump is being fitted). If required, shims are*

*available in 0.127 mm (0.005 inch), 0.254 mm (0.010 inch) and 0.508 mm (0.020 inch) sizes.*
**19** Fit new O-rings to each end of the transfer tubes and refit the tubes into the transfer housing. **Note:** *Use petroleum jelly to lubricate the O-rings.*
**20** Apply a thin coat of RTV sealant to the engine block-mounting surface of the transfer housing. Lift the transfer housing and tubes into place and push the front of the tubes in the back of the oil pump, until you can start the transfer housing-to-engine block bolts. Tighten the bolts to the torque listed in this Chapter's Specifications.
**21** Refit the remaining parts in the reverse order of removal.
**22** Add oil, start the engine and check for oil pressure and leaks.
**23** Recheck the engine oil level.

## 14 Driveplate -
### removal and refitting

### Removal

**1** Raise the car and support it securely on axle stands, then refer to Chapter 7 and remove the transmission. If it's leaking, now would be a very good time to renew the front pump seal/O-ring.

**13.14 Apply a thin coat anaerobic sealant (Loctite 510 or 518) to the pump cover sealing surface**

**13.17 Refit the original shim pack (arrowed) if the original pump is being used - if a new pump is being installed, refit a 0.38 mm (0.015-inch) shim pack**

**13.18 Check the oil pump and crankshaft sprocket alignment with a straightedge - add or subtract shims until the sprockets are aligned for smooth chain operation**

**14.2  Mark the driveplate and the crankshaft so they can be reassembled in the same relative position**

**14.3  Use a screwdriver to secure the flywheel while the bolts are removed**

**14.4  Pry off the driveplate spacer - if a driveplate is replaced, the spacer should be replaced also**

**2** Use a centre punch or paint to make alignment marks on the driveplate and crankshaft to ensure correct alignment during refitting **(see illustration)**.
**3** Remove the bolts that secure the driveplate to the crankshaft. If the crankshaft turns, wedge a screwdriver through a hole in the driveplate to keep it from turning **(see illustration)**.
**4** Remove the driveplate from the crankshaft. A spacer is located behind the driveplate **(see illustration)**. Pry it off and store it with the driveplate.

 **Warning: The ring-gear teeth may be sharp, wear gloves to protect your hands when handling the driveplate.**

### Refitting

**5** Clean the driveplate to remove grease and oil. Inspect the surface for cracks. Check for cracked and broken ring gear teeth. **Note:** *If there is any damage to the driveplate, replace the driveplate with a new driveplate, a new spacer and new bolts. Improved parts are available as a set from the dealer.*
**6** Clean and inspect the mating surfaces of the driveplate and the crankshaft. If the crankshaft rear seal is leaking, renew it before refitting the driveplate (see Section 15).
**7** Position the driveplate against the crankshaft. Be sure to align the marks made during removal. Some models may have an alignment dowel or staggered bolt holes to ensure correct refitting. Before refitting the bolts, apply thread-locking compound to the bolt threads.
**8** Wedge a screwdriver in the ring gear teeth to keep the driveplate from turning and tighten the bolts to the torque listed in this Chapter's Specifications. Follow a criss-cross pattern and work up to the final torque in three or four steps.
**9** The remainder of refitting is the reverse of the removal procedure.

## 15  Crankshaft rear oil seal - renewal

**1** The transmission adapter plate and driveplate must be removed from the car for this procedure (see Chapter 7).
**2** Remove the bolts, and detach the oil seal retainer. Remove the gasket material from the block and the seal retainer **(see illustration)**.
**3** Position the oil seal and retainer assembly between two wood blocks on a workbench and drive the old seal out from the backside **(see illustration)**.
**4** The new seal must be driven into the retainer plate from the engine side. Drive the

new seal into the retainer with a wood block or a section of pipe slightly smaller in diameter than the outside diameter of the seal **(see illustration)**. The seal should be driven in only until it is flush with the transmission side of the retainer.
*Caution: The new seal comes with a special plastic refitting sleeve inserted in the seal. It is designed to allow the seal to slide over the end of the crankshaft without displacing the seal lip. Do NOT remove this plastic sleeve until the retainer and seal have been installed on the engine.*
**5** Lubricate the seal area of the crankshaft with engine oil. Apply a bead of RTV sealant to the sealing surface of the retainer **(see illustration)**.

**15.2  Remove the bolts (arrowed) and the crankshaft rear oil seal retainer from the back of the engine block**

**15.3  After removing the retainer assembly from the engine block, support it between two wood blocks and drive out the old seal with a drift punch and hammer**

**15.4  Drive the new seal into the retainer with a wood block**

**15.5  Apply RTV sealant to the sealing surface**

15.6 Refit the retainer and oil seal onto the crankshaft

16.9 Front engine mount (A)
and retaining nut to engine bracket (B)

**6** Slowly and carefully press the seal and retainer squarely onto the crankshaft **(see illustration)**. The plastic sleeve may be pushed out as the retainer seats on the engine block. Remove the plastic sleeve.

**7** Refit and tighten the retainer bolts to the torque listed in this Chapter's Specifications.

**8** The remaining steps are the reverse of removal.

### 16 Engine mounts - check and renewal

**1** Engine mounts seldom require attention, but broken or deteriorated mounts should be renewed immediately or the added strain placed on the driveline components may cause damage or wear.

### Check

**2** During the check, the engine must be raised to remove the weight from the mounts.

**3** Raise the car and support it securely on axle stands, then position a jack under the engine sump. Place a large wood block between the jack head and the sump, then carefully raise the engine just enough to take the weight off the mounts. Do not position the wood block under the drain plug.

 *Warning: DO NOT place any part of your body under the engine when it's supported by a jack!*

**4** Check the front mounts to see if the rubber is cracked, hardened or separated from the metal plates. Sometimes the rubber will split down the centre.

**5** Check for relative movement between the mount plates and the engine or frame (use a large screwdriver or pry bar to attempt to move the mounts). If movement is noted, lower the engine and tighten the mount fasteners.

**6** Rubber preservative should be applied to the mounts to slow deterioration.

### Renewal

**7** Disconnect the battery negative cable.
*Caution: If the stereo in your vehicle is equipped with an anti-theft system, make sure you have the correct activation code before disconnecting the battery.*

**8** Raise the car and support it securely on axle stands. Support the engine as described in paragraph 3.
*Caution: Ensure the cooling fan doesn't hit the shroud as the engine is raised.*

**9** To remove either engine mount, remove the nut from the engine bracket, then raise the engine **(see illustration)**.

**10** From underneath the car, lower the steering gear (see Chapter 10) for access to the nut retaining the insulator to the chassis bracket.

**11** Refitting is the reverse of removal. Use thread-locking compound on the mount bolts/nuts and be sure to tighten them securely.

**12** See Chapter 7 for transmission mount renewal.

# Chapter 2  Part B
# Engine removal and overhaul procedures

## Contents

## Degrees of difficulty

| | | | | |
|---|---|---|---|---|
| **Easy,** suitable for novice with little experience  | **Fairly easy,** suitable for beginner with some experience  | **Fairly difficult,** suitable for competent DIY mechanic  | **Difficult,** suitable for experienced DIY mechanic  | **Very difficult,** suitable for expert DIY or professional |

## Specifications

### General

Cylinder compression pressure @ 300 rpm, warm
   Standard . . . . . . . . . . . . . . . . . . . . . . . . . . . . . . . . . . . . . . . . . . . . . 10.6 to 11.3 bar (150 to 160 psi)
   High compression models . . . . . . . . . . . . . . . . . . . . . . . . . . . . . . . . 11.3 to 12.1 bar (160 to 170 psi)
   Maximum variation between cylinders . . . . . . . . . . . . . . . . . . . . . . . 0.8 bar (10 psi)
Oil pressure (engine warm)
   At idle . . . . . . . . . . . . . . . . . . . . . . . . . . . . . . . . . . . . . . . . . . . . . . . 2.1 bar (30 psi) minimum
   At 4000 rpm . . . . . . . . . . . . . . . . . . . . . . . . . . . . . . . . . . . . . . . . . . 4.9 bar (70 psi) minimum

### Cylinder head

Resurfacing limit . . . . . . . . . . . . . . . . . . . . . . . . . . . . . . . . . . . . . . . . 0.25 mm (0.010 inch) maximum
Minimum thickness (see text)
   3.6 litre . . . . . . . . . . . . . . . . . . . . . . . . . . . . . . . . . . . . . . . . . . . . . . 129.6 mm (5.101 inches)
   3.2 and 4.0 litre . . . . . . . . . . . . . . . . . . . . . . . . . . . . . . . . . . . . . . . 129.7 mm (5.108 inches)

### Valves and related components

Valve stem-to-guide clearance . . . . . . . . . . . . . . . . . . . . . . . . . . . . . 0.038 to 0.076 mm (0.0015 to 0.0030 inch)
Valve springs, free length . . . . . . . . . . . . . . . . . . . . . . . . . . . . . . . . . 40.13 mm (1.580 inches)
Valve lifter
   Diameter . . . . . . . . . . . . . . . . . . . . . . . . . . . . . . . . . . . . . . . . . . . . . 33.34 to 33.35 mm (1.3126 to 1.3130 inches)
   Lifter-to-bore clearance . . . . . . . . . . . . . . . . . . . . . . . . . . . . . . . . . . 0.02 to 0.05 mm (0.0008 to 0.0020 inch)

### Crankshaft and connecting rods

Connecting rod journal
   Diameter . . . . . . . . . . . . . . . . . . . . . . . . . . . . . . . . . . . . . . . . . . . . . 52.97 to 52.99 mm (2.0856 to 2.0861 inches)
   Taper and out-of-round limits . . . . . . . . . . . . . . . . . . . . . . . . . . . . . 0.008 mm (0.0003 inch) maximum
   Bearing oil clearance
      3.6 litre . . . . . . . . . . . . . . . . . . . . . . . . . . . . . . . . . . . . . . . . . . . . 0.040 to 0.083 mm (0.0016 to 0.0033 inch)
      3.2 and 4.0 litre . . . . . . . . . . . . . . . . . . . . . . . . . . . . . . . . . . . . . 0.025 to 0.0068 mm (0.0010 to 0.0027 inch)
Connecting rod side clearance (endplay) . . . . . . . . . . . . . . . . . . . . . . 0.127 to 0.228 mm (0.005 to 0.009 inch)
Main bearing journal
   Diameter . . . . . . . . . . . . . . . . . . . . . . . . . . . . . . . . . . . . . . . . . . . . . 76.217 to 76.233 mm (3.0007 to 3.0012 inches)
   Taper and out-of-round limits . . . . . . . . . . . . . . . . . . . . . . . . . . . . . 0.008 mm (0.0003 inch) maximum
   Bearing oil clearance . . . . . . . . . . . . . . . . . . . . . . . . . . . . . . . . . . . 0.040 to 0.083 mm (0.0016 to 0.0033 inch)
Crankshaft endplay (standard) . . . . . . . . . . . . . . . . . . . . . . . . . . . . . 0.101 to 0.254 mm (0.004 to 0.010 inch)

## Engine block

Deck warpage limit ............................................. 0.076 mm (0.003 inch)
Cylinder bore diameter
  Standard
    Size group A ........................................ 90.990 to 91.003 mm (3.5823 to 3.5828 inches)
    Size group B ........................................ 91.005 to 91.018 mm (3.5829 to 3.5834 inches)
  Oversize
    0.25 mm (0.010 inch) OS ............................. 91.259 to 91.272 mm (3.5929 to 3.5934 inches)
    0.50 mm (0.020 inch) OS ............................. 91.513 to 91.526 mm (3.6029 to 3.6034 inches)

## Pistons and rings

Piston-to-bore clearance .................................. 0.017 to 0.043 mm (0.0007 to 0.0017 inch)
Piston ring end gap
  No.1 (top) compression ring ............................. 0.40 to 0.66 mm (0.016 to 0.026 inch)
  No.2 (middle) compression ring ......................... 0.40 to 0.66 mm (0.016 to 0.026 inch)
  Oil ring ................................................ 0.30 to 0.55 mm (0.012 to 0.022 inch)
Piston ring groove clearance
  No. 1 (top) compression ring .......................... 0.040 to 0.076 mm (0.0016 to 0.0030 inch)
  No. 2 (middle) compression ring ....................... 0.040 to 0.076 mm (0.0016 to 0.0030 inch)

## Torque wrench settings

| | Nm | lbf ft |
| --- | --- | --- |
| Main bearing cap bolts ................................... | 136 to 142 | 100 to 105 |
| Connecting rod cap nuts ................................. | 50 to 60 | 37 to 44 |

\* **Note:** *Refer to Part A for additional torque specifications.*

---

### 1  General information

Included in this portion of Chapter 2 are the general overhaul procedures for the cylinder head and internal engine components.

The information ranges from advice concerning preparation for an overhaul and the purchase of replacement parts to detailed, step-by-step procedures covering removal and refitting of internal engine components and the inspection of parts.

The following Sections have been written based on the assumption that the engine has been removed from the vehicle. For information concerning in-vehicle engine repair, as well as removal and refitting of the external components necessary for the overhaul, see Part A of this Chapter.

The Specifications included in this Part are only those necessary for the inspection and overhaul procedures which follow. Refer to Part A for additional Specifications.

### 2  Engine overhaul - general information

It's not always easy to determine when, or if, an engine should be completely overhauled, as a number of factors must be considered.

High mileage is not necessarily an indication that an overhaul is needed, while low mileage doesn't preclude the need for an overhaul. Frequency of servicing is probably the most important consideration. An engine that's had regular and frequent oil and filter changes, as well as other required maintenance, will most likely give many thousands of miles of reliable

service. Conversely, a neglected engine may require an overhaul very early in its life.

Excessive oil consumption is an indication that piston rings, valve seals and/or valve guides are in need of attention. Make sure that oil leaks aren't responsible before deciding that the rings and/or guides are bad. Perform a cylinder compression check to determine the extent of the work required (see Section 4). Also check the vacuum readings under various conditions (see Section 3).

Check the oil pressure with a gauge installed in place of the oil pressure sender unit **(see illustrations)** and compare it to this Chapter's Specifications. If it's extremely low, the bearings and/or oil pump are probably worn out.

Loss of power, rough running, knocking or metallic engine noises, excessive valve train noise and high fuel consumption rates may also point to the need for an overhaul, especially if they're all present at the same time. If a complete tune-up doesn't remedy the situation, major mechanical work is the only solution.

An engine overhaul involves restoring the internal parts to the specifications of a new engine. During an overhaul, the piston rings are replaced and the cylinder walls are reconditioned (rebored and/or honed). If a rebore is done by an automotive machine workshop, new oversize pistons will also be installed. The main bearings, big-end bearings and camshaft bearings are generally replaced with new ones and, if necessary, the crankshaft may be reground to restore the journals. Generally, the valves are serviced as well, since they're usually in less-than-perfect condition at this point. While the engine is being overhauled, other components, such as the distributor, starter and alternator, can be rebuilt as well. The end result should be a like new engine that will give many trouble free miles. **Note:** *Critical cooling system components such as the hoses, drivebelts, thermostat and water pump should be replaced with new parts when an engine is overhauled. The radiator should be checked carefully to ensure that it isn't clogged or leaking (see Chapter 3). If you purchase a*

2.4a  The oil pressure sender unit (arrowed) is located in the right front corner of the engine block, near the oil filter

2.4b The oil pressure can be checked by removing the sender unit and refitting a pressure gauge in its place

*rebuilt engine or short block, some rebuilders will not warranty their engines unless the radiator has been professionally flushed. Also, we don't recommend overhauling the oil pump - always refit a new one when an engine is rebuilt.*

Before beginning the engine overhaul, read through the entire procedure to familiarise yourself with the scope and requirements of the job. Overhauling an engine isn't difficult, but it is time-consuming. Plan on the vehicle being tied up for a minimum of two weeks, especially if parts must be taken to an automotive machine workshop for repair or reconditioning. Check on availability of parts and make sure that any necessary special tools and equipment are obtained in advance. Most work can be done with typical hand tools, although a number of precision measuring tools are required for inspecting parts to determine if they must be renewed. Often an automotive machine workshop will handle the inspection of parts and offer advice concerning reconditioning and renewal. **Note:** *Always wait until the engine has been completely dismantled and all components, especially the engine block, have been inspected before deciding what service and repair operations must be performed by an automotive machine workshop.* Since the engine block's condition will be the major factor to consider when determining whether to overhaul the original engine or buy a rebuilt one, never purchase parts or have machine work done on other components until the engine block has been thoroughly inspected. As a general rule, time is the primary cost of an overhaul, so it doesn't pay to refit worn or substandard parts.

If it turns out that a number of major components are beyond reconditioning, it may be cost effective to buy a factory-rebuilt engine from a Jaguar dealership.

As a final note, to ensure maximum life and minimum trouble from a rebuilt engine, everything must be assembled with care in a spotlessly-clean environment.

## 3 Vacuum gauge diagnostic checks

A vacuum gauge provides valuable information about what is going on in the engine at a low cost. You can check for worn rings or cylinder walls, leaking cylinder head or intake manifold gaskets, incorrect carburettor adjustments, restricted exhaust, stuck or burned valves, weak valve springs, improper ignition or valve timing and ignition problems.

Unfortunately, vacuum gauge readings are easy to misinterpret, so they should be used with other tests to confirm the diagnosis.

Both the absolute readings and the rate of needle movement are important for accurate interpretation. Most gauges measure vacuum

**3.4 The vacuum gauge is easily attached to a port on the intake manifold, and can tell a lot about an engine's state of tune**

in inches of mercury (in-Hg). As vacuum increases (or atmospheric pressure decreases), the reading will decrease. Also, for every 1000 foot increase in elevation above sea level; the gauge readings will decrease about one inch of mercury.

Connect the vacuum gauge directly to intake manifold vacuum, not to ported (above the throttle plate) vacuum **(see illustration)**. Be sure no hoses are left disconnected during the test or false readings will result.

Before you begin the test, allow the engine to warm up completely. Block the wheels and set the handbrake. With the transmission in Park, start the engine and allow it to run at normal idle speed.

 **Warning: Carefully inspect the fan blades for cracks or damage before starting the engine. Keep your hands and the vacuum tester clear of the fan and do not stand in front of the vehicle or in line with the fan when the engine is running.**

Read the vacuum gauge; an average, healthy engine should normally produce between 17 and 22 inches of vacuum with a fairly steady needle.

Refer to the following vacuum gauge readings and what they indicate about the engines condition:

**1** A low steady reading usually indicates a leaking gasket between the intake manifold and carburettor or throttle body, a leaky vacuum hose, late ignition timing or incorrect camshaft timing. Check ignition timing with a timing light and eliminate all other possible causes, utilising the tests provided in this Chapter before you remove the timing belt cover to check the timing marks.

**2** If the reading is three to eight inches below normal and it fluctuates at that low reading, suspect an intake manifold gasket leak at an intake port or a faulty injector.

**3** If the needle has regular drops of about two to four inches at a steady rate the valves are probably leaking. Perform a compression or leak-down test to confirm this.

**4** An irregular drop or down-flick of the needle can be caused by a sticking valve or an ignition misfire. Perform a compression or leak-down test and read the spark plugs.

**5** A rapid vibration of about four in-Hg vibration at idle combined with exhaust smoke indicates worn valve guides. Perform a leak-down test to confirm this. If the rapid vibration occurs with an increase in engine speed, check for a leaking intake manifold gasket or cylinder head gasket, weak valve springs, burned valves or ignition misfire.

**6** A slight fluctuation, say one inch up and down, may mean ignition problems. Check all the usual tune-up items and, if necessary, run the engine on an ignition analyser.

**7** If there is a large fluctuation, perform a compression or leak-down test to look for a weak or dead cylinder or a blown cylinder head gasket.

**8** If the needle moves slowly through a wide range, check for a clogged PCV system, incorrect idle fuel mixture, throttle body or intake manifold gasket leaks.

**9** Check for a slow return after revving the engine by quickly snapping the throttle open until the engine reaches about 2,500 rpm and let it shut. Normally the reading should drop to near zero, rise above normal idle reading (about 5 in.-Hg over) and then return to the previous idle reading. If the vacuum returns slowly and doesn't peak when the throttle is snapped shut, the rings may be worn. If there is a long delay, look for a restricted exhaust system (often the silencer or catalytic converter). An easy way to check this is to temporarily disconnect the exhaust ahead of the suspected part and redo the test.

## 4 Cylinder compression check

**1** A compression check will tell you what mechanical condition the upper end (pistons, rings, valves, cylinder head gasket) of your engine is in. Specifically, it can tell you if compression is down due to leakage caused by worn piston rings, defective valves and seats or a blown cylinder head gasket. **Note:** *The engine must be at normal operating temperature and the battery must be fully charged for this check.*

**2** Begin by cleaning the area around the spark plugs before you remove them (compressed air should be used, if available, otherwise a small brush or even a bicycle tyre pump will work). The idea is to prevent dirt from getting into the cylinders as the compression check is being done.

**3** Remove all of the spark plugs from the engine (see Chapter 1).

**4** Block the throttle wide open.

**5** Detach the coil wire from the centre of the distributor cap and ground it on the engine block. Use a jumper wire with alligator clips on each end to ensure a good earth. Also, remove the fuel pump relay (see Chapter 4) to disable the fuel pump during the compression test.

**4.6 A compression gauge with a threaded fitting for the spark plug hole is preferred over the type that requires hand pressure to maintain the seal - be sure to block open the throttle valve as far as possible during the compression check!**

**6** Refit the compression gauge in the spark plug hole **(see illustration)**.
**7** Crank the engine over at least seven compression strokes and watch the gauge. The compression should build up quickly in a healthy engine. Low compression on the first stroke, followed by gradually increasing pressure on successive strokes, indicates worn piston rings. A low compression reading on the first stroke, which doesn't build up during successive strokes, indicates leaking valves or a blown cylinder head gasket (a cracked cylinder head could also be the cause). Deposits on the undersides of the valve heads can also cause low compression. Record the highest gauge reading obtained.
**8** Repeat the procedure for the remaining cylinders and compare the results to this Chapter's Specifications.
**9** Add some engine oil (about three squirts from a plunger-type oil can) to each cylinder, through the spark plug hole, and repeat the test.
**10** If the compression increases after the oil is added, the piston rings are definitely worn. If the compression doesn't increase significantly, the leakage is occurring at the valves or cylinder head gasket. Leakage past the valves may be caused by burned valve seats and/or faces or warped, cracked or bent valves.
**11** If two adjacent cylinders have equally low compression, there's a strong possibility that the cylinder head gasket between them is blown. The appearance of coolant in the combustion chambers or the crankcase would verify this condition.
**12** If one cylinder is 20 percent lower than the others, and the engine has a slightly rough idle, a worn exhaust lobe on the camshaft could be the cause.
**13** If the compression is unusually high, the combustion chambers are probably coated with carbon deposits. If that's the case, the cylinder head(s) should be removed and decarbonised.
**14** If compression is way down or varies greatly between cylinders, it would be a good

idea to have a leak-down test performed by an automotive repair workshop. This test will pinpoint exactly where the leakage is occurring and how severe it is.

## 5  Engine removal - methods and precautions

If you've decided that an engine must be removed for overhaul or major repair work, several preliminary steps should be taken.
Locating a suitable place to work is extremely important. Adequate work space, along with storage space for the vehicle, will be needed. If a workshop or garage isn't available, at the very least a flat, level, clean work surface made of concrete or asphalt is required.
Cleaning the engine compartment and engine before beginning the removal procedure will help keep tools clean and organised.
An engine hoist or A-frame will also be necessary. Make sure the equipment is rated in excess of the combined weight of the engine and transmission. Safety is of primary importance, considering the potential hazards involved in lifting the engine out of the vehicle.
If the engine is being removed by a novice, a helper should be available. Advice and aid from someone more experienced would also be helpful. There are many instances when one person cannot simultaneously perform all of the operations required when lifting the engine out of the vehicle.
Plan the operation ahead of time. Arrange for or obtain all of the tools and equipment you'll need prior to beginning the job. Some of the equipment necessary to perform engine removal and refitting safely and with relative ease are (in addition to an engine hoist) a heavy duty trolley jack, complete sets of spanners and sockets as described in the front of this manual, wooden blocks and plenty of rags and cleaning solvent for mopping up spilled oil, coolant and petrol. If the hoist must be rented, make sure that you arrange for it in advance and perform all of the operations possible without it beforehand. This will save you money and time.
Plan for the vehicle to be out of use for quite a while. A machine workshop will be required to perform some of the work which the do-it-yourselfer can't accomplish without special equipment. These shops often have a busy schedule, so it would be a good idea to consult them before removing the engine in order to accurately estimate the amount of time required to rebuild or repair components that may need work.
Always be extremely careful when removing and refitting the engine. Serious injury can result from careless actions. Plan ahead, take your time and a job of this nature, although major, can be accomplished successfully.

## 6  Engine - removal and refitting

**Note:** *Read through the entire Section before beginning this procedure. It is recommended to remove the engine and transmission from the top as a unit, then separate the engine from the transmission on the workshop floor. If the transmission is not being serviced, it is possible to leave the transmission in the vehicle and remove the engine from the top by itself, by removing the crankshaft damper and tilting up the front end of the engine for clearance, but access to the upper bellhousing bolts is only practical when the rear transmission mount and driveshaft have been removed and the transmission is angled down with a trolley jack.*

### Removal

**1** Relieve the fuel system pressure (see Chapter 4).
**2** Disconnect the battery negative cable.
*Caution: If the stereo in your vehicle is equipped with an anti-theft system, make sure you have the correct activation code before disconnecting the battery.*
**3** Place protective covers on the wings and cowl and remove the bonnet (see Chapter 11).
**4** Remove the battery and battery tray.
**5** Remove the air cleaner assembly (see Chapter 4).
**6** Raise the vehicle and support it securely on axle stands. Drain the cooling system and engine oil and remove the drivebelts (see Chapter 1).
**7** Clearly label, then disconnect all vacuum lines, coolant and emissions hoses, wiring harness connectors and earth straps. Masking tape and/or a touch up paint applicator work well for marking items **(see illustration)**. Take instant photos or sketch the locations of components and brackets.
**8** Remove the cooling fan(s) and radiator (see Chapter 3).
**9** Disconnect the heater hoses.
**10** Release the residual fuel pressure in the tank by removing the petrol cap, then detach the fuel lines connecting the engine to the chassis (see Chapter 4). Plug or cap all open fittings.

**6.7 Label both ends of each wire and hose before disconnecting it**

6.20 Lift the engine high enough to clear the vehicle, tilting it up at the front to clear the front crossmember, then move it away and lower the hoist

6.21 With the engine on the floor but still supported by the hoist, remove the four large bolts (arrowed) and pull off the transmission adapter plate

**11** Disconnect the throttle linkage, transmission linkage (and dipstick tube) and speed control cable, if equipped, from the engine (see Chapters 4 and 7).

**12** Refer to Part A of this Chapter and remove the intake and exhaust manifolds.

**13** Unbolt the power steering pump (see Chapter 10). Tie the pump aside without disconnecting the hoses. Refer to Part A for removal of the hydraulic pump (if equipped) from the timing chain cover.

**14** On air-conditioned models, unbolt the compressor and set it aside. Do not disconnect the refrigerant hoses. **Note:** *Wire the compressor out of the way with a coat hanger, don't let the compressor hang on the hoses.*

**15** Refer to Part A of this Chapter and remove the drivebelts, water pump pulley and crankshaft pulley.

**16** Attach a lifting sling to the engine. Position a hoist and connect the sling to it. Take up the slack until there is slight tension on the hoist.

**17** With a trolley jack and piece of wood supporting the bottom of the transmission sump, refer to Chapter 8 and remove the driveshaft and rear transmission mount.

 *Warning: Do not place any part of your body under the engine/transmission when it's supported only by a hoist or other lifting device.*

**18** With the hoist taking the weight of the engine, unbolt the engine mounts (see Part A of this Chapter).

**19** Recheck to be sure nothing is still connecting the engine or transmission to the vehicle. Disconnect and label anything still remaining.

**20** Slowly lift the engine/transmission out of the vehicle **(see illustration)**. It may be necessary to pry the mounts away from the frame brackets.

**21** Move the engine away from the vehicle and carefully lower the hoist until the engine/transmission can be set on the floor. Refer to Chapter 7 and remove the transmission and converter. Refer to Part A of this Chapter for removal of the flywheel. With the flywheel removed, remove the four large bolts and the transmission adapter plate from the engine **(see illustration)**.

**22** Refer to Part A of this Chapter for removal of the rear main seal retainer plate from the back of the engine, then lift the engine to a position where it can be attached to a sturdy engine stand.

## Refitting

**23** Check the engine/transmission mounts. If they're worn or damaged, renew them.

**24** Attach the hoist and remove the engine from the stand. Refer to Part A of this Chapter and renew the rear main seal and retainer plate, then reattach the transmission adapter plate and refer to Chapter 7 for mounting the converter and transmission.

**25** Carefully lower the engine into the vehicle with the hoist. An assistant is helpful to guide the engine clear of accessories in the engine compartment as the engine is lowered into place.

**26** Refit the engine mount bolts and tighten them securely. Raise the back of the transmission with the trolley jack and reattach the transmission mount, driveshaft and shift linkage.

**27** Refit the remaining components and fasteners in the reverse order of removal.

**28** Add coolant, oil, power steering and transmission fluids as needed (see Chapter 1).

**29** Run the engine and check for proper operation and leaks. Shut off the engine and recheck the fluid levels.

## 7 Engine rebuilding alternatives

The do-it-yourselfer is faced with a number of options when performing an engine overhaul. The decision to renew the engine block, piston/connecting rod assemblies and crankshaft depends on a number of factors, with the number one consideration being the condition of the engine block. Other considerations are cost, access to machine workshop facilities, parts availability, time required to complete the project and the extent of prior mechanical experience on the part of the do-it-yourselfer.

Some of the rebuilding alternatives include:

**Individual parts** - If the inspection procedures reveal that the engine block and most engine components are in reusable condition, purchasing individual parts may be the most economical alternative. The engine block, cylinder head, crankshaft, and piston/connecting rod assemblies should all be inspected carefully. Even if the engine block shows little wear, the cylinder bores should be surface honed.

**Short block** - A short block consists of an engine block with a crankshaft and piston/connecting rod assemblies already installed. All new bearings are incorporated and all clearances will be correct. The existing camshafts, valve train components, cylinder head and external parts can be bolted to the short block with little or no machine workshop work necessary.

**Long block** - A long block consists of a short block plus an oil pump, sump, cylinder head, valve cover, camshaft and valve train components, timing sprockets and chain or gears and timing cover. All components are installed with new bearings, seals and gaskets incorporated throughout. The refitting of manifolds and external parts is all that's necessary. Engines in this rebuilt form are available from Jaguar dealers, and some independent rebuilders.

Give careful thought to which alternative is best for you and discuss the situation with local automotive machine shops, auto parts dealers and experienced rebuilders before ordering or purchasing replacement parts.

## 8  Engine overhaul - dismantling sequence

1 It's much easier to dismantle and work on the engine if it's mounted on a portable engine stand. A stand can often be rented quite cheaply from an equipment rental yard. Before the engine is mounted on a stand, the driveplate and rear oil seal retainer should be removed from the engine.

2 If a stand isn't available, it's possible to dismantle the engine with it blocked up on the floor. Be extra careful not to tip or drop the engine when working without a stand.

3 If you're going to obtain a rebuilt engine, all external components must come off first, to be transferred to the replacement engine, just as they will if you're doing a complete engine overhaul yourself. These include:

> Alternator and brackets
> Emissions control components
> Distributor, spark plug leads and spark plugs
> Thermostat and housing cover
> Water pump
> EFI components
> Intake/exhaust manifolds
> Oil filter
> Engine mounts
> Driveplate
> Transmission adapter plate

**Note:** *When removing the external components from the engine, pay close attention to details that may be helpful or important during refitting. Note the installed position of gaskets, seals, spacers, pins, brackets, washers, bolts and other small items.*

4 If you're obtaining a short block, which consists of the engine block, crankshaft, pistons and connecting rods all assembled, then the cylinder head, sump and oil pump will have to be removed as well from your engine so that your short-block can be turned in to the rebuilder as a core. See *Engine rebuilding alternatives* for additional information regarding the different possibilities to be considered.

5 If you're planning a complete overhaul, the engine must be dismantled and the internal components removed in the following order:

> Intake and exhaust manifolds
> Valve cover
> Upper timing chain and camshaft sprockets

> Camshafts
> Timing chain cover
> Cylinder head
> Sump
> Oil pump
> Piston/connecting rod assemblies
> Crankshaft rear oil seal retainer
> Crankshaft and main bearings

6 Before beginning the dismantling and overhaul procedures, make sure the following items are available. Also, refer to Section 21 for a list of tools and materials needed for engine reassembly.

> Common hand tools
> Small cardboard boxes or plastic bags for storing parts
> Gasket scraper
> Ridge reamer
> Micrometers
> Telescoping gauges
> Dial indicator set
> Valve spring compressor
> Cylinder surfacing hone
> Piston ring groove-cleaning tool
> Electric drill motor
> Tap and die set
> Wire brushes
> Oil gallery brushes
> Cleaning solvent

**Special Jaguar tools**
> Engine lifting brackets (18G 1465)
> Timing damper simulator (18E 1436)
> Camshaft TDC tool (18G 1433)

## 9  Cylinder head - dismantling

**Note:** *New and rebuilt cylinder heads are available from Jaguar and some independent rebuilders. Due to the fact that some specialised tools are necessary for the dismantling and inspection procedures, and replacement parts may not be readily available, it may be more practical and economical for the home mechanic to purchase a replacement cylinder head rather than taking the time to dismantle, inspect and recondition the original.*

**9.2  A small plastic bag, with an appropriate label, can be used to store the valve train components so they can be kept together and reinstalled in the correct guide**

1 Cylinder head dismantling involves removal of the intake and exhaust valves and related components. It's assumed that the lifters and camshafts have already been removed (see Part A as needed).

2 Before the valves are removed, arrange to label and store them, along with their related components, so they can be kept separate and reinstalled in the same valve guides they are removed from **(see illustration)**.

3 Compress the springs on the first valve with a spring compressor and remove the keepers **(see illustration)**. Carefully release the valve spring compressor and remove the retainer, the spring and the spring seat (if used). **Note:** *If your spring compressor does not have an end (such as the one shown) with cut-outs on the side, an adapter is available to use with a standard spring compressor.*
**Caution: Be very careful not to nick or otherwise damage the lifter bores when compressing the valve springs.**

4 Pull the valve out of the cylinder head, then remove the oil seal from the guide. If the valve binds in the guide (won't pull through), push it back into the cylinder head and deburr the area around the keeper groove with a fine file or whetstone.

5 Repeat the procedure for the remaining valves. Remember to keep all the parts for each valve together so they can be reinstalled in the same locations.

6 Once the valves and related components have been removed and stored in an organised manner, the cylinder head should be thoroughly cleaned and inspected. If a complete engine overhaul is being done, finish the engine dismantling procedures before beginning the cylinder head cleaning and inspection process.

## 10  Cylinder head - cleaning and inspection

1 Thorough cleaning of the cylinder head(s) and related valve train components, followed by a detailed inspection, will enable you to decide how much valve service work must be

**9.3  Compress the spring until the keepers can be removed with a small magnetic screwdriver or needle-nose pliers - use a valve spring compressor with an adapter (arrowed) to remove the keepers**

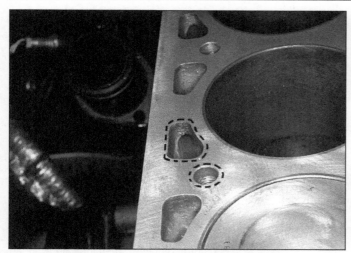

**10.12  Place the new head gasket on the engine block, and trace around the water passages and bolt holes - make sure there is no erosion of the aluminium beyond these lines**

**10.13  Check the cylinder head and engine block gasket surfaces for warpage by trying to slip a feeler gauge under a precision straightedge (see the Specifications for the maximum warpage allowed and use a feeler gauge of that thickness) - check both the cylinder head and engine block (shown)**

done during the engine overhaul. **Note:** *If the engine was severely overheated, the cylinder head is probably warped (see paragraph 12).*

### Cleaning

**2**  Scrape all traces of old gasket material and sealing compound off the cylinder head gasket, intake manifold and exhaust manifold sealing surfaces. Be very careful not to gouge the cylinder head. Special gasket-removal solvents that soften gaskets and make removal much easier are available at car accessory outlets.
**3**  Remove all built up scale from the coolant passages.
**4**  Run a stiff wire brush through the various holes to remove deposits that may have formed in them. If there are heavy deposits in the water passages, the bare head should be professionally cleaned at a machine workshop.
**5**  Run an appropriate-size tap into each of the threaded holes to remove corrosion and any thread sealant that may be present. If compressed air is available, use it to clear the holes of debris produced by this operation.

 *Warning: Wear eye protection when using compressed air!*

**6**  Clean the exhaust and intake manifold stud threads with a wire brush.
**7**  Clean the cylinder head with solvent and dry it thoroughly. Compressed air will speed the drying process and ensure that all holes and recessed areas are clean. **Note:** *Decarbonising chemicals are available and may prove very useful when cleaning cylinder heads and valve train components. They are very caustic and should be used with caution. Be sure to follow the instructions on the container.*
**8**  Clean the lifters with solvent and dry them

thoroughly. Compressed air will speed the drying process and can be used to clean out the oil passages. Don't mix them up during cleaning - keep them in a box with numbered compartments.
**9**  Clean all the valve springs, spring seats, keepers and retainers with solvent and dry them thoroughly. Work on the components from one valve at a time to avoid mixing up the parts.
**10**  Scrape off any heavy deposits that may have formed on the valves, then use a motorised wire brush to remove deposits from the valve heads and stems. Again, make sure that the valves don't get mixed up.

### Inspection

**Note:** *Be sure to perform all of the following inspection procedures before concluding that machine workshop work is required. Make a list of the items that need attention. The inspection procedures for the lifters and camshafts, can be found in Part A.*

#### Cylinder head

**11**  Inspect the cylinder head very carefully for cracks, evidence of coolant leakage and other damage. If cracks are found, check with an automotive machine workshop concerning repair. If repair isn't possible, a new cylinder head should be obtained.
**12**  A common problem on aluminium engines is erosion of the cylinder head or engine block coolant passages due to improper sealing. Using a new cylinder head gasket held against the cylinder head, trace the bolt holes and coolant passage outlines in pencil on the cylinder head. Use the gasket to trace the same on the top of the engine block **(see illustration)**. If the top of the engine block has eroded *outside* of the pattern around the

water passages or cylinder head bolt holes, the engine block must be renewed; the manufacturer doesn't recommend resurfacing it. If the cylinder head has eroded outside of the water passage holes but the erosion is *away from* the combustion chamber, the eroded area can be built up with metal-impregnated epoxy and machined flat again.
**13**  Using a straightedge and feeler gauge, check the cylinder head gasket mating surface (on the engine block and cylinder head) for warpage **(see illustration)**. If the warpage exceeds the limit found in this Chapter's Specifications, it can be resurfaced at an automotive machine workshop, but no more then 0.010-inch of material should be removed. If the cylinder head had been overheated, take it to the machinist for inspection before proceeding further. It's possible that the overheating could have annealed (softened) the aluminium of the cylinder head, making it unsuitable for machine work. In this case, a new cylinder head is required.
**Note 1:** *To check if a cylinder head has been machined previously, measure the height between the cylinder head gasket surface and the valve cover mounting surface with a large micrometer or vernier caliper and compare with Specifications.*
**Note 2:** *Jaguar aluminium cylinder heads require precision machine work. It is best to find a machine workshop that has considerable experience in servicing Jaguar cylinder heads.*
**14**  Examine the valve seats in each of the combustion chambers. If they're pitted, cracked or burned, the cylinder head will require valve service that's beyond the scope of the home mechanic.

**10.15 Use a small dial bore gauge to determine the inside diameter of the valve guides - subtract the valve stem diameter to determine the stem-to-guide clearance**

**10.17 The margin width on each valve must be as specified (if no margin exists, the valve cannot be re-used)**

## 11 Valves - servicing

1 Because of the complex nature of the job and the special tools and equipment needed, servicing of the valves, the valve seats and the valve guides, commonly known as a valve job, should be done by a professional.

2 The home mechanic can remove and dismantle the cylinder head(s), do the initial cleaning and inspection, then reassemble and deliver them to a dealer service department or an automotive machine workshop for the actual service work. Doing the inspection will enable you to see what condition the cylinder head(s) and valvetrain components are in and will ensure that you know what work and new parts are required when dealing with an automotive machine workshop.

3 The dealer service department, or automotive machine workshop, will remove the valves and springs, will recondition or renew the valves and valve seats, recondition the valve guides, check and renew the valve springs, spring retainers and keepers (as necessary), replace the valve seals with new ones, reassemble the valve components and make sure the installed spring height is correct. The cylinder head gasket surface will also be resurfaced if it's warped.

4 After the valve job has been performed by a professional, the cylinder head(s) will be in like new condition. When the cylinder heads are returned, be sure to clean them again before refitting on the engine to remove any metal particles and abrasive grit that may still be present from the valve service or cylinder head resurfacing operations. Use compressed air, if available, to blow out all the oil holes and passages.

**10.18 Measure the free length of each valve spring with a dial or vernier caliper**

**10.19 Check each valve spring for squareness**

### Valve components

18 Check each valve spring for wear (on the ends) and pits. Measure the free length and compare it to this Chapter's Specifications **(see illustration)**. Any springs that are shorter than specified have sagged and should not be re-used. The tension of all springs should be pressure checked with a special fixture before deciding that they're suitable for use in a rebuilt engine (take the springs to an automotive machine workshop for this check). **Note:** *If any valve springs are found broken on 1988 or 1989 engines, all springs should be replaced with the improved springs used in 1990 (after VIN 9EPCLA120245) and later engines. They are identified with a white stripe. If your engine has springs with white-stripes, they have already been replaced, and only broken ones need be replaced.*

19 Stand each spring on a flat surface and check it for squareness **(see illustration)**. If any of the springs are distorted or sagged, renew all of the springs.

20 Check the spring retainers and keepers for obvious wear and cracks. Any questionable parts should be renewed, as extensive damage will occur if they fail during engine operation.

21 If the inspection process indicates that the valve components are in generally poor condition and worn beyond the limits specified, which is usually the case in an engine that's being overhauled, reassemble the valves in the cylinder head and refer to Section 11 for valve servicing recommendations.

## 12 Cylinder head - reassembly

1 Regardless of whether or not the cylinder head was sent to an automotive machine workshop for valve servicing, make sure it's clean before beginning reassembly. Renew the cylinder head rear plate gasket any time that the engine is overhauled or the cylinder head is reconditioned (see Part A of this Chapter for renewal procedure).

2 If the cylinder head was sent out for valve servicing, the valves and related components will already be in place. Begin the reassembly procedure with paragraph 8.

3 Refit new seals on each of the valve guides. Gently push each valve seal into place until it's seated on the guide.

***Caution: Don't hammer on the valve seals once they're seated or you may damage them. Don't twist or cock the seals during refitting or they won't seat properly on the valve stems.***

15 Check the valve stem-to-guide clearance with a small hole gauge and micrometer, or a small dial bore gauge **(see illustration)**. Also, check the valve stem deflection with a dial indicator attached securely to the cylinder head. The valve must be in the guide and approximately 1/16-inch off the seat. The total valve stem movement indicated by the gauge needle must be noted, then divided by two to obtain the actual clearance value. If it exceeds the stem-to-guide clearance limit found in this Chapter's Specifications, the valve guides should be renewed. After this is done, if there's still some doubt regarding the condition of the valve guides they should be checked by an automotive machine workshop (the cost should be minimal).

### Valves

16 Carefully inspect each valve face for uneven wear, deformation, cracks, pits and burned areas. Check the valve stem for scuffing and galling and the neck for cracks. Rotate the valve and check for any obvious indication that it's bent. Look for pits and excessive wear on the end of the stem. The presence of any of these conditions indicates the need for valve service by an automotive machine workshop.

17 Measure the margin width on each valve **(see illustration)**. Any valve with a margin narrower than 1/32-inch will have to be replaced with a new valve.

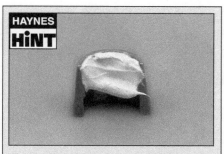

*The keepers are easier to fit if a small amount of grease is applied to keep them in place*

**4** Beginning at one end of the cylinder head, lubricate and refit the first valve. Apply moly-base grease or clean engine oil to the valve stem.

**5** Place the spring seat or shim(s) over the valve guide and set the valve spring and retainer in place.

**6** Compress the springs with a valve spring compressor and carefully refit the keepers in the upper groove, then slowly release the compressor and make sure the keepers seat properly. Apply a small dab of grease to each keeper to hold it in place if necessary **(see Haynes Hint)**.

**7** Repeat the procedure for the remaining valves. Be sure to return the components to their original locations - don't mix them up!

## 13 Pistons/connecting rods - removal

**Note :** *Prior to removing the piston/connecting rod assemblies, remove the cylinder head(s), the sump and the oil pump transfer tubes by referring to Chapter 2A.*

**1** Use your fingernail to feel if a ridge has formed at the upper limit of ring travel (about 1/4-inch down from the top of each cylinder). If carbon deposits or cylinder wear have produced ridges, they must be completely removed with a special tool **(see illustration)**. Follow the manufacturer's instructions provided with the tool. Failure to remove the ridges before attempting to remove the piston/connecting rod assemblies may result in piston damage.

**2** After the cylinder ridges have been removed, turn the engine upside-down so the crankshaft is facing up. Remove the screws and the front and rear baffle plates from the bottom of the engine block **(see illustration)**.

**3** Before the connecting rods are removed, check the endplay with a feeler gauge. Slide the blade between the first connecting rod and the crankshaft throw until the play is removed **(see illustration)**. The endplay is equal to the thickness of the feeler gauge(s). If the endplay exceeds the specified service limit, new connecting rods will be required. If

new rods (or a new crankshaft) are installed, the endplay may fall under the service limit (if it does, the rods will have to be machined to restore it - consult an automotive machine workshop for advice if necessary). Repeat the procedure for the remaining connecting rods.

**4** Check the connecting rods and caps for identification marks. If they aren't plainly marked, use a small centre punch to make the appropriate number of indentations on each rod and cap (1, 2, 3, etc, depending on the cylinder they're associated with) **(see illustration)**.

**5** Loosen each of the connecting rod cap nuts 1/2-turn at a time until they can be removed by hand. Remove the number one connecting rod cap and bearing insert. Don't drop the bearing insert out of the cap. **Note:** *These engines use special connecting rod and main bearing cap bolts that are designed to be used one time only. They can be used during Plastigage checks, but must be replaced with new bolts when the engine is finally reassembled.*

**6** Slip a short length of plastic or rubber hose over each connecting rod cap bolt to protect the crankshaft journal and cylinder wall as the piston is removed **(see illustration)**.

**7** Remove the bearing insert and push the connecting rod/piston assembly out through the top of the engine. Use a wooden hammer handle to push on the upper bearing surface in the connecting rod. If resistance is felt, double-check to make sure that all of the ridge was removed from the cylinder.

**13.1  A ridge reamer is required to remove the ridge from the top of each cylinder - do this before removing the pistons!**

**13.2  Remove the screws (arrowed) and remove the front and rear baffle plates**

**13.3  Check the connecting rod side clearance with a feeler gauge as shown**

**13.4  The connecting rods and caps should be marked by cylinder number - if they aren't, mark them with a centre punch to avoid confusion during reassembly**

**13.6  To prevent damage to the crankshaft journals and cylinder walls, slip sections of hose over the connecting rod bolts before removing the pistons**

14.1 Checking crankshaft endplay with a dial indicator

14.3 Checking crankshaft endplay with a feeler gauge

8 Repeat the procedure for the remaining cylinders. **Note:** *Turn the crankshaft as needed to position the piston/connecting rod assembly to be removed close to parallel with the cylinder bore - i.e. don't try to drive it out while at a large angle to the bore.*

9 After removal, reassemble the connecting rod caps and bearing inserts in their respective connecting rods and refit the cap nuts/bolts finger tight. Leaving the old bearing inserts in place until reassembly will help prevent the big-end bearing surfaces from being accidentally nicked or gouged.

10 Don't separate the pistons from the connecting rods (see Section 18 for additional information).

## 14 Crankshaft - removal

**Note:** *The rear main oil seal and retainer must be removed from the engine block before proceeding with crankshaft removal (see Part A of this Chapter).*

1 Before the crankshaft is removed, check the endplay. Mount a dial indicator to the front of the engine with the stem in line with, and just touching, the end of the crankshaft **(see illustration)**.

2 Push the crankshaft all the way to the rear and zero the dial indicator. Next, pry the crankshaft to the front as far as possible and check the reading on the dial indicator. The distance that it moves is the endplay. If it's greater than that specified in this Chapter's Specifications, check the crankshaft thrust surfaces for wear. If no wear is evident, new thrust washers should correct the endplay.

3 If a dial indicator isn't available, feeler gauges can be used. Gently pry or push the crankshaft all the way to the front of the engine. Slip feeler gauges between the crankshaft and the front face of the number 4 (thrust) main bearing to determine the clearance **(see illustration)**.

4 Check the main bearing caps to see if they're marked to indicate their locations. They should be numbered consecutively from the front of the engine to the rear. If they aren't, mark them with number stamping dies or a centre punch. Main bearing caps generally have a cast-in arrow, which points to the front of the engine. Loosen the main bearing cap bolts 1/4-turn at a time each, stating at the ends and working toward the centre, until they can be removed by hand.

5 The main bearing caps are numbered on the right side with corresponding numbers stamped into the sump rail on the same side **(see illustration)**. Gently tap the caps with a

soft-face hammer, then separate them from the engine block. If necessary, use the bolts as levers to remove the main bearing caps. Try not to drop the bearing inserts if they come out with the caps. **Note:** *The number four main bearing is the thrust bearing and is not numbered.*

6 Carefully lift the crankshaft out of the engine. It may be a good idea to have an assistant available, since the crankshaft is quite heavy. With the bearing inserts in place in the engine block and main bearing caps, return the main bearing caps to their respective locations on the engine block and tighten the bolts finger tight.

## 15 Engine block - cleaning

*Caution: The core plugs (also known as freeze or soft plugs) may be difficult or impossible to retrieve if they're driven completely into the engine block coolant passages.*

1 Using the blunt end of a punch, tap in on the outer edge of the core plug to turn the plug sideways in the bore. Then using pliers, pull the core plug from the engine block **(see illustrations)**.

14.5 The right side of each main bearing cap is stamped with a number (left arrow) that corresponds to the stamped number on the pan rail (right arrow)

15.1a A hammer and a large punch can be used to knock the core plugs sideways in their bores

15.1b Pull the core plugs from the engine block with pliers

**15.8  All bolt holes in the engine block - particularly the main bearing cap and cylinder head bolt holes - should be cleaned and restored with a tap (remove debris from holes after this is done)**

2  Using a gasket scraper, remove all traces of gasket material from the engine block. Be very careful not to nick or gouge the gasket sealing surfaces.

3  Remove the main bearing caps and separate the bearing inserts from the caps and the engine block. Tag the bearings, indicating which cylinder they were removed from and whether they were in the cap or the engine block, then set them aside.

4  Remove all of the threaded oil gallery plugs from the engine block. The plugs are usually very tight - they may have to be drilled out and the holes retapped. Use new plugs when the engine is reassembled.

5  If the engine is extremely dirty, it should be taken to an automotive machine workshop to be steam cleaned or hot tanked.

6  After the engine block is returned, clean all oil holes and oil galleries one more time. Brushes specifically designed for this purpose are available at most car accessory outlets. Flush the passages with warm water until the water runs clear, dry the engine block thoroughly and wipe all machined surfaces with a light, rust preventive oil. If you have access to compressed air, use it to speed the drying process and to blow out all the oil holes and galleries.

**15.10  A large socket on an extension can be used to drive the new core plugs into the bores**

> ⚠ **Warning: Wear eye protection when using compressed air!**

7  If the engine block isn't extremely dirty or sludged up, you can do an adequate cleaning job with hot soapy water and a stiff brush. Take plenty of time and do a thorough job. Regardless of the cleaning method used, be sure to clean all oil holes and galleries very thoroughly, dry the engine block completely and coat all machined surfaces with light oil.

8  The threaded holes in the engine block must be clean to ensure accurate torque readings during reassembly. Run the proper size tap into each of the holes to remove rust, corrosion, thread sealant or sludge and restore damaged threads **(see illustration)**. If possible, use compressed air to clear the holes of debris produced by this operation.

9  Refit the main bearing caps and tighten the bolts finger tight.

10  After coating the sealing surfaces of the new core plugs with suitable sealant, refit them in the engine block **(see illustration)**. Make sure they're driven in straight and seated properly or leakage could result. Special tools are available for this purpose, but a large socket, with an outside diameter that will just slip into the core plug, a 1/2-inch

drive extension and a hammer will work just as well.

11  Apply non-hardening sealant (such as Permatex no. 2 or Teflon pipe sealant) to the new oil gallery plugs and thread them into the holes in the engine block. Make sure they're tightened securely.

12  If the engine isn't going to be reassembled right away, cover it with a large plastic trash bag to keep it clean.

## 16  Engine block - inspection

1  Before the engine block is inspected, it should be cleaned as described in Section 15.

2  Visually check the engine block for cracks, rust and corrosion **(see illustration 10.12)**. Look for stripped threads in the threaded holes. It's also a good idea to have the engine block checked for hidden cracks by an automotive machine workshop that has the special equipment to do this type of work, especially if the vehicle had a history of overheating or using coolant. If defects are found, have the engine block repaired, if possible, or renewed. If the top of the engine block has been eroded by coolant leakage and the erosion is near the cylinder bores, the engine block must be renewed.

3  Check the cylinder bores for scuffing and scoring.

4  Check the cylinders for taper and out-of-round conditions as follows **(see illustrations)**:

5  Measure the diameter of each cylinder at the top (just under the ridge area), centre and bottom of the cylinder bore, parallel to the crankshaft axis.

6  Next, measure each cylinder's diameter at the same three locations perpendicular to the crankshaft axis.

7  The taper of each cylinder is the difference between the bore diameter at the top of the cylinder and the diameter at the bottom. The out-of-round specification of the cylinder bore

**16.4a  Measure the diameter of each cylinder at 90° to engine centreline (A), and parallel to engine centreline (B) - out-of-round is the difference between A and B; taper is the difference between A and B at the top of the cylinder and A and B at the bottom of the cylinder**

**16.4b  The ability to "feel" when the telescoping gauge is at the correct point will be developed over time, so work slowly and repeat the check until you're satisfied that the bore measurement is accurate**

**16.4c  The gauge is then measured with a micrometer to determine the bore size**

is the difference between the parallel and perpendicular readings. Compare your results to this Chapter's Specifications.

**8** If the cylinder walls are badly scuffed or scored, or if they're out-of-round or tapered beyond the limits given in this Chapter's Specifications, have the engine block rebored and honed at an automotive machine workshop. If a rebore is done, oversize pistons and rings will be required.

**9** Using a precision straightedge and feeler gauge, check the engine block deck (the surface that mates with the cylinder head) for distortion **(see illustration 10.13)**. If it's distorted beyond the specified limit, it can be resurfaced by an automotive machine workshop.

**10** If the cylinders are in reasonably good condition and not worn to the outside of the limits, and if the piston-to-cylinder clearances can be maintained properly, then they don't have to be rebored. Honing is all that's necessary (refer to Section 17).

## 17 Cylinder honing

**1** Prior to engine reassembly, the cylinder bores must be honed so the new piston rings will seat correctly and provide the best possible combustion chamber seal. **Note:** *If you don't have the tools or don't want to tackle the honing operation, most automotive machine shops will do it for a reasonable fee.*

**2** Before honing the cylinders, refit the main bearing caps (without bearing inserts) and tighten the bolts to the specified torque.

**3** Two types of cylinder hones are commonly available - the flex hone or "bottle brush" type and the more traditional surfacing hone with spring-loaded stones. Both will do the job, but for the less-experienced mechanic the "bottle brush" hone will probably be easier to use. You'll also need some paraffin or honing oil, rags and a variable-speed electric drill motor. The drill motor should be operated at a steady, slow speed. Proceed as follows:

a) *Mount the hone in the drill motor, compress the stones and slip it into the first cylinder* **(see illustration)**.

 **Warning: Be sure to wear safety goggles or a face shield!**

b) *Lubricate the cylinder with plenty of honing oil, turn on the drill and move the hone up-and-down in the cylinder at a pace that will produce a fine crosshatch pattern on the cylinder walls. Ideally, the crosshatch lines should intersect at approximately a 60° angle* **(see illustration)**. *Be sure to use plenty of lubricant and don't take off any more material than is absolutely necessary to produce the desired finish.* **Note:** *Piston ring manufacturers may specify a smaller*

**17.3a  A "bottle brush" hone will produce better results if you have never done cylinder honing before**

*crosshatch angle than the traditional 60° - read and follow any instructions included with the new rings.*

c) *Don't withdraw the hone from the cylinder while it's running. Instead, shut off the drill and continue moving the hone up-and-down in the cylinder until it comes to a complete stop, then compress the stones and withdraw the hone. If you're using a "bottle brush" type hone, stop the drill motor, then turn the chuck in the normal direction of rotation while withdrawing the hone from the cylinder.*

d) *Wipe the oil out of the cylinder and repeat the procedure for the remaining cylinders.*

**4** After the honing job is complete, chamfer the top edges of the cylinder bores with a small file so the rings won't catch when the pistons are installed. Be very careful not to nick the cylinder walls with the end of the file.

**5** The entire engine block must be washed again very thoroughly with warm, soapy water to remove all traces of the abrasive grit produced during the honing operation. **Note:** *The bores can be considered clean when a lint-free white cloth - dampened with clean engine oil - used to wipe them out doesn't pick up any more honing residue, which will show up as grey areas on the cloth. Be sure to run a brush through all oil holes and galleries and flush them with running water.*

**6** After rinsing, dry the engine block and apply a coat of light rust preventive oil to all machined surfaces. Wrap the engine block in a plastic bag to keep it clean and set it aside until reassembly.

**18.4a  The piston ring grooves can be cleaned with a special tool, as shown . . .**

**17.3b  The cylinder hone should leave a smooth, crosshatch pattern with the lines intersecting at approximately a 60° angle**

## 18 Pistons/connecting rods - inspection

**1** Before the inspection process can be carried out, the piston/connecting rod assemblies must be cleaned and the original piston rings removed from the pistons. **Note:** *Always use new piston rings when the engine is reassembled.*

**2** Using a piston ring refitting tool, carefully remove the rings from the pistons. Be careful not to nick or gouge the pistons in the process.

**3** Scrape all traces of carbon from the top of the piston. A hand-held wire brush or a piece of fine emery cloth can be used once the majority of the deposits have been scraped away. Do not, under any circumstances, use a wire brush mounted in a drill motor to remove deposits from the pistons. The piston material is soft and may be eroded away by the wire brush.

**4** Use a piston ring groove-cleaning tool to remove carbon deposits from the ring grooves. If a tool isn't available, a piece broken off the old ring will do the job. Be very careful to remove only the carbon deposits - don't remove any metal and do not nick or scratch the sides of the ring grooves **(see illustrations)**.

**5** Once the deposits have been removed, clean the piston/connecting rod assemblies with solvent and dry them with compressed air (if available). Make sure the oil return holes

**18.4b  . . . or a section of a broken ring**

**18.10 Check the ring groove clearance with a feeler gauge at several points around the groove**

**18.11 Measure the piston diameter at a 90° angle to the piston pin, at the bottom of the piston pin area - a precision caliper may be used if a micrometer isn't available**

**19.5 Measure the diameter of each crankshaft journal at several points to detect taper and out-of-round conditions**

in the back sides of the ring grooves and the oil hole in the lower end of each rod are clear.

6 If the pistons and cylinder walls aren't damaged or worn excessively, and if the engine block is not rebored, new pistons won't be necessary. Normal piston wear appears as even vertical wear on the piston thrust surfaces and slight looseness of the top ring in its groove. New piston rings, however, should always be used when an engine is rebuilt.

7 Carefully inspect each piston for cracks around the skirt, at the pin bosses and at the ring lands.

*Caution: Some early 1988 3.6 litre engines (before engine no. 9D 121113) have incorrectly-stamped pistons. On these, the word FRONT is actually stamped on the rear of the pistons. Correct pistons will have the cast arrows on the inside of the skirt to your left when facing the word FRONT.*

8 Look for scoring and scuffing on the thrust faces of the skirt, holes in the piston crown and burned areas at the edge of the crown. If the skirt is scored or scuffed, the engine may have been suffering from overheating and/or abnormal combustion, which caused excessively high operating temperatures. The cooling and lubrication systems should be checked thoroughly. A hole in the piston crown is an indication that abnormal combustion (pre-ignition) was occurring. Burned areas at the edge of the piston crown are usually evidence of spark knock (detonation). If any of the above problems exist, the causes must be corrected or the damage will occur again. The causes may include intake air leaks, incorrect air/fuel mixture, incorrect ignition timing and EGR system malfunctions.

9 Corrosion of the piston, in the form of small pits, indicates that coolant is leaking into the combustion chamber and/or the crankcase. Again, the cause must be corrected or the problem may persist in the rebuilt engine.

10 Measure the piston ring groove clearance by laying a new piston ring in each ring groove and slipping a feeler gauge in beside it **(see illustration)**. Check the clearance at three or four locations around each groove. Be sure to

use the correct ring for each groove - they are different. If the clearance is greater than that listed in this Chapter's Specifications, new pistons will have to be used.

11 Check the piston-to-bore clearance by measuring the bore (see Section 16) and the piston diameter. Make sure the pistons and bores are correctly matched. Measure the piston across the skirt, at a 90° angle to the piston pin **(see illustration)**. Subtract the piston diameter from the bore diameter to obtain the clearance. If it's greater than specified, the engine block will have to be rebored and new pistons and rings installed.

12 Check the piston-to-rod clearance by twisting the piston and rod in opposite directions. Any noticeable play indicates excessive wear, which must be corrected.

13 If the pistons must be removed from the connecting rods for any reason, the rods should be taken to an automotive machine workshop, to be checked for bend and twist, since automotive machine shops have special equipment for this purpose.

14 Check the connecting rods for cracks and other damage. Temporarily remove the rod caps, lift out the old bearing inserts, wipe the connecting rod and cap bearing surfaces clean and inspect them for nicks, gouges and scratches. After checking the connecting rods, renew the old bearings, slip the caps into place and tighten the nuts finger tight.
**Note:** *If the engine is being rebuilt because of a connecting rod knock, be sure to refit new rods.*

**19 Crankshaft** - inspection

1 Clean the crankshaft with solvent and dry it with compressed air (if available). Be sure to clean the oil holes with a stiff brush and flush them with solvent.

2 Check the main and connecting rod bearing journals for uneven wear, scoring, pits and cracks.

3 Remove all burrs from the crankshaft oil holes with a stone, file or scraper.

4 Check the remainder of the crankshaft for cracks and other damage. It should be magnafluxed to reveal hidden cracks - an automotive machine workshop will handle the procedure.

5 Using a micrometer, measure the diameter of the main and connecting rod journals and compare the results to this Chapter's Specifications **(see illustration)**. By measuring the diameter at a number of points around each journal's circumference, you'll be able to determine whether or not the journal is out-of-round. Take the measurement at each end of the journal, near the crank throws, to determine if the journal is tapered. Crankshaft runout should be checked also, but large V-blocks and a dial indicator are needed to do it correctly. If you don't have the equipment, have a machine workshop check the runout.

6 If the crankshaft journals are damaged, tapered, out-of-round or worn beyond the limits given in the Specifications, have the crankshaft reground by an automotive machine workshop. Be sure to use the correct size bearing inserts if the crankshaft is reconditioned.

7 Check the oil seal journals at each end of the crankshaft for wear and damage. If the seal has worn a groove in the journal, or if it's nicked or scratched, the new seal may leak when the engine is reassembled. In some cases, an automotive machine workshop may be able to repair the journal by pressing on a thin sleeve. If repair isn't feasible, a new or different crankshaft should be installed.

8 Refer to Section 20 and examine the main and big-end bearing inserts.

**20 Main and big-end bearings -** inspection and selection

*Inspection*

1 Even though the main and big-end bearings should be replaced with new ones during the engine overhaul, the old bearings should be retained for close examination, as they may

FATIGUE FAILURE — CRATERS OR POCKETS

IMPROPER SEATING — BRIGHT (POLISHED) SECTIONS

SCRATCHED BY DIRT — SCRATCHES — DIRT IMBEDDED INTO BEARING MATERIAL

LACK OF OIL — OVERLAY WIPED OUT

EXCESSIVE WEAR — OVERLAY GONE FROM ENTIRE SURFACE

TAPERED JOURNAL — RADIUS RIDE

**20.1 When inspecting the main and big-end bearings, look for these problems**

**20.9 Later model 4.0 litre engines have graded journals and bearings, with the markings indicated on the front throw of the crankshaft - "A" indicates the front of the engine, "B" indicates the codes for the main journals/bearings, and "C" indicates the connecting rod journal grades**

reveal valuable information about the condition of the engine **(see illustration)**.

**2** Bearing failure occurs because of lack of lubrication, the presence of dirt or other foreign particles, overloading the engine and corrosion. Regardless of the cause of failure, it must be corrected before the engine is reassembled to prevent it from happening again.

**3** When examining the bearings, remove them from the engine block, the main bearing caps, the connecting rods and the rod caps and lay them out on a clean surface in the same general position as their location in the engine. This will enable you to match any bearing problems with the corresponding crankshaft journal.

**4** Dirt and other foreign particles get into the engine in a variety of ways. It may be left in the engine during assembly, or it may pass through filters or the PCV system. It may get into the oil, and from there into the bearings. Metal chips from machining operations and normal engine wear are often present. Abrasives are sometimes left in engine components after reconditioning, especially when parts are not thoroughly cleaned using the proper cleaning methods. Whatever the source, these foreign objects often end up embedded in the soft bearing material and are easily recognised. Large particles will not embed in the bearing and will score or gouge the bearing and journal. The best prevention for this cause of bearing failure is to clean all parts thoroughly and keep everything spotlessly clean during engine assembly. Frequent and regular engine oil and filter changes are also recommended.

**5** Lack of lubrication (or lubrication breakdown) has a number of interrelated causes. Excessive heat (which thins the oil), overloading (which squeezes the oil from the bearing face) and oil leakage or throw off (from excessive bearing clearances, worn oil pump or high engine speeds) all contribute to lubrication breakdown. Blocked oil passages, which usually are the result of misaligned oil holes in a bearing shell, will also oil starve a bearing and destroy it. When lack of lubrication is the cause of bearing failure, the bearing material is wiped or extruded from the steel backing of the bearing. Temperatures may increase to the point where the steel backing turns blue from overheating.

**6** Driving habits can have a definite effect on bearing life. Low speed operation in too high a gear (labouring the engine) puts extremely high loads on bearings, which tends to squeeze out the oil film. These loads cause the bearings to flex, which produces fine cracks in the bearing face (fatigue failure). Eventually the bearing material will loosen in pieces and tear away from the steel backing. Short trip driving leads to corrosion of bearings because insufficient engine heat is produced to drive off the condensed water and corrosive gases. These products collect in the engine oil, forming acid and sludge. As the oil is carried to the engine bearings, the acid attacks and corrodes the bearing material.

**7** Incorrect bearing refitting during engine assembly will lead to bearing failure as well. Tight-fitting bearings leave insufficient bearing oil clearance, and this will lead to oil starvation. Dirt or foreign particles trapped behind a bearing insert result in high spots on the bearing which lead to failure.

### Selection

**8** If the original bearings are worn or damaged, or if the oil clearances are incorrect (see Sections 23 or 25), the following procedures should be used to select the correct new bearings for engine reassembly. However, if the crankshaft has been reground, new undersize bearings must be installed - the following procedure should not be used if undersize bearings are required! The automotive machine workshop that reconditions the crankshaft will provide or help you select the correct-size bearings. Regardless of how the bearing sizes are determined, use the oil clearance, measured with Plastigage, as a guide to ensure the bearings are the right size.

**9** If you need to use a STANDARD size main or big-end bearing, refit one that has the same number as the original bearing. **Note:** *4.0 litre engines after #164637 have sized crankshafts and bearings in three grades, indicated by colour and letter. The codes are stamped into the front throw of the crankshaft* **(see illustration)**. *Match replacement bearings by the colour codes: pink (P), white (W) or green (G) for main bearings; red (R), yellow (Y) or blue (B) for the three grades of big-end bearings.*

**10** Remember, the oil clearance is the final judge when selecting new bearing sizes. If you have any questions or are unsure which bearings to use, get help from a dealer parts or service department.

**22.3  When checking piston ring end gap, the ring must be square in the cylinder bore (this is done by pushing the ring down with the top of a piston as shown)**

**22.4  With the ring square in the cylinder, measure the end gap with a feeler gauge**

**22.5  If the end gap is too small, clamp a file in a vice and file the ring ends (from the outside in only) to enlarge the gap slightly**

## 21 Engine overhaul - reassembly sequence

1  Before beginning engine reassembly, make sure you have all the necessary new parts, gaskets and seals as well as the following items on hand:

*Common hand tools*
*A 1/2-inch drive torque wrench*
*Piston ring refitting tool*
*Piston ring compressor*
*Short lengths of rubber or plastic hose  to fit over connecting rod bolts*
*Plastigauge*
*Feeler gauges*
*A fine-tooth file*
*New engine oil*
*Engine assembly lube or moly-base grease*
*Gasket sealer*
*Thread locking compound*

**Special Jaguar tools:**
*Engine lifting brackets (18G 1465)*
*Timing damper simulator (18E 1436)*
*Camshaft TDC tool (18G 1433)*

2  In order to save time and avoid problems, engine reassembly must be done in the following general order:

*Piston rings (Part B)*
*Crankshaft and main bearings (Part B)*
*Piston/connecting rod assemblies (Part B)*
*Rear main (crankshaft) oil seal (Part B)*
*Auxiliary shaft (Part A)*
*Timing chains and sprockets (Part A)*
*Oil pump (Part A)*
*Timing chain cover (Part A)*
*Cylinder head and lifters (Part A)*
*Camshafts (Part A)*
*Oil pick-up (Part A)*
*Sump (Part A)*
*Intake and exhaust manifolds (Part A)*
*Valve cover (Part A)*
*Flywheel/driveplate (Part A)*

## 22 Piston rings - refitting

1  Before refitting the new piston rings, the ring end gaps must be checked. It's assumed that the piston ring groove clearance has been checked and verified correct (see Section 18).
2  Lay out the piston/connecting rod assemblies and the new ring sets so the ring sets will be matched with the same piston and cylinder during the end gap measurement and engine assembly.
3  Insert the top (number one) ring into the first cylinder and square it up with the cylinder walls by pushing it in with the top of the piston **(see illustration)**. The ring should be near the bottom of the cylinder, at the lower limit of ring travel.
4  To measure the end gap, slip feeler gauges between the ends of the ring until a gauge equal to the gap width is found **(see illustration)**. The feeler gauge should slide between the ring ends with a slight amount of drag. Compare the measurement to that found in this Chapter's Specifications. If the gap is larger or smaller than specified, double-check to make sure you have the correct rings before proceeding.
5  If the gap is too small, it must be enlarged or the ring ends may come in contact with each other during engine operation, which can cause serious damage to the engine. The end gap can be increased by filing the ring ends very carefully with a fine file. Mount the

file in a vice equipped with soft jaws, slip the ring over the file with the ends contacting the file face and slowly move the ring to remove material from the ends **(see illustration)**.
*Caution: When performing this operation, file only from the outside in, and after the correct gap is achieved, deburr the filed ends of the rings with a fine whetstone.*
6  Excess end gap isn't critical unless it's greater than Specifications. Again, double-check to make sure you have the correct rings for your engine.
7  Repeat the procedure for each ring that will be installed in the first cylinder and for each ring in the remaining cylinders. Remember to keep rings, pistons and cylinders matched.
8  Once the ring end gaps have been checked/corrected, the rings can be installed on the pistons.
9  The oil control ring (lowest one on the piston) is usually installed first. It's composed of three separate components. Slip the spacer/expander into the groove **(see illustration)**. If an anti-rotation tang is used, make sure it's inserted into the drilled hole in the ring groove. Next, refit the lower side rail. Don't use a piston ring refitting tool on the oil ring side rails, as they may be damaged. Instead, place one end of the side rail into the groove between the spacer/expander and the ring land, hold it firmly in place and slide a finger around the piston while pushing the rail into the groove **(see illustrations)**. Next, refit the upper side rail in the same manner.
10  After the three oil ring components have been installed, check to make sure that both

**22.9a  Refit the spacer/expander in the oil control ring groove**

**22.9b  DO NOT use a piston ring refitting tool when refitting the oil ring side rails**

22.12 Refit the compression rings with a ring expander - the mark must face up

23.10 Lay the Plastigauge strips on the main bearing journals, parallel to the crankshaft centreline

the upper and lower side rails can be turned smoothly in the ring groove.

**11** The number two (middle) ring is installed next. It's usually stamped with a mark which must face up, toward the top of the piston. **Note:** *Always follow the instructions on the ring package or box - different manufacturers may require different approaches. Do not mix up the top and middle rings, as they have different cross sections.*

**12** Use a piston ring refitting tool and make sure the ring's identification mark is facing the top of the piston, then slip the ring into the middle groove on the piston **(see illustration)**. Don't expand the ring any more than necessary to slide it over the piston.

**13** Refit the number one (top) ring in the same manner. Make sure the mark is facing up. Be careful not to confuse the number one and number two rings.

**14** Repeat the procedure for the remaining pistons and rings.

### 23 Crankshaft - refitting and main bearing oil clearance check

**1** Crankshaft refitting is the first major step in engine reassembly. It's assumed at this point that the engine block and crankshaft have been cleaned, inspected and repaired or reconditioned.

**2** Position the engine with the bottom facing up.

**3** Remove the main bearing cap bolts and lift out the caps. Lay the caps out in the proper order.

**4** If they're still in place, remove the old bearing inserts from the engine block and the main bearing caps. Wipe the main bearing surfaces of the engine block and caps with a clean, lint free cloth. They must be kept spotlessly clean!

### Main bearing oil clearance check

**5** Clean the back sides of the new main bearing inserts and lay the bearing half with the oil groove in each main bearing saddle in

the engine block. Lay the other bearing half from each bearing set in the corresponding main bearing cap. Make sure the tab on each bearing insert fits into the recess in the engine block or cap. Also, the oil holes in the block must line up with the oil holes in the bearing insert.

**Caution: Do not hammer the bearings into place and don't nick or gouge the bearing faces. No lubrication should be used at this time.**

**6** The thrust bearings (washers) must be installed in the number four main bearing cap and saddle.

**7** Clean the faces of the bearings in the engine block and the crankshaft main bearing journals with a clean, lint free cloth. Check or clean the oil holes in the crankshaft, as any dirt here can go only one way - straight through the new bearings.

**8** Once you're certain the crankshaft is clean, carefully lay it in position in the main bearings.

**9** Before the crankshaft can be permanently installed, the main bearing oil clearance must be checked.

**10** Trim several pieces of the appropriate size Plastigauge (they must be slightly shorter than the width of the main bearings) and place one piece on each crankshaft main bearing journal, parallel with the journal axis **(see illustration)**.

**11** Clean the faces of the bearings in the caps and refit the caps in their respective positions (don't mix them up) with the arrows pointing toward the front of the engine. Don't disturb the Plastigauge. Apply a light coat of oil to the bolt threads and the undersides of the bolt heads, then refit them. **Note:** *Use the old bolts for this step (save the new bolts for final refitting).*

**12** Tighten the main bearing cap bolts, in three steps, to the torque listed in this Chapter's Specifications. Don't rotate the crankshaft at any time during this operation!

**13** Remove the bolts and carefully lift off the main bearing caps or cap assembly. Keep them in order. Don't disturb the Plastigauge or rotate the crankshaft. If any of the main bearing caps are difficult to remove, tap them gently from side-to-side with a soft-face hammer to loosen them.

**14** Compare the width of the crushed Plastigauge on each journal to the scale printed on the Plastigauge envelope to obtain the main bearing oil clearance **(see illustration)**. Check the Specifications to make sure it's correct.

**15** If the clearance is not as specified, the bearing inserts may be the wrong size (which means different ones will be required - see Section 20). Before deciding that different inserts are needed, make sure that no dirt or oil was between the bearing inserts and the caps or engine block when the clearance was measured. If the Plastigauge is noticeably wider at one end than the other, the journal may be tapered (see Section 19).

**16** Carefully scrape all traces of the Plastigauge material off the main bearing journals and/or the bearing faces. Don't nick or scratch the bearing faces.

### *Final crankshaft refitting*

**17** Carefully lift the crankshaft out of the engine. Clean the bearing faces in the engine block, then apply a thin, uniform layer of clean moly-base grease or engine assembly lube to each of the bearing surfaces. Coat the thrust washers as well.

**18** Lubricate the crankshaft surfaces that contact the oil seals with moly-base grease, engine assembly lube or clean engine oil.

**19** Make sure the crankshaft journals are clean, then lay the crankshaft back in place in the engine block. Clean the faces of the bearings in the main bearing caps, then apply lubricant to them. Refit the main bearing caps in their respective positions with the arrows pointing toward the front of the engine. **Note:** *Be sure to refit the thrust washers (lubricated) with the number 4 main journal.* The upper (block side) thrust washers can be rotated into position around the crankshaft with the crankshaft installed in the engine block, with the thrust washer grooves facing OUT. The lower thrust washers should be placed on the main bearing caps with their grooves OUT.

**20** For the final assembly, use only **new** bolts, for both the main bearings and the

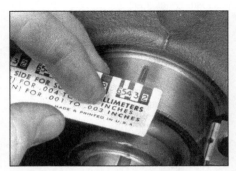

23.14 Compare the width of the crushed Plastigauge to the scale on the envelope to determine the main bearing oil clearance (always take the measurement at the widest point of the Plastigauge). Be sure to use the correct scale - imperial and metric scales are included

connecting rods. Apply a light coat of oil to the bolt threads and the under sides of the bolt heads, then refit them. Tighten all main bearing cap bolts to the torque listed in this Chapter's Specifications, starting in the centre and working out to the ends.

**21** Rotate the crankshaft a number of times by hand to check for any obvious binding.

**22** Check the crankshaft endplay with a feeler gauge or a dial indicator as described in Section 14. The endplay should be correct if the crankshaft thrust faces aren't worn or damaged and new thrust washers have been installed. **Note:** *If the end-play is too great, even with the new thrust bearings, oversized thrust bearings are available. There are two sizes, 0.005-inch and 0.010-inch oversize.*

**23** Refit a new rear main oil seal, then bolt the retainer to the engine block (see Section 24).

## 24 Rear main oil seal refitting

**1** The crankshaft must be installed first and the main bearing caps bolted in place, then the new seal should be installed in the retainer and the retainer bolted to the engine block.

**2** Check the seal contact surface on the crankshaft very carefully for scratches and nicks that could damage the new seal lip and cause oil leaks. If the crankshaft is damaged, the only alternative is a new or different crankshaft.

**3** Refer to Part A of this Chapter for refitting of the new rear seal, using the plastic alignment tool supplied with the engine overhaul gasket set.

## 25 Pistons/connecting rods - refitting and big-end bearing oil clearance check

**1** Before refitting the piston/connecting rod assemblies, the cylinder walls must be perfectly clean, the top edge of each cylinder must be chamfered, and the crankshaft must be in place.

**2** Remove the cap from the end of the number one connecting rod (refer to the marks made during removal). Remove the original bearing inserts and wipe the bearing surfaces of the connecting rod and cap with a clean, lint-free cloth. They must be kept spotlessly clean.

### Big-end bearing oil clearance check

**3** Clean the back side of the new upper bearing insert, then lay it in place in the connecting rod. Make sure the tab on the bearing fits into the recess in the rod so the oil holes line up. Don't hammer the bearing insert into place and be very careful not to nick or gouge the bearing face. Don't lubricate the bearing at this time.

**25.5 Stagger the ring end gaps around the piston as shown**

    A  *Oil ring rail gaps*
    B  *Second compression ring gap*
    C  *Oil ring spacer gap*
    D  *Top compression ring gap*

**4** Clean the back side of the other bearing insert and refit it in the rod cap. Again, make sure the tab on the bearing fits into the recess in the cap, and don't apply any lubricant. It's critically important that the mating surfaces of the bearing and connecting rod are perfectly clean and oil free when they're assembled.

**5** Position the piston ring gaps at staggered intervals around the piston **(see illustration)**.

**6** Slip a section of plastic or rubber hose over each connecting rod cap bolt.

**7** Lubricate the piston and rings with clean engine oil and attach a piston ring compressor to the piston. Leave the skirt protruding about 1/4-inch to guide the piston into the cylinder. The rings must be compressed until they're flush with the piston.

**8** Rotate the crankshaft until the number one connecting rod journal is at BDC (bottom dead centre) and apply a coat of engine oil to the cylinder wall.

**9** With the word FRONT (or the arrow) on top of the piston facing the front of the engine **(see illustration)**, gently insert the piston/connecting rod assembly into the number one cylinder bore and rest the bottom edge of the ring compressor on the engine block.

**10** Tap the top edge of the ring compressor to make sure it's contacting the engine block around its entire circumference.

**25.11 The piston can be driven (gently) into the cylinder bore with the end of a wooden or plastic hammer handle**

**25.9 Pistons must be installed with the arrow (right arrow) or FRONT facing the front of the engine - left arrow indicates piston size letter**

**11** Gently tap on the top of the piston with the end of a wooden hammer handle (see illustration) while guiding the end of the connecting rod into place on the crankshaft journal. The piston rings may try to pop out of the ring compressor just before entering the cylinder bore, so keep some downward pressure on the ring compressor. Work slowly, and if any resistance is felt as the piston enters the cylinder, stop immediately. Find out what's hanging up and fix it before proceeding.

***Caution: Do not, for any reason, force the piston into the cylinder - you might break a ring and/or the piston.***

**12** Once the piston/connecting rod assembly is installed, the big-end bearing oil clearance must be checked before the rod cap is permanently bolted in place.

**13** Cut a piece of the appropriate size Plastigauge slightly shorter than the width of the big-end bearing and lay it in place on the number one connecting rod journal, parallel with the journal axis **(see illustration)**.

**14** Clean the connecting rod cap bearing face, remove the protective hoses from the connecting rod bolts and refit the rod cap. Make sure the mating mark on the cap is on the same side as the mark on the connecting rod. Check the cap to make sure the front mark is facing the timing chain of the engine.

**15** Apply a light coat of oil to the under sides of the nuts, then refit and tighten them to the torque listed in this Chapter's Specifications,

**25.13 Lay the Plastigauge strips on each big-end bearing journal, parallel to the crankshaft centreline**

**25.17  Measure the width of the crushed Plastigauge to determine the big-end bearing oil clearance**

working up to it in three steps. **Note:** *Use the old bolts for this step (save the new bolts for final refitting).* Use a thin-wall socket to avoid erroneous torque readings that can result if the socket is wedged between the rod cap and nut. If the socket tends to wedge itself between the nut and the cap, lift up on it slightly until it no longer contacts the cap. Do not rotate the crankshaft at any time during this operation.

**16** Remove the nuts and detach the rod cap, being careful not to disturb the Plastigauge.

**17** Compare the width of the crushed Plastigauge to the scale printed on the envelope to obtain the oil clearance **(see illustration)**. Compare it to this Chapter's Specifications to make sure the clearance is correct.

**18** If the clearance is not as specified, the bearing inserts may be the wrong size (which means different ones will be required). Before deciding that different inserts are needed, make sure that no dirt or oil was between the bearing inserts and the connecting rod or cap when the clearance was measured. Also, recheck the journal diameter. If the Plastigauge was wider at one end than the other, the journal may be tapered (refer to Section 19).

### Final connecting rod refitting

**19** Carefully scrape all traces of the Plastigauge material off the rod journal and/or bearing face. Be very careful not to scratch

the bearing, use your fingernail or the edge of a credit card to remove the Plastigauge.

**20** Make sure the bearing faces are perfectly clean, then apply a uniform layer of clean moly-base grease or engine assembly lube to both of them. You'll have to push the piston higher into the cylinder to expose the face of the bearing insert in the connecting rod, be sure to slip the protective hoses over the connecting rod bolts first.

**21** At this time, remove the original connecting rod bolts/nuts and replace them with new bolts/nuts. They are of a design which requires they be used only once. The old ones are OK for Plastigauge checking, but for final assembly use only new connecting rod bolts/nuts. Refit the rod cap and tighten the nuts to the torque listed in this Chapter's Specifications. Again, work up to the torque in three steps.

**22** Repeat the entire procedure for the remaining pistons/connecting rod assemblies.

**23** The important points to remember are:

a) *Keep the back sides of the bearing inserts and the insides of the connecting rods and caps perfectly clean during assembly..*

b) *Make sure you have the correct piston/ connecting rod assembly for each cylinder.*

c) *The dimple on the piston must face the front of the engine.*

d) *Lubricate the cylinder walls with clean oil.*

e) *Lubricate the bearing faces when refitting the rod caps after the oil clearance has been checked.*

**24** After all the piston/connecting rod assemblies have been properly installed, rotate the crankshaft a number of times by hand to check for any obvious binding.

**25** As a final step, the connecting rod endplay must be checked. Refer to Section 13 for this procedure.

**26** Compare the measured endplay to this Chapter's Specifications to make sure it's correct. If it was correct before dismantling and the original crankshaft and connecting rods were reinstalled, it should still be right. However, if new connecting rods or a new crankshaft were installed, the endplay may be

inadequate. If so, the connecting rods will have to be removed and taken to an automotive machine workshop for resizing.

## 26 Initial start-up and running-in after overhaul

*Warning: Have a suitable fire extinguisher handy when starting the engine for the first time.*

**1** Once the engine has been installed in the vehicle, double-check the engine oil and coolant levels.

**2** With the spark plugs out of the engine and the ignition system and fuel pump disabled, crank the engine until oil pressure registers on the gauge or the light goes out.

**3** Refit the spark plugs, hook up the plug leads and restore the ignition system and fuel pump functions.

**4** Start the engine. It may take a few moments for the fuel system to build up pressure, but the engine should start without a great deal of effort.

**5** After the engine starts, it should be allowed to warm up to normal operating temperature. While the engine is warming up, make a thorough check for fuel, oil and coolant leaks.

**6** Shut the engine off and recheck the engine oil and coolant levels.

**7** Drive the vehicle to an area with no traffic, accelerate from 30 to 50 mph, then allow the vehicle to slow to 30 mph with the throttle closed. Repeat the procedure 10 or 12 times. This will load the piston rings and cause them to seat properly against the cylinder walls. Check again for oil and coolant leaks.

**8** Drive the vehicle gently for the first 500 miles (no sustained high speeds) and keep a constant check on the oil level. It is not unusual for an engine to use oil during the running-in period.

**9** At approximately 500 to 600 miles, change the oil and filter.

**10** For the next few hundred miles, drive the vehicle normally. Do not pamper it or abuse it.

**11** After 2000 miles, change the oil and filter again and consider the engine run-in.

# Chapter 3
# Cooling, heating and air conditioning systems

## Contents

## Degrees of difficulty

| Easy, suitable for novice with little experience  | Fairly easy, suitable for beginner with some experience  | Fairly difficult, suitable for competent DIY mechanic  | Difficult, suitable for experienced DIY mechanic  | Very difficult, suitable for expert DIY or professional |
|---|---|---|---|---|

## Specifications

### General

| | |
|---|---|
| Radiator cap pressure rating ................................ | 13.5 to 117.5 psi |
| Thermostat rating ......................................... | 180 to 207° F |

### Torque wrench settings

| | Nm | lbf ft |
|---|---|---|
| Coolant pipe to block ..................................... | 22 to 28 | 16 to 21 |
| Fan assembly-to-drive hub nuts .............................. | 22 to 28 | 16 to 21 |
| Fan clutch-to-fan blade bolts ................................ | 22 to 28 | 16 to 21 |
| Thermostat cover bolts..................................... | 22 to 28 | 16 to 21 |
| Thermostat housing-to-block bolts ........................... | 22 to 28 | 16 to 21 |
| Water pump bolts ........................................ | 22 to 28 | 16 to 21 |

## 1 General information

### Engine cooling system

All vehicles covered by this manual employ a pressurised engine cooling system with thermostatically-controlled coolant circulation. An impeller type water pump mounted on the front of the block pumps coolant through the engine. The coolant flows around each cylinder and toward the rear of the engine. Cast-in coolant passages direct coolant around the intake and exhaust ports, near the spark plug areas and in proximity to the exhaust valve guides.

A wax-pellet type thermostat is located in the thermostat housing at the front of the engine. During warm up, the closed thermostat prevents coolant from circulating through the radiator. When the engine reaches normal operating temperature, the thermostat opens and allows hot coolant to travel through the radiator, where it is cooled before returning to the engine.

The cooling system is sealed by a pressure-type radiator cap. This raises the boiling point of the coolant, and the higher boiling point of the coolant increases the cooling efficiency of the radiator. If the system pressure exceeds the cap pressure-relief value, the excess pressure in the system forces the spring-loaded valve inside the cap off its seat and allows the coolant to escape through the overflow tube into a coolant reservoir. When

the system cools, the excess coolant is automatically drawn from the reservoir back into the radiator. This type of cooling system is known as a closed design because coolant that escapes past the pressure cap is saved and reused.

The Jaguar cooling system on 1988 and 1989 models has both a manifold tank and a coolant recovery tank. The manifold tank is the highest point in the cooling system and is the location of the "radiator" cap (the cap is not on the radiator). The recovery tank down in the passenger's footwell collects heated coolant as described above. Models from 1990 to 1994 do not have a coolant recovery tank, but have an enlarged manifold tank. In all models, the recovery tank has a sensor in it to detect a low coolant level, and the instrument panel has a warning light to that effect.

## Heating system

The heating system consists of two blower fans, one under the dash on the right and one on the left, and a heater core located within the heater/air conditioning assembly which is under the dash and behind the console. Hoses connect the heater core to the engine cooling system. Heater function is controlled by the heater/air conditioning control head on the dashboard. Hot engine coolant is circulated through the heater core. When the heater mode is activated, a flap door opens to expose the heater box to the passenger compartment. A fan switch on the control head activates the blower motor, which forces air through the core, heating the air.

## Air conditioning system

The air conditioning system consists of a condenser mounted in front of the radiator, an evaporator mounted in the heat/air conditioning assembly behind the console and under the centre of the dash, a compressor mounted on the engine, a filter-drier which contains a high pressure relief valve and the plumbing connecting all of the above.

A blower fan forces the warmer air of the passenger compartment through the evaporator core (sort of a radiator-in-reverse), transferring the heat from the air to the refrigerant. The liquid refrigerant boils off into low pressure vapour, taking the heat with it when it leaves the evaporator. The compressor keeps refrigerant circulating through the system, pumping the warmed coolant through the condenser where it is cooled and then circulated back to the evaporator.

## 2  Antifreeze/coolant -
general information

⚠️ **Warning: Do not allow antifreeze to come in contact with your skin or painted surfaces of the vehicle. Rinse off spills immediately with** plenty of water. Antifreeze is highly toxic if ingested. Never leave antifreeze lying around in an open container or in puddles on the floor; children and pets are attracted by it's sweet smell and may drink it. Check with local authorities about disposing of used antifreeze. Many communities have collection centres which will see that antifreeze is disposed of safely. Never dump used antifreeze on the ground or into drains.

**Note:** Non-toxic antifreeze is now manufactured and available at local car accessory outlets, but even these types should be disposed of properly.

The cooling system should be filled with a water/ethylene-glycol based antifreeze solution, which will prevent freezing down to at least -20° F, or lower if local climate requires it. It also provides protection against corrosion and increases the coolant boiling point.

The cooling system should be drained, flushed and refilled every 24,000 miles or every two years (see Chapter 1). The use of antifreeze solutions for periods of longer than two years is likely to cause damage and encourage the formation of rust and scale in the system. If your tap water is "hard", i.e. contains a lot of dissolved minerals, use distilled water with the antifreeze.

Before adding antifreeze to the system, check all hose connections, because antifreeze tends to leak through very minute openings. Engines do not normally consume coolant. Therefore, if the level goes down, find the cause and correct it.

The exact mixture of antifreeze-to-water you should use depends on the relative weather conditions. The mixture should contain at least 50-percent antifreeze, but should never contain more than 70-percent antifreeze. Consult the mixture ratio chart on the antifreeze container before adding coolant. Hydrometers are available at most car accessory outlets to test the ratio of antifreeze to water **(see illustration)**. Use antifreeze which meets the vehicle manufacturer's specifications.

## 3  Thermostat -
check and renewal

⚠️ **Warning: Do not attempt to remove the radiator cap, coolant or thermostat until the engine has cooled completely.**

### Check

1 Before assuming the thermostat is responsible for a cooling system problem, check the coolant level (Chapter 1), drivebelt tension (Chapter 1) and temperature gauge (or light) operation.
2 If the engine takes a long time to warm up (as indicated by the temperature gauge or heater operation), the thermostat is probably stuck open. Renew the thermostat.
3 If the engine runs hot, use your hand to check the temperature of the lower radiator hose.

⚠️ **Warning: Do this check with the engine off. Do not get your hands near the fan blades. If the hose is not hot, but the engine is, the thermostat is probably stuck in the closed position, preventing the coolant inside the engine from travelling through the radiator. Renew the thermostat. Do not drive the vehicle without a thermostat. The computer may stay in open loop and emissions and fuel economy will suffer.**

4 If the lower radiator hose is hot, it means that the coolant is flowing and the thermostat is open. Consult the *Troubleshooting* section at the front of this manual for further diagnosis.

### Renewal

5 Disconnect the battery negative cable.
**Caution: If the stereo in your vehicle is equipped with an anti-theft system, make sure you have the correct activation code before disconnecting the battery.**
6 Drain the coolant from the radiator (see Chapter 1).
7 Remove the bolts from the thermostat cover **(see illustration)**. If the cover doesn't

**2.4  An inexpensive hydrometer can be used to test the condition of your coolant**

**3.7 Remove the two bolts (small arrows) holding the thermostat cover to the housing (large arrow)**

3.9 The thermostat is fitted with the spring end towards the cylinder head - use a new O-ring (A) and position jiggle pin (B) up

4.8 Remove the four nuts (arrows indicate three shown here) holding the fan/clutch assembly to the front of the water pump

pull loose, tap it with a soft-faced hammer. Do not use a screwdriver between the cover and the thermostat housing.

8 Remove the thermostat, noting the direction in which it was installed in the housing, and thoroughly clean the sealing surfaces.

9 Refit a new O-ring onto the thermostat (see illustration). Make sure it is evenly fitted all the way around.

10 Apply a bead of RTV sealant to the thermostat housing. Refit the thermostat and housing, positioning the jiggle pin at the highest point. **Note:** *The thermostat is usually marked TOP on the radiator side for proper orientation.*

11 Tighten the cover fasteners to the torque listed in this Chapter's Specifications.

12 Refill the cooling system, run the engine and check for leaks and proper operation.

### 4 Engine cooling fans - check and renewal

## Mechanical fan (1988 to 1992 models)

⚠️ **Warning:** *Keep hands, hair, tools and clothing away from the fan when the engine is running. To*

avoid injury or damage DO NOT operate the engine with a damaged fan. Do not attempt to repair fan blades - renew a damaged fan .

### Check

⚠️ *Warning: In order to check the fan clutch, the engine will need to be at operating temperature, so while going through checks prior to Step 6 be careful that the ignition is NOT switched on. Severe personal injury can result!*

1 Symptoms of failure of the fan clutch are continuous noisy operation, looseness, vibration and evidence of silicone fluid leaks.

2 Rock the fan back and forth by hand to check for excessive bearing play.

3 With the engine cold, turn the blades by hand. The fan should turn freely.

4 Visually inspect for substantial fluid leakage from the fan clutch assembly, a deformed bi-metal spring or grease leakage from the cooling fan bearing. If any of these conditions exist, renew the fan clutch.

5 When the engine is fully warmed up, turn off the ignition switch and disconnect the cable from the negative battery terminal. Turn the fan by hand. Some resistance should be felt. If the fan turns easily, renew the fan clutch.

*Caution: If the stereo in your vehicle is equipped with an anti-theft system, make*

sure you have the correct activation code before disconnecting the battery.

### Removal and refitting

6 Leave the battery cable disconnected (see the Caution in Step 5).

7 Remove the fan's drivebelt (see Chapter 1).

8 Remove the nuts holding the fan assembly to the water pump (see illustration). **Note:** *You'll have to "walk" the fan assembly forward as you loosen the nuts. There is not enough room to remove them all the way at one time.*

9 The fan can be removed without removing the shroud, if you are only renewing the fan or clutch (see illustration). Be careful not to allow the blades contact the radiator fins.

10 Remove the two fan shroud mounting clips at the top of the shroud (see illustration).

11 Lift the shroud up and out of the engine compartment. The bottom of the fan shroud does not have any fasteners. It has two tangs on the bottom that slip out of slots in the body when pulled up.

12 The fan clutch can be unbolted from the fan blade assembly for renewal (see illustration).

*Caution: To prevent silicone fluid from draining from the clutch assembly into the fan drive bearing and ruining the lubricant, DON'T place the clutch in a position with the rear pointing down. Store the clutch in its upright position if possible.*

4.9 The fan can be removed with the shroud in place by angling it out of the shroud

4.10 Pry out the two clips (arrow indicates the left one) at the top of the fan shroud and lift out the shroud

4.12 Separate the fan clutch from the fan by removing the four bolts (arrowed)

**4.15 Disconnect the electrical connector (A) from the thermostatic switch (B) in the radiator and bypass it with a jumper wire (C) - the fan should operate now with the ignition on**

**4.17 Disconnect the fan wiring connector and connect jumper wires from there directly to the positive and negative terminals of the battery - the purple wire's terminal should receive the battery power and the black wire's terminal should be earthed**

13 Refitting is the reverse of removal. Tighten the fan clutch-to-fan blade bolts and the fan assembly-to-drive hub nut to the torque listed in this Chapter's Specifications.

### Electric fans

#### Check

 *Warning: Keep your hands or clothing away from the fan blades at all times.*

14 On 1988 through 1992 models, a single electric fan is mounted in front of the radiator, controlled by a thermostatic switch. Access to the fan is with the grille removed. The 1993 and 1994 models have a fan shroud assembly that includes two electric fans, and a "twin" thermostatic switch, with the assembly mounted on the engine side of the radiator.

15 If the electric fan does not come on at any time, bypass the thermostatic switch by disconnecting the electrical connector at the switch and connecting the two pins with a jumper wire **(see illustration)**. If the fan now operates, renew the thermostatic switch. If the fan doesn't operate, the problem is either the fan relay or the fan motor. On 1993 and 1994 models with twin electric fans, jumpering one set of connections in the plug from the switch should make both fans operate at slow speed (fans in series) and jumpering the other two should run both fans at higher speed (fans in parallel). In normal operation, the fans operate at the higher-speed only when the air conditioning is on, or when coolant temperature exceeds 212° F. When the coolant cools down to below 200° F, the fans revert to the normal speed.

16 To renew a defective thermostatic switch, allow the vehicle to cool off and drain the coolant (see Chapter 1). Remove the switch from the radiator and refit the new switch. Connect the electrical connector and test again for proper fan operation.

17 To test an inoperative fan motor (one that doesn't come on when the engine gets hot or when the air conditioner is on), first check the fuses and/or fusible links (see Chapter 12). Then disconnect the electrical connector at the motor (refer to Chapter 11 for removal of the grille for access on front-mounted-fan models) and use fused jumper wires to connect the fan directly to the battery and to chassis ground **(see illustration)**. If the fan still does not work, renew the fan motor.

 *Warning: Do not allow the test clips to contact each other or any metallic part of the vehicle.*

18 If the motor tested OK in the previous test but is still inoperative, then the fault lies in the relay, fuse, or wiring. The fan relay can be tested for continuity (see Chapter 12).

### Renewal

19 Disconnect the negative battery cable.
*Caution: If the stereo in your vehicle is equipped with an anti-theft system, make sure you have the correct activation code before disconnecting the battery.*

**4.20 Disconnect the fan's electrical connector (large arrow) and remove the bolts (small arrows) on single-fan models - grille is removed here**

20 Access the 1988 through 1992 single electric fan with the grille removed (see Chapter 11 for grille removal). Disconnect the electrical connector and remove the bolts holding the fan assembly to the body **(see illustration)**.

21 On 1993 and 1994 models, remove the two bolts holding the fan shroud to the top of the radiator and lift the shroud/fans assembly from the vehicle.

22 If the fan on 1988 to 1992 models must be renewed, renew the fan, motor and shroud as a unit. The fan is separate from the shroud on later models.

23 Refitting is the reverse of removal. If the thermostatic switch was renewed, refill the cooling system.

---

**5 Radiator, expansion tank and coolant reservoir -** removal and refitting

 *Warning: Do not start this procedure until the engine is completely cool.*

### Radiator

#### Removal

1 Disconnect the negative battery cable.
*Caution: If the stereo in your vehicle is equipped with an anti-theft system, make sure you have the correct activation code before disconnecting the battery.*

2 Drain the coolant into a container (see Chapter 1).

3 Remove both the upper and lower radiator hoses, and the small expansion tank hose from the top left of the radiator **(see illustration)**.

4 Remove the cooling fan and shroud (see Section 4).

5.3 Remove the clamp and the hose going to the expansion tank

5.5a At the left side of the radiator, disconnect the automatic transmission cooler lines (small arrows) and the lower radiator hose (larger arrow)

5.5b Disconnect the power steering cooler lines (small arrows) at the right side of the radiator, and the upper radiator hose (large arrow)

**5** If equipped with an automatic transmission, disconnect the cooler lines from the radiator **(see illustrations)**. Disconnect the cooling fan switch connector **(see illustration 4.15)**. Place a drip pan to catch the fluid and cap the fittings. **Note:** *The transmission oil cooler lines enter the radiator on the left, while the power steering cooler lines attach on the right side of the radiator. On 1993 and 1994 models, the cooler fittings require a spring-lock coupling tool, normally used on fuel lines or air conditioning lines.*

**6** Remove the four bolts from the radiator cowl panel and take off the panel **(see illustration)**.

**7** Lift out the radiator. Be aware of dripping fluids and the sharp fins. Take care not to damage the radiator fins by contact with other parts.

**8** With the radiator removed, it can be inspected for leaks, damage and internal blockage. If repairs are necessary, have a radiator specialist or dealer service department perform the work, as special techniques are required. Check the rubber mounting pads on the bottom of the radiator **(see illustration)**. If they're cracked or damaged, get new ones before refitting the radiator.

**9** Bugs and dirt can be cleaned from the radiator with compressed air and a soft brush. Don't bend the cooling fins as this is done.

 *Warning: Wear eye protection.*

### Refitting

**10** Refitting is the reverse of the removal procedure. Be sure the rubber mounts are in place on the bottom of the radiator.

**11** After refitting, fill the cooling system with the proper mixture of antifreeze and water. Refer to Chapter 1 if necessary.

**12** Start the engine and check for leaks. Allow the engine to reach normal operating temperature, indicated by both radiator hoses becoming hot. Recheck the coolant level and add more if required.

**13** On automatic transmission equipped models, check and add fluid as needed and check the power steering fluid level as well.

### Expansion tank and coolant reservoir, removal and refitting

**14** The expansion tank is located at the top of the left-hand side inner wing. With the cooling system drained below the level of the expansion tank, remove the hoses, the coolant level probe and the two screws mounting it to the body **(see illustration)**.

**15** Wash out and inspect the reservoir for cracks and chafing. Renew it if damaged.

5.6 Remove the bolts (arrowed) and take off the radiator cowl panel

5.14 The expansion tank is located on the left inner wing

A *Hose to recovery tank (where applicable)*
B *Hose to radiator*
C *Hose to thermostat housing*
D *Hose to water pump housing*
E *Mounting screws*
F *Low-coolant-level sensor*

**16** If the low-coolant level light has been showing on the instrument panel, even when the coolant level is correct, disconnect the sensor's connector and test it with an ohmmeter **(see illustration)**. The sensor should be renewed if the resistance at the connections is over 150 ohms.

*Caution: Using a long-necked funnel to add coolant can damage the sensor, which is just below the expansion tank filler neck.*

5.8 There are rubber mounts (arrowed) for the radiator and the condenser - they must be in place when these components are reinstalled

5.16 The low-coolant-level sensor can be tested with an ohmmeter - resistance should be below 150 ohms - gently use a pair of long-neck pliers to move the sensor up and down in the tank to get a reading

**5.17 The recovery bottle (arrowed) on 1988 and 1989 models is located in the footwell - disconnect the hoses and the two mounting screws**

**6.2 Disconnect the two metal oil lines (arrowed) where they mount to the bottom of the cooler - use two spanners**

17 A coolant recovery bottle is used on 1988 and 1989 models, located in the passenger's inner wing. The plastic inner wing splash shield must be removed for access to the recovery bottle (see Chapter 11). Disconnect the recovery hose and remove the mounting screws to renew the recovery bottle **(see illustration)**. Models from 1990 on do not have the recovery bottle, but do have a larger expansion tank.

18 Refitting of either expansion tank or recovery bottle is the reverse of removal.

## 6 Engine oil cooler - renewal

1 Models from 1988 through 1991 have a engine oil cooler, mounted ahead of the radiator. The engine's mechanical fan draws air through the oil cooler, cooling off hot engine oil that is circulated from the engine by steel tubes. Access to the cooler is with the grille removed (refer to Chapter 11 for grille removal).

2 To renew the oil cooler, first disconnect the

**6.3 Remove the mounting nuts (arrowed) to take the oil cooler out**

two fittings connecting the lines to the cooler **(see illustration)**.

*Caution: The engine should be cool for this procedure, and you should have a small drain pan handy because the fittings are on the bottom of the cooler and will probably drip some oil on dismantling.*

3 Remove the mounting nuts to take the cooler out of the vehicle **(see illustration)**.

4 The other ends of the oil cooler tubes mount to a block just below the oil filter. With a drain pan handy, remove the nut retaining both pipes to the block.

5 Refitting the oil cooler and oil lines is the reverse of removal. When refitting the lines to the block or the cooler, use new O-rings.

## 7 Water pump - check

1 A failure in the water pump can cause serious engine damage due to overheating.

2 With the engine running and warmed to normal operating temperature, squeeze the upper radiator hose. If the water pump is working properly, a pressure surge should be felt as the hose is released.

 *Warning: Keep hands away from fan blades!*

3 Water pumps are equipped with weep or vent holes **(see illustration)**. If a failure occurs in the pump seal, coolant will leak from this hole. In most cases it will be necessary to use a flashlight to find the hole on the water pump by looking through the space behind the pulley just below the water pump shaft.

4 If the water pump shaft bearings fail there may be a howling sound at the front of the engine while it is running. Bearing wear can be felt if the water pump pulley is rocked up and

down. Do not mistake drivebelt slippage, which causes a squealing sound, for water pump failure. Spray automotive drivebelt dressing on the belts to eliminate the belt as a possible cause of the noise.

## 8 Water pump and pipes - renewal

 *Warning: Do not start this procedure until the engine is completely cool.*

1 Disconnect the negative battery cable and drain the cooling system (see Chapter 1).

*Caution: If the stereo in your vehicle is equipped with an anti-theft system, make sure you have the correct activation code before disconnecting the battery.*

2 Refer to Section 4 to remove the mechanical fan and clutch (if applicable to your model).

3 Refer to Chapter 1 for removal of the drivebelts.

**7.3 Check the weep hole (arrowed) for signs of leakage (pump removed for clarity) - grey discolouration is normal, large brown stains indicates seal failure**

**8.4 Remove the water pump mounting bolts (arrows indicate five visible here)**

**8.8a Once the water pump is removed, the rear housing (arrowed) is held in place only by the hoses - check them for leakage and condition whenever the pump is disturbed**

**8.8b The water pipe (arrowed) may need new gaskets where it meets the block - the pipe is best accessed from below or with the intake manifold unbolted**

**4** Remove the water pump mounting bolts **(see illustration)**.
**Note 1:** *The water pump is sold as a complete assembly, including the rear housing with the hose connections. Unless the rear housing is corroded or cracked, many Jaguar mechanics only refit the pump assembly itself, using the original rear housing with all its hoses intact. However, if the engine has a great deal of years or mileage on it, it would be a good idea to renew those hoses as well, in which case the new rear housing can be installed.*
**Note 2:** *There are three different lengths of water pump bolts. The longer bolts retain the pump and rear housing to the engine* **(see illustration 7.3).**
**5** If the pump doesn't come loose right away, tap it with a soft-faced hammer to break the gasket seal. Be careful not to hit the radiator fins with the pump during removal.
**6** Thoroughly clean all sealing surfaces, removing all traces of gasket or sealant from the back of the pump and the face of the housing.
**7** Apply a bead of RTV sealant to the sealing surface on the back of the pump. Refit the pump and bolts, tightening the bolts to the torque listed in this Chapter's Specifications.
**8** Refit the remaining parts in the reverse order of removal. **Note:** *If the pump has been renewed after many miles of usage, it's a good idea to also renew the hoses connected to the water pump housing* **(see illustrations)**. *Refer to Chapter 2A for intake manifold removal to access the coolant pipes and hoses. If you have noticed water leaks or stains on the left side of the engine, the leaks may be coming from these pipes and hoses.*
**9** Refill the cooling system (see Chapter 1), run the engine and check for leaks and proper operation.

## 9 Coolant temperature sender unit - check and renewal

⚠ *Warning: Do not start this procedure until the engine is completely cool.*

### Check

**1** If the coolant temperature gauge is inoperative, check the fuses first (Chapter 12).
**2** If the temperature gauge indicates excessive temperature after running awhile, see the *Fault finding* section at the rear of the manual.
**3** If the temperature gauge indicates Hot as soon as the engine is started cold, disconnect the wire at the coolant temperature sender **(see illustration)**. If the gauge reading drops, renew the sender unit. If the reading remains high, the wire to the gauge may be shorted to ground, or the gauge is faulty.
**4** If the coolant temperature gauge fails to show any indication after the engine has been warmed up, (approx. 10 minutes) and the fuses checked out OK, shut off the engine. Disconnect the wire at the sender unit and, using a jumper wire, connect the wire to a clean ground on the engine. Briefly turn on the ignition without starting the engine. If the gauge now indicates Hot, renew the sender unit.
**5** If the gauge fails to respond, the circuit may be open or the gauge may be faulty - see Chapter 12 for additional information.

### Renewal

**6** Drain the coolant (see Chapter 1).
**7** Disconnect the electrical connector from the sender unit.

**9.3 The coolant temperature sender unit (arrowed) is located in the top of the thermostat housing - it is the sender unit with the single wire**

**8** Using a deep socket or a spanner, remove the sender unit.
**9** Refit the new unit and tighten it securely. Do not use thread sealant as it may electrically insulate the sender unit.
**10** Reconnect the wiring connector, refill the cooling system and check for coolant leakage and proper gauge function.

## 10 Heating and air conditioning blower motors - circuit check and component renewal

⚠ *Warning: Later models are equipped with airbags. To prevent accidental deployment of the airbag, which could cause personal injury or damage to the airbag system, DO NOT work in the vicinity of the steering wheel or instrument panel. Jaguar recommends that, on airbag-equipped models, the following procedure should be left to a dealer service department or other repair workshop because of the special tools and techniques required to disable the airbag system.*
**1** Disconnect the battery negative cable.
*Caution: If the stereo in your vehicle is equipped with an anti-theft system, make sure you have the correct activation code before disconnecting the battery.*
**2** There are two blower motors, one under the left side of the dash and one behind the glove compartment **(see illustration)**. If the blower doesn't work, check the fuse and all connections in the circuit for looseness and corrosion. Make sure the battery is fully charged. To access the right blower, remove the glove compartment liner, the glove compartment door and the right lower dash panel (see Chapter 11).

⚠ *Warning: When working around the area behind the glove box, watch out for a strip of sheet metal bracing that has a very sharp edge (see illustration). Apply some heavy duct tape to the edge of the brace before beginning work in this area, or you could injure your hands.*

10.2a  The right blower housing (arrowed) is located behind the glove box area of the dash

10.2b  Apply heavy duct tape to the sharp edge of this brace (dotted line) when working behind the glove box area of the dash - the metal is very sharp

10.3a  Remove the screw (A) holding the wiring harness in place, then remove the two lower cruise-control ECU screws (B) . . .

10.3b  . . . then remove the upper ECU screw (arrowed) and pull down the ECU, then remove the ECU mounting plate

10.5  Two bolts (arrow indicates the left bolt) hold the top of the blower housing to the cowl

10.6  Pull down and out on the housing until it clears the sheet metal brace below it

10.7  Remove this brace rod (small arrow) for clearance to remove the left blower motor housing (large arrow)

10.10  Remove the five clips (two shown here with arrows) and one screw holding the halves of the housing together

**3** Remove the screws holding the cruise-control ECU in place **(see illustrations)**, then remove the four screws holding the ECU mounting plate in place.

**4** Disconnect the vacuum lines and electrical connectors at the blower housing, identifying each connection with marked masking tape for reassembly, or write down the colour codes of the vacuum tubing. Remove the duct tape connecting the blower housing to the duct from the heater/air conditioning unit.

**5** Remove the two bolts holding the top of the blower housing to the cowl **(see illustration).**

**6** Pull down and back on the housing until it

squeezes past the metal brace below it **(see illustration).** It will take some force at first.

**7** To access the left blower motor, remove the left-hand brace rod from the steering column forward to the body **(see illustration)**, then repeat Steps 4 and 5 on the left blower housing. The blower housing should now drop straight down and out.

**8** If the blower motor does not operate, disconnect the electrical connectors at the blower motor and connect the black wire terminal to chassis ground, and the purple wire terminal to a fused source of battery voltage. If the blower doesn't operate, it

should be renewed. If it does operate, there is a problem in the feed or earth circuit.

**9** If the motor is good, but doesn't operate at any speed, the problem could be in the heater/air conditioning control assembly or the heating/air conditioning computer. Diagnosis either of these electronic components is beyond the scope of the home mechanic, and should be referred to your Jaguar dealer or other qualified repair facility.

**10** If either blower motor must be renewed, remove the five clips and one screw holding the blower housing halves together **(see illustration).**

10.11a  Separate the housing halves - the blower motor (arrowed) is attached to a plastic plate sandwiched between the two housing halves

10.11b  Loosen the clamp bolt (arrowed) on the motor bracket and then pull the motor and fan out as an assembly

11  Separate the housing halves and pull up the plastic plate holding the motor and fan **(see illustration)**. The fan doesn't come off the motor, but loosen the clamp-bolt on the motor's mount bracket and slide the motor and fan out for renewal **(see illustration)**. **Note:** *Some 1988 models had problems with cracking of the fan blades and noise from the blowers. These blowers and fans have been superseded with improved parts, available from your Jaguar dealer.*

12  When either blower housing is separated, you'll find two relays mounted inside **(see illustration)**. These are the blower isolation relay and blower relay. Before refitting the blower housing in the car, refer to Chapter 12 for testing of these relays.

13  Refitting is the reverse of removal. Check for proper operation.

## 11  Heater core - removal and refitting

**Warning: Later model vehicles are equipped with airbags. To prevent the accidental deployment of the airbag, which could cause personal injury or damage to the airbag system, DO NOT work in the vicinity of the steering wheel or instrument panel. The manufacturer recommends that, on airbag-equipped models, the following procedure should be left to a dealer service department or other repair workshop because of the special tools and techniques required to disable the airbag system.**

1  Disconnect the battery negative cable.
*Caution: If the stereo in your vehicle is equipped with an anti-theft system, make sure you have the correct activation code before disconnecting the battery.*

2  Drain the cooling system (see Chapter 1). Disconnect the heater hoses where they enter the bulkhead **(see illustration)**. **Note:** *Use compressed air in one of the pipes to blow out any remaining coolant and collect it. This will prevent any spills on the carpeting when the heater core is removed. Plug the pipes to prevent any remaining coolant from spilling out.*

3  Refer to Chapter 11 for removal of the under-dash panels on both the driver and passenger sides, and removal of the glovebox.

**Warning: When working around the area behind the glove box, watch out for a strip of sheet**

10.12  Inside the blower case are the blower and isolation relays (arrowed) - while the case is apart, test these relays for proper operation

11.2  Disconnect the heater hoses from the pipes at the bulkhead (small arrows) - the large arrow indicates the evaporator case retaining nut

**11.4 Remove these screws (small arrows) to remove the plastic plate over the heater core pipes on the left side**

**11.5 With the cover off, remove the Allen bolts (arrows indicate three of the four) to pull the coolant pipes out of the left side of the heater core**

**11.6a Remove three screws (one arrowed; one at the top-back and one below) to take out the climate-control computer on right side of heater/air conditioning assembly**

**11.6b Pull away the climate control computer (arrowed)**

**11.7 Remove the four screws (arrowed) and the heater core cover plate**

**11.8 Pull the heater core out to the right**

**11.9 Retain the original foam insulation on the heater core or transfer to the new core, and replace the two O-rings (arrowed)**

metal bracing that has a very sharp edge (see illustration 10.2b). Apply some heavy duct tape to the edge of the brace before beginning work in this area, or you could injure your hands.

**4** On the passenger's side, under the dash, remove the screws holding the plastic cover where the heater pipes enter the heater/air conditioning housing **(see illustration)**.

**5** With the cover off, there is access to remove the four Allen bolts holding the two pipes to the heater core **(see illustration)**.

**6** Move to the right side and unbolt the climate control computer and pull it down and away from the heater/air conditioning housing **(see illustrations)**.

**7** Remove the four small screws and remove the plastic plate over the heater core, right behind where the climate control computer had been **(see illustration)**.

**8** Carefully slide the heater core out from the right side of the heating/air conditioning housing **(see illustration)**. **Note:** *Keep plenty of towels or rags on the carpeting to catch any coolant that may drip.*

**9** Refitting is the reverse order of removal. When refitting the heater core, make sure all of the foam insulation strips are in place and refit new O-rings where the heater pipes enter the core **(see illustration)**.

**10** Refill the cooling system, reconnect the battery and run the engine. Check for leaks and proper system operation.

## 12 Heater and air conditioning control assembly - check, removal and refitting

 **Warning:** *Later models are equipped with airbags. To prevent the accidental deployment of the airbag, which could cause personal injury or damage to the airbag system, DO NOT work in the vicinity of the steering wheel or instrument panel. The manufacturer recommends that, on airbag-equipped models, the following procedure should be left to a dealer service department or other repair workshop*

because of the special tools and techniques required to disable the airbag system.

### Removal and refitting

**1** Disconnect the battery negative cable. *Caution: If the stereo in your vehicle is equipped with an anti-theft system, make sure you have the correct activation code before disconnecting the battery.*

**2** Refer to Chapter 11 for removal of the console heater control/radio assembly trim bezel.

**3** Remove the mounting screws retaining the heater/air conditioning control assembly to the console **(see illustrations)**. Pull the assembly out, and disconnect the electrical connectors.

**12.3a Remove these six screws (arrowed) to release the control panel/radio assembly from the console**

**12.3b  Remove the four screws (three are shown here) holding the control assembly in the control/radio housing**

**12.11  Check the operation of the vacuum servo motors; in this case, vacuum is applied to the servo on the right blower case - the flapper door (arrowed) should operate**

**4** Refitting is the reverse of the removal procedure.

**5** Run the engine and check for proper functioning of the heater (and air conditioning, if equipped).

### Control checks

**6** The climate-control system uses an all-electronic control panel that sends digital information to the climate control computer. There is little the home mechanic can do to troubleshoot or test the system. The factory recommends that diagnosis be performed at a dealership.

**7** If there is a problem in just one area of climate control, put the controls through their entire range of operation and check the system responses, i.e. set the controls to COLD, the fan to low and the temperature to 65° F. In this mode the Manual LED should be lit and the air conditioning compressor should engage. Try all of the fan speeds and try the temperature on HOT, then feel for warm air coming from the ducts. *Note: Between each try of the different controls, wait 20 seconds or so for the heater/air conditioning system to adjust before checking for a response.*

**8** When each control button is pushed two times, its LED light should go on or off. Renew the control assembly if any of the warning lights don't work.

**9** On 1988 and 1989 models, if the climate controls do not respond to any driver input, check with your Jaguar dealer before renewing the ECU or control panel. A service part is available (a resistor, #JLM 1901) that can be installed at one of the control panel terminals that may fix the problem without any other parts being renewed. Instructions are included with the part.

**10** Check the vacuum lines to the several vacuum motors that operate the heater/air conditioning functions. Look for pinched or blocked hoses and leaks.

**11** Each of the vacuum "servo motors" in the system can be checked with a hand-held vacuum pump **(see illustration)**. Apply vacuum and watch that the door or control it operates is working.

**12** Further diagnosis of the controls or climate control ECU are best left to a Jaguar dealership or other qualified repair facility.

---

**13  Air conditioning and heating system** - check and maintenance

---

### Air conditioning system

⚠️ *Warning: The air conditioning system is under high pressure. Do not loosen any hose fittings or remove any components until the system has been discharged. Air conditioning refrigerant should be properly discharged into an EPA-approved recovery/recycling unit by a dealer service department or an automotive air conditioning repair facility. Always wear eye protection when working near air conditioning system fittings.*

**1** The following maintenance checks should be performed on a regular basis to ensure that the air conditioner continues to operate at peak efficiency:

a) *Inspect the condition of the compressor drivebelt. If it is worn or deteriorated, renew it (see Chapter 1).*

b) *Check the drivebelt tension and, if necessary, adjust it (see Chapter 1).*

c) *Inspect the system hoses. Look for cracks, bubbles, hardening and deterioration. Inspect the hoses and all fittings for oil bubbles or seepage. If there is any evidence of wear, damage or leakage, renew the hose(s).*

d) *Inspect the condenser fins for leaves, bugs and any other foreign material that may have embedded itself in the fins. Use a "fin comb" or compressed air to remove debris from the condenser.*

e) *Make sure the system has the correct refrigerant charge.*

**2** It's a good idea to operate the system for about ten minutes at least once a month. This is particularly important during the winter months because long term non-use can cause hardening, and subsequent failure, of the seals.

**3** Leaks in the air conditioning system are best spotted when the system is brought up to operating temperature and pressure, by running the engine with the air conditioning ON for five minutes. Shut the engine off and inspect the air conditioning hoses and connections. Traces of oil usually indicate refrigerant leaks.

**4** Because of the complexity of the air conditioning system and the special equipment required to effectively work on it, accurate troubleshooting of the system should be left to a professional technician.

**5** If the air conditioning system doesn't operate at all, check the fuse panel and the air conditioning relay (refer to Chapter 12 for relay locations and testing). See Sections 4, 9 and 12 for electrical checks of heating/air conditioning system components.

**6** The most common cause of poor cooling is simply a low system refrigerant charge. If a noticeable drop in cool air output occurs, the following quick check will help you determine if the refrigerant level is low.

### Checking the refrigerant charge

**7** Warm the engine up to normal operating temperature.

**8** Place the air conditioning temperature selector at the coldest setting and put the

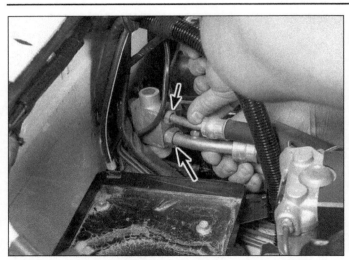

13.9 Feel the inlet (small arrow) and outlet (large arrow) pipes at the bulkhead leading to the air conditioning evaporator (battery removed here for clarity only)

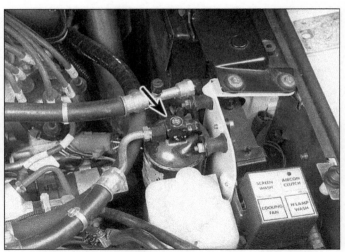

13.11 The sight glass (arrowed) is located on the top of the receiver/drier, to the right of the radiator

blower at the highest setting. Open the doors (to make sure the air conditioning system doesn't cycle off as soon as it cools the passenger compartment).

9  With the compressor engaged - the clutch will make an audible click and the centre of the clutch will rotate. After the system reaches operating temperature, feel the two pipes connected to the evaporator at the bulkhead (see illustration).

10  The pipe (thinner tubing) leading from the condenser outlet to the evaporator should be cold, and the evaporator outlet line (the thicker tubing that leads back to the compressor) should be slightly colder (3 to 10° F). If the evaporator outlet is considerably warmer than the inlet, the system needs a charge. Insert a thermometer in the centre air distribution duct while operating the air conditioning system - the temperature of the output air should be 35 to 40° F below the ambient air temperature (down to approximately 40° F). If the ambient (outside) air temperature is very high, say 110° F, the duct air temperature may be as high as 60° F, but generally the air conditioning is 30 to 50° F cooler than the ambient air. If the air isn't as cold as it used to be, the system probably needs a charge. Further inspection or testing of the system is beyond the scope of the home mechanic and should be left to a professional.

11  Inspect the sight glass (see illustration). If the refrigerant looks foamy when running, it's low. When ambient temperatures are very hot, bubbles may show in the sight glass even with the proper amount of refrigerant. With the proper amount of refrigerant, when the air conditioning is turned off, the sight glass should show refrigerant that foams, then clears. Note: 1993 and 1994 models are equipped with R-134a refrigerant systems and do not have a sight glass.

### Heating systems

12  If the air coming out of the heater vents isn't hot, the problem could stem from any of the following causes:

a) The thermostat is stuck open, preventing the engine coolant from warming up enough to carry heat to the heater core. Renew the thermostat (see Section 3).

b) A heater hose is blocked, preventing the flow of coolant through the heater core. Feel both heater hoses at the bulkhead. They should be hot. If one of them is cold, there is an obstruction in one of the hoses or in the heater core, or the heater control valve is shut. Detach the hoses and back flush the heater core with a water hose. If the heater core is clear but circulation is impeded, remove the two hoses and flush them out with a water hose.

c) If flushing fails to remove the blockage from the heater core, the core must be renewed. (see Section 11).

13  If the blower motor speed does not correspond to the setting selected on the blower switch, the problem could be a bad

13.16 This drain hose (arrowed) from the heater/air conditioning unit should be kept clear to allow drainage of condensation

fuse, circuit, control panel or climate control computer (see Sections 10 and 12).

14  If there isn't any air coming out of the vents:

a) Turn the ignition ON and activate the fan control. Place your ear at the heating/air conditioning register (vent) and listen. Most motors are audible. Can you hear the motor running?

b) If you can't (and have already verified that the blower switch and the blower motor resistor are good), the blower motor itself is probably bad (see Section 10).

15  If the carpet under the heater core is damp, or if antifreeze vapour or steam is coming through the vents, the heater core is leaking. Remove it (see Section 11) and refit a new unit (most radiator shops will not repair a leaking heater core).

16  Inspect the drain hose from the heat/AC assembly at the right side of the bulkhead, make sure it is not clogged (see illustration). If there is a humid mist coming from the system ducts, this hose may be plugged. In some early models, the hose may have been pinched during assembly or blocked with insulation or underseal.

### 14  Air conditioning receiver/drier - removal and refitting

Warning: The air conditioning system is under high pressure. Do not loosen any hose fittings or remove any components until the system has been discharged. Air conditioning refrigerant should be properly discharged into an EPA-approved recovery/recycling unit by a dealer service department or an automotive air conditioning

**14.2  After the system has been discharged, unbolt the two refrigerant lines (left arrows) from the top of the receiver/drier and cap them - use two spanners when loosening or tightening these lines - right arrows indicate the two top mounting bolts**

**15.4  Disconnect the electrical connector (small arrow) at the compressor, then disconnect the bolt (large arrow) at the retaining plate that holds the two hoses in place**

*repair facility. Always wear eye protection when working near air conditioning system fittings.*

**1** Have the refrigerant discharged and recovered by an air conditioning technician.

**2** Disconnect the refrigerant lines **(see illustration)** from the receiver/drier and cap the open fittings to prevent entry of moisture.

**3** Remove the three nuts holding the receiver/drier to the radiator support and remove the receiver/drier. **Note:** *On 1993 and 1994 models, the receiver/drier is a long tubular style mounted to the top-front of the radiator support. The grille must be removed for access on these models (see Chapter 11 for grille removal).*

**4** Refitting is the reverse of removal.

**5** Have the system evacuated, charged and leak tested by the workshop that discharged it. If the receiver/drier was renewed, have them add new refrigeration oil to the compressor, about 28 cc (one ounce). Use only the refrigerant oil compatible with the refrigerant of your system (R-12 or R-134a).

## 15  Air conditioning compressor - removal and refitting

⚠ *Warning: The air conditioning system is under high pressure. Do not loosen any hose fittings or remove any components until the system has been discharged. Air conditioning refrigerant should be properly discharged into an EPA-approved recovery/recycling unit by a dealer service department or an automotive air conditioning repair facility. Always wear eye protection when disconnecting air conditioning system fittings.*

**1** Have the refrigerant discharged by an automotive air conditioning technician.

**2** Disconnect the battery negative cable.
*Caution: If the stereo in your vehicle is equipped with an anti-theft system, make sure you have the correct activation code before disconnecting the battery.*

**3** Remove the drivebelt from the compressor (see Chapter 1).

**4** Detach the electrical connector and disconnect the flexible refrigerant lines **(see illustration)**.

**5** Unbolt the compressor and lift it from the vehicle **(see illustration)**.

**6** If a new or rebuilt compressor is being installed, drain the fluid from the new unit by opening the drain plug and by tilting the compressor to the rear so that any remaining oil will come out the ports in the back normally covered by the plate and hard lines. Refit the drain plug and end-plate and add 199 cc (7 fluid ounces) of new oil of a type compatible with the type refrigerant in your system.

**7** Refitting is the reverse of removal. Renew any O-rings with new ones specifically made for the type of refrigerant in your system and lubricate them with refrigerant oil, also designed specifically for your refrigerant.

**8** Have the system evacuated, recharged and tested by the workshop that discharged it.

## 16  Air conditioning condenser - removal and refitting

⚠ *Warning: The air conditioning system is under high pressure. Do not loosen any hose fittings or remove any components until the system has been discharged. Air conditioning refrigerant should be properly discharged into an EPA-approved recovery/recycling unit by a dealer service department or an automotive air conditioning repair facility. Always wear eye protection when disconnecting air conditioning system fittings.*

**1** Have the refrigerant discharged and recovered by an air conditioning technician.

**2** Remove the radiator cowl panel as described in Section 5.

**3** Using two spanners to avoid twisting the fittings, disconnect the inlet and outlet lines from the condenser **(see illustration)**.

**4** Pull the condenser straight up and out of the vehicle.

**5** Refitting is the reverse of removal. When refitting the condenser, be sure the rubber

**15.5  Remove the lower mounting bolts and the adjuster bolt (arrowed)**

**16.3  Disconnect the two lines, then pull up on the condenser (arrowed)**

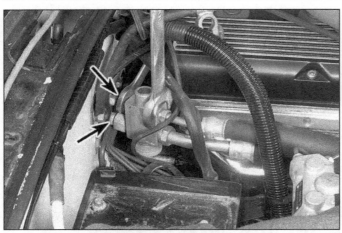

17.2 Use two spanners when disconnecting the air conditioning lines (arrowed) at the bulkhead, on the backside of the expansion valve - one spanner holds the body of the expansion valve

17.4 Remove the housing retaining nut (arrowed) on the engine side of the bulkhead, near the expansion valve - another nut is on the right, near the heater core pipes

cushions fit on the mounting points and that any foam insulator strips are still in place or transferred to the new condenser.

**6** Reconnect the refrigerant lines, using new O-rings. If a new condenser has been installed, add 84 cc (3 fluid ounces) of new refrigerant oil. **Note:** *The oil and O-rings must be compatible with the type of refrigerant you are using.*

**7** Refit the remaining parts in the reverse order of removal.

**8** Have the system evacuated, charged and leak tested by the workshop that discharged it.

---

**17 Air conditioning evaporator and expansion valve -** removal and refitting

⚠️ *Warning 1: The air conditioning system is under high pressure. Do not loosen any hose fittings or remove any components until the system has been discharged. Air conditioning refrigerant should be properly discharged into an EPA-approved recovery/recycling unit by a dealer service department or an automotive air conditioning repair facility. Always wear eye protection when disconnecting air conditioning system fittings.*

⚠️ *Warning 2: Later model vehicles are equipped with airbags. To prevent the accidental deployment of the airbag, which could cause personal injury or damage to the airbag system, DO NOT work in the vicinity of the steering wheel or instrument panel. The manufacturer recommends that, on airbag-equipped models, the following procedure should be left to a dealer service department or other repair workshop because of the special tools and techniques required to disable the airbag system.*

**1** Refer to Chapter 11 for removal of the glove compartment, under-dash panels and console. **Note:** *The removal of the heater/evaporator housing is difficult and time-consuming, much more so than the removal of the heater core (see Section 11). For some home mechanics, the job is better left to a Jaguar dealership or other qualified repair workshop.*

**2** Disconnect the air conditioning lines from the backside of the expansion valve (at the bulkhead, just to the right of the engine), using two spanners **(see illustration)**. Cap the open fittings and expansion valve after dismantling to prevent the entry of air or dirt.

**3** Refer to Section 11 for moving the climate-control computer aside and disconnecting the heater core pipes.

**4** From the engine side of the bulkhead, near the expansion valve, remove the nut retaining the heat/air conditioning assembly housing **(see illustration)**. Another mounting nut is on the left side, under the wiper motor **(see illustration 11.2)**.

**5** Disconnect the defroster ducts on the left and right side of the evaporator housing **(see illustration)**.

**6** Identify all of the vacuum motor lines with masking tape and a felt pen, then disconnect the lines. **Note:** *Most vacuum lines are colour-coded. Make notes on which ones go to which devices.*

**7** Tag and disconnect the wiring plugs connected to the heating/air conditioning housing.

**8** At the bottom left and bottom right of the housing, pull off the rubber drain tubes that go into the flooring.

**9** Remove the four rod-type support braces. Two support the dash, and two connect the case to the floor of the car **(see illustrations)**.

17.5 Left duct (large arrow) can be removed by pulling off the clip (small arrow) - right duct pulls out without a clip

17.9a Unbolt the four support braces (small arrows) from the case (large arrow) and floor

17.9b Black case-support rods are held with nuts (arrowed), the gold dash-support rods are retained by a bolt/nut to the dash

**10** With everything disconnected, pull the heat-air conditioning housing back and out from under the dash.

*Caution: Do not force anything. If the unit gets stuck, determine where the interference is before a duct, wire or hose is broken.*

**11** Pry off the series of black metal clips connecting the main housing to the evaporator case, then separate the evaporator case and pull out the evaporator core. **Note:** *When refitting the evaporator core into the case, be sure to refit the foam insulation in the same way it was installed originally.*

**12** The evaporator core can be cleaned with a "fin comb" and blown off with compressed air.

**13** The expansion valve is located on the right side of the bulkhead on the engine side. To renew it, remove the battery (Chapter 5) for better access. Disconnect the lines from the back of the valve as in Step 2. Disconnect the high and low-pressure hoses from the *front* of the expansion valve **(see illustration)**.

**14** If the evaporator core is renewed, make sure the technician adds 1.4 ounces of new refrigerant oil (of a type compatible with your type of refrigerant) to the system.

**15** The remainder of the refitting is the reverse of the removal process. Be sure to use new O-rings, and new gaskets on the expansion valve.

**16** Have the system evacuated, charged and leak tested by the workshop that discharged it.

**17.13 Disconnect the lines at the front of the expansion valve - always use two spanners to avoid twisting a line - one spanner holds the body of the valve**

# Notes

# Chapter 4
# Fuel and exhaust systems

## Contents

## Degrees of difficulty

| Easy, suitable for novice with little experience  | Fairly easy, suitable for beginner with some experience  | Fairly difficult, suitable for competent DIY mechanic  | Difficult, suitable for experienced DIY mechanic  | Very difficult, suitable for expert DIY or professional |
|---|---|---|---|---|

## Specifications

### Fuel system
| Fuel pressure: | kPa | psi |
|---|---|---|
|   Ignition ON, engine not running ........................... | 260 to 300 | 38 to 44 |
|   Engine idling: | | |
|     Vacuum hose detached from fuel pressure regulator ........... | 280 to 320 | 40 to 46 |
|     Vacuum hose attached to fuel pressure regulator ............. | 210 to 260 | 30 to 38 |
|   Fuel system hold pressure ................................. | 145 | 21 |
| Fuel injector resistance .................................... | 2.0 to 3.0 ohms | |

### Idle speed .............................................. Must be set by authorised service department

### Torque wrench settings
| | Nm | lbf ft |
|---|---|---|
| Throttle body mounting bolts ............................... | 19 | 14 |
| Fuel rail mounting bolts ................................... | 12 | 9 |

---

## 1  General information

The fuel system consists of a fuel tank, an electric fuel pump either located externally, next to the fuel tank (1988 to 1990 models) or in the fuel tank (1991 to 1994 models), an EFI fuel pump relay and main relay, an inertia switch, fuel injectors and fuel rail, an air cleaner assembly and a throttle body unit.

### Multi Point Fuel Injection (MPFI) system

Multi point fuel injection uses timed impulses to sequentially inject the fuel directly into the intake port of each cylinder. The injectors are controlled by the Electronic Control Unit (ECU). The ECU monitors various engine parameters and delivers the exact amount of fuel, in the correct sequence, into the intake ports. The throttle body serves only to control the amount of air passing into the system. Because each cylinder is equipped with an injector mounted immediately adjacent to the intake valve, much better control of the fuel/air mixture ratio is possible.

### Fuel pump and lines

Fuel is circulated from the fuel tank to the fuel injection system, and back to the fuel tank, through a pair of metal lines running along the underside of the vehicle. On early models (1988 to 1990), an electric fuel pump is attached to the chassis next to the fuel tank. On later models (1991 to 1994), the fuel pump and fuel level sender unit are located inside the fuel tank. A vapour return system routes all vapours and hot fuel back to the fuel tank through a separate return line.

The fuel pump will operate as long as the engine is cranking or running and the ECU is receiving ignition reference pulses from the electronic ignition system (see Chapter 5). If there are no reference pulses, the fuel pump will shut off after 2 or 3 seconds.

### Inertia switch

These models are equipped with an inertia switch that is wired in the circuit between the fuel pump relay, the ignition switch and the fuel pump (refer to the wiring diagrams at the end of Chapter 12). The inertia switch is a

2.3a Relay locations on a 1988 model

2.3b Relay locations on a 1989 model

special electrical device that provides circuit protection by switching off the ignition and fuel pump upon impact in the event of vehicle collision. Later Jaguar models are equipped with an additional specialised inertia switch. This later device switches OFF all ignition fed circuits, locks the fuel filler cap, locks the boot (only if doors are locked) and unlocks the doors if they are locked during the accident. All these functions are directed by the inertia switch. The inertia switch is located behind the left kick panel. Refer to Chapter 12 for more information.

### Exhaust system

The exhaust system includes an exhaust manifold equipped with an exhaust oxygen sensor, a catalytic converter, an exhaust pipe, and a silencer.

The catalytic converter is an emission control device added to the exhaust system to reduce pollutants. A single-bed converter is used in combination with a three-way (reduction) catalyst. See Chapter 6 for more information regarding the catalytic converter.

### 2 Fuel pressure relief

*Warning: Petrol is extremely flammable, so take extra precautions when you work on any part of the fuel system. Don't smoke or allow open flames or bare light bulbs near the work area, and don't work in a garage where a natural gas-type appliance (such as a water heater or a clothes dryer) with a pilot light is present. Since petrol is carcinogenic, wear latex gloves when there's a possibility of being exposed to fuel, and, if you spill any fuel on your skin, rinse it off immediately with soap and water. Mop up any spills immediately and do not store fuel-soaked rags where*

*they could ignite. The fuel system is under constant pressure, so, if any fuel lines are to be disconnected, the fuel pressure in the system must be relieved first. When you perform any kind of work on the fuel system, wear safety glasses and have a Class B type fire extinguisher on hand.*

1 Before servicing any fuel system component, you must relieve the fuel pressure to minimise the risk of fire or personal injury.
2 Remove the fuel filler cap - this will relieve any pressure built up in the tank.
3 Remove the fuel pump relay from the main relay panel **(see illustrations)**. **Note:** *These models are equipped with a fuel pump relay that is located in various areas of the vehicle depending on the year. On 1988 and 1989 models, the fuel pump relay is under the glovebox. On 1990 to 1992 models, the fuel pump relay is in the engine compartment on the left side, attached to the brake pedal hanger. On 1993 models, the fuel pump relay is in the boot. On 1994 models, it's in the engine compartment on the right side of the bulkhead. Refer to the relay location charts in Chapter 12 for additional information.*
4 Start the engine and wait for the engine to stall, then turn the ignition key to Off. Disconnect the cable from the negative

2.3c On 1992 models, the fuel pump relay is located in the left rear corner of the engine compartment

terminal of the battery before beginning any work on the fuel system.
*Caution: If the stereo in your vehicle is equipped with an anti-theft system, make sure you have the correct activation code before disconnecting the battery.*
5 The fuel system is now depressurised.
**Note:** *Place a rag around the fuel line before removing any hose clamp or fitting to prevent any residual fuel from spilling onto the engine.*

### 3 Fuel pump/fuel pressure - check

*Warning: Petrol is extremely flammable, so take extra precautions when you work on any part of the fuel system. See the Warning in Section 2.*
**Note:** *To perform the fuel pressure test, you will need to obtain a fuel pressure gauge and adapter set (fuel line fittings).*
**Note:** *On 1988 to 1990 models, the fuel pump may chatter excessively and the engine may stall frequently during hot weather. If stalling occurs, the engine will restart after a cool-down period. Dual fuel pumps can be installed by a dealer service department or other qualified repair facility to remedy this problem.*

### Preliminary inspection

1 Should the fuel system fail to deliver the proper amount of fuel, or any fuel at all, inspect it as follows. Remove the fuel filler cap. Have an assistant turn the ignition key to the ON position (engine not running) while you listen at the fuel filler opening. You should hear a whirring sound that lasts for a couple of seconds. On 1988 to 1990 models, listen behind the left rear wheel (external fuel pump) for the fuel pump sound.
2 If you don't hear anything, check the fuel pump relay **(see illustration 2.3a, b or c)** and

3.3a  Checking for battery voltage at the fuel pump relay connector ( 1989 model)

3.3b  Checking for battery voltage to the main relay (1989 model)

circuit. If all circuits are intact and not damaged, check the inertia switch. **Note:** *The inertia switch is a special device that shuts down power to the ignition and the fuel pump in the event of an accident. See Chapter 12 for checking and resetting procedures for the inertia switch.*

**3** Remove the relay and check for battery voltage to the fuel pump relay connector **(see illustration)**. If there is battery voltage present, check the relay for proper operation. Refer to the relay checking procedure in Chapter 12. **Note:** *If battery voltage is not available, check for battery voltage to the main relay* **(see illustration)**. *Refer to the relay location diagrams in Chapter 12. The main relay, which is located next to the fuel pump relay, supplies voltage to the fuel pump and ignition system.*

**4** If battery voltage is present, check for battery voltage directly at the fuel pump electrical connector **(see illustrations)**, within two seconds of the ignition key being turned On. If there is no voltage, check the fuel pump circuit. If there is voltage present, renew the pump (see Section 4). **Note:** *It will be necessary to raise the vehicle and support it securely on axle stands to gain access to the fuel pump electrical connectors. Have an assistant operate the ignition key and be sure to block the front wheels to avoid any movement of the vehicle.*

### Operating pressure check

**5** Relieve the fuel system pressure (see Section 2). Detach the cable from the negative battery terminal.
*Caution: If the stereo in your vehicle is equipped with an anti-theft system, make sure you have the correct activation code before disconnecting the battery.*
**6** Detach the fuel line from the fuel rail and connect a fuel pressure gauge **(see illustrations)** between the fuel pulsation

damper and the fuel rail. Tighten the hose clamps securely.
**7** Attach the cable to the negative battery terminal. Start the engine.
**8** Note the fuel pressure and compare it with the pressure listed in this Chapter's Specifications.
**9** Disconnect the vacuum hose from the fuel

pressure regulator and hook up a hand-held vacuum pump **(see illustration)** to the port on the fuel pressure regulator.
**10** Read the fuel pressure gauge with vacuum applied to the pressure regulator and also with no vacuum applied. The fuel pressure should decrease as vacuum increases (and increase as vacuum decreases).

3.4a  Remove the rubber boot from the fuel pump electrical connector and check for voltage while an assistant turns the ignition key (1989 model shown)

3.4b  Check for battery voltage to the fuel pump on the harness connector near the fuel tank on models with in-tank fuel pumps

3.6a  Remove the fuel line from the fuel pulsation damper . . .

3.6b  . . . then refit the fuel pressure gauge between the fuel rail and the fuel pressure damper using a T-fitting

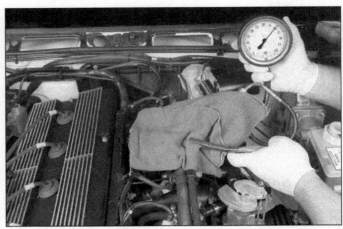

**3.9 Check fuel pressure without vacuum applied to the fuel pressure regulator, then with vacuum applied; fuel pressure should DECREASE as vacuum INCREASES**

**3.12 Using a pair of pliers, squeeze the return line and observe the fuel pressure increase (wrap a rag around the fuel line so you don't damage it)**

**11** Reconnect the vacuum hose to the regulator and check the fuel pressure at idle, comparing your reading with the value listed in this Chapter's Specifications. Disconnect the vacuum hose and watch the gauge - the pressure should jump up considerably as soon as the hose is disconnected. If it doesn't, check for a vacuum signal to the fuel pressure regulator (see Step 14).

**12** If the fuel pressure is low, pinch the fuel return line shut **(see illustration)** and watch the gauge. If the pressure doesn't rise, the fuel pump is defective or there is a restriction or leak in the fuel feed line, or the pump is faulty. If the pressure rises sharply, renew the pressure regulator.

**13** If the fuel pressure is too high, turn the engine off. Disconnect the fuel return line and blow through it to check for a blockage. If there is no blockage, renew the fuel pressure regulator.

**14** Connect a vacuum gauge to the pressure regulator vacuum hose. Start the engine and check for vacuum **(see illustration)**. The fuel pressure regulator receives manifold vacuum that decreases (increases fuel pressure) when the engine speed is raised (acceleration). If there isn't vacuum present, check for a clogged hose or vacuum port. If the amount of

vacuum is adequate but the pressure is too high, renew the fuel pressure regulator.

**15** Turn the ignition switch to OFF, wait five minutes and recheck the pressure on the gauge. Compare the reading with the specified hold pressure. If the hold pressure is less than specified:

a) The fuel lines may be leaking.
b) The fuel pressure regulator may be allowing the fuel pressure to bleed through to the return line.
c) A fuel injector (or injectors) may be leaking.
d) The fuel pump may be defective.

### 4 Fuel pump - removal and refitting

> ⚠️ **Warning: Petrol is extremely flammable, so take extra precautions when you work on any part of the fuel system. See the Warning in Section 2.**

**Note 1:** *On early models (1988 to 1990), an electric fuel pump is attached to the chassis next to the fuel tank. On later models (1991 to 1994), the fuel pump is inside the fuel tank.*

**Note 2:** *On 1988 to 1990 models, the fuel pump may chatter excessively and the engine may stall frequently during hot weather. If stalling occurs, the engine will restart after a cool-down period. Dual fuel pumps can be installed by a dealer service department or other qualified repair facility to remedy this problem.*

**1** Remove the fuel tank filler cap to relieve any pressure in the fuel tank. Relieve the fuel pressure (see Section 2).

**2** Disconnect the cable from the negative terminal of the battery.

*Caution: If the stereo in your vehicle is equipped with an anti-theft system, make sure you have the correct activation code before disconnecting the battery.*

### External fuel pumps

**3** Raise the vehicle and support it securely on axle stands.

**4** Disconnect the fuel lines from the fuel pump.

**5** Disconnect the electrical connectors from the fuel pump **(see illustration 3.4a)**.

**6** Remove the fuel pump bracket retaining nuts **(see illustration)**.

**7** Carefully withdraw the fuel pump from the rubber case inside the fuel pump bracket and angle the fuel pump over the rear suspension and out near the wheel on the left side of the vehicle.

**8** Refitting is the reverse of removal.

### In-tank fuel pumps

**9** Raise the vehicle and support it securely on axle stands.

**10** Disconnect the fuel pump and fuel level sender unit electrical connectors and the fuel lines.

**11** Remove the fuel tank from the boot (see Section 7).

**12** Disconnect the fuel lines from the evaporative flange **(see illustration)**. Remove the lock ring with a hammer and brass punch, tapping the lock ring anti-clockwise.

**13** Withdraw the fuel pump module from the fuel tank. **Note:** *The fuel pump module is*

**3.14 Connect a vacuum gauge to the vacuum line leading to the fuel pressure regulator and check the vacuum source**

**4.6 Remove the fuel pump mounting nuts (arrowed) and slide the fuel pump out of the rubber casing (1989 model shown)**

4.12 Exploded view of the in-tank fuel pump and the fuel tank on 1991 to 1994 models

*indexed near the bottom, therefore it will be necessary to turn the module slightly to unlock it from the rubber holder mounted on the bottom of the fuel tank.*

**14** Renew the fuel pump module as a single unit.

**15** Refitting is the reverse of removal.

---

### 5  Fuel level sender unit - check and renewal

> **Warning: Petrol is highly flammable, so take precautions when you work on any part of the fuel system. See the Warning in Section 2.**

**Note:** *Some 1994 models may be equipped with faulty fuel level sender units. A tight float rod bushing may cause the float to stick and indicate high fuel levels while the tank is almost empty.*

### Check

**1** Before performing any tests on the fuel level sender unit, completely fill the tank with fuel.

**2** Remove the boot liner (see Chapter 12) to expose the fuel level sender unit access cover.

**3** Disconnect the fuel level sender unit electrical connector located on the access cover. **Note:** *1991 to 1994 models are equipped with a fuel pump module and a sender unit assembly while 1988 and 1989 models are equipped with only the fuel level sender unit inside the tank.*

**4** Position the ohmmeter probes on the electrical connector terminals **(see illustration)** and check for resistance. Use the 200 ohm scale on the ohmmeter.

**5** With the fuel tank completely full, the resistance should be about 18 to 20 ohms.

**6** Reconnect the electrical connector and drive it until the tank is nearly empty.

**7** Check the resistance. The resistance of the sender unit should be about 190 to 200 ohms.

**8** If the readings are incorrect, renew the sender unit. **Note:** *The test can also be performed with the fuel level sender unit removed from the fuel tank. Using an ohmmeter, check the resistance of the sender unit with the swing arm completely down (tank empty) and with the arm up (tank full)* **(see illustration)**. *The resistance should change steadily from 200 ohms to around 18 ohms.*

### Renewal

> **Warning: The fuel level in the tank must be less than half full to safely remove the fuel pump/sender unit assembly from the fuel**

5.4 Connect the probes of the ohmmeter to the fuel level sender unit terminals and check the resistance of the float assembly

5.8 An accurate check of the sender unit can be made by removing it from the fuel tank and observing the resistance with the float down (empty) and then extended (full)

5.10  Use a brass punch and remove the lock ring by tapping on it in an anti-clockwise direction

5.11  Lift the fuel level sender unit assembly from the fuel tank at an angle so as not to damage the float or arm

*tank. If there is any doubt about the amount of fuel in the tank, drain the fuel tank completely before attempting this procedure (Section 7, paragraph 1).*

9 Disconnect the cable from the negative terminal of the battery. Disconnect the fuel level sender unit/fuel pump electrical connector.

*Caution: If the stereo in your vehicle is equipped with an anti-theft system, make sure you have the correct activation code before disconnecting the battery.*

10 Using a brass punch, tap on the lock ring anti-clockwise **(see illustration)** until the tabs align with the indentations in the fuel tank.

11 Carefully angle the sender unit out of the opening without damaging the fuel level float **(see illustration)**.

12 Refitting is the reverse of removal.

### 6  Fuel lines and fittings - inspection and renewal

> **Warning: Petrol is extremely flammable, so take extra precautions when you work on any part of the fuel system. See the Warning in Section 2.**

**Note:** *If there is a distinct knocking noise coming from the dash when the engine is idling, the fuel feed hose may have hardened, restricting fuel flow and causing abnormal sounds. Replace the fuel inlet (feed) hose with a new one.*

## Inspection

1 Once in a while, you will have to raise the vehicle to service or renew some component (an exhaust pipe hanger, for example). Whenever you work under the vehicle, always inspect fuel lines and all fittings and connections for damage or deterioration.

2 Check all hoses and pipes for cracks, kinks, deformation or obstructions.

3 Make sure all hoses and pipe clips attach their associated hoses or pipes securely to the underside of the vehicle.

4 Verify all hose clamps attaching rubber hoses to metal fuel lines or pipes are a tight fit between the hoses and pipes.

## Renewal

5 If you must renew any damaged sections, use hoses or pipes constructed from exactly the same material as the section you are replacing. Do not refit substitutes constructed from inferior or inappropriate material or you could cause a fuel leak or a fire.

6 Always, before detaching or disassembling any part of the fuel line system, note the routing of all hoses and pipes and the orientation of all clamps and clips to assure that new sections are identically installed.

7 Before detaching any part of the fuel system, be sure to relieve the pressure in the tank by removing the fuel tank cap, then relieve the fuel system pressure (Section 2). Cover the fitting being disconnected with a rag to absorb any fuel that may leak out.

### 7  Fuel tank - removal and refitting

> **Warning: Petrol is extremely flammable, so take extra precautions when you work on**

7.6  Remove the clamp that retains the fuel filler assembly to the filler neck

*any part of the fuel system. See the Warning in Section 2.*

1 This procedure is much easier to perform if the fuel tank is empty. Some models may have a drain plug for this purpose. If for some reason the drain plug can't be removed, postpone the job until the tank is empty or siphon the fuel into an approved container using a siphoning kit (available at most motor factors).

> **Warning: Do not start the siphoning action by mouth!**

2 Remove the fuel filler cap to relieve fuel tank pressure.

3 Detach the battery negative cable.

*Caution: If the stereo in your vehicle is equipped with an anti-theft system, make sure you have the correct activation code before disconnecting the battery.*

4 If the tank is full or nearly full, drain the fuel into an approved container.

5 Raise the vehicle and place it securely on axle stands.

6 Remove the filler neck vent tube clamp **(see illustration)** and separate the tube from the fuel filler neck.

7 Remove the fuel filler assembly bolts **(see illustration)** and slide the large rubber boot down the neck of the fuel tank. **Note:** *These vehicles are susceptible to clogging of the fuel overflow line. If this happens, excess fuel or*

7.7a  Remove bolts (arrowed) that retain the fuel filler assembly to the body and slide the assembly down the filler neck of fuel tank

**7.7b Direct low pressure compressed air into the hole for the overflow line if clogged**

**7.8 Remove the bolts (arrowed) from the spare tyre bracket and lift out the assembly**

**7.9a Disconnect the flexible fuel lines from the metal fuel lines**

**7.9b Disconnect the vapour return line from the fuel tank**

**7.9c Disconnect the canister purge line from the fuel tank**

Be careful to angle the fuel filler neck away from the body.
**12** Remove the tank from the vehicle.
**13** Refitting is the reverse of removal.

---

## 8 Fuel tank cleaning and repair - general information

**1** Any repairs to the fuel tank or filler neck should be carried out by a professional who has experience in this critical and potentially dangerous work. Even after cleaning and flushing of the fuel system, explosive fumes can remain and ignite during repair of the tank.
**2** If the fuel tank is removed from the vehicle, it should not be placed in an area where sparks or open flames could ignite the fumes coming out of the tank. Be especially careful inside garages where a natural petrol-type appliance is located, because the pilot light could cause an explosion.

---

## 9 Air cleaner assembly - removal and refitting

**1** Detach the clips and remove the air filter cover and the filter element (see Chapter 1).
**2** Remove the bolts and remove the air cleaner assembly from the engine compartment **(see illustrations)**.
**3** Refitting is the reverse of removal.

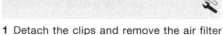

**7.9d Remove the clips (arrowed) that retain the fuel lines to the fuel tank using needle-nose pliers**

**7.10 Remove the tank strap bolts (arrowed) from the body**

*water in the fuel filler cap recess could flow into the boot, causing a dangerous condition and/or an unpleasant mess. To correct this condition, direct low-pressure compressed air into the overflow hole (see illustration), which should be enough to clear any obstruction in the line.*
**8** Remove the spare tyre and the spare tyre bracket assembly **(see illustration)**.
**9** Disconnect the fuel lines, the vapour return line and the canister vent line **(see illustrations)**. Note: *Be sure to plug the hoses to prevent leakage and contamination of the fuel system.* Remove the driveline to gain access to the fuel line connectors next to the tank (see Chapter 8). Working under the vehicle, remove the pins using a needle-nose pliers, turn the connectors slightly to loosen them from the grommets and pull the fuel lines out of the tank.

**10** Remove the retaining bolts from the fuel tank retaining straps **(see illustration)**.
**11** Pull the fuel tank out into the boot area.

**9.2a Remove the bolts (arrowed) from the air cleaner assembly**

**9.2b Also, remove the bolt that retains the air intake duct to the MAF sensor and lift the assembly from the compartment**

**10.2 Loosen the locknuts on the accelerator cable**

**10.3 Rotate the bellcrank and remove the cable end from the slot**

**10.4 Remove circlip (arrowed) and separate cable from the accelerator pedal by pulling the pin from the pedal assembly**

**10.9 Make sure the throttle closes completely and there is a slight amount of flex in the cable**

## 10 Accelerator cable - removal, refitting and adjustment

### Removal

**1** Detach the cable from the negative terminal of the battery.
*Caution: If the stereo in your vehicle is equipped with an anti-theft system, make sure you have the correct activation code before disconnecting the battery.*
**2** Loosen the locknut on the threaded portion of the throttle cable at the throttle body **(see illustration)**.
**3** Rotate the throttle lever, then slip the throttle cable end out of the slot in the lever **(see illustration)**.
**4** Detach the throttle cable from the accelerator pedal **(see illustration)**.
**5** From inside the vehicle, pull the cable through the bulkhead.

### Refitting and adjustment

**6** Refitting is the reverse of removal.
**7** To adjust the cable, fully depress the accelerator pedal and check that the throttle is fully opened.
**8** If not fully opened, loosen the locknuts, depress accelerator pedal and adjust the cable until the throttle is fully open.
**9** Tighten the locknuts and recheck the adjustment. Make sure the throttle closes fully when the pedal is released **(see illustration)**.
**10** After the cable is adjusted, check the adjustment of the bellcrank. Use a small clamp and a straight rod or stiff wire (coat hanger) and attach it to the brake master cylinder in such a way that the tip acts as a pointer. Align the pointer with "A" (automatic transmission) or "M" (manual transmission) on the bellcrank **(see illustration)**,depending on what type of transmission is installed in the vehicle.
**11** Slowly rotate the bellcrank until it reaches the throttle stop (wide open throttle) and

check to make sure the pointer aligns with the notch in the bellcrank **(see illustration)**.
**12** If necessary, adjust the position of the throttle stop using a spanner and turn the throttle stop screw until the bellcrank reaches the correct position. Lock the throttle stop screw in place.

**10.10 Attach a strong wire (coat hanger) to the master cylinder using a clamp and align it with the notch on the bellcrank**

**10.11 Rotate the bellcrank until it reaches wide open throttle and make sure the pointer aligns with the A on the bellcrank. Adjust if necessary**

13 Allow the bellcrank to return to the idle position and test the adjustment once again until the correct adjustment has been attained.

## 11 Electronic Fuel Injection (EFI) system - general information

1 These models are equipped with an Electronic Fuel Injection (EFI) system. This fuel injection system is designed by Bosch but licensed by Lucas and is called the Lucas LH Engine Management system. The EFI system is composed of three basic sub systems: fuel system, air induction system and electronic control system **(see illustration)**.

### Fuel system

2 An electric fuel pump is located on the chassis of the rear suspension (external) (1988 to 1990) or inside the fuel tank (1991 to 1994) The fuel pump supplies fuel under constant pressure to the fuel rail, which distributes fuel evenly to all injectors. From the fuel rail, fuel is injected into the intake ports, just above the intake valves, by fuel injectors. The amount of fuel supplied by the injectors is precisely controlled by an Electronic Control Unit (ECU). A pressure regulator controls system pressure in relation to intake manifold vacuum. A fuel filter between the fuel pump and the fuel rail filters fuel to protect the components of the system.

### Air induction system

3 The air system consists of an air filter housing, a Mass Air Flow (MAF) sensor (airflow meter), Intake Air Temperature (IAT) sensor and a throttle body. The MAF sensor is an information gathering device for the ECU.

A heated element determines the temperature differential by measuring the current changes which in turn measures the mass (weight and volume) of air entering the engine. This information helps the ECU determine the amount of fuel to be injected by the injectors. The throttle plate inside the throttle body is controlled by the driver. As the throttle plate opens, the amount of air that can pass through the system increases, so the potentiometer opens further and the ECU signals the injectors to increase the amount of fuel delivered to the intake ports. Refer to Chapter 6 for additional information on the fuel injection system sensors, test procedures and renewal procedures.

### Electronic control system

4 The Computer Control System controls the EFI and other systems by means of an Electronic Control Unit (ECU), which employs a microcomputer. The ECU receives signals from a number of information sensors which monitor such variables as intake air volume, intake air temperature, coolant temperature, engine rpm, acceleration/deceleration and exhaust oxygen content. These signals help the ECU determine the injection duration necessary for the optimum air/fuel ratio. Some

**11.1 Fuel injection and emission control component locations for the 3.6 litre 1989 XJ6**

| | | |
|---|---|---|
| 1 Fuel pressure regulator (under fuel rail) | 4 Bellcrank | 8 Mass Airflow (MAF) sensor | 11 Fuel injector |
| 2 Idle Speed Control (ISC) motor | 5 Throttle body (below bellcrank) | 9 Throttle potentiometer (under throttle body) | 13 Ignition amplifier (below block valve) |
| 3 Fuel pressure damper | 6 Intake Air Temp. (IAT) sensor | 10 Fuel rail | 14 Distributor |
| | 7 Supplementary air valve | | |

12.7 Use a stethoscope or a screwdriver to determine if the injectors are working properly - they should make a steady clicking sound that rises and falls with engine speed changes

12.8 Refit the "noid" light into the fuel injector electrical connector and check to see that it blinks with the engine running

of these sensors and their corresponding ECU-controlled relays are not contained within EFI components, but are located throughout the engine compartment. For further information regarding the ECU and its relationship to the engine electrical and ignition system, see Chapter 6.

## 12 Electronic Fuel Injection (EFI) system - check

1 Check the earth wire connections for tightness. Check all wiring and electrical connectors that are related to the system. Loose electrical connectors and poor grounds can cause many problems that resemble more serious malfunctions.
2 Check to see that the battery is fully charged, as the control unit and sensors depend on an accurate supply voltage in order to properly meter the fuel.
3 Check the air filter element - a dirty or partially blocked filter will severely impede performance and economy (see Chapter 1).
4 If a blown fuse is found, renew it and see if it blows again. If it does, search for a shorted wire in the harness related to the system.
5 Check the air intake duct from the MAF sensor to the intake manifold for leaks, which will result in an excessively lean mixture. Also check the condition of the vacuum hoses connected to the intake manifold.
6 Remove the air intake duct from the throttle body and check for carbon and residue build-up. If it's dirty, clean with aerosol carburettor cleaner (make sure the can says it's safe for use with oxygen sensors and catalytic converters) and a toothbrush.
7 With the engine running, place a stethoscope against each injector, one at a time, and listen for a clicking sound, indicating operation (see illustration).

8 If there is a problem with an injector, purchase a special injector test light (noid light) and refit it into the injector electrical connector (see illustration). Start the engine and make sure that each injector connector flashes the noid light. This will test for the proper voltage signal to the injector. *Caution: If the engine will not start and the noid light indicates that each injector is receiving the proper signal, there is a good possibility that the injector(s) is stuck open and allowing fuel into the combustion chamber in excessive amounts.* If the spark plugs are fouled, detach the primary (low voltage) wires from the ignition coil, disable the fuel pump by removing the fuel pump relay (see Section 2), remove the spark plugs and crank the engine over. If fuel sprays from the spark plug holes, the engine is flooded and the fuel must be removed from the combustion chambers.
9 With the engine OFF and the fuel injector electrical connectors disconnected, measure the resistance of each injector (see illustration). Each injector should measure about 2.0 to 3.0 ohms. If not, the injector is probably faulty.

12.9 Using an ohmmeter, measure the resistance across both terminals of the injector

10 The remainder of the system checks should be left to a Jaguar service department or other qualified repair workshop, as there is a chance that the control unit may be damaged if not performed properly.

## 13 Electronic Fuel Injection (EFI) system - component check and renewal

 **Warning: Petrol is extremely flammable, so take extra precautions when you work on any part of the fuel system. See the Warning in Section 2.**
*Caution: If the stereo in your vehicle is equipped with an anti-theft system, make sure you have the correct activation code before disconnecting the battery.*

### Throttle body

#### Check

1 Verify that the throttle linkage operates smoothly.
2 Start the engine, detach each vacuum hose and, using your finger, check the vacuum at each port on the throttle body with the engine at idle and above idle. The vacuum available from the throttle body is ported. Raise the engine rpm and watch as vacuum increases. It may be necessary to use a vacuum gauge. Refer to Chapter 2B for additional information concerning vacuum checks.

#### Renewal

**Warning: Wait until the engine is completely cool before beginning this procedure.**

3 Detach the cable from the negative terminal of the battery *(see the* **Caution** *at the beginning of this Section).*
4 Drain the radiator (see Chapter 1).

**13.7  Push up on the clip and remove the harness connector from the MAF sensor**

**13.8  Remove the air intake duct clamp from the MAF sensor housing**

**5** Remove the air cleaner (see Chapter 1) and the air cleaner housing (see Section 9).

**6** Remove the air intake duct.

**7** Detach the electrical connector from the MAF sensor **(see illustration)**.

**8** Remove the clamp that retains the MAF sensor to the air intake duct **(see illustration)** and lift the MAF sensor assembly from the engine compartment.

**9** Detach the throttle cable from the bellcrank (see Section 10), then remove the bellcrank assembly from the throttle body **(see illustration)**.

**10** Detach the kickdown cable from the bellcrank and set the cable and brackets aside (see Chapter 7).

**11** Clearly label, then detach, all vacuum and coolant hoses from the throttle body.

**12** Disconnect the electrical connector from the throttle potentiometer.

**13** Remove the four throttle body mounting bolts and detach the throttle body from the intake manifold.

**14** Using a soft brush and carburettor cleaner, thoroughly clean the throttle body casting, then blow out all passages with compressed air.

*Caution: Do not clean the throttle position sensor with any solvents or sprays. Just wipe it off with a clean, soft cloth.*

**15** Refitting of the throttle body is the reverse of removal.

**16** Be sure to tighten the throttle body mounting bolts to the torque listed in this Chapter's Specifications.

### Adjustment

**17** Remove the air intake duct to expose the throttle body and butterfly valve.

**18** Make sure the throttle body is clean and free of burrs, nicks or carbon build-up **(see illustration)**.

**19** Measure the clearance between the butterfly valve (throttle plate) and the wall of the throttle body **(see illustration)**. It should be 0.05 mm (0.002 inch).

**20** If the gap is incorrect, loosen the throttle stop locknut **(see illustration)** and turn the throttle stop screw until the correct clearance is attained.

**21** Refit the air intake duct and surrounding components.

### Idle Speed Control (ISC) motor

**Note:** *The minimum idle speed is pre-set at the factory and should not require adjustment under normal operating conditions; however if*

**13.9  Remove the bellcrank assembly bolts (arrowed) and separate it from the throttle body**

**13.18  The area inside the throttle body near the throttle plate suffers from sludge build-up because the PCV hose vents crankcase vapour into the intake duct**

*the throttle body has been replaced or you suspect the minimum idle speed has been tampered with (for example, if the idle speed screw was removed from the throttle body) have the vehicle checked by a dealer service department or a qualified automotive repair workshop.*

### Check

**22** Start the engine and allow it to reach normal operating temperature. Switch on the

**13.19  Measure clearance between the butterfly valve and the throttle body**

**13.20  Adjust the butterfly angle by loosening the locknut on the throttle stop and turning the adjustment bolt**

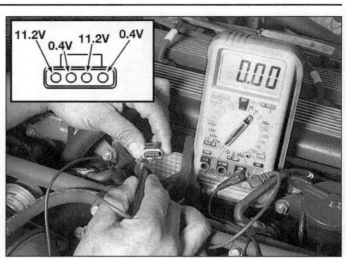

**13.23a To check the ISC motor, turn the ignition key ON (engine not running) and check for the proper voltage amounts at the harness connector (1989 model shown)**

**13.23b Later models are equipped with a different shape ISC connector but the voltage values should be the same as the early style**

headlights or heated rear window and confirm that the engine rpm decreases at first and then increases. This check monitors the ISC motor as it is signalled by the computer to increase idle speed due to additional amperage required from the charging system. As the headlights draw current from the charging system, the alternator will create resistance on the belt as it works to produce the additional energy. If the rpm does not increase, check the ISC motor.

**23** Check for approximately 11.2 volts to the ISC stepper motor **(see illustrations)**. Disconnect the ISC harness connector and working on the harness side, check for 11.2 volts with the ignition key ON (engine not running). Also, check the corresponding terminals for the correct voltage amounts. If the correct voltage does not exist, check the wiring harness. Refer to the wiring diagrams at the end of Chapter 12.

**24** The ISC motor or stepper motor can be checked for correct operation but a special tool is required to activate the internal coils. Have the stepper motor checked by a dealer service department or other qualified repair workshop.
**25** Reconnect the ISC motor electrical connector.

### Renewal

**26** Detach the cable from the negative terminal of the battery *(see **Caution** at the beginning of this Section)*.
**27** Use a large open-end spanner and unscrew the ISC motor from the housing **(see illustration)**.
**28** Refitting is the reverse of removal, but be sure to use a new gasket.

### Fuel rail and fuel injectors

**Note:** *If there is a distinct knocking noise coming from the dash when the engine is idling, the fuel feed hose may have hardened*

*restricting fuel flow and causing abnormal sounds. Replace the fuel inlet (feed) hose with a new part from the dealer parts department.*

### Check

**29** Refer to the fuel injection system checking procedure (see Section 12).

### Renewal

**30** Relieve the fuel pressure (see Section 2).
**31** Detach the cable from the negative terminal of the battery *(see **Caution** at the beginning of this Section)*.
**32** Disconnect the fuel injector wiring connectors and set the injector wire harness aside.
**33** Detach the vacuum sensing hose from the fuel pressure regulator.
**34** Disconnect the fuel lines from the fuel pressure regulator and the fuel rail **(see illustration 3.6a)**
**35** Remove the fuel rail mounting bolts **(see illustration)**.

**13.27 Use a large open end spanner to remove the ISC motor from the intake manifold**

**13.35 Remove the fuel rail mounting bolts (arrowed) . . .**

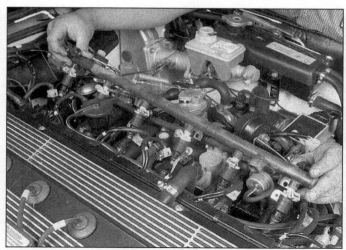

13.36 . . . and remove the fuel rail with the fuel injectors attached

13.37 Remove the fuel injector retaining clips from the fuel rail using a small screwdriver

**36** Remove the fuel rail with the fuel injectors attached **(see illustration)**.

**37** Prise off the clips and remove the fuel injector(s) from the fuel rail **(see illustration)**.

**38** If you are replacing the injector(s), discard the old injector. If you intend to re-use the same injectors, renew the grommets and O-rings **(see illustrations)**.

**39** Refitting of the fuel injectors is the reverse of removal. Apply a light film of clean engine oil to the O-rings before refitting them.

**40** Tighten the fuel rail mounting bolts to the torque listed in this Chapter's Specifications.

### *Fuel pressure regulator*

#### Check

**41** Refer to the fuel pump/fuel pressure check procedure (see Section 3).

#### Renewal

**42** Relieve the fuel pressure (see Section 2) and detach the cable from the negative terminal of the battery *(see the* **Caution** *at the beginning of this Section)*.

**43** Detach the vacuum hose from the regulator.

**44** Remove the fuel rail and the injectors as an assembly (see Steps 30 to 39).

**45** Remove the fuel line from the fuel pressure regulator **(see illustration)**.

**46** Remove the fuel pressure regulator mounting bolts and detach the pressure regulator from the engine.

**47** The remainder of refitting is the reverse of removal. Make sure the fuel lines are secure and there are no leaks before using the car.

### *Supplementary air valve*

#### Check

**48** The supplementary air valve provides additional throttle valve bypass air during cold starting and cold running conditions below 15° F. This output actuator is controlled by the computer (ECU) in response to information

received from the coolant temperature sensor, intake air temperature sensor and other information sensors working with the fuel injection system.

**49** Check for battery voltage to the supplementary air valve. With the engine cold, backprobe the electrical connector using a long pin and check for battery voltage **(see illustration)**. Voltage should exist.

**50** Because of the special tools required to test the supplementary air valve, have it tested by a dealer service department or other qualified repair facility.

13.38a If you plan to refit the original injectors, remove and discard the O-rings and grommets and fit new ones

13.45 Disconnect the fuel pressure regulator from the fuel return line

### Renewal

**51** Remove the intake hoses, the mounting screws and detach the supplementary air valve from the engine.

**52** Refitting is the reverse of removal.

**53** Be sure to use a new gasket when refitting the idle-up valve.

### *Air intake plenum*

**Note:** *The air intake plenum is removed and installed as a complete unit with the intake manifold. In the event of damage or leaks, remove the air intake plenum and intake*

13.38b Pick out the old injector seal but make sure the injector body is not damaged in the process

13.49 Check for battery voltage to the supplementary air valve

*manifold as a single unit and have it repaired by a dealer service department. Refer to Chapter 2 for removal and refitting procedures.*

## 14 Exhaust system servicing - general information

**Warning: Inspection and repair of exhaust system components should be done only after the components have cooled.**

**1** The exhaust system consists of the exhaust manifold, catalytic converter, the silencer, the tailpipe and all connecting pipes, brackets, hangers and clamps. The exhaust system is attached to the body with mounting brackets and rubber hangers **(see illustrations)**. If any of these parts are damaged or deteriorated, excessive noise and vibration will be transmitted to the body. **Note:** *The exhaust system configuration changes with later model updates. Earlier models (1988 and 1989) are equipped with a pre-catalytic converter near the exhaust manifold incorporating a single exhaust pipe to the silencer. Later models are equipped with dual exhaust pipes, dual catalytic converters and silencers.*

**2** Conducting regular inspections of the exhaust system will keep it safe and quiet. Look for any damaged or bent parts, open seams, holes, loose connections, excessive corrosion or other defects which could allow exhaust fumes to enter the vehicle. Deteriorated exhaust system components should not be repaired - they should be replaced with new parts.

**3** If the exhaust system components are extremely corroded or rusted together, they will probably have to be cut from the exhaust system. The convenient way to accomplish this is to have a silencer repair workshop remove the corroded sections with a cutting torch. If, however, you want to save money by doing it yourself and you don't have an oxy/acetylene welding outfit with a cutting torch, simply cut off the old components with a hacksaw. If you have compressed air, special pneumatic cutting chisels can also be

**14.1a The rear tailpipe section is fastened to the chassis with a special rubber mount (arrowed) that pivots with road movement. Check for deterioration and alignment**

**14.1c On dual silencer models, check the condition of the mount (arrowed) and the clamps**

used. If you do decide to tackle the job at home, be sure to wear eye protection to protect your eyes from metal chips and work gloves to protect your hands.

**4** Here are some simple guidelines to apply when repairing the exhaust system:

a) *Work from the back to the front when removing exhaust system components.*

b) *Apply penetrating oil to the exhaust system component fasteners to make them easier to remove* **(see illustration)**.

c) *Use new gaskets, hangers and clamps when refitting exhaust system components.*

d) *Apply anti-seize compound to the threads of all exhaust system fasteners during reassembly.*

**14.1b Check the condition of the flexible rubber mounts that hang the silencer to the chassis**

**14.4 Use penetrating spray on the exhaust flange nuts before attempting to remove them**

e) *Be sure to allow sufficient clearance between newly installed parts and all points on the underbody to avoid overheating the floor pan and possibly damaging the interior carpet and insulation. Pay particularly close attention to the catalytic converter and its heat shield.*

**Warning: The catalytic converter operates at very high temperatures and takes a long time to cool. Wait until it's completely cool before attempting to remove the converter. It's a good idea to wear suitable gloves. Failure to observe these points could result in serious burns.**

# Chapter 5
# Engine electrical systems

## Contents

## Degrees of difficulty

| Easy, suitable for novice with little experience  | Fairly easy, suitable for beginner with some experience  | Fairly difficult, suitable for competent DIY mechanic  | Difficult, suitable for experienced DIY mechanic  | Very difficult, suitable for expert DIY or professional  |
|---|---|---|---|---|

## Specifications

### Ignition system

| | |
|---|---|
| Ignition timing (all models) ............................... | Not adjustable |
| Ignition coil resistance (at 68°F): | |
|   Primary resistance ...................................... | 0.4 to 0.5 ohms |
|   Secondary resistance ................................... | 6.0 to 6.5 k-ohms |

### Charging system

| | |
|---|---|
| Charging voltage ........................................ | 13.9 to 15.1 volts |
| Standard amperage: | |
|   No load ............................................... | Less than 10 amps |
|   Full load .............................................. | 30 amps or more |

## 1  General information

The engine electrical systems include all ignition, charging and starting components. Because of their engine related functions, these components are discussed separately from chassis electrical devices such as the fuses, relays, lights, etc. (which are included in Chapter 12).

Always observe the following precautions when working on the electrical systems:

a) *Be extremely careful when servicing engine electrical components. They are easily damaged if checked, connected or handled improperly.*

b) *Never leave the ignition switch on for long periods of time (10 minutes maximum) with the engine off.*

c) *Don't disconnect the battery cables while the engine is running.*

d) *Maintain correct polarity when connecting a battery cable from another vehicle during jump starting.*

e) *Always disconnect the negative cable first and hook it up last or the battery may be shorted by the tool being used to loosen the cable clamps.*

It's also a good idea to review the safety-related information regarding the engine electrical systems in the *Safety first* section near the front of this manual before beginning any operation included in this Chapter.

## 2  Battery - emergency jump starting

See *"Jump starting"* in *"Roadside repairs"* at the front of this Manual.

## 3  Battery - removal and refitting

1 Disconnect the negative terminal, then the positive terminal from the battery. On 1989 to 1992 models, the battery is located in the engine compartment on the passenger side bulkhead and on 1993 and 1994 models, it is located in the boot.

*Caution: If the stereo in your vehicle is equipped with an anti-theft system, make sure you have the correct activation code before disconnecting the battery.*

2 Remove the battery hold-down clamp.

3 Lift out the battery. Be careful, it's heavy.

4 While the battery is out, inspect the carrier (tray) for corrosion.

5 If you are replacing the battery, make sure that you get one that's identical, with the

same dimensions, amperage rating, cold cranking rating, etc. as the original.

6 Refitting is the reverse of removal.

## 4 Battery cables - check and renewal

*Caution: If the stereo in your vehicle is equipped with an anti-theft system, make sure you have the correct activation code before disconnecting the battery.*

1 Periodically inspect the entire length of each battery cable for damage, cracked or burned insulation and corrosion. Poor battery cable connections can cause starting problems and decreased engine performance.

2 Check the cable-to-terminal connections at the ends of the cables for cracks, loose wire strands and corrosion. The presence of white, fluffy deposits under the insulation at the cable terminal connection is a sign that the cable is corroded and should be renewed. Check the terminals for distortion, missing mounting bolts and corrosion.

3 When removing the cables, always disconnect the negative cable first and hook it up last or the battery may be shorted by the tool used to loosen the cable clamps. Even if only the positive cable is being renewed, be sure to disconnect the negative cable from the battery first (see Chapter 1 for further information regarding battery cable removal).

4 Disconnect the cables from the battery, then trace each of them to their opposite ends and detach them from the starter solenoid and earth terminals. Note the routing of each cable to ensure correct refitting.

5 If you are replacing either or both of the old cables, take them with you when buying new items. It is vitally important that you replace the cables with identical parts. Cables have characteristics that make them easy to identify: positive cables are usually red, larger in cross-section and have a larger diameter battery post clamp; earth cables are usually black, smaller in cross-section and have a slightly smaller diameter clamp for the negative post.

6 Clean the threads of the solenoid or earth connection with a wire brush to remove rust and corrosion. Apply a light coat of battery terminal corrosion inhibitor, or petroleum jelly, to the threads to prevent future corrosion.

7 Attach the cable to the solenoid or earth connection and tighten the mounting nut/bolt securely.

8 Before connecting a new cable to the battery, make sure that it reaches the battery post without having to be stretched.

9 Connect the positive cable first, followed by the negative cable.

## 5 Ignition system - general information and precautions

1 All models are equipped with a computerised ignition system. The ignition system consists of the ignition coil, the crankshaft position sensor, the amplifier and the electronic control unit (ECU). The ignition ECU controls the ignition timing and advance characteristics for the engine. The ignition timing is not adjustable, therefore, changing the position of the distributor will not change the timing in any way. **Note:** *In the event the distributor must be removed from the engine, be sure to follow the precautions described in Section 9 and mark the engine and distributor with paint to ensure correct refitting. If the distributor is not marked and lhe crankshaft is turned while the distributor is out of the engine, have the distributor installed by a dealer service department. The distributor must be installed using a special alignment tool.*

2 The distributor is driven by the intermediate shaft which also drives the power steering pump. The crankshaft position sensor is located on the front timing cover. It detects crank position by pulsing an electronic signal to the ECU. This signal is sent to the ECU to provide ignition timing specifications.

3 The computerised ignition system provides complete control of the ignition timing by determining the optimum timing in response to engine speed, coolant temperature, throttle position and vacuum pressure in the intake manifold. These parameters are relayed to the ECU by the crankshaft position sensor, throttle potentiometer, coolant temperature sensor and MAF sensor. Ignition timing is altered during warm-up, idling and warm running conditions by the ECU. This electronic ignition system also consists of the ignition switch, battery, coil, distributor, spark plug leads and spark plugs.

4 Refer to a dealer parts department or car accessory outlet for any questions concerning the availability of the distributor parts and assemblies. Testing the crankshaft position sensor is covered in Chapter 6.

5 When working on the ignition system, take the following precautions:

a) *Do not keep the ignition switch on for more than 10 seconds if the engine will not start.*

b) *Always connect a tachometer in accordance with the manufacturer's instructions. Some tachometers may be incompatible with this ignition system. Consult a dealer service department before buying a tachometer for use with this vehicle.*

c) *Never allow the ignition coil terminals to touch earth. Earthing the coil could result in damage to the igniter and/or the ignition coil.*

d) *Do not disconnect the battery when the engine is running.*

## 6 Ignition system - check

⚠ *Warning: Because of the high voltage generated by the ignition system, extreme care should be taken when working on the ignition components. This not only includes the amplifier, coil, distributor and spark plug leads, but related components such as connectors, tachometer and other test equipment also.*

1 With the ignition switch turned to the "ON" position, a "Battery" light or an "Oil Pressure" light is a basic check for ignition and battery supply to the ECU.

2 Check all ignition wiring connections for tightness, cuts, corrosion or any other signs of a bad connection.

3 Use a calibrated ignition tester to verify adequate secondary voltage (25,000 volts) at each spark plug **(see illustration)**. A faulty or poor connection at that plug could also result in a misfire. Also, check for carbon deposits inside the spark plug boot.

4 Check for carbon tracking on the coil. If carbon tracking is evident, renew the coil and be sure the secondary wires related to that coil are clean and tight. Excessive wire resistance or faulty connections could damage the coil.

5 Check for battery voltage to the ignition coil **(see illustration)**. If battery voltage is available, check the ignition coil primary and secondary resistance (see Section 8).

6 Check the distributor cap for any obvious signs of carbon tracking, corroded terminals or cracks (see Chapter 1).

7 Using an ohmmeter, check the resistance of the spark plug leads. Each wire should measure less than 25,000 ohms.

8 Check for battery voltage to the ignition amplifier (see Section 7). If battery voltage does not exist, check the circuit from the ignition switch (refer to the wiring diagrams at the end of Chapter 12).

**6.3 To use a calibrated ignition tester (available at most car accessory outlets), remove a plug lead from a cylinder, connect the spark plug boot to the tester and clip the tester to a good earth - if there is enough voltage to fire the plug, sparks will be clearly visible between the electrode tip and the tester body**

**6.5 Check for battery voltage to the coil (+) terminal**

**6.9 Check for battery voltage to the IGN ON relay**

**6.11 Refit the LED test light to the coil negative (-) terminal, crank the engine over and observe the light flash in response to the trigger signal from the computer**

**7.1 Remove the clip that retains the harness connector to the amplifier**

**7.2 Check for battery voltage to the ignition amplifier**

9 Check for battery voltage to the Ignition ON relay **(see illustration)**. If battery voltage does not exist, check the circuit from the ignition ON relay to the battery (refer to the wiring diagrams at the end of Chapter 12). **Note:** *See Chapter 12 for the location of the Ignition ON relay.*

10 Check the operation of the crankshaft position sensor (see Chapter 6).

11 If all the checks are correct, check the voltage signal from the computer. Using an LED type test light, backprobe the coil power lead (negative terminal) on the ignition coil **(see illustration)**. Remove the coil secondary wire and earth the terminal to the engine. Now have an assistant crank the engine over and observe that the test light pulses on and off. If there is no flashing from the test light, most likely the computer is damaged. Have the ECU diagnosed by a dealer service department.

12 Additional checks should be performed by a dealer service department or an automotive repair workshop.

## 7 Amplifier - check and renewal

⚠️ **Warning: Because of the high voltage generated by the ignition system, extreme care should be taken whenever an operation is performed involving ignition**

components. This not only includes the amplifier, coil, distributor and spark plug leads, but related components such as connectors, tachometer and other test equipment also.

**Note:** *Because of the complexity and the special tools required to test the amplifier, the following procedure only describes a test to verify battery voltage is reaching the amplifier. If the wiring harness and the relays are working properly and battery voltage is available to the amplifier, have the ignition system and the ECU diagnosed by a dealer service department.*

### Check

1 Disconnect the amplifier electrical connector **(see illustration)**.

2 Turn the ignition key ON (engine not running), check for battery voltage **(see illustration)** to the amplifier.

3 If no battery voltage is present, check the harness from the ignition switch to the amplifier. Refer to the wiring diagrams at the end of Chapter 12.

### Renewal

4 Disconnect the negative battery terminal.
*Caution: If the stereo in your vehicle is equipped with an anti-theft system, make sure you have the correct activation code before disconnecting the battery.*

5 Remove the amplifier mounting bolts **(see illustration)**.

6 Refitting is the reverse of removal.

## 8 Ignition coil - check and renewal

### Check

1 Detach the cable from the negative terminal of the battery.
*Caution: If the stereo in your vehicle is equipped with an anti-theft system, make*

**7.5 Remove the amplifier mountings screws (arrowed) and lift the unit from the engine compartment**

**8.3a To check the primary resistance of the coil, measure the resistance between the positive and the negative terminals**

**8.3b To check the secondary resistance of the coil, measure the resistance between the positive terminal and the HT terminal**

**8.7 Remove the nuts from the coil mounting bracket (arrowed)**

sure you have the correct activation code before disconnecting the battery.

2 Disconnect the electrical connectors and the coil wire from the coil.

3 Using an ohmmeter, check the coil resistance:

a) Measure the resistance between the positive and negative terminals **(see illustration)**. Compare your reading with the specified coil primary resistance listed in this Chapter's Specifications.

b) Measure the resistance between the positive terminal and the high tension (HT) terminal **(see illustration)**. Compare your reading with the specified coil secondary resistance listed in this Chapter's Specifications.

4 If either of the above tests yield resistance values outside the specified amount, renew the coil.

### Renewal

5 Detach the battery negative cable.

*Caution: If the stereo in your vehicle is equipped with an anti-theft system, make sure you have the correct activation code before disconnecting the battery.*

6 Label and disconnect the electrical wires from the coil terminals.

7 Remove the coil mounting fasteners **(see illustration)**.

8 Refitting is the reverse of removal.

### 9 Distributor - removal and refitting

**Note:** *The timing on this ignition system cannot be adjusted by turning the distributor. Ignition timing is maintained by the ECU at all times. In the event the distributor must be removed from the engine, be sure to follow the precautions described in this section and mark the engine and distributor with paint to ensure correct refitting. If the distributor is not marked, and the crankshaft is turned while the distributor is out of the engine, have the distributor installed by a dealer service department. The distributor must be installed using a special alignment tool.*

### Removal

1 Detach the battery negative cable.

*Caution: If the stereo in your vehicle is equipped with an anti-theft system, make sure you have the correct activation code before disconnecting the battery.*

2 Disconnect the electrical connectors from the distributor.

3 Look for a raised "1" on the distributor cap. This marks the location for the number one cylinder spark plug lead terminal. If the cap does not have a mark for the number one terminal, locate the number one spark plug and trace the wire back to the terminal on the cap.

4 Remove the distributor cap (see Chapter 1) and rotate the engine until the rotor is pointing toward the number one spark plug terminal.

5 Make a mark on the edge of the distributor base directly below the rotor tip and in line with it. Also, mark the distributor base and the engine block to ensure that the distributor is installed correctly **(see illustrations)**.

6 Remove the distributor hold-down bolt, then pull the distributor out to remove it.

*Caution: DO NOT turn the crankshaft while the distributor is out of the engine, or the alignment marks will be useless.*

**9.5a Paint or scribe a mark (arrowed) on the edge of the distributor housing below the rotor tip to ensure that the rotor is pointing in the same direction when the distributor is reinstalled**

**9.5b Paint or scribe another mark across the cylinder head and the distributor body (arrowed) to ensure that the distributor is aligned correctly when it is reinstalled**

## Refitting

**7** Insert the distributor into the engine in exactly the same relationship to the block that it was in when removed.

**8** If the distributor does not seat completely, recheck the alignment marks between the distributor base and the block to verify that the distributor is in the same position it was in before removal. Also check the rotor to see if it's aligned with the mark you made on the edge of the distributor base.

**9** Refit the distributor hold-down bolt(s).

**10** The remainder of refitting is the reverse of removal.

### 10  Charging system - general information and precautions

The charging system includes the alternator, an internal voltage regulator, a charge indicator light, load dump module, the battery, an ignition ON relay, an in-line fuse and the wiring between all the components **(see illustration)**. The charging system supplies electrical power for the ignition system, the lights, the radio, etc. The alternator is driven by a drivebelt at the front of the engine.

The purpose of the voltage regulator is to limit the alternator's voltage to a preset value. This prevents power surges, circuit overloads, etc., during peak voltage output.

The alternator load dump module protects the electrical circuits from excessive voltage surges. When the battery cables are removed large amounts of transient voltage is released through the electrical circuits. This device diverts up to 30 load volts of excess voltage to earth by way of a voltage dependent resistor.

The in-line fuse is a special fuse installed into the circuit with the engine compartment wiring harness (see Chapter 12). The in-line fuse protects the electrical system in the event of excess voltage surges or a power to earth short circuit. Refer to Chapter 12 for additional information concerning the in-line fuses and their locations.

1993 and 1994 models have a Starter Logic Relay. This microprocessor (computer) gathers information from the ignition switch, linear gear position switch, park/neutral switch, the security switch and the electronic door lock system. If all the conditions are in order, the computer allows battery voltage to be transferred from the ignition switch to the starter/solenoid assembly.

The charging system doesn't ordinarily require periodic maintenance. However, the drivebelt, battery and wires and connections should be inspected at the intervals outlined in Chapter 1.

The dashboard warning light should come on when the ignition key is turned to Start, then should go off immediately. If it remains on, there is a malfunction in the charging system. Some vehicles are also equipped with a voltage gauge. If the voltage gauge

**10.1  Schematic of a typical charging system**

indicates abnormally high or low voltage, check the charging system (see Section 11).

Be very careful when making electrical circuit connections to a vehicle equipped with an alternator and note the following:

a) *When reconnecting wires to the alternator from the battery, note their polarity.*

b) *Before using arc welding equipment to repair any part of the vehicle, disconnect the wires from the alternator and the battery terminals.*

c) *Never start the engine with a battery charger connected.*

d) *Always disconnect both battery leads before using a battery charger.*

e) *The alternator is driven by an engine drivebelt which could cause serious injury if your hand, hair or clothes become entangled in it with the engine running.*

f) *Because the alternator is connected directly to the battery, it could arc or cause a fire if overloaded or shorted out.*

g) *Wrap a plastic bag over the alternator and secure it with rubber bands before steam cleaning the engine.*

### 11  Charging system - check

**Note:** *1993 and 1994 models are equipped with a Starter Logic Relay. This microprocessor (computer) gathers information from the*

*ignition switch, linear gear position switch, park/neutral switch, the security switch and the electronic door lock system. If all the conditions are in order, the computer allows battery voltage to be transferred from the ignition switch to the starter/solenoid assembly. If all the components of the charging system are working properly and the system still does not charge properly, have the Starter Logic Relay diagnosed by a dealer service department.*

**1** If a malfunction occurs in the charging circuit, don't automatically assume that the alternator is causing the problem. First check the following items:

a) *Check the drivebelt tension and its condition. Renew it if worn or damaged.*

b) *Make sure the alternator mounting and adjustment bolts are tight.*

c) *Inspect the alternator wiring harness and the electrical connectors at the alternator and voltage regulator. They must be in good condition and tight.*

d) *Check the fusible link (if equipped) located between the starter solenoid and the alternator or the large main fuses in the engine compartment. If it's burned, determine the cause, repair the circuit and renew the link or fuse (the vehicle won't start and/or the accessories won't work if the fusible link or fuse blows).*

e) *Check all the in-line fuses that are in series with the charging system circuit (see Chapter 12). The location of these fuses and fusible links may vary from year and*

**11.2 Connect the probes of a voltmeter to the battery terminals and observe battery voltage with the engine OFF and then with the engine running**

**11.9 The load dump module is located on the bulkhead next to the MAF sensor**

model but the designations are the same. Refer to the wiring diagrams at the end of Chapter 12.

f) *Start the engine and check the alternator for abnormal noises (a shrieking or squealing sound indicates a bad bushing).*

g) *Check the specific gravity of the battery electrolyte. If it's low, charge the battery (doesn't apply to maintenance free batteries).*

h) *Make sure that the battery is fully charged (one bad cell in a battery can cause overcharging by the alternator).*

i) *Disconnect the battery cables (negative first, then positive). **Caution:** If the stereo in your vehicle is equipped with an anti-theft system, make sure you have the correct activation code before disconnecting the battery. Inspect the battery posts and the cable clamps for corrosion. Clean them thoroughly if necessary (see Chapter 1). Reconnect the positive cable, then the negative cable.*

**2** Using a voltmeter, check the battery voltage with the engine off. It should be approximately 12 volts **(see illustration)**.

**3** Start the engine and check the battery voltage again. It should now be approximately 13.5 to 15.1 volts.

**4** Turn on the headlights. The voltage should drop and then come back up, if the charging system is working properly.

**5** If the voltage reading is greater than the specified charging voltage, renew the alternator.

**6** If you have an ammeter, connect it up to the charging system according to its maker's instructions. If you don't have a professional-type ammeter, you can also use an inductive-type current indicator. This device is inexpensive, readily available at car accessory outlets and accurate enough to perform simple amperage checks like the following test.

**7** With the engine running at 2000 rpm, check the reading on the ammeter with all accessories and lights off (no load), then again with the high-beam headlights on and the heater blower switch turned to the HI position (full load). Compare your readings to the standard amperage listed in this Chapter's Specifications.

**8** If the ammeter reading is less than standard amperage, repair or renew the alternator.

**9** If the alternator is working but the charging system still does function properly, check the operation of the load dump module **(see illustration)**. Have this component checked at a dealer service department.

## 12 Alternator - removal and refitting

**1** Detach the cable from the negative terminal of the battery.

***Caution: If the stereo in your vehicle is equipped with an anti-theft system, make sure you have the correct activation code before disconnecting the battery.***

**2** Detach the electrical connectors from the alternator.

**3** Loosen the alternator adjustment and pivot bolts **(see illustration)** and detach the drivebelt.

**4** Remove the adjustment and pivot bolts **(see illustration)** from the alternator adjustment bracket.

**5** If you are replacing the alternator, take the old alternator with you when purchasing a replacement unit. Make sure that the new/rebuilt unit is identical to the old alternator. Look at the terminals - they should be the same in number, size and locations as the terminals on the old alternator. Finally, look at the identification markings - they will be stamped in the housing or printed on a tag or plaque affixed to the housing. Make sure that these numbers are the same on both alternators.

**6** Many new/rebuilt alternators do not have a pulley installed, so you may have to switch the pulley from the old unit to the new/rebuilt one. When buying an alternator, find out the policy regarding refitting of pulleys - some shops will perform this service free of charge.

**7** Refitting is the reverse of removal.

**12.3 Loosen the lock bolt and back-off the adjustment bolt (arrowed) to remove the drivebelt**

**12.4 Remove the pivot bolt and nut**

8 After the alternator is installed, adjust the drivebelt tension (see Chapter 1).
9 Check the charging voltage to verify proper operation of the alternator (see Section 11).

## 13 Starting system - general information and precautions

The sole function of the starting system is to crank the engine over quickly enough to allow it to start.

The starting system consists of the battery, the starter motor, the starter solenoid, the starter relay and the electrical circuit connecting the components. The solenoid is mounted directly on the starter motor.

The solenoid/starter motor assembly is installed on the upper part of the engine, next to the transmission bellhousing.

When the ignition key is turned to the START position, the starter solenoid is actuated through the starter control circuit. The starter solenoid then connects the battery to the starter. The battery supplies the electrical energy to the starter motor, which does the actual work of cranking the engine.

The starter on a vehicle equipped with an automatic transmission can be operated only when the transmission selector lever is in Park or Neutral.

These vehicles are equipped with either a Bosch or Lucas starter assembly. The Lucas unit is distinguished by the separate earth strap from the solenoid to the starter body. Bosch starter assemblies are equipped with a solid metal earthing bar.

The starting system circuit is equipped with a relay. The relay allows the ignition switch to power the starter solenoid.

Always observe the following precautions when working on the starting system:

a) *Excessive cranking of the starter motor can overheat it and cause serious damage. Never operate the starter motor for more than 15 seconds at a time without pausing to allow it to cool for at least two minutes.*
b) *The starter is connected directly to the battery and could arc or cause a fire if mishandled, overloaded or short circuited.*
c) *Always detach the cable from the negative terminal of the battery before working on the starting system.*

**Caution: *If the stereo in your vehicle is equipped with an anti-theft system, make sure you have the correct activation code before disconnecting the battery.***

## 14 Starter motor - testing in vehicle

1 Make sure that the battery is charged and that all cables, both at the battery and starter solenoid terminals, are clean and secure.

**14.5 With the ignition key ON (engine not running), check for battery voltage to the starter relay**

2 If the starter motor does not turn at all when the switch is operated, make sure that the shift lever is in Neutral or Park (automatic transmission) or that the clutch pedal is depressed (manual transmission).
3 If the starter motor spins but the engine is not cranking, the overrunning clutch in the starter motor is slipping and the starter motor must be renewed.
4 If, when the switch is actuated, the starter motor does not operate at all but the solenoid clicks, then the problem lies with either the battery, the main solenoid contacts or the starter motor itself (or the engine is seized).
5 If the solenoid plunger cannot be heard when the switch is actuated, the battery is bad, the in-line fuse is burned (the circuit is open), the starter relay **(see illustration)** is defective or the starter solenoid itself is defective.
6 To check the solenoid, connect a jumper lead between the battery (+) and the ignition switch terminal (the small terminal) on the solenoid. If the starter motor now operates, the solenoid is OK and the problem is in the ignition switch, linear switch (1988 to 1992), rotary switch (1993 and 1994) or in the wiring.
7 If the starter motor still does not operate, remove the starter/solenoid assembly for dismantling, testing and repair.
8 If the starter motor cranks the engine at an abnormally slow speed, first make sure that the battery is charged and that all terminal

**15.4a Disconnect the solenoid electrical connector at the harness connector located near the bulkhead behind the cylinder head (arrowed)**

connections are tight. If the engine is partially seized, or has the wrong viscosity oil in it, it will crank slowly.
9 Run the engine until normal operating temperature is reached, then disconnect the coil wire from the distributor cap and earth it on the engine.
10 Connect a voltmeter positive lead to the battery positive post and connect the negative lead to the negative post.
11 Crank the engine and take the voltmeter readings as soon as a steady figure is indicated. Do not allow the starter motor to turn for more than 15 seconds at a time. A reading of nine volts or more, with the starter motor turning at normal cranking speed, is normal. If the reading is nine volts or more but the cranking speed is slow, the motor is faulty. If the reading is less than nine volts and the cranking speed is slow, the solenoid contacts are probably burned, the starter motor is bad, the battery is discharged or there is a bad connection.

## 15 Starter motor - removal and refitting

1 Detach the cable from the negative terminal of the battery.
**Caution: *If the stereo in your vehicle is equipped with an anti-theft system, make sure you have the correct activation code before disconnecting the battery.***
2 Raise the vehicle and support it securely using axle stands.
3 Drain the transmission fluid (see Chapter 7) and remove the transmission fluid filler tube from the transmission.
4 Detach the electrical connectors from the starter/solenoid assembly **(see illustrations)**.
5 Place a trolley jack under the tail section of the transmission, remove the rear transmission mount (see Chapter 7) and lower the transmission slightly to gain access to the upper transmission bellhousing bolts. Using an extension with a swivel socket, remove the upper starter mounting bolt **(see illustration)**.

**15.4b From underneath the vehicle, remove the battery terminal from the solenoid (cylinder head removed for clarity)**

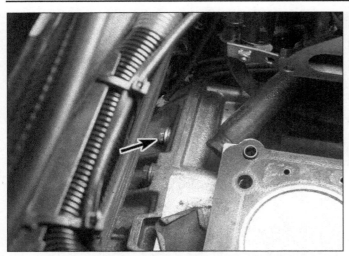

**15.5 The upper starter bolt can be reached from underneath the vehicle using a long extension and swivel socket (cylinder head removed for clarity)**

**16.4 Remove the three solenoid mounting screws (arrowed) and separate the solenoid from the starter assembly**

**6** Working forward of the transmission, reach up into the engine bellhousing area, under the intake manifold and remove the lower starter mounting bolt.

**7** Tilt the starter down and carefully lower the starter assembly through the front, ahead of the transmission.

**8** Refitting is the reverse of removal.

## 16 Starter solenoid - removal and refitting

**1** Remove the starter motor (see Section 15).
**2** Scribe or paint a mark across the starter motor and solenoid assembly.

**3** Disconnect the strap from the solenoid to the starter motor terminal (if equipped).
**4** Remove the screws which secure the solenoid to the starter drive end housing **(see illustration)**.
**5** Separate the solenoid from the starter.
**6** Refitting is the reverse of removal. Be sure to align the paint or scribe mark.

# Chapter 6
# Emissions and engine control systems

## Contents

## Degrees of difficulty

| | | | | |
|---|---|---|---|---|
| **Easy,** suitable for novice with little experience  | **Fairly easy,** suitable for beginner with some experience  | **Fairly difficult,** suitable for competent DIY mechanic  | **Difficult,** suitable for experienced DIY mechanic  | **Very difficult,** suitable for expert DIY or professional |

## Specifications

**EGR gas temperature sensor resistance**

Temperature:

| | |
|---|---|
| 212° F .................................................. | 60 to 100 k-ohms |
| 400° F .................................................. | 3 to 8 k-ohms |
| 662° F .................................................. | 250 to 350 ohms |

| **Torque wrench setting** | **Nm** | **lbf ft** |
|---|---|---|
| Crankshaft sensor bolt .................................... | 27 | 20 |

## 1  General information

To minimise pollution of the atmosphere from incompletely burned and evaporating gases and to maintain good driveability and fuel economy, a number of emission control systems are used on these vehicles. They include the:

    *Air Injection Reactor (AIR) system*
    *Crankcase Ventilation system*
    *Exhaust Gas Recirculation (EGR) system*
    *Electronic Fuel Injection (EFI) system*
    *Evaporative Emission Control (EVAP) system*
    *Three-way catalytic converter (TWC) system*

The sections in this chapter include general descriptions, checking procedures within the scope of the home mechanic and component renewal procedures (when possible) for each of the systems listed above.

Before assuming an emissions control system is malfunctioning, check the fuel and ignition systems carefully (Chapters 4 and 5). The diagnosis of some emission control devices requires specialised tools, equipment and training. If checking and servicing become too difficult or if a procedure is beyond the scope of your skills, consult your dealer service department or other repair workshop.

This doesn't mean, however, that emission control systems are particularly difficult to maintain and repair. You can quickly and easily perform many checks and do most of the regular maintenance at home with common tune-up and hand tools. **Note:** *The most frequent cause of emission problems is simply a loose or broken electrical connector or vacuum hose, so always check the electrical connectors and vacuum hoses first.*

Pay close attention to any special precautions outlined in this chapter. It should be noted that the illustrations of the various systems may not exactly match the system installed on your vehicle because of changes made by the manufacturer during production or from year-to-year.

The Vehicle Emissions Control Information (VECI) label and a vacuum hose diagram are located under the bonnet **(see illustrations)**. These contain important emissions specifications and setting procedures, and a vacuum hose schematic with emissions

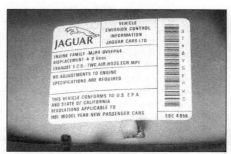

**1.6a  The Vehicle Emissions Control Information (VECI) label shows the types of emission control systems installed, engine information, etc (1992 model shown)**

**1.6b  Typical vacuum hose routing label (1992 model shown)**

components identified. When servicing the engine or emissions systems, the VECI label in your particular vehicle should always be checked for up-to-date information.

## 2 Electronic control system and ECU

### General description

**Note:** *These models are susceptible to ECU damage if water is allowed to build up in the front cowl drain and overspill into the dash area near the computer. Inspect and clear the front cowl drain as a regular maintenance item to keep the water draining properly. Remove the duckbill-type rubber hose and inspect it for clogging, collapsing or deterioration.*

**1** The Lucas LH Engine Management system controls the fuel injection system by means of a microcomputer known as the Electronic Control unit (ECU).

**2** The ECU receives signals from various sensors which monitor changing engine operating conditions such as intake air mass, intake air temperature, coolant temperature, engine rpm, acceleration/deceleration, exhaust oxygen content, etc. These signals are utilised by the ECU to determine the correct injection duration.

**3** The system is analogous to the central nervous system in the human body: The sensors (nerve endings) constantly relay signals to the ECU (brain), which processes the data and, if necessary, sends out a command to change the operating parameters of the engine (body).

**4** Here's a specific example of how one portion of this system operates: An oxygen sensor, located in the exhaust manifold, constantly monitors the oxygen content of the exhaust gas. If the percentage of oxygen in the exhaust gas is incorrect, an electrical signal is sent to the ECU. The ECU takes this information, processes it and then sends a command to the fuel injection system telling it to change the air/fuel mixture. This happens in a fraction of a second and it goes on continuously when the engine is running. The end result is an air/fuel mixture ratio which is constantly maintained at a predetermined ratio, regardless of driving conditions.

**5** In the event of a sensor malfunction, a backup circuit will take over to provide driveability until the problem is identified and fixed.

### Precautions

**6** Follow these steps:

a) *Always disconnect the power by either turning off the ignition switch or disconnecting the battery terminals before removing electrical connectors.*

 **Warning:** *Later models are equipped with airbags. To prevent accidental deployment of*

*the airbag, which could cause personal injury, DO NOT work in the vicinity of the steering column or instrument panel. The manufacturer recommends that, on airbag equipped models, the following procedure should be left to a dealer service department or other repair workshop because of the special tools and techniques required to disable the airbag system.*
**Caution:** *If the stereo in your vehicle is equipped with an anti-theft system, make sure you have the correct activation code before disconnecting the battery.*

b) *When refitting a battery, be particularly careful to avoid reversing the positive and negative battery cables. Also, make sure the ignition key is in the Off position when connecting or disconnecting the battery.*
c) *Do not subject EFI components, emissions-related components or the ECU to severe impact during removal or refitting.*
d) *Do not be careless during fault diagnosis. Even slight terminal contact can invalidate a testing procedure and damage one of the numerous transistor circuits.*
e) *Never attempt to work on the ECU or open the ECU cover. The ECU is protected by a government-mandated extended warranty that will be nullified if you tamper with or damage the ECU.*
f) *If you are inspecting electronic control system components during rainy weather, make sure that water does not enter any part. When washing the engine compartment, do not spray these parts or their electrical connectors with water.*
g) *These models are susceptible to ECU damage if water is allowed to build up in the front cowl drain and overspill into the dash area. Inspect and clear the front cowl drain system as a regular maintenance item to keep the water draining properly. Remove the duckbill type rubber hose and inspect it for clogging, collapsing or deterioration.*

### ECU removal and refitting

**7** Disconnect the negative cable from the battery (see Chapter 5).

 **Warning:** *Later models are equipped with airbags. To prevent the accidental deployment of the airbag, which could cause personal injury, DO NOT work in the vicinity of the steering column or instrument panel. The manufacturer recommends that, on airbag equipped models, the following procedure should be left to a dealer service department or other repair workshop because of the special tools and techniques required to disable the airbag system.*
**Caution:** *If the stereo in your vehicle is equipped with an anti-theft system, make sure you have the correct activation code before disconnecting the battery.*

**2.10 The ECU is located behind the passenger's side glovebox near the footrest area. Remove the mounting screws (arrowed) and carefully lower the ECU**

**8** Remove the lower instrument panel on the passenger side under the glove compartment (see Chapter 11).
**9** Remove the glove compartment from the passenger compartment (see Chapter 11).
**10** Remove the screws from the ECU bracket **(see illustration)**.
**11** Lower the ECU and unplug the electrical connectors.
**12** Refitting is the reverse of removal.

## 3 On Board Diagnosis (OBD) system - description and fault code access

**Note:** *1990 and 1991 models may set Code 69 erroneously. If the battery voltage drops sufficiently and the ignition key is switched quickly from OFF to START, battery voltage will be lowered and during cranking causing a delayed park/neutral signal from the decoder module to the ECU. Check all the battery connections and the condition of the battery and then check the rotary switch adjustment in Chapter 7 to remedy this code.*

### General information

**1** The ECU contains a built-in self-diagnosis system which detects and identifies malfunctions occurring in the network. When the ECU detects a problem, three things happen: the CHECK ENGINE light comes on, the fault is identified and a diagnostic code is recorded and stored. The ECU stores the failure code assigned to the specific problem area until the diagnosis system is cancelled.
**Note:** *1988 and 1989 models are not equipped with long term memory. It is possible to access the codes but the operator must remember to NOT turn the ignition key to the OFF position after the CHECK ENGINE light has been noticed. The codes will be lost and it will be necessary to start the engine and operate the vehicle through a complete drive cycle to allow the fault code(s) to be set once again. Instead of turning the ignition key to the OFF position, simply stop at position II (key ON but engine not running) to retain the fault codes.*

**2** The CHECK ENGINE warning light, which is located on the instrument panel, comes on when the ignition switch is turned to ON and the engine is not running. When the engine is started, the warning light should go out. If the light remains on, the self-diagnosis system has detected a malfunction. **Note:** *The CHECK ENGINE light on early models is displayed on the dashboard VCM panel on the right side. Later models are equipped with a separate CHECK ENGINE light on the left side of the instrument cluster.* **Note:** *Not all the codes will cause the CHECK ENGINE light to activate. When performing any fuel or emissions systems diagnosis, always check for codes that may be stored but not indicated by the CHECK ENGINE light.*

## Obtaining fault code output

**3** To obtain an output of diagnostic codes, verify first that the battery voltage is above 11 volts, the throttle is fully closed, the transmission is in Park, the accessory switches are off and the engine is at normal operating temperature.

**4** Turn the ignition switch to ON but don't start the engine (Position II). **Note:** *On 1988 and 1989 models, remember to turn the ignition switch to position II without turning the key to OFF.*

**5** Press the VCM button on the display panel **(see illustration)** and observe the LED display on the dash for the designated codes. An asterisk next to the code indicates that there are multiple codes stored.

**6** The numerical values will be displayed on the trip computer display on the dashboard.

**7** If there are any malfunctions in the system, the corresponding fault codes are displayed in numerical order, lowest to highest.

## Cancelling a diagnostic code

**8** After the faulty component has been repaired/renewed, the fault code(s) stored in computer memory must be cancelled.

 a) *On 1988 to 1991 vehicles, simply drive the vehicle faster than 19 mph and the computer will automatically erase the stored fault code from memory.*

**3.5 To access the self-diagnosis system fault codes, locate the VCM button on the dash and with the ignition key ON (engine not running) press it to display the codes**

### Fault code chart for 1988 and 1989 models

| Code | System affected | Probable cause |
|---|---|---|
| 1 | Oxygen sensor | Open oxygen sensor circuit |
| 2 | Airflow sensor | Not in operating range |
| 3 | Coolant temperature sensor | Not in operating range |
| 4 | Oxygen sensor | System indicates full rich |
| 5 | Throttle potentiometer/airflow sensor | Low throttle potentiometer signal with high airflow sensor signal |
| 6 | Throttle potentiometer/airflow sensor | High throttle potentiometer signal with low airflow sensor signal |
| 7 | Throttle potentiometer | Idle fuel adjustment failure |
| 8 | Intake air temperature sensor | Open or shorted circuit in IAT sensor harness |

### Fault code chart for 1990 to 1994 models

| Code | System affected | Probable cause |
|---|---|---|
| 11 | Idle potentiometer | Not in operating range |
| 12 | Airflow sensor | Not in operating range |
| 14 | Coolant temperature sensor | Not in operating range |
| 16 | Air temperature sensor | Not in operating range |
| 17 | Throttle potentiometer | Not in operating range |
| 18 | Throttle potentiometer/airflow sensor | Signal resistance low at wide open throttle |
| 19 | Throttle potentiometer/airflow sensor | Signal resistance high at idle |
| 22 | Heated oxygen sensor | Open or short circuit |
| 22 | Fuel pump circuit | Open or short circuit |
| 23 | Fuel supply | Rich exhaust Indicated |
| 24 | Ignition amplifier circuit | Open or short circuit |
| 26 | Oxygen sensor circuit | Lean exhaust/vacuum leak |
| 29 | ECU | Self check |
| 33 | Fuel injector circuit | Open or short circuit |
| 34 | Fuel injector circuit | Faulty injector indicated |
| 37 | EGR solenoid circuit | Short or open circuit |
| 39 | EGR circuit | Faulty system operation |
| 44 | Oxygen sensor circuit | Rich or lean condition |
| 46 | Idle speed control valve - (coil 1) | Open or short circuit |
| 47 | Idle speed control valve - (coil 2) | Open or short circuit |
| 48 | Idle speed control valve | Not within specification |
| 68 | Road speed sensor | Incorrect signal voltage |
| 69 | Neutral safety switch circuit | Engine cranks in Drive (adjust or renew switch) |
| 89 | Purge control valve circuit | Open or short circuit |

 b) *On 1992 to 1994 models, disconnect the negative battery lead for 30 seconds or more to erase the stored fault codes.*

**Caution: If the stereo in your vehicle is equipped with an anti-theft system, make sure you have the correct activation code before disconnecting the battery.**

**9** A stored code can also be cancelled on early models by removing the cable from the battery negative terminal, but other items with memory (such as the clock and radio presets) will also be cancelled.

**10** If the diagnosis code is not cancelled, it will be stored by the ECU and appear with any new codes in the event of future trouble.

**11** Should it become necessary to work on engine components requiring removal of the battery terminal, always check to see if a diagnostic code has been recorded before disconnecting the battery.

## 4  Information sensors

**Note**: *Refer to Chapters 4 and 5 for additional information on the location and the diagnostic procedures for the output actuators (ISC motor, air supplementary valve, distributor, amplifier, etc.) that are not directly covered in this section.*

### Coolant temperature sensor

#### General description

**1** The coolant temperature sensor is a thermistor (a resistor which varies the value of its voltage output in accordance with temperature changes) which is threaded into the thermostat housing. As the sensor temperature DECREASES, the resistance values will INCREASE. As the sensor

**4.2 The coolant temperature sensor is in the thermostat housing. To check the coolant temperature sensor, use an ohmmeter to measure the resistance between the two sensor terminals**

**4.3 Check for reference voltage to the electrical connector for the coolant sensor with the ignition key ON (engine not running). It should be approximately 5.0 volts**

temperature INCREASES, the resistance values will DECREASE. A failure in this sensor circuit should set a Code 3 (1988 and 1989) or 13 (1990 to 1994). This code indicates a failure in the coolant temperature sensor circuit, so in most cases the appropriate solution to the problem will be either repair of a connector or wire, or renewal of the sensor.

### Check

**2** To check the sensor, measure its resistance value **(see illustration)** while it is completely cold (60 to 80° F = 1500 to 3000 ohms). Next, start the engine and warm it up until it reaches operating temperature. The resistance should be lower (180 to 200° F = 280 to 350 ohms).
**3** If the resistance values of the coolant temperature sensor are correct, check the circuit for the proper signal voltage. Turn the ignition key ON (engine not running) and check for reference voltage with a high-impedance digital voltmeter **(see illustration)**. It should be approximately 5 volts.

### Renewal

 **Warning: Wait until the engine is completely cool before beginning this procedure.**
**4** To remove the sensor, depress the locking tabs, unplug the electrical connector, then carefully unscrew the sensor.
*Caution: Handle the coolant sensor with care. Damage to this sensor will affect the operation of the entire fuel injection system.*
**5** Before refitting the new sensor, wrap the threads with Teflon sealing tape to prevent leakage and thread corrosion.
**6** Refitting is the reverse of removal.

## Oxygen sensor

**Note:** *An oxygen sensor splash shield is equipped on models from VIN 664941 (mid-*

*1990) to present. This shield prevents the self diagnosis system from setting an intermittent and erroneous code 44. Whenever replacing an oxygen sensor, make sure the splash shield is in place.*

### General description

**7** These models are equipped with a heated oxygen sensor system. The oxygen sensor is mounted ahead of the front catalytic converter and monitors the exhaust gases before they are changed. The electrical heating system incorporated into the oxygen sensor allows for quicker warm-up time and more efficient oxygen content monitoring. The oxygen sensor monitors the oxygen content of the exhaust gas stream. The oxygen content in the exhaust reacts with the oxygen sensor to produce a voltage output which varies from 0.1 volts (high oxygen, lean mixture) to 0.9 volts (low oxygen, rich mixture). The ECU constantly monitors this variable voltage output to determine the ratio of oxygen to fuel in the mixture. The ECU alters the air/fuel mixture ratio by controlling the pulse width (open time) of the fuel injectors. A mixture ratio of 14.7 parts air to 1 part fuel is the ideal mixture ratio for minimising exhaust emissions, thus allowing the catalytic converter to operate at maximum efficiency. This ratio of 14.7 to 1 is the one which the ECU and the oxygen sensor attempt to maintain at all times.
**8** The oxygen sensor produces no voltage when it is below its normal operating temperature of about 600° F. During this initial period before warm-up, the ECU operates in open loop mode.
**9** If the engine reaches normal operating temperature and/or has been running for two or more minutes, and if the oxygen sensor is producing a steady signal voltage below 0.45 volts at 1500 or more rpm, the ECU will set a Code 4 (1988 and 1989) or 26 (1990 to 1994).
**10** When there is a problem with the oxygen sensor or its circuit, the ECU operates in the

open loop mode - that is, it controls fuel delivery in accordance with a programmed default value instead of feedback information from the oxygen sensor.
**11** The proper operation of the oxygen sensor depends on four conditions:

a) *Electrical - The low voltages generated by the sensor depend upon good, clean connections which should be checked whenever a malfunction of the sensor is suspected or indicated.*
b) *Outside air supply - The sensor is designed to allow air circulation to the internal portion of the sensor. Whenever the sensor is removed and installed or renewed, make sure the air passages are not restricted.*
c) *Proper operating temperature - The ECU will not react to the sensor signal until the sensor reaches approximately 600° F. This factor must be taken into consideration when evaluating the performance of the sensor.*
d) *Unleaded fuel - The use of unleaded fuel is essential for proper operation of the sensor. Make sure the fuel you are using is of this type.*

**12** In addition to observing the above conditions, special care must be taken whenever the sensor is serviced.

a) *The oxygen sensor has a permanently attached pigtail and electrical connector which should not be removed from the sensor. Damage to or removal of the pigtail or electrical connector can adversely affect operation of the sensor.*
b) *Grease, dirt and other contaminants should be kept away from the electrical connector and the louvered end of the sensor.*
c) *Do not use cleaning solvents of any kind on the oxygen sensor.*
d) *Do not drop or roughly handle the sensor.*

4.13 To test the oxygen sensor heater, disconnect the electrical connector, and working on the sensor side, check the resistance across the two terminals. Heater resistance should be 5 to 6 ohms

4.15 Refit a pin into the backside of the oxygen sensor connector into the correct terminal and check for a millivolt output signal generated by the sensor as it warms up. The SIGNAL wire is easily recognised by the rubber sheath covering the terminal (arrowed)

e) *The silicone boot must be installed in the correct position to prevent the boot from being melted and to allow the sensor to operate properly.*

### Check

**13** Locate the oxygen sensor electrical connector and inspect the oxygen sensor heater. Disconnect the oxygen sensor electrical connector and connect an ohmmeter between the two terminals **(see illustration)**. It should be around 5 to 6 ohms.

**14** Also, check for proper supply voltage to the oxygen sensor heater. Measure the voltage with the electrical connector connected. Insert a long pin into the backside of the electrical connector on the correct wire. With the ignition key ON (engine not running), check for voltage. There should be approximately 12 volts. **Note:** *Battery voltage to the heater is supplied by the main relay (1988 to 1990) or the oxygen sensor relay (1991 to 1994). Check the oxygen sensor relay and the wiring harness if battery voltage is not available to the heater. Refer to the wiring diagrams at the end of Chapter 12 and the relay locator schematics also in Chapter 12.*

**15** Next, check for a millivolt signal from the oxygen sensor. Locate the oxygen sensor electrical connector and insert a long pin into the oxygen sensor signal wire terminal **(see illustration)**. The SIGNAL wire is the single wire with the rubber sheath covering its terminal.

**16** Monitor the voltage signal (millivolts) as the engine goes from cold to warm.

**17** The oxygen sensor will produce a steady voltage signal at first (open loop) of approximately 0.1 to 0.2 volts with the engine cold. After a period of approximately two minutes, the engine will reach operating temperature and the oxygen sensor will start

to fluctuate between 0.1 to 0.9 volts (closed loop). If the oxygen sensor fails to reach the closed loop mode or there is a very long period of time until it does switch into closed loop mode, or if the voltage doesn't fluctuate well (indicating a "lazy" sensor), renew the oxygen sensor with a new part.

### Renewal

**Note:** *Because it is installed in the exhaust manifold or pipe, which contracts when cool, the oxygen sensor may be very difficult to loosen when the engine is cold. Rather than risk damage to the sensor (assuming you are planning to reuse it in another manifold or pipe), start and run the engine for a minute or two, then shut it off. Be careful not to burn yourself during the following procedure.*

**18** Disconnect the cable from the negative terminal of the battery.

**Caution: If the stereo in your vehicle is equipped with an anti-theft system, make sure you have the correct activation code before disconnecting the battery.**

**19** Raise the vehicle and place it securely on axle stands.

**20** Disconnect the electrical connectors from the sensor pigtail lead.

**21** Unscrew the oxygen sensor from the exhaust system **(see illustration)**.

**Caution: Excessive force may damage the threads.**

**22** Anti-seize compound must be used on the threads of the sensor to facilitate future removal. The threads of new sensors will already be coated with this compound, but if an old sensor is removed and reinstalled, recoat the threads.

**23** Refit the sensor and tighten it securely.

**24** Reconnect the electrical connectors to the main engine wiring harness.

**25** Lower the vehicle and reconnect the cable to the negative terminal of the battery.

## *Throttle potentiometer*

### General description

**26** The throttle potentiometer is located on the end of the throttle shaft on the bottom section of the throttle body. By monitoring the output voltage from the throttle potentiometer, the ECU can alter fuel delivery based on throttle valve angle (driver demand). A broken or loose throttle potentiometer will cause bursts of fuel from the injectors and an unstable idle because the ECU thinks the throttle is moving. Throttle body removal procedures are covered in Chapter 4.

### Check

**27** Check for the proper reference voltage to the throttle potentiometer. Carefully back-probe the throttle potentiometer electrical connector using a pin on the reference voltage wire and ground **(see illustration)**. With the ignition key ON (engine not running) the reference voltage should be about 5.0 volts.

4.21 Unscrew the oxygen sensor from the exhaust system

**4.27 Backprobe the throttle potentiometer electrical connector with a pin and with the ignition key ON (engine not running) there should be 5.0 volts REFERENCE available**

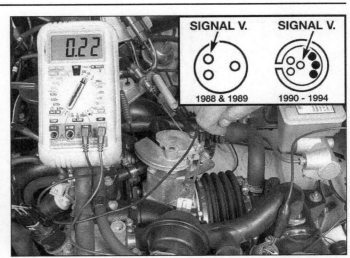

**4.28 First check the throttle potentiometer SIGNAL voltage with the throttle closed (idle). It should be 0.2 to 0.5 volts . . .**

**4.29 . . . then check the SIGNAL voltage with the throttle wide open. It should be between 4.5 and 5.0 volts**

**4.39 Check for battery voltage to the MAF sensor on terminal number 5**

**4.40 With the engine idling, raise the engine rpm and observe the voltage changes on terminal number 3**

**28** Check the signal voltage from the potentiometer. Carefully backprobe the electrical connector on the signal voltage wire (-) with the ignition key ON (engine not running) **(see illustration)**. There should be approximately 0.5 volts.

**29** Next, rotate the throttle lever manually and confirm that the reference voltage increases to approximately 4.8 volts **(see illustration)**.

**30** If the voltage does not increase, renew the throttle potentiometer with a new part.

### Renewal

**31** Remove the throttle body from the intake manifold (see Chapter 4).

**32** Remove the two mounting bolts and separate the throttle potentiometer from the throttle body. **Note:** *The throttle potentiometer is difficult to reach and adjustment requires that the home mechanic tighten the bolts after the final adjustment using a mirror. Be sure to mark the mounting position of the old throttle potentiometer before refitting the new part.*

**33** Refitting is the reverse of removal.

### Adjustment

**34** Refit the throttle body with the throttle potentiometer mounting bolts just loose enough to move the potentiometer. Be sure the bolts are tight and the potentiometer does not rotate easily.

**35** Backprobe the signal wire and the ground wire (see Step 28) and with the throttle closed (idle position), rotate the potentiometer until the voltmeter reads between 0.2 and 0.5 volts. **Note:** *The throttle potentiometer is difficult to reach. Be sure to rotate the potentiometer slowly and do not interfere with the voltmeter and the electrical connectors to the gauge.*

**36** Rotate the throttle lever and confirm that the voltage increases to around 4.8 volts. If the voltage range is correct, the throttle potentiometer is installed correctly.

**37** Tighten the throttle potentiometer bolts. If necessary, use a small mirror to locate the bolts.

### Mass airflow (MAF) sensor

#### General Information

**38** The mass airflow sensor (MAF) is located on the air intake duct. This sensor uses a hot wire sensing element to measure the amount of air entering the engine. The air passing over the hot wire causes it to cool. Consequently, this change in temperature can be converted into an analogue voltage signal to the ECU which in turn calculates the required fuel injector pulse width.

#### Check

**39** Check for power to the MAF sensor. Backprobe the MAF sensor electrical plug. Working on the harness side with the ignition ON (engine not running), check for battery voltage on terminal number 5 **(see illustration)**.

**40** Remove the pin and backprobe the MAF sensor electrical connector terminal number 3 with the voltmeter **(see illustration)**. The voltage should be less than 1.0 volt with the ignition switch ON (engine not running). Raise the engine rpm. The signal voltage from the MAF sensor should increase to about 2.0 volts. It is impossible to simulate load conditions in the driveway but it is necessary to observe the voltmeter for a fluctuation in voltage as the engine speed is raised. The vehicle will not be under load conditions but MAF sensor voltage should vary slightly.

**41** If the voltage readings are correct, check the wiring harness for open circuits or a damaged harness (see Chapter 12).

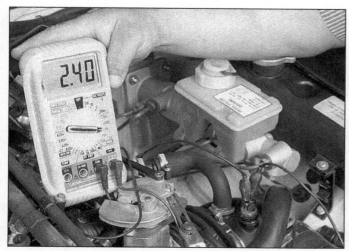

**4.51 The air intake temperature sensor resistance will DECREASE when the temperature of the air INCREASES**

**4.57 Location of the crankshaft position sensor**

42  Also, check the reference voltage to the MAF sensor from the computer. Backprobe terminal number 6 and make sure that approximately 5 volts is present.

### Renewal

43  Disconnect the electrical connector from the MAF sensor.
44  Remove the air cleaner assembly (see Chapter 4).
45  Remove the four bolts and separate the MAF sensor from the air intake duct.
46  Refitting is the reverse of removal.

## Intake air temperature (IAT) sensor

### General description

47  The intake air temperature sensor is located inside the air intake duct. This sensor acts as a resistor which changes value according to the temperature of the air entering the engine. Low temperatures produce a high resistance value (for example, at 68° F the value is 2.0 to 2.6 k-ohms) while high temperatures produce low resistance values (at 176° F the resistance is 260 to 330 ohms. The ECU supplies around 5 volts (reference voltage) to the air temperature sensor. The voltage will change according to the temperature of the incoming air. The voltage will be high when the air temperature is cold and low when the air temperature is warm. Any problems with the air temperature sensor will usually set a code 8 (1988 and 1989) or code 16 (1990 to 1994).

### Check

48  To check the air temperature sensor, disconnect the two prong electrical connector and turn the ignition key ON but do not start the engine.
49  Measure the voltage (reference voltage), which should be approximately 5 volts.
50  If the voltage signal is not correct, have

the ECU diagnosed by a dealer service department or other repair workshop.
51  Measure the resistance across the air temperature sensor terminals **(see illustration)**. The resistance should be HIGH when the air temperature is LOW. Next, start the engine and let it idle. Wait awhile and let the engine reach operating temperature. Turn the ignition OFF, disconnect the air temperature sensor and measure the resistance across the terminals. The resistance should be LOW when the air temperature is HIGH. If the sensor does not exhibit this change in resistance, renew it with a new part.

## EGR gas temperature sensor (1991 to 1994 models)

### General description

52  The EGR gas temperature sensor is mounted in the exhaust gas transfer pipe. This sensor detects the temperature of the exhaust moving through the EGR valve. The information is sent to the ECU so the EGR on/off time is regulated precisely and efficiently.

### Check

53  Disconnect the harness connector for the EGR gas temperature sensor and measure the resistance of the sensor at the various temperatures. Refer to the Specifications listed in this Chapter for a list of the temperatures and the resistance values.

### Removal and refitting

54  Disconnect the harness connector for the EGR gas temperature sensor and using an open-end spanner, remove the sensor from the EGR adapter under the intake manifold.
55  Refitting is the reverse of removal.

## Speed sensor

### General description

56  The speed sensor is mounted on the

differential housing and monitors vehicle speed by sensing the rotational speed of the rear axle. A problem with this sensor or circuit will set a code 68 and may also be the cause of an inoperative speedometer. If the speedometer doesn't work, the problem lies in the speed sensor, the instrument cluster, the ECU or the wiring in between. For further diagnosis, take the vehicle to a dealer service department or other suitably-equipped and qualified repair workshop.

## Crankshaft position sensor

57  The crankshaft position sensor is located in the front timing cover near the crankshaft pulley **(see illustration)**. The crankshaft position sensor relays a signal to the ECU to indicate the exact position (angle) of the crankshaft.

### Check

58  The crankshaft sensor cannot be diagnosed without the proper tools. The Jaguar dealer uses a diagnostic scope/computer called the JDS. Have the crankshaft sensor diagnosed by the dealer service department or other qualified repair workshop.

### Renewal

59  To renew the sensor, disconnect the electrical connector and remove the bolt from the crankshaft position sensor. Refitting is the reverse of removal.
60  To renew the crankshaft sensor gear, remove the front pulley (refer to Chapter 2A).
61  Be sure there is a small gap between the crankshaft sensor and the teeth on the gear. It should be between 0.46 to 1.07 mm (0.018 to 0.042 inch).
62  Refitting is the reverse of removal. Tighten the crankshaft sensor bolt to the torque listed in this Chapter's Specifications.

5.2 Schematic of the Air Injection Reactor (AIR) system

5.5 Location of the AIR pump relay on a 1992 model

## 5 Air Injector Reactor (AIR) system

### General information

1 The air injection reactor system reduces carbon monoxide and hydrocarbon content in the exhaust gases by injecting fresh air into the hot exhaust gases leaving the exhaust ports. When fresh air is mixed with hot exhaust gases, oxidation is increased, reducing the concentration of hydrocarbons and carbon monoxide and converting them into harmless carbon dioxide and water.

2 The air injection system is composed of an air pump, diverter valve (bypass), check valve, air injection manifold, vacuum delay valve, vacuum control solenoid, air pump magnetic clutch, air pump clutch relay and hoses (see illustration). The air pump is driven by a belt from the crankshaft and supplies compressed air to the exhaust manifold(s). The check valve prevents the reverse flow of exhaust gases into the system. The vacuum-operated (early models) or electrically-operated (later models)

air cut-off valve prevents air from being drawn into the exhaust when the air pump is switched off. System vacuum to the air cut-off valve is controlled by the solenoid vacuum valve in parallel circuit with the air pump. A delay valve prevents vacuum loss to the solenoid valve during wide open throttle operation.

3 Injected air is controlled by the computer, the air pump clutch and the air pump clutch relay. The AIR system is used during warm-up (58 to 83° F) to control emissions while the engine is running rich. The oxygen sensor feedback system cannot function while the AIR system is operating. The computer controls both systems during warm-up and operating temperatures. If problems occur with the AIR system relay or circuit, the on-board diagnosis system will set a code 66.

### Check

4 Check the condition of the air pump drivebelt, the injection hoses and the injection manifold. Make sure that all components are intact and there are no leaks.

5 Check the operation of the air pump clutch relay (see illustration) and the air pump clutch. First remove the relay and check for

battery voltage to the relay. Also, check the relay itself. Refer to the relay checking procedure in Chapter 12. Extract codes from the self-diagnosis system (see Section 3) and check for a code 66, AIR relay malfunction.

6 Make sure the electrical connector is securely fastened to the diverter valve (see illustration). If everything appears OK but a fault code still sets, have the system diagnosed by a dealer service department or other qualified repair workshop.

### Air pump renewal

7 Disconnect the cable from the negative terminal of the battery.
*Caution: If the stereo in your vehicle is equipped with an anti-theft system, make sure you have the correct activation code before disconnecting the battery.*

8 Disconnect the electrical connector from the air pump clutch.

9 Loosen the clips from the air inlet and outlet hose and separate them from the air injection pump.

10 Loosen the adjuster and pivot bolts (see illustration) and nuts but do not remove them from the air injection pump brackets.

5.6 Location of the AIR diverter valve on a 1992 model - check the hoses for cracking and the electrical connector for security

5.10 Loosen the pivot bolt and then the adjustment nut to remove the drivebelt from the air pump. The adjustment nut has a lock bolt that must be loosened before the pump will move down the adjuster

6.2  Schematic of the EGR system

Labels: EGR Valve, Transfer Pipe, Intake Manifold, EGR Temp. Sensor Adaptor, EGR Solenoid

49011-6-6.2 HAYNES

6.4  Apply vacuum to the EGR valve and confirm that the valve opens and allows exhaust gases to circulate. Once it is activated, the EGR valve should hold steady (no loss in vacuum)

11  Swing the pump toward the engine and remove the drivebelt from the pump.

12  Remove the link arm through-bolt.

13  Remove the pivot bolt and front spacer, rear cone and air injection pump from the engine compartment.

14  Remove the nut securing the front pulley on the air injection pump.

15  Remove the clutch snap-ring and the clutch.

16  Refitting is the reverse of removal.

### 6  Exhaust Gas Recirculation (EGR) system

**Note 1:** *Some 1990 models have the EGR vacuum hose routed incorrectly through the bulkhead securing straps, thereby restricting the vacuum signal to the EGR valve. Remove the EGR vacuum hose from the bulkhead harness and refit a new hose. Secure it to the engine compartment using tie-wraps and do not allow any restrictions in the hose.*

**Note 2:** *Some models have copper sealing washers that soften and leak around the EGR valve causing engine performance and starting problems. Refit steel washers and pipe adapters into the EGR system. Contact a Jaguar dealer for the VIN numbers and years of the models that are affected by this defect.*

1  To reduce oxides of nitrogen emissions, some of the exhaust gases are recirculated through the EGR valve to the intake manifold to lower combustion temperatures.

2  The EGR system consists of the EGR valve, an EGR solenoid, an EGR gas temperature sensor and the transfer pipe **(see illustration)**.

### Check

#### EGR valve

3  Start the engine and allow it to idle.

4  Detach the vacuum hose from the EGR valve and attach a hand vacuum pump in its place **(see illustration)**.

5  Apply vacuum to the EGR valve. Vacuum should remain steady and the engine should run poorly. **Note:** *This action will raise the pintle and allow exhaust gases to recirculate*

into the intake system and cause rough running condition at idle. Double-check the movement of the pintle by checking the diaphragm using the tip of your finger **(see illustration)**. If the EGR diaphragm moves smoothly and holds steady when vacuum is applied, the EGR valve is working properly.

⚠ **Warning: Don't burn yourself. If the EGR valve is hot, wear a glove or wait until it cools.**

a) *If the vacuum doesn't remain steady and the engine doesn't run poorly, renew the EGR valve and recheck it.*

b) *If the vacuum remains steady but the engine doesn't run poorly, remove the EGR valve and check the valve and the intake manifold for blockage. Clean or renew parts as necessary and recheck.*

#### EGR system

6  Disconnect the hose from the EGR valve, refit a vacuum gauge and check for vacuum to the EGR valve. There should be vacuum present with the engine warmed to operating temperature (above 140° F) and between 1000 and 4000 rpm **(see illustration)**.

6.5  Use a fingertip to move the diaphragm inside the EGR valve

6.6  Check for vacuum to the EGR valve from the throttle body

**6.8  Check for battery voltage to the EGR control solenoid**

**7** Start the engine and observe the vacuum gauge. At idle, there should be no vacuum present. Raise the engine rpm and observe the vacuum increase. This is a ported vacuum source and therefore it should only register vacuum when throttled.

**8** Check the operation of the EGR control solenoid. Check for battery voltage to the EGR control solenoid harness **(see illustration)**. If battery voltage is not available, check the harness. Refer to the wiring diagrams at the end of Chapter 12.

**9** If battery voltage is available to the EGR control solenoid, have the EGR system diagnosed by a dealer service department or other qualified repair workshop.

### EGR valve renewal

**10** Detach the vacuum hose, disconnect the fitting that attaches the EGR pipe to the EGR valve and remove the EGR valve from the exhaust manifold and check it for sticking and heavy carbon deposits. If the valve is sticking or clogged with deposits, clean or renew it.

**11** Refitting is the reverse of removal.

---

**7   Evaporative Emission Control (EVAP) system**

---

**Note:** *Some models may have charcoal canister vent plugs installed in the canister from the factory. These blanking plugs must be removed to allow proper pressure and release within the EVAP system. Check the charcoal canister for these additional plugs and remove them. With the blanking plugs installed, the fuel tank will collapse causing rough running and hesitation and loss of power under load.*

### General description

**1** This system is designed to trap and store fuel that evaporates from the fuel tank, throttle body and intake manifold that would normally enter the atmosphere in the form of hydrocarbon (HC) emissions.

**2** The Evaporative Emission Control (EVAP) system consists of a charcoal-filled canister, the lines connecting the canister to the fuel tank, tank pressure control valve, purge

**7.2  Schematic of the EVAP system**

control valve and thermal vacuum valve (TVV) **(see illustration)**. **Note:** *1993 and 1994 models have a purge control solenoid that is controlled by the ECU. This solenoid switches vacuum to the purge control valve.*

**3** Fuel vapours are transferred from the fuel tank and throttle body to a canister where they're stored when the engine isn't running. When the engine is running, the fuel vapours are purged from the canister by intake airflow and consumed in the normal combustion process. **Note:** *The ECU will set a code 89 if the purge control valve is defective or the circuit has shorted.*

**4** The fuel tank is equipped with a pressure control valve. This valve opens and closes according to the pressure increase and decrease in the fuel tank.

### Check

**5** Poor idle, stalling and poor driveability can all be caused by an inoperative pressure relief valve, split or cracked hoses or hoses connected to the wrong fittings. Check the fuel tank filler cap for a damaged or deformed gasket.

**6** Evidence of fuel loss or fuel odour can be caused by liquid fuel leaking from fuel lines, a cracked or damaged canister, an inoperative fuel tank control valve, disconnected, misrouted, kinked, deteriorated or damaged vapour or control hoses.

**7** Inspect each hose attached to the canister for kinks, leaks and cracks along its entire length. Repair or renew as necessary.

**8** Look for fuel leaking from the bottom of the

**7.11a  Check for vacuum to the thermal vacuum valve (TVV)**

**7.11b  Check for vacuum from the TVV before and after the engine has reached normal operating temperature**

**7.12  Remove the front spoiler to gain access to the purge control valve (see Chapter 11). Apply vacuum to the valve and make sure the valve holds vacuum**

**7.14  Remove the bolts (arrowed) and lower the charcoal canister from the wing**

## 8  Crankcase ventilation system

### General information

**1** The crankcase ventilation system reduces hydrocarbon emissions by scavenging crankcase vapours. It does this by circulating fresh air from the air cleaner through the crankcase, where it mixes with blow-by gases and is then re-routed through a heating element to the intake manifold **(see illustration).**

**2** The main components of the crankcase ventilation system are the control orifice, a heating element and the vacuum hoses connecting these components with the engine.

**3** Piston blow-by gasses are collected from the crankcase and the camshaft housing via the oil filler tube. These gasses are fed into the intake manifold at part throttle through the part throttle orifice and when the engine is at full throttle, the gasses are fed through the air intake elbow.

**4** To prevent possible icing-up during cold weather operation, the control orifice and the hose to the intake system is electronically heated. The heater element is energised by a relay signal from the windscreen washer jet temperature sensor.

### Check

**5** Remove the tubes and elbows that connect the crankcase ventilation system and inspect them for obstructions, oil deposits or clogging. Make sure the ventilation system is free of all

canister. If fuel is leaking, renew the canister and check the hoses and hose routing.

**9** Inspect the canister. If it's cracked or damaged, renew it.

**10** Check for a clogged filter or a damaged pressure relief valve. Using low pressure compressed air (such as from a tyre pump), blow into the canister tank pipe. Air should flow freely from the other pipes. If a problem is found, renew the canister.

**11** Check the operation of the thermal vacuum valve (TVV). With the engine cold and idling, check for ported vacuum to the temperature vacuum switch. Vacuum should be present **(see illustration)**. Now warm the engine to operating temperature (above 115°F/43°C) and confirm that ported vacuum passes through the TVV **(see illustration)**. Renew the valve if the test results are incorrect.

**12** Check the operation of the purge control valve. Apply vacuum to the purge control valve using a hand-held vacuum pump and observe that the valve holds vacuum steadily **(see illustration)**. If the valve holds vacuum and the valve is opening, it is working properly.

### Charcoal canister renewal

**13** Clearly label, then detach the vacuum hoses from the canister.

**14** Remove the mounting clamp bolts **(see illustration)**, lower the canister with the

bracket, disconnect the hoses from the check valve and remove it from the vehicle.

**15** Refitting is the reverse of removal.

**8.1  Schematic of the crankcase ventilation system**

Oil fill tube

Electronic heating element

To intake

Control orifice

Air intake elbow

49011-6-8.1 HAYNES

**8.7 Disconnect the electrical connector from the electronic heating element**

obstructions to ensure complete recirculation of gasses from the crankcase back into the intake manifold. In the event of clogging, the pressure will increase causing blow-by and oil leaks through seals and gaskets.

6 Check the operation of the heating element. Check for battery voltage to the element while the engine is cold. If no voltage is available to the heating element, check the circuit from the windscreen washer jet temperature sensor.

### Renewal

7 Disconnect the electrical connector from the heating element **(see illustration)**.

8 Remove the clamps from the hoses and separate the heating element from the engine.

9 Remove the hoses from the intake manifold. These crankcase ventilation hoses are specially formed and must be replaced with special factory parts from Jaguar.

10 Refitting is the reverse of removal.

## 9  Catalytic converter

### General description

1 To reduce hydrocarbon, carbon monoxide and oxides of nitrogen emissions, all vehicles are equipped with a three-way catalyst system which oxidises and reduces these chemicals, converting them into harmless nitrogen, carbon dioxide and water.

2 The catalytic converter fits into the exhaust system much like a silencer. **Note:** *The exhaust system configuration changes with later model updates. Older models (1988 and 1989) are equipped with a pre-catalytic converter near the exhaust manifold incorporating a single exhaust pipe to the silencer. Later models are equipped with dual exhaust pipes, dual catalytic converters and dual silencers.*

### Check

3 Periodically inspect the catalytic converter-to-exhaust pipe mating flanges and bolts. Make sure that there are no loose bolts and no leaks between the flanges.

4 Look for dents in or damage to the catalytic converter protector. If any part of the protector is damaged or dented enough to touch the converter, repair or renew it.

5 Inspect the heat insulator for damage. Make sure there is enough clearance between the heat insulator and the catalytic converter.

### Renewal

6 To renew the catalytic converter, refer to Chapter 4. It is recommended that catalytic converters be renewed at a qualified silencer workshop because of the numerous tack welds on the exhaust pipes.

# Chapter 7
# Automatic transmission

## Contents

## Degrees of difficulty

| Easy, suitable for novice with little experience  | Fairly easy, suitable for beginner with some experience  | Fairly difficult, suitable for competent DIY mechanic  | Difficult, suitable for experienced DIY mechanic  | Very difficult, suitable for expert DIY or professional |

## Specifications

| Torque wrench settings | Nm | lbf ft |
| --- | --- | --- |
| Driveplate-to-torque converter bolts | 49 to 54 | 36 to 40 |
| Oil cooler banjo bolt | 32 to 36 | 24 to 26 |
| Transmission-to-adapter bolts | 49 to 54 | 36 to 40 |
| Valve body bolts | 8 | 6 |

## 1 General information

All models covered by this manual are equipped with a four-speed automatic transmission with a lock-up torque converter. 1988 and 1989 models are equipped with a ZF 4 HP 22. Under loads such as hills or passing situations, this unit is downshifted by a kickdown cable, which can be adjusted and replaced. 1990 and later models use a ZF 4 HP 24 E9 electronic transmission. This unit does not use a kickdown cable; it uses a kickdown switch (under the accelerator pedal) that signals the transmission computer to initiate a downshift. The kickdown switch must be serviced by a Jaguar dealer service department.

Because of the complexity of the clutch mechanisms and the hydraulic and electronic control systems, and because of the special tools and expertise needed to rebuild an automatic transmission, transmission servicing is usually beyond the scope of the home mechanic. The procedures in this Chapter are therefore limited to general diagnosis, routine maintenance, adjustments and transmission removal and refitting.

Should the transmission require major repair work, take it to a dealer service department or a transmission repair workshop. You can, however, save the cost of removing and refitting the transmission by doing it yourself.

If you have to replace the transmission with a new or rebuilt unit, make sure you purchase the right unit. The transmission identification plate is on the left side of the housing, behind the manual valve lever **(see illustration)**.

If the transmission warning light on a 1990 or later model comes on:

a) Check the transmission oil level (see Chapter 1).
b) Check the kickdown cable (see Section 3).
c) Check the shift cable adjustment (see Section 4).
d) Check the state of tune of the engine (see Chapter 1).

**1.4 The transmission identification label is located on the left side of the transmission; always refer to this tag when replacing the transmission**

After performing the above, note whether the transmission warning light still comes on. If it does, take the vehicle to a dealer. Further diagnosis should be left to a Jaguar dealer service department or competent Jaguar independent garage.

## 2 Diagnosis - general

**Note:** *Automatic transmission problems may be caused by five general conditions: poor engine performance, improper adjustments, hydraulic malfunctions, mechanical malfunctions, or malfunctions in the computer or its signal network. Diagnosis of these problems should always begin with a check of the easily repaired items: fluid level and condition (see Chapter 1), kickdown cable adjustment and shift cable adjustment. Next, perform a road test to determine if the problem has been corrected or if more diagnosis is necessary. If the problem persists after the preliminary tests and corrections are completed, additional diagnosis should be done by a dealer service department or transmission specialist. Refer to the* Fault Finding *section for information on symptoms of transmission problems.*

### Preliminary checks

1 Drive the vehicle to warm the transmission to normal operating temperature.

**2** Check the fluid level (see Chapter 1):

a) *If the fluid level is unusually low, add enough fluid to bring the level within the designated area of the dipstick, then check for external leaks (see below).*

b) *If the fluid level is abnormally high, drain off the excess, then check the drained fluid for contamination by coolant. The presence of engine coolant in the automatic transmission fluid indicates that a failure has occurred in the internal radiator walls that separate the coolant from the transmission fluid (see Chapter 3).*

c) *If the fluid is foaming, drain it and refill the transmission, then check for coolant in the fluid or a high fluid level.*

**3** Check the engine idle speed. **Note:** *If the engine is malfunctioning, do not proceed with the preliminary checks until it has been repaired and runs normally.*

**4** Check the kickdown cable for freedom of movement. Adjust it if necessary (refer to Section 3). **Note:** *The kickdown cable may function properly when the engine is shut off and cold, but it may malfunction once the engine is hot. Check it cold and at normal operating temperature.*

**5** Inspect the shift cable (see Section 4). Make sure that it's properly adjusted and that the cable operates smoothly.

### Fluid leak diagnosis

**6** Most fluid leaks are easy to locate visually. Repair usually consists of replacing a seal or gasket. If a leak is difficult to find, the following procedure may help.

**7** Identify the fluid. Ensure it's transmission fluid, not engine oil or brake fluid (automatic transmission fluid is a deep red colour).

**8** Try to pinpoint the source of the leak. Drive the vehicle several miles, then park it over a large sheet of cardboard. After a minute or two, you should be able to locate the leak by determining the source of the fluid dripping onto the cardboard.

**9** Make a careful visual inspection of the suspected component and the area immediately around it. Pay attention to gasket mating surfaces. A mirror is often helpful for finding leaks in areas that are hard to see.

**10** If the leak still cannot be found, clean the suspected area thoroughly with a degreaser or solvent, then dry it.

**11** Drive the vehicle for several miles at normal operating temperature and varying speeds. After driving the vehicle, visually inspect the suspected component again.

**12** Once the leak has been located, the cause must be determined before it can be properly repaired. If a gasket is replaced but the sealing flange is bent, the new gasket will not stop the leak. The bent flange must be straightened.

**13** Before attempting to repair a leak, check to make sure that the following conditions are corrected or they may cause another leak. **Note:** *Some of the following conditions cannot be fixed without highly specialized tools and expertise. Such problems must be referred to a transmission repair workshop or a dealer service department.*

### Gasket leaks

**14** Check the pan periodically. Make sure the bolts are tight, no bolts are missing, the gasket is in good condition and the pan is flat (dents in the pan may indicate damage to the valve body inside).

**15** If the pan gasket is leaking, the fluid level or the fluid pressure may be too high, the transmission breather (on top of the extension housing) may be plugged, the pan bolts may be too tight, the pan sealing flange may be warped, the sealing surface of the transmission housing may be damaged, the gasket may be damaged or the transmission casting may be cracked or porous. If sealant instead of gasket material has been used to form a seal between the pan and the transmission housing, it may be the wrong sealant.

### Seal leaks

**16** If a transmission seal is leaking, the fluid level or pressure may be too high, the transmission breather (on top of the extension housing) may be plugged, the seal bore may be damaged, the seal itself may be damaged or improperly installed, the surface of the shaft protruding through the seal may be damaged or a loose bearing may be causing excessive shaft movement.

**17** Make sure the dipstick is a tight fit inside the filler tube. If the seal at the top of the dipstick is worn or damaged, renew the seal or the dipstick. If fluid continues to leak from the top of the dipstick tube, inspect the breather, which is a plastic cap secured by a clip to the top of the extension housing. This breather can be plugged by the noise-deadening foam installed in the transmission tunnel, causing transmission fluid to leak from the top of the dipstick tube.

### Case leaks

**18** If the case itself appears to be leaking, the casting is porous and will have to be repaired or renewed.

**19** Make sure the oil cooler hose fittings are tight and in good condition.

### Fluid comes out vent pipe or fill tube

**20** If this happens, the transmission is overfilled, there is coolant in the fluid, the case is porous, the dipstick is incorrect, the vent is plugged or the drain back holes are plugged.

**3 Kickdown cable (1988 and 1989 models) - adjustment and renewal**

### Adjustment

**Note:** *The following procedure does not apply to 1990 and later models, which utilize a kickdown switch instead of a kickdown cable. The switch must be serviced by a Jaguar service department.*

**1** Adjust the accelerator cable (refer to Chapter 4).

**2** Open the throttle bellcrank to the kickdown (full-throttle) position (you should be able to feel the kickdown detent as the bellcrank is moved). Measure the distance from the cable housing to the cable plug **(see illustration)**. It should be 39 to 40 mm (1.54 to 1.58 inches). If the measurement is outside this range, renew the cable.

**3** Return the bellcrank to the idle position and measure the gap between the cable plug and the cable housing **(see illustration)**. It should be 0.76 ± 0.51 mm (0.030 ± 0.020 inch). If the

**3.2 Open the throttle bellcrank to the kickdown (full-throttle) position and measure the distance from the cable housing to the cable plug**

**3.3 Return the bellcrank to the idle position and measure the gap between the cable plug and the cable housing**

3.4 Depress the accelerator pedal, hold it to the floor and measure the distance between the plug and the cable housing

3.6a To disengage the kickdown cable from the throttle bellcrank, disconnect the return spring . . .

3.6b . . . pry off the C-clip, remove the washer . . .

3.6c . . . lift off the return spring link . . .

3.6d . . . pull out the pin, swing the cruise control link out of the way . . .

3.6e . . . disengage the cable from the bellcrank . . .

measurement is outside this range, loosen the locknut and adjust the cable until this dimension is within the specified range.

**4** Depress the accelerator pedal and hold it to the floor. Measure the distance between the plug and the cable housing **(see illustration)**. It should be at least 44 mm (1.74 inches). If the measured dimension is less than the specified dimension, recheck the throttle cable adjustment (see Chapter 4).

### *Renewal*

**5** Place the shift lever in the Neutral position.
**6** Disengage the kickdown cable from the throttle bellcrank, loosen the cable locknuts and detach the cable from its bracket **(see illustrations)**.
**7** Raise the vehicle and place it securely on axle stands.
**8** Drain the transmission fluid (see Chapter 1).
**9** Remove the transmission sump (see Chapter 1).
**10** Pull down the upper end of the kickdown cable between the engine and the bulkhead.
**11** Remove the transmission filter (see Chapter 1).
**12** Remove the valve body **(see illustration)**.
**13** Rotate the cam and disengage the cable from the cam **(see illustrations)**.
**14** The cable housing is routed through the transmission case, and locked into place by four nylon tangs. Pull the cable up until the

3.6f . . . loosen the locknuts and detach the cable from its bracket

3.12 To remove the valve body, remove these T30 Torx bolts (arrowed)

3.13a Pull on the cable to rotate the cam . . .

3.13b . . . and disengage the cable from the cam

**3.14 To remove the cable from the transmission, use a small socket to squeeze the nylon locking tangs together while pulling up on the cable from above**

**3.15 Make sure that the O-ring on the new cable is properly seated (arrowed), then lubricate it with clean automatic transmission fluid before inserting the cable into the transmission case**

plug stops against these tangs, then squeeze the tangs together with a small socket **(see illustration)** while pulling on the cable from above.

**15** Remove the old cable assembly and refit the new cable. Before inserting the lower end of the new cable through the transmission, make sure the O-ring **(see illustration)** is properly seated, lubricate the O-ring with clean automatic transmission fluid.

**16** Insert the cable through the transmission case and pull it down with a pair of pliers until the four locking tangs snap into place **(see illustration)**.

**17** Rotate the cam and refit the new cable end plug into the slot in the cam. Pull on the cable from above a couple of times to verify that the cable is properly engaged in its track in the cam and the locking tangs are fully seated.

**18** Refit the valve body, make sure the manual lever pawl is properly engaged with the manual control valve **(see illustration)** and tighten the valve body bolts to the torque listed in this Chapter's Specifications.

**19** Refit the sump and tighten the sump bolts to the torque wrench setting listed in the Chapter 1 Specifications.

**20** Route the cable up between the engine and the bulkhead.

**21** Lower the vehicle.

**22** Route the cable through its mounting bracket and connect the cable end to the throttle bellcrank **(see illustrations 3.6a to 3.6f)**.

**23** Adjust the cable (see above) before tightening the locknuts.

**24** Refill the transmission with the recommended fluid (see Chapter 1).

**4 Shift cable -**
renewal and adjustment

### Renewal

**Note:** *The illustrations accompanying this procedure depict a 1988 or 1989 model, which uses a linear type Neutral start/reversing light switch. If you are replacing or adjusting the shift cable on a 1990 or later model, you'll see a rotary type Neutral start/reversing light switch at the manual lever shaft on the transmission. But even though it appears different at the transmission end of the cable, the cable renewal and adjustment procedures are identical.*

**1** Remove the centre console (refer to Chapter 11).

**3.16 Pull down on the cable tangs until they snap into place (arrowed); pull up on the cable from above and make sure it's locked in**

**3.18 When you refit the valve body, make sure the manual lever pawl is properly engaged with the manual valve as shown**

**4.2  To detach the shift cable from the shift lever, remove the nut on the end of the cable (arrowed); to detach the cable from the shift lever base, remove the two locknuts (arrowed); don't loosen the retaining screws (arrowed) for the neutral start/reversing light switch unless you plan to readjust or replace the switch**

**4.4  To detach the lower end of the shift cable from the transmission, remove the nut (arrowed) which secures the cable end pin to the manual lever and remove the bolts (arrowed) which attach the cable bracket to the transmission**

**2** Detach the cable from the shift lever **(see illustration)**.

**3** Raise the vehicle and place it securely on axle stands.

**4** Remove the bolts securing the cable bracket to the transmission **(see illustration)**. Some early models may be equipped with a slightly different bracket than shown; on these models, the cable is attached to the bracket by a clamp and bolt, it's not necessary to remove

the bracket - simply remove the bolt and clamp and detach the cable from the bracket.

**5** On some early models, you'll find a cable bracket at the rear of the transmission; loosen the locknuts and disengage the cable from the bracket.

**6** Disengage the shift cable from the manual lever **(see illustration 4.4)**.

**7** Pry the cable grommet out of the floorpan **(see illustration)** and remove the shift cable.

**8** Refitting is the reverse of removal. Be sure to adjust the cable (see below) before refitting the Neutral start/reversing light switch, console and shift lever trim panel.

### Adjustment

**9** Place the shift lever in the Park position.

**10** Raise and support the car on axle stands.

**11** Loosen the cable adjuster locknut **(see illustration)**.

**12** Remove the nut that secures the cable to the manual lever **(see illustration)**.

**13** Place the manual lever in Park (the most forward detent position).

**14** Adjust the cable so that the pin on the end of the cable fits into the manual lever without moving the lever **(see illustration)**. If the pin pushes or pulls on the lever, pull out the pin, rotate the adjuster one turn in or out as necessary, then insert the pin back through the lever and check it again.

**15** When the pin on the end of the cable fits loosely into the manual lever as shown, refit the cable-to-manual lever retaining nut and tighten it securely.

**16** Tighten the adjuster locknut securely.

**17** Lower the vehicle.

**18** Adjust the Neutral start/reversing light switch (see Section 5).

**4.7  Pry the cable grommet out of the floor with a screwdriver**

**4.11  Loosen the cable adjust locknut**

**4.12  Remove the nut that secures the cable pin to the manual lever**

**4.14  With the shift lever and the manual lever in Park, the cable must fit loosely through the manual lever as shown**

### 5  Neutral start/reversing light switch - check and renewal

### Check

**Note:** *Due to production changes, the wire colours used in the following checks may not match your vehicle. If this is the case, some experimentation may be necessary to find the correct wire terminals for testing.*

**5.3a On 1988 and 1989 models, disconnect the black electrical connector to the Neutral start/reversing light switch. Check for continuity between white/pink and black/pink wire terminals (on the switch side of the connector) with the shift lever in Park and Neutral and no continuity with the shift lever in Drive, 2 and 3**

**5.3b On 1988 and 1989 models, place the shift lever in Reverse and verify that there's continuity between the terminal for the black wire and the terminal for the red wire and the grey/light green wire (again, on the *switch* side of the connector)**

**1** If the engine can be started with the shift lever in any position other than Park or Neutral, or if the reversing lights do not come on when the shift lever is placed in Reverse, check the neutral start/reversing light switch.
**2** Remove the centre console (refer to Chapter 11).

### 1988 and 1989 models

**3** Place the shift lever in Park, disconnect the black electrical connector to the Neutral start/reversing light switch, then connect an ohmmeter between the terminals for the white/pink wire and the black/pink wire (on the *switch* side of the connector) and verify that there's continuity. Place the shift lever in Neutral and verify that there's still continuity between these same terminals **(see illustrations)**. Place the shift lever in Drive, 2 and 3, and verify there's no continuity. Place the shift lever in Reverse and verify that there's continuity between the terminal for the black wire and the terminal for the red wire and the grey/light green wire (again, on the *switch* side of the connector).
**4** If the switch fails the above tests, place the shift lever in Park, loosen the switch retaining screws **(see illustration 4.2)**, hook up the ohmmeter leads to the white/pink and black/pink wire terminals, move the switch until you get continuity, tighten the retaining screws, then recheck the Neutral and Reverse positions. If the switch can't be adjusted to give continuity in Park, or if it still fails to produce continuity in Neutral or Reverse even after being adjusted, renew it (see below).
**5** Refit the centre console (see Chapter 11).

### 1990 and later models

**6** Place the shift lever in Park.
**7** Disconnect the electrical connector from the Neutral start/reversing light switch, then connect an ohmmeter to the terminals for the

white/purple wire and the red/white wire (1990 to 1992 models), or the terminals for the red/orange and the green/orange wires (1993 and later models), and verify that there's continuity. Place the shift lever in Neutral and verify that there's still continuity between the same terminals. Place the shift lever in Reverse and hook up the ohmmeter leads to the terminals for the grey/light green wire and the black wire and verify that there's continuity between these terminals.
**8** If the switch fails the first of the above tests (Park), place the shift lever in Park, loosen the switch retaining screws, hook up the ohmmeter leads to the terminals for the Park position (white/purple wire and red/white wire on 1990 to 1992 models, red/orange and green/orange wires on 1993 and later models), and adjust the switch until there's continuity. If the switch can't be adjusted to give continuity in Park, or if it still fails to produce continuity in Neutral or Reverse even after being adjusted, renew it (see below).
**9** Refit the centre console (see Chapter 11).

**5.13a On 1990 and later models, remove these two bolts (arrowed) and remove the protective cover for the Neutral start/reversing light switch**

### Renewal

**Note:** *If you're replacing the switch on a 1990 or later model, you'll need a special switch adjustment tool (Jaguar tool no. JD161) to adjust the switch.*
**10** Remove the centre console (Chapter 11).
**11** On 1990 and later models, raise the vehicle and place it securely on axle stands.
**12** Disconnect the electrical connector(s) from the switch (on 1990 and later models, the switch is located at the transmission and the electrical connector is routed through the top of the tunnel and into the console).
**13** Remove the switch retaining nuts **(1988 and 1989 models, see illustration 4.2; 1990 and later models, see illustrations 5.13a and 5.13b)** and remove the switch.
**14** Place the shift lever in Neutral, refit the switch and refit the switch retaining nuts, but don't tighten them yet.

**5.13b To remove a rotary type Neutral start/reversing light switch, disconnect the plug (in the console area inside the car), feed the wiring through the grommet in the tunnel, and remove these nuts (arrowed); the rubber plug (arrowed) must be removed to fit the special switch adjustment tool**

**5.16 To adjust a rotary type Neutral start/reversing light switch on 1990 and later models, refit this special tool (Jaguar tool no. JD161) as shown, then tighten the switch retaining nuts**

**6.5 Using a hooked seal removal tool or a large screwdriver, carefully pry the torque converter seal out of the transmission**

**15** On 1988 and 1989 models, hook up an ohmmeter to the Neutral terminals (see paragraph 3) and adjust the switch to produce continuity between these terminals with the shift lever in Neutral. Tighten the nuts.

**16** On 1990 and later models, remove the small rubber plug, fit the special switch adjustment tool (JD161) as shown **(see illustration)**. This tool aligns the switch to produce continuity when the shift lever is in Neutral. If you don't have the special tool, use an ohmmeter to adjust the switch to produce continuity in Neutral (see Step 8), but you may have to experiment before determining which wires to use. Once the switch is adjusted, tighten the switch nuts. Refit the switch protective cover and tighten the two bolts.

**17** On 1990 and later models, route the wire harness for the new switch through the grommet in the tunnel. Lower the vehicle.

**18** Plug in the electrical connector(s).

**19** Refit the console (see Chapter 11).

**20** Check the operation of the switch. Make sure the engine can be started in Park and Neutral, but not in any other gear, and that the reversing lights come on when the shift lever in placed in Reverse.

## 6 Oil seal - renewal

**1** There are three seals in the automatic transmission - the torque converter seal, the manual valve seal and the transmission output shaft seal - that can cause transmission fluid leaks. If the torque converter seal is leaking, you'll find transmission fluid in the bottom of the bellhousing. If the manual valve seal leaks, you'll see fluid on the side of the transmission case and the fluid pan. If the output shaft seal leaks, you'll find fluid on the extension housing and the front of the driveshaft.

**2** You can renew all of these seals without

dismantling, although replacing the torque converter seal requires removal of the transmission and the torque converter .

### Torque converter seal

**3** Remove the transmission and the torque converter (see Section 8).

**4** Inspect the bushing in the torque converter hub. If it's worn, the new seal will soon leak. Try removing any sharp edges or burrs with fine emery cloth. If the hub is deeply scored, the torque converter must be renewed.

**5** Using a hooked seal removal tool or screwdriver, pry the seal out of the transmission case **(see illustration)**. Make sure you don't gouge the surface of the seal bore.

**6** Lubricate the lip of the new seal with automatic transmission fluid and carefully drive it into place with a socket or a section of pipe with an outside diameter slightly smaller than the outside diameter of the seal.

**7** Refit the torque converter, making sure it is completely engaged with the front pump (to do this, turn the converter as you push it into place - continue turning and pushing until you're sure it's fully seated). Refit the transmission/converter assembly (see Section 8).

### Manual valve seal

**8** Raise and support the car on axle stands.

**9** Remove the manual valve lever from the transmission. Do not disconnect the linkage from the lever or you'll have to readjust it.

**10** Pry out the seal with a small hooked seal removal tool or a small screwdriver. Ensure you don't gouge the surface of the seal bore.

**11** Lubricate the lip of the new seal with automatic transmission fluid and carefully drive it into place with a socket or a section of pipe with an outside diameter slightly smaller than the outside diameter of the seal.

**12** Refit the manual lever and tighten the nut to the specified torque. If you didn't disconnect the linkage, it's unnecessary to readjust the linkage.

### Output shaft seal

**13** Raise the rear of the vehicle and support it securely on axle stands. Be sure to block the front wheels to keep the vehicle from rolling.

**14** Remove the exhaust system (Chapter 4).

**15** Remove the driveshaft (see Chapter 8).

**16** Pry out the lockplate **(see illustration)**, immobilize the flange by inserting a bolt and jamming it against a reinforcing rib as shown, then remove the flange nut **(see illustration)**. Remove the flange from the output shaft. Use a puller, if necessary.

**17** Using a seal removal tool or a small

**6.16a Pry out the locking plate . . .**

**6.16b . . . insert a bolt through the flange to lock it, then remove the flange nut**

7.3 Support the transmission with a jack; place a wood block between the jack head and the transmission to protect the pan

7.5a With an assistant pushing up on the crossmember, remove these four nuts (arrowed) . . .

7.5b . . . then remove this retaining clip and clevis pin from the travel limiter strap

7.6a To dismantle the transmission mount, remove this retaining screw (arrowed) . . .

7.6b . . . place the mount/crossmember assembly in a bench vice, remove these two bolts (arrowed) from one side . . .

7.6c . . . and this bolt (arrowed) from the other side . . .

7.6d . . . place the assembly on a work bench and remove the upper spring . . .

7.6e . . . the retainer . . .

7.6f . . . the bump-stop . . .

screwdriver, carefully pry out the old oil seal. Make sure you don't damage the seal bore when you pry out the seal.

18 Apply a light coat of oil to the lip of the new seal, clean off the end of the output shaft, slide the seal onto the shaft and carefully drive it into place using a short section of pipe with an outside diameter slightly smaller than the outside diameter of the seal.

19 Refit the flange. Coat the side of the nut that contacts the flange with sealant to prevent oil leaks. Tighten the flange nut to the torque listed in this Chapter's Specifications. Refit a new lockplate by tapping it into place with a brass punch and hammer. Make sure the lockplate is fully seated.

20 The remainder of refitting is the reverse of removal.

### 7 Transmission mount - check and renewal

1 If you hear a rumbling sound coming from the tunnel when the vehicle is driven over rough roads, expansion joints, bumpy surfaces, etc., the rear transmission mount may be defective.

2 Raise the vehicle and support it securely on axle stands.

3 Place a transmission jack or trolley jack under the transmission (see illustration).

4 Remove the central exhaust pipe section (see Chapter 4).

5 With an assistant supporting the mount crossmember, remove the crossmember retaining nuts (see illustration) and lower the mount/crossmember assembly until you can see the travel limiter strap. To disconnect the strap, remove the retaining clip and clevis pin (see illustration).

6 Dismantle the mount assembly as shown (see illustrations).

7 Inspect the rubber bump-stop for cracks, tears and deformation. If it's damaged or worn, renew it.

8 Refitting is otherwise the reverse of removal. Have your assistant hold the mount/crossmember assembly in position while you reattach the mount to the travel limiter strap with the clevis pin and retaining clip (see illustration 7.5b). Then raise the mount/crossmember all the way up, refit the crossmember nuts and tighten them securely.

7.6g ... the upper insulator ...

7.6h ... the lower spring ...

7.6i ... and the lower insulator

## 8 Automatic transmission - removal and refitting

**Caution: On 1994 models with engine numbers ranging from 9E-185496 to 9E-186799, four of the ten bolts that attach the transmission to the adapter plate were originally manufactured to substandard material specifications. These four bolts are black in colour. Once these bolts are removed, discard them, DO NOT reuse these bolts. There is no danger of these bolts failing unless they are removed and reused.**

1 Disconnect the cable from the negative battery terminal.
**Caution: If the radio in your vehicle is equipped with an anti-theft system, make sure you have the correct activation code before disconnecting the battery.**
2 On 1988 and 1989 models, if you're planning on refitting the original transmission, disconnect the kickdown cable from the throttle linkage and from its mounting bracket (see Section 3). If you're planning on refitting a new or rebuilt transmission, the cable should be disconnected from the transmission after the vehicle is lifted.
3 Remove the dipstick tube retaining bolt **(see illustration)**.
4 Raise the vehicle and support it securely on axle stands.
5 Drain the transmission fluid (see Chapter 1).
6 Place a drain pan underneath the dipstick tube, remove the tube, drain the oil in the tube and plug the hole.

7 Disconnect the oil cooler lines **(see illustration)**.
8 Remove the front exhaust pipe and hang the remainder of the exhaust system out of the way (see Chapter 4).
9 If you're renewing the transmission on a 1988 or 1989 model, disconnect the kickdown cable (see Section 3).
10 Disconnect the shift cable from the mounting bracket on the left side of the transmission and from the manual lever (see Section 4).
11 Support the engine from above with an engine hoist (see Chapter 2).
**Caution: Do not allow the engine to remain unsupported while removing the transmission, or damage may occur.**
12 Support the transmission with a transmission jack or a trolley jack. If you use a trolley jack, place a wood block between the jack head and the sump to protect the pan.
13 Remove the transmission mount (see Section 7).
14 Remove the torque converter access covers **(see illustrations)**, mark the relationship of the torque converter to the driveplate and remove the bolts that attach the torque converter to the driveplate **(see illustrations)**.
15 On vehicles with a 4 HP 24 E9 transmission (1990 and later models), disconnect the control unit electrical connector from the left side of the transmission, just above the pan **(see illustration)**.

8.3 Remove the dipstick tube retaining bolt (arrowed)

8.7 Disconnect the oil cooler line fittings (arrowed)

8.14a Pry out the rubber torque converter access cover ...

8.14b ... and the plastic grille in the bellhousing ...

8.14c ... mark the relationship of the torque converter to the driveplate ...

**8.14d ... and remove the bolts that attach the torque converter to the driveplate**

**16** Lower the engine and transmission. Ensure the engine doesn't contact the steering gear.

*Caution: Do NOT allow the torque converter shaft to support the weight of the transmission or you will damage the torque converter or transmission.*

**17** Remove the bolts that attach the transmission bellhousing to the engine adapter plate **(see illustration)**, pull the transmission to the rear until it's free, then carefully lower the jack enough to make a last-minute check for anything that might still be connected to the transmission. As you lower the transmission, make sure the kickdown cable doesn't hang up on anything.

**18** If you're renewing the transmission, remove the torque converter and refit it on the new/rebuilt unit. To remove the torque converter from the transmission, refit two long bolts halfway into the converter mounting holes and pull evenly on both bolts.

**19** Refitting is basically the reverse of removal, but note the following:

a) *Tighten the transmission and torque converter bolts to the torque listed in this Chapter's Specifications.*

b) *Before reattaching the cooler lines, flush them with clean automatic transmission fluid, to remove any friction lining particles that could clog the new or rebuilt transmission.*

c) *Use a new gasket on the pan drain plug and a new O-ring on the dipstick/filler tube connection at the pan.*

**20** Refill the transmission with clean automatic transmission fluid of the specified type (see Chapter 1).

**21** Adjust the kickdown cable and the shift cable (see Sections 3 and 4, respectively).

**8.15 On vehicles with a 4 HP 24 E9 transmission (1990 and later models), disconnect the control unit electrical connector from the left side of the transmission, just above the pan**

**8.17 Transmission bellhousing bolts (arrowed)**

# Chapter 8
# Drivetrain

## Contents

## Degrees of difficulty

| Easy, suitable for novice with little experience  | Fairly easy, suitable for beginner with some experience  | Fairly difficult, suitable for competent DIY mechanic  | Difficult, suitable for experienced DIY mechanic  | Very difficult, suitable for expert DIY or professional |
|---|---|---|---|---|

## Specifications

### Torque wrench settings

| | Nm | lbf ft |
|---|---|---|
| **Propshaft** | | |
| U-joint-to-flange (front or rear) | 95 to 105 | 70 to 77 |
| Flexible coupling-to-pinion flange | 81 | 60 |
| Centre bearing assembly | | |
| Crossmember-to-body bolts | 22 to 28 | 16 to 20 |
| Bearing-to-crossmember bolts | 22 to 24 | 16 to 17 |
| **Driveshafts** | | |
| U-joint to output flange | 78 to 95 | 58 to 70 |
| Driveshaft nut | 300 to 320 | 221 to 236 |
| **Differential** | | |
| Pinion flange nut | 4 to 6 | 3 to 4 |
| Output shaft housing bolts | 51 to 58 | 38 to 42 |

## 1  General information

### Propshaft

Power is transmitted from the transmission to the rear axle by a two-piece propshaft joined ahead of the centre bearing by a "slip joint," a sliding, splined coupling. The slip joint allows slight fore-and-aft movement of the propshaft. The forward end of the propshaft (and the rear end, on some early models) is attached to the extension housing output flange by a conventional universal joint. The rear end of the propshaft is attached to the pinion flange of the differential by a flexible rubber coupling. This flex coupling, sometimes referred to as a "Jurid" coupling or a "flex-disc," isolates the differential from the sudden torque forces of the propshaft. (If you have an early model with a U-joint at the rear end of the propshaft, a flexible coupling can be retrofitted; see your Jaguar dealer for

details.) The middle of the propshaft is supported by the centre bearing, which is rubber-mounted to isolate propshaft vibrations. The centre bearing crossmember is bolted to the vehicle body.

### Differential assembly

The rear-mounted differential assembly includes the drive pinion, the ring gear, the differential and the output flanges. The drive pinion, which drives the ring gear, is also known as the differential input shaft. It's connected to the propshaft via an input flange. The differential is bolted to the ring gear and drives the rear wheels through a pair of output flanges bolted to driveshafts with U-joints at either end. The differential allows the wheels to turn at different speeds when cornering (the outside wheel must travel farther - and therefore faster - than the inside wheel in the same period of time). The differential assembly is bolted to a large crossmember and to various suspension pieces. To renew it, you'll have to drop the entire rear axle/suspension assembly.

Major repair work on the differential assembly components (drive pinion, ring-and-pinion and differential) requires many special tools and a high degree of expertise, and therefore should not be attempted by the home mechanic. If major repairs become necessary, we recommend that they be performed by a dealer service department or other repair workshop.

### Driveshafts and universal joints

The driveshafts deliver power from the differential output flanges to the rear wheels. The driveshafts are equipped with U-joints at each end. The differential assembly, the driveshafts and the wheels are never in perfect alignment; U-joints allow the driveshafts to deliver power to the rear wheels while moving up and down with the rear suspension.

The inner U-joints are connected to flanges which are bolted to the differential output flanges. The outer U-joints are connected to stub shafts which engage the splines of the wheel hubs and are secured by an axle nut.

2.3a Paint or scribe alignment marks across the transmission output flange and front U-joint flange

2.3b . . . and across the rear flexible coupling (shown), or U-joint, and the pinion flange

## 2 Propshaft - removal and refitting

### Removal

1 Raise the car, and support on axle stands.
2 Remove the central section of the exhaust system (see Chapter 4).
3 Using paint, a punch or a scribe, make alignment marks across the transmission output flange and, and across the rear flexible coupling (or U-joint, on later models), to insure that the propshaft is reinstalled in the same position **(see illustrations)**. **Note:** *If you're simply renewing a rear flexible coupling, it's not necessary to remove the propshaft; all you have to do is unbolt it from the flexible coupling* (see Section 3).
4 Support the propshaft at the centre. Remove the two bolts that attach the centre bearing to the crossmember, then remove the crossmember bolts **(see illustration)** and pull out the crossmember.
5 Remove the propshaft assembly.
6 If you're renewing a U-joint or flexible coupling, refer to Section 3. If you're renewing the centre bearing, refer to Section 4.

7 Refitting is the reverse of removal. Be sure to tighten all fasteners to the torque listed in this Chapter's Specifications.

## 3 Propshaft universal joint and flexible coupling - check and renewal

### Check

#### Universal joint(s)

1 U-joint wear is characterised by vibration in the transmission, noise during acceleration or metallic squeaking and grating sounds as the bearings disintegrate.
2 It's easy to check the U-joint(s) for wear with the propshaft installed. To check the rear U-joint, try to turn the propshaft while immobilising the differential input flange. To check the front U-joint, try to turn the propshaft while holding the transmission output flange. Freeplay between the propshaft and the front or rear flanges indicates excessive wear.
3 If the propshaft is already removed, you can check the universal joints by holding the shaft in one hand and turning the yoke or flange with the other. If the axial movement is excessive, renew the propshaft.

#### Flexible coupling

4 Although there's no maintenance interval for the flexible coupling, you should inspect it whenever you're working under the vehicle. The coupling is made of rubber, so it's vulnerable to road grit, heat generated by the exhaust system, and the twisting torque of the propshaft. Inspect the coupling for cracks, tears, missing pieces and distortion. If it's cracked or generally worn, renew it.

### Renewal

#### U-joint

5 Remove the propshaft (see Section 2).
6 Remove the snap-rings from the bearing cups. Use a punch to free them if they're stuck.
7 Place the propshaft in a vice with the yokes of the propshaft (not the flange) resting on the open vice jaws (remember that the propshaft is hollow and easily damaged by too much vice pressure).
8 Using a hammer and a socket which just fits over the bearing cups, gently tap the flange yoke down so that the uppermost bearing cup protrudes from the yoke **(see illustration)**. Remove the cup **(see illustration)**.
9 Rotate the propshaft 180-degrees and repeat this operation on the opposite bearing.

2.4 Remove the crossmember bolts (arrowed) and remove the crossmember

3.8a Tap the flange yoke down . . .

3.8b . . . and remove the bearing cup

3.12 Spider, bearings and snap-rings

3.13a Place the spider in the yoke . . .

3.13b . . . and refit a bearing cup

3.14a Pressing the bearing cup
into the yoke

3.14b Refitting the snap-ring

3.15a Tap the first cup into the
shaft yoke . . .

3.15b . . . refit the other cup . . .

3.15c . . . and press it into place
with the vice

3.22 Remove three nuts (not visible) and
bolts (arrowed) and remove the coupling

**10** The flange can now be removed from the propshaft and the same procedure used to remove the spider from the shaft.

**11** Clean the bearing seats in the flange and propshaft yokes.

**12** Remove the bearings from the new spider **(see illustration)** and make sure that the needle bearings are well greased. If not, thoroughly lubricate them with chassis grease.

**13** Place the spider in the flange yoke **(see illustration)** and refit one bearing cup onto the yoke **(see illustration)**.

**14** Using the vice and a socket of suitable diameter, press the bearing cup into the yoke **(see illustration)**. Refit the snap-ring **(see illustration)**.

**15** Repeat this procedure on the opposite side, then refit the flange yoke and spider on the propshaft yoke (remember to match up your alignment marks) and refit the remaining bearing cups **(see illustrations)**.

**16** Refit the rest of the bearing retaining snap-rings.

**17** Check the joint for full and free movement. If it feels too tight, rest it on the vice and gently tap it with a plastic mallet. This should centre the bearings and free the joint.

**18** Refit the propshaft (see Section 2).

### Flexible coupling

**19** Raise the vehicle and place it securely on axle stands.

**20** Make alignment marks between the propshaft, the coupling and the pinion flange **(see illustration 2.3b)**.

**21** Unbolt the propshaft from the coupling.

**22** Remove the nuts and bolts which hold the coupling to the flange **(see illustration)** and remove the coupling.

**23** Refitting is the reverse of removal. Be sure to match up the alignment marks on the propshaft and the pinion flange.

### 4 Propshaft centre bearing -
check and renewal

### *Check*

**1** The centre bearing consists of a ball-bearing assembly encircled by a rubber mount. The bearing assembly is pressed onto the propshaft and is secured by a snap-ring. The centre bearing is protected by dust caps on either side, but water and dirt can still enter the bearing and ruin it. Propshaft vibration can also lead to bearing failure. To inspect the centre bearing properly, you'll need to remove the propshaft (see Section 2). Conversely, whenever the propshaft is removed for any reason, always inspect the bearing. Rotate the bearing and see if it turns smoothly; if it's difficult to turn, or if it has a gritty feeling, renew it. Also inspect the rubber portion. If it's cracked or deteriorated, renew it.

### *Renewal*

**2** Remove the propshaft assembly.

**3** Take the propshaft to an automotive machine workshop to have the old bearing pressed off and a new bearing pressed on.

### 5  Pinion oil seal - renewal

**1** Raise the rear of the vehicle and place it securely on axle stands.

**2** Disconnect the propshaft and flexible coupling or rear U-joint from the pinion flange (see Section 2).

**3** Make matching marks on the pinion shaft, the flange nut and the flange **(see illustration)**.

**4** Hold the input flange stationary and remove the flange nut.

**5** Using a puller, remove the input flange.

**6** Pry out the old seal with a seal removal tool or a screwdriver. Make sure you don't nick or gouge the seal bore.

**7** Dip the new seal in differential lubricant and drive it into position with a seal driver. If you don't have a seal driver, a large socket or some pipe of the correct diameter will work.

**5.3  Mark the relationship of the pinion flange, nut and shaft**

**8** Lightly lubricate the input shaft and press the input flange back on, but don't bottom it out. Refit the flange nut and, using a torque wrench, slowly tighten the nut, noting the torque at which the marks line up - it should be within or very near the torque range listed in this Chapter's Specifications. If the nut is tightened and the marks are in alignment, but the torque required to align the marks isn't fairly close to the specified torque, the pinion shaft sleeve probably needs to be renewed. Due to the special tools required and the critical nature of the job, renewal of the pinion shaft sleeve should be left to a dealer service department or other qualified repair workshop.

*Caution: If the specified torque is reached before the match marks line up, don't continue to turn the nut until they do. Don't tighten the nut past the match marks and then back it off, as this could over-compress the pinion shaft sleeve.*

### 6  Driveshaft - removal and refitting

**1** Set the handbrake firmly. Loosen the rear wheel nuts, raise the rear of the vehicle and support it securely on axle stands. Remove the wheel.

**2** Remove the brake caliper and disc, disconnect the handbrake cable from the handbrake assembly and unbolt the ABS sensor (see Chapter 9).

**3** Remove the driveshaft nut and washer **(see illustrations)**.

**4** Pull the carrier outward and detach the outer end of the driveshaft from the carrier **(see illustration)**. If the driveshaft is stuck in the hub splines, use a puller to push the driveshaft through the hub.

**5** Remove the four nuts **(see illustration)** which attach the inner U-joint flange to the differential output shaft flange.

**6.3a  Refit a couple of wheel nuts, insert a large prybar between them to hold the hub assembly, and break loose the driveshaft nut**

**6.3b  After removing the driveshaft nut, remove this washer**

**6.4  Swing the carrier assembly out and down and disengage the outer end of the driveshaft from the carrier (disconnect the handbrake cable and ABS sensor first, or they will be damaged)**

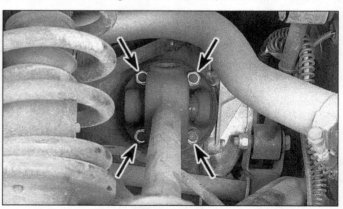

**6.5  To detach the inner driveshaft U-joint from the differential output shaft flange, remove these four nuts (arrowed)**

---

6 Remove the driveshaft assembly.
7 Refitting is the reverse of removal. Be sure to tighten the inner U-joint flange nuts and the driveshaft nut to the torque listed in this Chapter's Specifications.

## 7 Driveshaft universal joints - check and renewal

1 Remove the driveshaft (see Section 6).
2 Renew the U-joints following the procedure described in Section 3.
3 Refit the driveshaft (see Section 6).

## 8 Differential output shaft bearing and seal - renewal

1 Raise the rear of the vehicle and support it securely on axle stands.
2 Drain the differential lubricant (Chapter 1).
3 Separate the driveshaft from the differential (see Section 6) and suspend it out of the way with a piece of wire.
4 Remove the output shaft housing bolts (see illustration) and remove the flange and housing assembly from the differential.
5 Take the flange and housing assembly to a Jaguar service department or an automotive machine workshop to have the bearing and seal renewed.
6 Refitting is the reverse of removal. Be sure to tighten the housing bolts to the torque listed in this Chapter's Specifications.

**8.4 To detach the output shaft housing from the differential, remove these bolts (arrowed) (upper bolts not visible)**

## 9 Differential - removal and refitting

### Removal

**Warning: Do not attempt the following procedure without some help. The differential and rear suspension assembly is heavy. You will need an assistant to help you balance the assembly on the jack as it's lowered to the ground.**

1 Loosen the rear wheel nuts. Raise the rear of the vehicle and place it securely on axle stands. Remove the wheels.
2 Drain the differential lubricant (Chapter 1).
3 Disconnect the propshaft from the pinion flange (see Section 2). Support the end of the propshaft with a piece of wire so the centre bearing isn't damaged. Remove the pinion flange (see Section 5).

4 Remove the brake calipers and hang them out of the way (see Chapter 9). Remove the brake discs. Disconnect the handbrake cables from the handbrake shoes and snake the cables out of the crossmember. Unbolt and remove the ABS sensors. Remove all brackets and cut all cable ties which attach handbrake hoses or lines, ABS electrical harnesses and handbrake cables to the rear suspension. Hang all hoses, lines, harnesses and cables out of the way so that they won't be damaged when the rear suspension/differential assembly is lowered.
5 Unbolt the speed sensor (see illustration) and hang it out of the way (don't hang it by the electrical harness - use a piece of wire).
6 Disconnect the fuel lines (see Chapter 4) and tuck them out of the way. Make sure that the fuel pump, fuel filter and fuel return lines are all clear of the crossmember before proceeding.
7 Support the differential/crossmember assembly with a transmission jack or a floor jack equipped with a transmission holding fixture. Make sure the jack is positioned directly in the centre of the crossmember/differential/suspension assembly, and secure the assembly to the jack with safety chains. Raise the jack just enough to take the weight of the crossmember mounting bolts.
8 Unbolt the lower ends of the shock absorbers from the control arms (Chapter 10).
9 Disconnect the tie bars from the differential (see illustration 9.5).
10 Remove the crossmember mounting bracket bolts (see illustration).
11 Lower the crossmember/differential/rear suspension assembly and remove it from under the vehicle.

**9.5 To detach the speed sensor from the differential, remove these two bolts (arrowed), then hang the sensor out of the way with a piece of wire; to disconnect the tie bars from the differential, remove the nut (lower arrow) and bolt (left tie bar shown)**

**9.10 To detach the crossmember from the body, remove these bolts (arrowed) from each mounting bracket (left bracket shown)**

**9.12a To detach the front of the differential from the crossmember, remove these four nuts (arrowed) (two upper nuts not visible)**

**9.12b To detach the crossmember from the underside of the differential, remove these bolts (arrowed) (assembly is shown still attached to vehicle)**

**9.14 To detach the front and rear control arm mounting brackets from the differential, remove these nuts (arrowed) and bolts (rear bracket shown)**

**12** Disconnect the crossmember from the differential **(see illustrations)**.

**13** Disconnect the driveshafts from the differential (see Section 6).

**14** Disconnect the rear control arms from the differential (see Chapter 10). Unbolt the front and rear control arm brackets from the differential **(see illustration)**.

**15** Refitting is the reverse of removal. Be sure to tighten all critical fasteners to the torque listed in this Chapter's Specifications and the Chapter 9 and 10 Specifications.

### Refitting

**16** Position the differential housing in place against its mounts and loosely refit the bolts (don't tighten any of them until they are all installed), then tighten all fasteners securely.

**17** Refitting is now the reverse of removal.

# Chapter 9
# Braking system

## Contents

## Degrees of difficulty

| | | | | |
|---|---|---|---|---|
| **Easy,** suitable for novice with little experience  | **Fairly easy,** suitable for beginner with some experience  | **Fairly difficult,** suitable for competent DIY mechanic  | **Difficult,** suitable for experienced DIY mechanic  | **Very difficult,** suitable for expert DIY or professional |

## Specifications

### General

| | |
|---|---|
| Brake fluid type . . . . . . . . . . . . . . . . . . . . . . . . . . . . . . . . . . . . . . . . . | See Chapter 1 |
| Minimum brake pad thickness . . . . . . . . . . . . . . . . . . . . . . . . . . . . . . . | See Chapter 1 |
| Brake disc minimum permissible thickness . . . . . . . . . . . . . . . . . . . . . | Cast into disc |
| Parallelism . . . . . . . . . . . . . . . . . . . . . . . . . . . . . . . . . . . . . . . . . . . . . | 0.013 mm (0.0005 inch) maximum |
| Runout . . . . . . . . . . . . . . . . . . . . . . . . . . . . . . . . . . . . . . . . . . . . . . . . | 0.102 mm (0.004 inch) maximum |

### Torque wrench settings

| | Nm | lbf ft |
|---|---|---|
| Brake servo mounting nuts . . . . . . . . . . . . . . . . . . . . . . . . . . . . . . . . . | 10 | 7 |
| Caliper bolts (front and rear) . . . . . . . . . . . . . . . . . . . . . . . . . . . . . . . . | 31 to 40 | 23 to 29 |
| Caliper bracket bolts | | |
|   Front bracket . . . . . . . . . . . . . . . . . . . . . . . . . . . . . . . . . . . . . . . | 102 to 128 | 75 to 94 |
|   Rear bracket . . . . . . . . . . . . . . . . . . . . . . . . . . . . . . . . . . . . . . . . | 55 to 62 | 40 to 45 |
| Master cylinder-to-brake servo nuts . . . . . . . . . . . . . . . . . . . . . . . . . . | 22 to 28 | 16 to 20 |
| Wheel nuts . . . . . . . . . . . . . . . . . . . . . . . . . . . . . . . . . . . . . . . . . . . . . | See Chapter 1 Specifications | |

## 1 General information

All models covered by this manual are equipped with hydraulically operated front and rear disc brake systems. Both front and rear brakes are self adjusting.

### Hydraulic system

The hydraulic system is divided into two separate circuits. The master cylinder has separate reservoirs for the two circuits, and, in the event of a leak or failure in one hydraulic circuit, the other circuit will remain operative. All models are equipped with an Anti-lock Braking System (ABS).

### Brake servo

A hydraulic brake servo system is used on all models covered by this manual. This system uses hydraulic pressure from an engine-driven pump on models equipped with a power hydraulic system, and an electric pump on models without the power hydraulic system.

### Handbrake

The handbrake lever operates the rear brakes through cable actuation. It's activated by a lever mounted in the centre console. The handbrake assembly uses a pair of brake shoes located inside the rear hub/brake disc.

### Brake pad wear warning system

The brake pad wear warning system turns on a red light in the instrument cluster when the brake pads have worn down to the point at which they must be replaced. Do NOT ignore this reminder. If you don't renew the pads shortly after the brake pad wear warning light comes on, the brake discs will be damaged.

The wear sensors are attached to the brake pads. Once the pads wear down to the point at which they're flush with the sensor, the disc grinds away the side of the sensor facing the disc, the wire inside the sensor is broken, the circuit is opened and the red light on the instrument panel comes on.

Always check the sensor(s) when replacing the pads. If you change the pads before the warning light comes on, the sensor(s) may still be good; once the light has come on, renew the sensor.

### Service

After completing any operation involving dismantling of any part of the brake system, always test drive the vehicle to check for proper braking performance before resuming normal driving. When testing the brakes, perform the tests on a clean, dry, flat surface. Conditions other than these can lead to inaccurate test results.

Test the brakes at various speeds with both light and heavy pedal pressure. The vehicle should stop evenly without pulling to one side or the other. Avoid locking the brakes, because this slides the tyres and diminishes braking efficiency and control of the vehicle.

Tyres, vehicle load and wheel alignment are factors which also affect braking performance.

## 2 Anti-lock Brake system (ABS) - general information

The Anti-lock Brake System is designed to maintain vehicle steerability, directional stability and optimum deceleration under severe braking conditions on most road surfaces. It does so by monitoring the rotational speed of each wheel and controlling the brake line pressure to each wheel during braking. This prevents the wheels from locking up.

The ABS system has three main units - the wheel speed sensors, the electronic control unit and the modulator (hydraulic control unit). The sensors - one at each wheel - send a variable voltage signal to the electronic control unit, which monitors these signals, compares them to its program and determines whether a wheel is about to lock up. When a wheel is about to lock up, the control unit signals the hydraulic unit to reduce hydraulic pressure (or not increase it further) at that wheel's brake caliper. Pressure modulation is handled by three electrically-operated solenoid valves - one for each front wheel and one for the rear wheels - inside the modulator.

If a problem develops within the system, an "ABS" warning light will glow on the dashboard. Sometimes, a visual inspection of the ABS system can help you locate the problem. Carefully inspect the ABS wiring harness. Pay particularly close attention to the harness and connections near each wheel. Look for signs of chafing and other damage caused by incorrectly routed wires. If a wheel sensor harness is damaged, the sensor should be replaced (the harness and sensor are integral).

⚠ *Warning: Do NOT try to repair an ABS wiring harness. The ABS system is sensitive to even the*

*smallest changes in resistance. Repairing the harness could alter resistance values and cause the system to malfunction. If the ABS wiring harness is damaged in any way, it must be replaced.*
*Caution: Make sure the ignition is turned off before unplugging or reattaching any electrical connections.*

### Diagnosis and repair

If a dashboard warning light comes on and stays on while the vehicle is in operation, the ABS system requires attention. Although special electronic ABS diagnostic testing tools are necessary to properly diagnose the system, you can perform a few preliminary checks before taking the vehicle to a dealer service department or other qualified repair workshop.

a) *Check the brake fluid level in the master cylinder reservoir.*
b) *Verify that all ABS system electrical connectors in the engine compartment are plugged in.*
c) *Check the fuses.*
d) *Follow the wiring harness to each front wheel and to the differential sensor and verify that all connections are secure and that the wiring is undamaged.*

If the above preliminary checks do not rectify the problem, the vehicle should be diagnosed by a dealer service department. Due to the complex nature of this system, all actual repair work must be done by a dealer service department or other qualified repair workshop.

## 3 Disc brake pads - renewal

⚠ *Warning: Disc brake pads must be replaced on both front wheels or both rear wheels at the same time - never renew the pads on only one wheel. Also, the dust created by the brake system may contain asbestos, which is harmful to your health. Never blow it out with compressed air and don't inhale any of it. An approved filtering mask should be worn when working on the brakes. Do not, under any circumstances, use petroleum-based solvents to clean brake parts. Use brake system cleaner only!*
**Note:** *The following procedure applies to both the front and rear brake pads.*

1 Remove the cap from the brake fluid reservoir and siphon off about two-thirds of the fluid from the reservoir. Failing to do this could result in fluid overflowing when the caliper pistons are pressed into their bores.
2 Loosen the wheel nuts, raise the front of the vehicle and support it securely on axle stands.
3 Remove the front wheels. Work on one brake assembly at a time, using the assembled brake for reference if necessary.
4 Inspect the brake disc (see Section 5).
5 Follow the accompanying photos, beginning with **illustration 3.5a**, for the pad removal procedure. Be sure to stay in order and read the caption under each illustration.

**3.5a  Before starting, wash down the caliper and disc with brake cleaner**

**3.5b  Attach a hose to the bleed screw, open the bleed screw slightly and depress the piston into the caliper. Tighten the bleed screw when the piston bottoms**

**3.5c  Remove the caliper mounting bolts (upper bolt arrowed); use another spanner to hold the flats of the caliper guide pins while you back out the caliper bolts**

**3.5d  Remove the caliper . . .**

**3.5e  . . . and suspend it out of the way with a piece of wire**

3.5f  Remove the outer brake pad

3.5g  Remove the inner brake pad

3.5h  Pull out the wear sensor, trace the sensor lead back to its plug, detach the lead from the suspension, and discard it

3.5i  Remove the caliper guide pins and boots (lower pin and boot shown) . . .

3.5j  . . . clean them off, inspect the pin and boot for damage, renew as necessary, then lubricate the pins with brake grease and refit them in the caliper bracket

3.5k  Apply anti-squeal compound to the new brake pads

**6** Be sure to buy new pads with wear sensors. Pattern pads may not have wear sensors; refitting pads without wear sensors will cause the dash warning light to come on.
**7** To refit the new pads, reverse the removal procedure. When refitting the caliper, be sure to tighten the mounting bolts to the torque listed in this Chapter's Specifications.
**8** After the job is completed, depress the brake pedal a few times to bring the pads into contact with the discs. The pedal should be at normal height above the floorpan and firm. Check the brake fluid level and add enough to top it up (see Chapter 1). Inspect carefully for leaks and check the operation of the brakes before placing the vehicle into normal service.
**9** Tighten the wheel nuts to the specified torque.

3.5l  Insert the new wear sensor into the inner pad as shown . . .

3.5m  . . . then refit the inner pad onto the caliper bracket

---

**4  Disc brake caliper** - removal, overhaul and refitting

> ⚠️ **Warning: Dust created by the brake system may contain asbestos, which is harmful to your health. Never blow it out with compressed air and don't inhale any of it. An approved filtering mask should be worn when working on the brakes. Do not, under any circumstances, use petroleum-based solvents to clean brake parts. Use brake system cleaner only!**

**Note 1:** *The following procedure applies to both front and rear calipers.*
**Note 2:** *If an overhaul is indicated, explore all options before beginning the job. New and*

3.5n  Refit the outer pad

3.5o  Refit the caliper, then tighten the mounting bolts to the specified torque

*factory rebuilt calipers are available on an exchange basis, which makes this job quite easy. If you decide to rebuild the calipers, make sure a rebuild kit is available before proceeding. Always rebuild the calipers in pairs - never rebuild just one of them.*

### Removal

**1** Loosen the wheel nuts, raise the front or rear of the vehicle and place it securely on axle stands. Remove the wheel.
**2** If you're just removing the caliper for access to other components, it isn't

4.2 Use a flare-nut spanner to protect the brake hose fitting when unscrewing it from the caliper

4.5 With the caliper padded to catch the piston, use compressed air to force the piston out of its bore - make sure your fingers are not between the piston and the caliper

necessary to detach the brake line. If you're removing the caliper for overhaul, detach the hose from the metal line at the frame bracket (see Section 8), then disconnect the brake line from the caliper with a flare-nut spanner to protect the fitting **(see illustration)**. Plug the metal line to keep contaminants out of the brake system and to prevent losing brake fluid.

**3** Refer to illustration 3.5c and unbolt the front or rear caliper.

### *Overhaul*

**4** Before you remove the piston, place a wood block between the piston and caliper to prevent damage as it is removed.

**5** To remove the piston from the caliper, apply compressed air to the brake fluid hose connection on the caliper body **(see illustration)**. Use only enough pressure to ease the piston out of its bore. Remove the dust boot.

 *Warning: Be careful not to place your fingers between the piston and the caliper as the piston may come out with some force. Be sure to wear eye protection when using compressed air.*

**6** Inspect the mating surfaces of the piston and caliper bore wall. If there is any scoring, rust, pitting or bright areas, renew the complete caliper unit with a new one.

**7** If these components are in good condition, remove the piston seal from the caliper bore using a wooden or plastic tool **(see illustration)**. Metal tools may damage the cylinder bore.

**8** Remove the caliper guide pins and the rubber dust boots from the caliper bracket.

**9** Wash all the components in brake system cleaner.

**10** Using the correct rebuild kit for your vehicle, reassemble the caliper as follows.

**11** Submerge the new rubber seal in clean brake fluid and refit it in the lower groove in the caliper bore, making sure it isn't twisted.

**12** Coat the piston with clean brake fluid and stretch the new dust boot over the bottom of the piston. Hold the piston over the caliper bore and insert the rubber flange of the dust boot into the upper groove in the bore. Start with the side farthest from you and work your way around toward the front until it is completely seated. Push the piston into the caliper bore until it is bottomed in the bore, then seat the top of the dust boot in the groove in the piston.

**13** Lubricate the sliding surfaces of the guide pins with silicone-based grease (usually supplied in the kit), then refit the new dust boots and pins into the caliper bracket.

### *Refitting*

**14** Refit the caliper by reversing the removal procedure (see Section 3).

**15** If the brake hose was disconnected from the caliper, bleed the brake system (see Section 9).

4.7 Remove the piston seal from the caliper bore using a wooden or plastic tool (metal tools may damage the cylinder bore)

## 5 Brake disc - inspection, removal and refitting

**Note:** *The following procedure applies to both the front and rear brake discs.*

### *Inspection*

**1** Loosen the wheel nuts, raise the vehicle and support it securely on axle stands. Remove the wheel and refit three nuts to hold the disc in place. If the rear brake disc is being worked on, release the handbrake.

**2** Remove the brake caliper as outlined in Section 4. It is not necessary to disconnect the brake hose. After removing the caliper, suspend it out of the way with a piece of wire.

**3** Visually inspect the disc surface for scoring or damage. Light scratches and shallow grooves are normal after use and may not always be detrimental to brake operation, but deep scoring - over 0.015 inch - requires disc removal and refinishing by an automotive machine shop. Be sure to check both sides of the disc **(see illustration)**. If pulsating has

5.3 The brake pads on this vehicle were obviously neglected, as they wore down to the rivets and cut deep grooves into the disc - this disc must be replaced

**5.4a To check disc runout, mount a dial indicator as shown and rotate the disc**

**5.4b Using a swirling motion, remove the glaze from the disc surface with sandpaper or emery cloth**

**5.5a The disc thickness can be checked with a micrometer**

**5.5b Compare your measurement with the minimum thickness stamped into the disc**

**5.6a Before you can remove the caliper mounting bracket bolts (arrowed) and the bracket, you'll have to cut the safety wire between them with a pair of diagonal cutters (rear bracket shown)**

**5.6b On front caliper brackets, remove the ABS wheel speed sensor bolt (centre arrow) and pull out the sensor before removing the bracket bolts (upper and lower arrows) and bracket**

been noticed during application of the brakes, suspect disc runout.

**4** To check disc runout, place a dial indicator at a point about 1/2-inch from the outer edge of the disc **(see illustration)**. Set the indicator to zero and turn the disc. The indicator reading should not exceed the specified allowable runout limit. If it does, the disc should be refinished by an automotive machine workshop. **Note:** *It is recommended that the discs be resurfaced regardless of the dial indicator reading, as this will impart a smooth finish and ensure a perfectly flat surface, eliminating any brake pedal pulsation or other undesirable symptoms related to questionable discs. At the very least, if you elect not to have the discs resurfaced, remove*

*the glazing from the surface with emery cloth or sandpaper using a swirling motion* **(see illustration)**.

**5** It is absolutely critical that the disc not be machined to a thickness under the specified minimum allowable thickness. The disc thickness can be checked with a micrometer **(see illustration)**. Then compare your measurement to the minimum wear (or discard) thickness stamped into the hub of the disc after the disc is removed **(see illustration)**.

### Removal

**6** Cut the safety wire from the caliper bracket mounting bolts **(see illustration)**. On front caliper brackets, remove the ABS wheel

speed sensor **(see illustration)**, then remove the caliper bracket bolts and remove the bracket.

**7** Remove the disc retaining screw **(see illustration)** and remove the disc from the hub. If the disc sticks, give it a few sharp raps with a hammer **(see illustration)**. If the disc is stuck to the hub, spray a generous amount of penetrant onto the area between the hub and the disc and allow the penetrant a few minutes to loosen the rust between the two components. If a rear disc still sticks, insert a thin, flat-bladed screwdriver or brake adjusting tool through the hub flange, rotate the star wheel on the handbrake adjusting screw and contract the handbrake shoes **(see illustration)**.

**5.7a Using an impact driver, if necessary, remove the disc retaining screw, then remove the disc from the hub**

**5.7b If the disc is stuck to the hub, give it a few sharp raps with a hammer**

**5.7c If a rear disc is stuck to the hub, insert a suitable tool through the hub flange and retract the handbrake shoes**

6.4 Trace the electrical lead back from the reservoir cap and disconnect the low fluid level sensor

6.5 Loosen the hydraulic brake line fittings with a flare-nut spanner to protect the corners of the nuts

## Refitting

8 Place the disc on the hub and refit the disc retaining screw. Tighten the screw securely.
9 Refit the caliper mounting bracket, using a new safety wire on the mounting bolts.
10 Refit the brake pads and caliper (see Section 3). Tighten all fasteners to the torque listed in this Chapter's Specifications.
11 Refit the wheel and wheel nuts, then lower the vehicle to the ground. Tighten the wheel nuts to the specified torque (see Chapter 1 Specifications). Depress the brake pedal a few times to bring the brake pads into contact with the disc.
12 Adjust the handbrake shoes, if necessary.
13 Check the operation of the brakes carefully, if possible before driving the vehicle on public roads.

## 6 Master cylinder - removal, overhaul and refitting

**Note:** *Although master cylinder parts and rebuild kits are available for most models, we recommend replacing the master cylinder with a new or remanufactured unit, if possible.*

## Removal

1 The master cylinder is connected to the brake servo, which is attached to the pedal box, in front of the bulkhead on the driver's side of the engine compartment.
2 Remove as much fluid as you can from the reservoir with a syringe.
3 Place rags under the line fittings and prepare caps or plastic bags to cover the ends of the lines once they are disconnected. *Caution: Brake fluid will damage paint. Cover all body parts and be careful not to spill fluid during this procedure.*
4 Disconnect the electrical connector for the low fluid level warning light **(see illustration)**.
5 Loosen the brake line fittings at the master

cylinder **(see illustration)**. Use a flare-nut spanner to prevent rounding off the nuts. Pull the brake lines away from the master cylinder slightly and plug the ends to prevent contamination.
6 Remove the nuts attaching the master cylinder to the servo **(see illustration)**. Pull the master cylinder off the studs and lift it out of the engine compartment. Again, be careful not to spill fluid as this is done.

## Overhaul

7 Follow the accompanying photo sequence, beginning with **illustration 6.7a**. Stay in order,

don't skip steps, read each caption and study the photo carefully.
8 Once you have dismantled the master cylinder, clean everything thoroughly, blow the parts dry with compressed air and carefully inspect the secondary piston and the bore of the master cylinder with a bright light. If the secondary piston or the master cylinder bore is damaged or worn, renew the master cylinder with a new or rebuilt unit.

## Bench bleeding procedure

9 Before refitting a new or rebuilt master cylinder it should be bench bled. Because it

6.6 Remove the two master cylinder mounting nuts

6.7a Knock out the roll pin that secures the reservoir to the master cylinder

6.7b Carefully pry off the reservoir by inserting a screwdriver between the reservoir and each grommet; this takes firm pressure, so don't slip and damage the reservoir or the master cylinder

6.7c Remove the grommets, noting the position of each one

6.7d Pry off the end cap

6.7e Locate the stopper pin (arrowed) inside the forward grommet hole . . .

6.7f . . . insert a punch into the pocket of the primary piston, place the master cylinder vertically as shown, push down on the master cylinder to depress the pistons and pull out the stopper pin with a magnet

6.7g Remove the primary piston

6.7h Remove the secondary piston

6.7i If the secondary piston is stuck, rap the master cylinder on a wood block to dislodge it

6.7j Remove the seals and cups from the pistons - be very careful not to scratch the piston surface - then wash the secondary piston with clean brake fluid and inspect it; if the secondary piston is damaged, you must renew the master cylinder with a new or rebuilt unit (a new primary piston is included with the rebuild kit)

6.7k Refit the new O-ring seals and cups as shown; make sure the cups on the primary piston (the one on the left) face forward as shown (toward the spring), and the cups on the secondary piston (the one on the right) face out, away from the piston (the one on the left faces toward the primary piston, the one on the right faces toward the spring)

6.7l The master cylinder assembly

1  Roll pin
2  Reservoir
3  Grommets
4  End plate
5  Primary piston
6  Secondary piston stopper pin
7  Secondary piston

6.7m Apply some clean brake fluid to the secondary piston and refit it with the slot oriented with the stopper pin hole, so that the stopper pin will go through the slot

6.7n Apply a coat of clean brake fluid to the primary piston and refit it into the bore

6.7o Using the same technique as in illustration 6.7f, depress the pistons and refit the stopper pin

6.7p Refit the end plate as shown, with the bend in the plate flange aligned with the groove in the master cylinder flange

6.7q Using a hammer and punch, stake the end plate as shown (there's a dimple in the side of the plate for this purpose)

6.7r Refit the grommets

will be necessary to apply pressure to the master cylinder piston and, at the same time, control flow from the brake line outlets, it is recommended that the master cylinder be mounted in a vice. Use caution not to clamp the vice too tightly, or the master cylinder body might crack.

**10** Insert threaded plugs into the brake line outlet holes and snug them down so that there will be no air leakage past them, but not so tight that they cannot be easily loosened.

**11** Fill the reservoir with brake fluid of the recommended type (see *Recommended lubricants and fluids* in Chapter 1).

**12** Remove one plug and push the piston assembly into the master cylinder bore to expel the air from the master cylinder. A large Phillips screwdriver can be used to push on the piston assembly.

**13** To prevent air from being drawn back into the master cylinder, the plug must be replaced and tightened before releasing the pressure on the piston assembly.

**14** Repeat the procedure until only brake fluid is expelled from the brake line outlet hole. When only brake fluid is expelled, repeat the procedure with the other outlet hole and plug. Be sure to keep the master cylinder reservoir filled with brake fluid to prevent the introduction of air into the system.

**15** Since high pressure is not involved in the bench bleeding procedure, an alternative to the removal and renewal of the plugs with

6.7s Align the reservoir pipes with the grommets as shown . . .

6.7t . . . and squeeze the reservoir and master cylinder together; make sure the reservoir is fully seated

6.7u Refit the reservoir roll pin . . .

6.7v . . . and tap it into place

each stroke of the piston assembly is available. Before pushing in on the piston assembly, remove the plug as described in

Step 12. Before releasing the piston, however, instead of replacing the plug, simply put your finger tightly over the hole to keep air from

7.5 Use a flare-nut spanner to loosen the fittings, then pull the lines back from the brake servo and plug them to prevent contamination

7.6 Pry off the two rubber caps from the pedal box

7.7 To detach the brake servo from the pedal box, remove these four nuts (arrowed) (lower right nut not visible in this photo)

being drawn back into the master cylinder. Wait several seconds for brake fluid to be drawn from the reservoir into the piston bore, then depress the piston again, removing your finger as brake fluid is expelled. Be sure to put your finger back over the hole each time before releasing the piston, and when the bleeding procedure is complete for that outlet, renew the plug and snug it up before going on to the other port.

### Refitting

16 Refit the master cylinder over the studs on the brake servo and tighten the mounting nuts only finger tight at this time.
17 Thread the brake line fittings into the master cylinder. Since the master cylinder is still a bit loose, it can be moved slightly to allow the fitting threads to start easily. Do not strip the threads as the fittings are tightened.
18 Tighten the brake fittings securely and the mounting nuts to the torque listed in this Chapter's Specifications.
19 Fill the master cylinder reservoir with fluid, then bleed the master cylinder and the brake system (see Section 9).
20 To bleed the master cylinder on the vehicle, have an assistant pump the brake pedal several times and then hold the pedal to the floor. Loosen the fitting nut to allow air and fluid to escape, then tighten the nut. Repeat this procedure on both fittings until the fluid is clear of air bubbles. Test the operation of the brake system carefully before placing the vehicle into service.

### 7 Brake servo - general information, removal and refitting

### General information

1 A hydraulic brake servo system assists braking when the brake pedal is depressed. The booster unit, located between the brake pedal box and the master cylinder, is operated by hydraulic pressure generated by an engine-driven pump (on early models) or by an electric pump (on later models). When the engine is

running, the pump supplies hydraulic pressure to an accumulator. The accumulator stores and regulates the pressure to the hydraulic brake servo. When you depress the brake pedal, the pressure in the booster helps actuate the master cylinder, reducing pedal effort.
2 The hydraulic brake servo isn't rebuildable; if it fails, it must be replaced. Basic operation can be checked (see Chapter 1, Section 15), but in-depth testing of the system requires special tools, so diagnosis is beyond the scope of the home mechanic. If the system fails, take it to a dealer service department or other qualified repair workshop for repairs. However, if the unit must be replaced, you can do it yourself as follows.

### Removal and refitting

3 With the engine off, discharge the hydraulic accumulator by depressing the brake pedal several times until it feels hard to depress.
4 Remove the master cylinder (see Section 6).
5 Clean the area around the return and supply tube nuts, then disconnect them with a flare-nut spanner (see illustration). Plug the lines to prevent dirt from entering the system.
*Caution: Even a particle of dirt can damage the servo system, so be extremely careful to prevent dirt from entering the system while the lines are disconnected.*
6 To disconnect the brake servo pushrod from the brake pedal, remove the access plugs from both sides of the pedal box (see illustration), remove the clevis pin retaining clip and drive out the clevis pin.
7 Remove the four mounting nuts and remove the brake servo (see illustration).
8 Refitting is the reverse of removal. Tighten the hydraulic line fittings securely.
9 When you're done, adjust the brake light switch (see Section 13).

### 8 Brake hoses and lines - inspection and renewal

### Inspection

1 About every six months, with the vehicle

raised and placed securely on axle stands, the flexible hoses which connect the steel brake lines with the front and rear brake assemblies should be inspected for cracks, chafing of the outer cover, leaks, blisters and other damage. These are important and vulnerable parts of the brake system and inspection should be complete. A light and mirror will prove helpful for a thorough check. If a hose exhibits any of the above conditions, renew it with a new one.

### Flexible hose renewal

2 Clean all dirt away from the ends of the hose.
3 To disconnect the hose at the frame end, use a second spanner on the hex-shaped fitting on the end of the flexible hose and loosen the nut on the metal brake line (see illustrations). If the nut is stuck, soak it with penetrating oil. After the hose is disconnected from the metal line, remove the nut right above the bracket and detach the hose from the bracket.
4 To detach the flexible hose from the caliper, simply unscrew it.
5 Refitting is the reverse of the removal procedure. Make sure the brackets are in good condition and the locknuts are tightened securely.

8.3a To remove a front flexible brake hose from a metal brake line, use one spanner to hold the hose fitting just below the bracket (lower spanner), then break loose the nut on the metal line (upper spanner); to disconnect the flex hose from the bracket, remove the centre nut (arrowed) just above the bracket

8.3b **The connection (arrowed) for the rear hose and line is located right above the mounting bracket for the front corner of the differential crossmember; remove the hose as described in the previous illustration**

6 Carefully check to make sure the suspension and steering components do not make contact with the hoses. Have an assistant push on the vehicle and also turn the steering wheel from lock-to-lock during inspection.

7 Bleed the brake system (see Section 9).

### Metal brake line renewal

8 When replacing brake lines, use the proper parts only. Do not use copper line for any brake system connections. Purchase steel brake lines from a dealer or motor factors..

9 Unless you're using factory renewal brake lines, you may need a tubing bender to bend the lines to the proper shape.

10 First, remove the line you intend to renew, lay it on a clean workbench and measure it carefully. Obtain a new line of the same length and bend it to match the pattern of the old line.

 *Warning: Do not crimp or damage the line. No bend should have a smaller radius than 9/16-inch. Make sure the protective coating on the new line is undamaged at the bends.*

11 When refitting the new line, make sure it's well supported by the brackets, the routing matches the original and there's plenty of clearance between moving or hot components.

12 After refitting, check the master cylinder fluid level and add fluid as necessary. Bleed the brake system as outlined in Section 9 and test the brakes carefully before driving the vehicle. Be sure there are no leaks.

### 9 Brake hydraulic system - bleeding

 *Warning: Wear eye protection when bleeding the brake system. If the fluid comes in contact with your eyes, immediately rinse them with water and seek medical attention.*

9.9 **When bleeding the brakes, a hose is connected to the bleed screw at the caliper or wheel cylinder and then submerged in brake fluid - air will be seen as bubbles in the tube and container (all air must be expelled before moving to the next brake)**

**Note:** *Bleeding the hydraulic system is necessary to remove any air which has entered the system during removal and refitting of a hose, line, caliper or master cylinder.*

1 It will probably be necessary to bleed the system at all four brakes if air has entered the system due to low fluid level or if the brake lines have been disconnected at the master cylinder.

2 If a brake line was disconnected at only one wheel, then only that caliper or wheel cylinder must be bled.

3 If a brake line is disconnected at a fitting located between the master cylinder and any of the brakes, that part of the system served by the disconnected line must be bled.

4 Bleed the right rear, the left rear, the right front and the left front caliper, in that order, when the entire system is involved.

5 Remove any residual vacuum from the servo and pressure in the anti-lock braking system (if equipped) by applying the brake about 30 times with the engine off.

6 Remove the master cylinder reservoir cover and fill the reservoir with brake fluid. Refit the cover. **Note:** *Check the fluid level often during the bleeding operation and add fluid as necessary to prevent the fluid level from falling low enough to allow air into the master cylinder.*

7 Have an assistant on hand, as well as a supply of new brake fluid, an empty clear plastic container, a length of 3/16-inch clear tubing to fit over the bleed screws and a spanner to open and close the bleed screws.

8 Beginning at the right rear wheel, loosen the bleed screw slightly, then tighten it to a point where it is snug but can still be loosened quickly and easily.

9 Place one end of the tubing over the bleed valve and submerge the other end in brake fluid in the container **(see illustration)**.

10 Have the assistant pump the brakes a few times to build pressure in the system, then hold the pedal firmly depressed.

11 While the pedal is held depressed, open the bleed screw just enough to allow fluid to flow from the caliper. Watch for air bubbles to

exit the submerged end of the tube. When the fluid flow slows after a couple of seconds, close the screw and have your assistant release the pedal.

12 Repeat Steps 10 and 11 until no more air is seen leaving the tube, then tighten the bleed screw and proceed to the left rear wheel, the right front wheel and the left front wheel, in that order, and perform the same procedure. Be sure to check the fluid in the master cylinder reservoir frequently.

13 Never reuse old brake fluid. It contains contaminates and moisture which could damage the braking system.

14 Refill the master cylinder with fluid at the end of the operation.

15 Check the operation of the brakes. The pedal should feel solid when depressed, with no sponginess. If necessary, repeat the entire process.

 *Warning: Do not drive the car if in doubt about the effectiveness of the brake system.*

### 10 Handbrake cable - adjustment

1 Slowly apply the handbrake and count the number of clicks at the lever. It should be fully applied within three to five clicks. If the lever is still not fully applied by the fifth click, adjust the handbrake cable as follows:

2 Raise the vehicle and place it securely on axle stands.

3 Loosen the locknut **(see illustration)** and tighten the cable adjuster until all slack has been removed. Tighten the locknut. Make sure the wheels turn freely with the handbrake lever released

4 Lower the vehicle and recheck the handbrake lever. It should now be properly adjusted. If it's now fully applied within three to five clicks, raise the vehicle again and readjust the cable at the adjuster.

5 Make sure the handbrake holds the vehicle on an incline.

10.3 **To adjust the handbrake cable, loosen the locknut, then turn the adjuster to remove any slack in the cable; be sure to tighten the locknut when the cable is properly adjusted**

11.2 To disconnect the forward end of the front cable from the handbrake lever, remove this cotter pin, washer and clevis pin

11.3 To disconnect the rear end of the front cable from the adjuster lever, remove this cotter pin, washer and clevis pin (arrowed)

11.5 To disconnect the intermediate cable, remove the cotter pins, washers and clevis pins (arrowed) from the adjuster lever and the yoke

## 11 Handbrake cable(s) - renewal

1 Raise the vehicle and place it securely on axle stands.

### Front cable

2 Remove the cotter pin, washer and clevis pin from the forward end of the front cable **(see illustration)**. Disconnect the forward end of the front cable from the handbrake lever.
3 Follow the cable back to the adjuster lever and remove the cotter, washer and clevis pin **(see illustration)**. Remove the front cable.
4 Refitting is the reverse of removal.

### Intermediate cable

5 Remove the cotter pins, washers and clevis pin from both ends of the intermediate cable **(see illustration)**. Remove the cable.
6 Refitting is the reverse of removal.

### Rear cables

7 Remove the cotter pin, washer and clevis pin from the intermediate cable-to-rear cable yoke **(see illustration)**.
8 Disconnect the rear end of each cable from the handbrake assembly **(see illustration)**., then pry the cable out of the carrier.
9 Refitting is the reverse of removal.

### All cables

10 Be sure to adjust the handbrake cable when you're done (see Section 10). The rear wheels should turn freely with the handbrake lever released.
11 Remove the axle stands and lower the vehicle. Apply the handbrake lever, make sure it's fully applied within three to five clicks and that it holds the vehicle on an incline. If it doesn't, readjust it (see Section 10).

## 12 Handbrake shoes - check and renewal

**Warning: Dust created by the brake system may contain asbestos, which is harmful to your health. Never blow it out with compressed air and don't inhale any of it. An approved filtering mask should be worn when working on the brakes. Do not, under any circumstances, use petroleum-based solvents to clean brake parts. Use brake system cleaner only!**

### Check

1 The handbrake system should be checked regularly. With the car parked on a hill, apply the brake, place the transmission in Neutral and check that the handbrake alone will hold the car (be sure to stay in the car during this check). However, every 24 months (or

11.7 To disconnect the rear cables and yoke from the intermediate cable, remove this cotter pin, washer and clevis pin (arrowed)

11.8 The rear handbrake cable-to-handbrake shoe connection is hidden behind the lower part of the brake backing plate, on the underside of the carrier (this view is looking straight up from underneath the carrier). To disconnect either rear handbrake cable, swing this clip (arrowed) to the side and remove it - the rear cable is now disconnected

**12.5a Wash down the handbrake assembly with brake cleaner before dismantling**

**12.5b Back off the star wheel on the adjuster, then disengage the adjuster mechanism from the handbrake shoes**

**12.5c Remove the front hold-down spring, washers and pin; note that one washer goes below the spring and one above it**

**12.5d Remove the rear hold-down spring, washers and pin; put the parts in a plastic bag so you don't lose them**

**12.5e Push the shoes together and disengage the upper return spring from the rear shoe . . .**

**12.5f . . . and from the front shoe**

**12.5g Pull the shoes apart and remove them with the lower spring attached as shown, then disengage the lower return spring from both shoes**

**12.5h The handbrake shoe assembly**

| | |
|---|---|
| 1  Adjuster | 3  Upper return spring |
| 2  Hold down springs and washers | 4  Lower return spring |
| | 5  Handbrake shoes |

whenever a fault is suspected), the assembly itself should be visually inspected.

**2** Loosen the wheel nuts, raise the rear of the vehicle and place it securely on axle stands. Remove the rear wheels.

**3** Remove the rear brake calipers and discs (see Sections 3, 4 and 5). Support the caliper assemblies with a coat hanger or heavy wire and do not disconnect the brake line from the caliper.

**4** With the disc removed, the handbrake components are visible and can be inspected for wear and damage. The linings should last the life of the vehicle. However, they can wear down if the handbrake system has been improperly adjusted. There is no minimum thickness specification for the handbrake shoes, but as a rule of thumb, if the shoe material is less 1/32-inch thick, you should renew them. Also check the springs and

adjuster mechanism and inspect the drum for deep scratches and other damage.

### Renewal

**5** Loosen the wheel nuts, raise the rear of the vehicle and place it securely on axle stands. Remove the rear wheels. Remove the brake discs (see Section 5). Follow the accompanying photo sequence beginning with **illustration 12.5a**. Work on only one side

12.5i Lubricate the six friction points (two arrowed) on the backing plate with high-temperature brake grease

12.5j Place the front shoe in position, insert the pin through the backing plate and the shoe . . .

12.5k . . . and refit the hold-down spring and washers

12.5l Hook the lower return spring into its hole in the front shoe . . .

12.5m . . . hook the other end of the lower spring into the rear shoe . . .

12.5n . . . stretch the spring over the top of the handbrake lever box . . .

at a time, so you can use the other side as a reference during reassembly.

**6** Refitting is the reverse of removal.

**7** After refitting the brake disc, adjust the handbrake shoes. Temporarily refit two nuts, turn the adjuster **(see illustration 5.7c)** and expand the shoes until the disc locks, then back off the adjuster until you can spin the disc without the shoes dragging.

**8** Adjust the handbrake cable (Section 10).

**9** Remove the axle stands and lower the vehicle. Tighten the wheel nuts to the specified torque (see Chapter 1 Specifications).

12.5o . . . place the rear shoe in position, insert the pin through the backing plate and the shoe and refit the rear washers and hold-down spring

12.5p Hook the upper return spring into the front shoe . . .

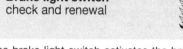

## 13 Brake light switch - check and renewal

**1** The brake light switch activates the brake lights when the brake pedal is depressed. It's located at the top of the brake pedal, inside the pedal box.

**2** If the brake lights don't come on when the brake pedal is depressed, check the fuses (the fuse for the left brake light is in the left fuse panel and the fuse for the right brake light is in the right panel).

**3** If the fuses are okay, check the brake light bulbs (see Chapter 12).

**4** If the fuses and bulbs are okay, either the switch isn't getting voltage (there's an open-circuit between the voltage source and the switch), voltage isn't reaching the brake light

12.5q . . . and into the rear shoe

12.5r Pull the shoes apart and refit the adjuster mechanism

bulbs (open-circuit between the switch and the bulbs), or the switch is defective.

**5** To remove the switch, reach up under the dash and unplug the two electrical connectors - one for the brake lights and one for the cruise control system. Locate the two pairs of leads coming down the pedal box and trace them to their connectors on or near the steering column.

**6** Remove the three switch-plate retaining bolts and remove the switch assembly **(see illustrations)**. Inspect the switch-plate rubber gasket for cracks or deterioration and renew it if it's damaged or worn.

**7** Place the switch assembly on a workbench and connect an ohmmeter to the brake light switch terminals. With the switch plunger in its normal, extended position (brake pedal not applied), there should be no continuity (infinite resistance) **(see illustration)**; when the plunger is depressed (brake pedal applied), there should be continuity (zero resistance) **(see illustration)**. If the switch doesn't perform as described, renew it. If the switch works in an opposite fashion, i.e. continuity when the plunger is free, no continuity when the plunger is depressed, you've tested the cruise control switch! Switch the ohmmeter leads to the other connector and recheck.

**8** To remove the switch from the plate, remove the two small nuts on the back of the plate **(see illustration)**.

**9** Refit the switch assembly and the switch plate bolts but don't tighten the bolts yet.

**10** Plug in the brake light and cruise control connectors.

**11** The holes in the switch plate are slotted for adjustment. While an assistant presses the brake pedal, verify that the brake lights come on; with the pedal released, make sure the brake lights are off. If the lights don't come on when the pedal is depressed, or stay on when the pedal is released, adjust the switch by moving the plate until proper operation is achieved. Tighten the switch-plate bolts.

**12** After tightening the switch-plate bolts, check the switch again to make sure it performs properly.

**13.6a  To remove the brake light switch, remove the three mounting plate screws (arrowed) . . .**

**13.6b  . . . and carefully pry the switch plate away from the pedal box - be careful not to damage the gasket**

**13.7a  To check the brake light switch, connect an ohmmeter to the switch terminals; with the switch plunger released, there should be no continuity (infinite resistance)**

**13.7b  With the switch plunger depressed, there should be continuity (zero resistance)**

**13.8  If you're replacing the switch, remove these two nuts (arrowed) and transfer the retaining plate to the new switch**

# Chapter 10
# Suspension and steering systems

## Contents

## Degrees of difficulty

| | | | | |
|---|---|---|---|---|
| **Easy,** suitable for novice with little experience  | **Fairly easy,** suitable for beginner with some experience  | **Fairly difficult,** suitable for competent DIY mechanic | **Difficult,** suitable for experienced DIY mechanic  | **Very difficult,** suitable for expert DIY or professional |

## Specifications

### General

Power steering fluid type ................................. See Chapter 1

### Torque wrench settings

| | Nm | lbf ft |
|---|---|---|
| **Front suspension** | | |
| Balljoints | | |
|   Retaining bolts ......................................... | 55 to 62 | 41 to 45 |
|   Ball stud nuts ......................................... | 47 to 68 | 35 to 50 |
| Lower control arm | | |
|   Spring pan bolts ....................................... | 26 to 34 | 19 to 25 |
|   Pivot nuts/bolts ....................................... | 43 to 68 | 32 to 50 |
| Shock absorber | | |
|   Lower nut ............................................. | 61 to 68 | 45 to 50 |
|   Upper nut ............................................. | 35 to 43 | 26 to 31 |
| Anti-roll bar | | |
|   Bushing bracket bolts | | |
|     Upper ............................................. | 22 to 28 | 16 to 20 |
|     Lower ............................................. | 24 to 30 | 18 to 22 |
|   Link nuts ............................................. | 55 to 60 | 41 to 44 |
| Upper control arm pivot nuts/bolts ......................... | 61 to 75 | 45 to 55 |
| **Rear suspension** | | |
| Carrier-to-control arm bolt/nut ............................. | 70 to 80 | 51 to 59 |
| Rear control arm-to-crossmember bolt/nut ................... | 85 to 105 | 62 to 77 |
| Shock absorber/coil spring assembly | | |
|   Lower shock-to-control arm bolt/nut .................... | 160 to 200 | 118 to 147 |
|   Upper shock-to-body bolts ............................. | 22 to 28 | 16 to 20 |
| **Steering** | | |
| Steering wheel-to-steering shaft nut ........................ | 35 to 45 | 26 to 33 |
| Steering shaft-to-steering gear pinion shaft U-joint pinch bolt ....... | 19 to 24 | 14 to 17 |
| Steering gear mounting bracket bolts/nuts ................... | 26 to 29 | 19 to 21 |
| Tie-rod end-to-steering knuckle nut ........................ | 61 to 68 | 45 to 50 |

**1.1 Front suspension and steering systems**

1  Anti-roll bar
2  Anti-roll bar bushing brackets
3  Anti-roll bar links
4  Lower control arms
5  Steering knuckles
6  Tie-rod ends
7  Tie-rods
8  Steering gear boots
9  Steering gear
10 Suspension crossmember
11 Lower control arm crossbrace

**1.2 Front suspension (left corner)**

1  Anti-roll bar bushing bracket
2  Anti-roll bar link
3  Anti-roll bar
4  Coil spring pan
5  Lower control arm
6  Coil spring
7  Upper control arm
8  Lower balljoint
9  Steering knuckle
10 Tie-rod end
11 Tie-rod
12 Steering gear boot

**1.3 Rear suspension**

1 Hub carrier    2 Control arms    3 Crossmember mounting brackets    4 Crossmember

# 1  General information

⚠️ **Warning: Whenever any of the suspension or steering fasteners are loosened or removed, they must be inspected and if necessary, replaced with new ones of the same part number or of original equipment quality and design. Torque wrench settings must be followed for proper reassembly and component retention. Never attempt to heat, straighten or weld any suspension or steering component. Instead, renew any bent or damaged part.**

The front suspension **(see illustrations)** consists of unequal-length upper and lower control arms, shock absorbers and coil springs. The upper ends of the shocks are attached to the body; the lower ends are attached to the lower control arms. The upper ends of the coil springs are seated against the suspension crossmember; the lower ends are seated against removable plates which are bolted to the lower control arms. The steering knuckles are attached to balljoints in the upper and lower control arms. An anti-roll bar is attached to the suspension crossmember with a pair of bushing brackets and to the lower control arms via a connecting link at each end.

The independent rear suspension **(see illustration)** uses control arms and integral shock absorber/coil spring units. The upper ends of the shocks are attached to the body; the lower ends are connected to the control arms.

The steering system consists of the steering wheel, a steering column, a universal joint on the lower end of the steering shaft, a rack-and-pinion power steering gear, a power steering pump and a pair of tie-rods which connects the steering gear to the steering knuckles **(see illustration)**.

# 2  Self-levelling rear suspension system

1988 to 1992 models were equipped with a system that provided hydraulic power for the rear suspension and for the power brakes. As the vehicle is loaded or unloaded, the rear suspension is automatically adjusted to maintain a constant ride height.

The system was discontinued on 1993 and later models, which are equipped with conventional shock absorber/coil spring units. A kit is available from your Jaguar dealer should you decide to retrofit the later, conventional shocks to a pre-1993 vehicle. Complete instructions for refitting the kit are included in Section 10.

# 3  Anti-roll bar (front) - removal and refitting

1 Raise the front of the vehicle and support it securely on axle stands.
2 Remove the bolts from the anti-roll bar brackets that attach the anti-roll bar to the suspension crossmember **(see illustration)**.
3 Remove the nuts that attach the anti-roll bar to the links **(see illustration)**. If you're replacing the links themselves, or removing the control arm, remove the nuts attaching the links to the lower control arms.

**3.2 To detach the anti-roll bar from the suspension crossmember, remove these two bolts (arrowed) from each bushing bracket**

**3.3 To disconnect the anti-roll bar from the link, remove the upper nut (arrowed); to disconnect the link from the lower control arm, remove the lower nut (arrowed)**

**4.3 To disconnect the lower end of the shock absorber from the lower control arm, remove this nut and bolt**

4 Remove the anti-roll bar from the vehicle.
5 Refitting is the reverse of the removal procedure. Be sure to tighten all fasteners to the torque listed in this Chapter's Specifications.

### 4 Shock absorber (front) - removal and refitting

**Note:** *Always renew both left and right shocks at the same time to prevent handling peculiarities and abnormal ride quality.*

1 Loosen but do not remove the front wheel nuts. Raise the front of the vehicle and support it on axle stands. Remove the wheels.
2 Support the lower control arm with a trolley jack **(see illustration)**. Place a block of wood between the jack head and the control arm to protect the arm and spring plate.
3 Remove the nut and bolt that attach the lower end of the shock absorber to the lower control arm **(see illustration)**.
4 Remove the nut that attaches the upper end of the shock to the body **(see illustration)**.
5 Remove the shock absorber.
6 Refitting is the reverse of removal. Tighten the fasteners to the torque listed in this Chapter's Specifications.

**4.2 Support the lower control arm with a jack; put a block of wood between the jack head and the control arm to protect the arm and coil spring plate**

**4.4 To disconnect the upper end of the shock absorber from the body, remove this nut (arrowed)**

### 5 Balljoints - check and renewal

#### Check

1 Raise the vehicle and support it securely on axle stands.
2 Visually inspect the rubber boot between the balljoints and the steering knuckle for cuts, tears or leaking grease. If you note any of these conditions, renew the balljoint.
3 Place a large crowbar between each

**5.7 To detach the upper balljoint from the steering knuckle, loosen the ballstud nut, fit a small puller and break the ballstud loose from the knuckle**

control arm and the steering knuckle. If you can see or feel any movement during either check, a worn-out balljoint is indicated.
4 Have an assistant grasp the tyre at the top and bottom and shake the top of the tyre with an in-and-out motion. Touch the balljoint stud nut. If any looseness is felt, suspect a worn-out balljoint stud or a widened hole in the steering knuckle. If the latter problem exists, the steering knuckle should be replaced as well as the balljoint.

#### Renewal

5 Loosen the wheel nuts, raise the vehicle and support it securely on axle stands. Remove the wheel.
6 Support the lower control arm with a trolley jack **(see illustration 4.2)**. Place a block of wood between the jack head and the control arm as shown to protect the arm and spring plate.

#### Upper balljoint

7 Loosen - but don't remove - the ball stud nut, fit a small puller **(see illustration)** and pop the ball stud loose from the steering knuckle.
8 Remove the two bolts that attach the balljoint to the upper arm **(see illustration)**. Count the number of shims installed and set them aside.
9 Refitting is the reverse of removal. Don't forget to refit the same number of shims. Tighten the bolts to the torque listed in this Chapter's Specifications.
10 Remove the jack from under the control arm, refit the front wheel, lower the vehicle and tighten the wheel nuts to the torque listed in the Chapter 1 Specifications. Drive the vehicle to an alignment workshop to have the wheel alignment checked, and if necessary, adjusted.

#### Lower balljoint

11 Loosen - but don't remove - the ball stud nut, then give the steering knuckle a few sharp raps with a hammer to pop the ball stud loose **(see illustration)**. Remove the ball stud nut.

**5.8 Remove the bolts and shims from the upper balljoint; be sure to put the shims back when refitting the new balljoint**

**5.11  Strike the steering knuckle in this area to pop the lower ball stud loose from the steering knuckle**

**5.12  To detach the lower balljoint from the lower control arm, remove these four bolts (arrowed)**

**5.13  To detach the dust boot from the steering knuckle, pry the lower lip of the boot out of its groove in the knuckle**

**12** Remove the four balljoint retaining bolts **(see illustration)**.

**13** If the dust boot is damaged, pry it out **(see illustration)**.

**14** Remove the balljoint.

**15** Refitting is the reverse of removal. Tighten the balljoint bolts and the ball stud nut to the torque listed in this Chapter's Specifications.

**16** Remove the jack from under the control arm, refit the front wheel. Lower the vehicle and tighten the wheel nuts to the torque listed in the Chapter 1 Specifications.

## 6  Steering knuckle -
### removal and refitting

**1** Loosen the wheel nuts, raise the front of the vehicle and place it securely on axle stands. Remove the wheel.

**2** Remove the front brake caliper and mounting bracket (see Chapter 9). Do not disconnect the brake hose. Hang the caliper out of the way with a piece of wire.

**3** Remove the brake disc (see Chapter 9).

**4** Remove the ABS sensor **(see illustration)**.

**5** Remove the brake shield **(see illustration)**.

**6** Disconnect the tie-rod end from the steering knuckle (see Section 15).

**7** Disconnect the upper and lower balljoints from the steering knuckle (see Section 5).

**8** Remove the steering knuckle.

**9** Refitting is the reverse of removal. Tighten the balljoint nuts and the tie-rod end nuts to the specified torque. Tighten the brake fasteners to the torque values listed in the Chapter 9 Specifications.

## 7  Upper control arm -
### removal and refitting

**1** Loosen the wheel nuts, raise the vehicle and support it securely on axle stands. Remove the wheel.

**2** Support the lower control arm with a trolley jack **(see illustration 4.2)**.

**3** Disconnect the upper balljoint from the steering knuckle (see Section 5).

**4** If you're removing the right upper control arm on a vehicle equipped with the power hydraulic system, remove the three Torx screws which attach the accumulator **(see illustration)** and push the assembly aside just far enough to clear the pivot bolt.

**5** Remove the upper control arm pivot bolt and nut **(see illustration)**. When removing the nut, note the number of washers used and the order in which they're installed. Put these parts in a plastic bag.

**6** Remove the upper control arm. Inspect the bushings at either end of the arm and renew them if they're damaged or worn.

**7** Refitting is the reverse of removal. Be sure to refit the washers in the same order in which they were removed. Raise the suspension

**6.4  To detach the ABS sensor from the steering knuckle, remove this bolt**

**7.4  Remove these three Torx screws (arrowed) and move the accumulator assembly to the side a little to provide clearance for pulling out the pivot bolt**

**6.5  To detach the brake shield from the steering knuckle, remove these three screws (arrowed)**

**7.5  To detach the upper control arm from the crossmember, remove the nut (at the rear) and pull the bolt out from the front; note the fitted order of the spacer washers**

with the trolley jack to simulate normal ride height, then tighten the upper control arm pivot bolt and nut to the torque listed in this Chapter's Specifications.

## 8  Coil spring (front) -
### removal and refitting

> **Warning: The coil springs cannot be removed without a special spring compressor tool (Jaguar tool JD115). Do not try to remove a coil spring without this special tool. If you do, you could be seriously injured.**

**1** Loosen the wheel nuts, raise the vehicle

8.2a When refitting the spring compressor tool (JD115), insert the upper end of the rod into the cross-shaped slot in the suspension crossmember, then rotate the rod 90° so this pin on the upper end of the tool locks into the crossmember

8.2b This is how the spring compressor tool (JD115) looks when it's installed; note how the offset collet is oriented so that it's flush with the coil spring pan

8.3 To detach the coil spring pan from the lower control arm, compress the spring and remove these six bolts (arrowed)

and support it securely on axle stands. Remove the wheel.

**2** Refit the special spring compressor tool (JD115) as shown **(see illustrations)**.

**3** Tighten the tool until the spacer is tight against the spring pan, then remove the spring pan bolts **(see illustration)**.

**4** Slowly back off the wingnut on the special tool until all tension is relieved from the spring. Remove the tool, remove the pan, and remove the coil spring.

**5** Refitting is the reverse of removal. Place the coil spring in position with the spring pan below it, refit the special tool and carefully tighten the wingnut until the spring is compressed enough to allow the pan to be positioned and bolted to the lower control arm. Be sure to tighten the pan bolts to the torque listed in this Chapter's Specifications.

## 9 Lower control arm - removal and refitting

⚠️ **Warning: The lower control arms cannot be removed without a special spring compressor tool (Jaguar tool JD115). Do not try to remove a lower control arm without this tool, or you could be seriously injured.**

**1** Loosen the wheel nuts, raise the vehicle and support it securely on axle stands. Remove the wheel.

**2** Remove the spring pan and the coil spring (see Section 8).

**3** Detach the steering gear (see Section 17) and lower it far enough to provide clearance for the lower control arm pivot bolt.

**4** Remove the pivot bolt and nut **(see illustration)**. Note any washers behind the nut and store them in a plastic bag.

**5** Remove the lower control arm.

**6** Refitting is the reverse of removal. Be sure to refit any washers removed. Raise the suspension with the trolley jack to simulate normal ride height, then tighten the pivot bolt and nut to the torque listed in this Chapter's Specifications. Refer to Section 8 for coil spring refitting.

## 10 Shock absorber/coil spring (rear) - removal and refitting

**Note 1:** *Always renew both left and right shocks at the same time to prevent handling peculiarities and abnormal ride quality.*
**Note 2:** *If you're replacing the shock absorbers on an earlier vehicle with the self-levelling system, we strongly recommend (and so does*

*Jaguar) that you renew the self-levelling units with conventional units (available at the dealer as a retrofit kit for older vehicles equipped with the self-levelling system).*

**1** Loosen the rear wheel nuts. Raise the rear of the vehicle and support it securely on axle stands. Remove the rear wheels. Support the control arm with a trolley jack. Place a block of wood on the jack head to serve as a cushion.

**2** If you are removing/replacing the shocks on a vehicle equipped with the self-levelling rear suspension system, depressurise the system by pumping the brake pedal until it feels hard to push (this dissipates the pressure inside the accumulator), then locate the hydraulic line valve block just in front of the upper end of the left rear shock **(see illustration)**. Attach a plastic hose to the bleeder screw **(see illustration)**, put the other end of the hose in a catch bottle, crack the bleeder and drain off as much fluid as possible. Disconnect the hydraulic line that connects the left shock to the valve block. Now locate the other valve block just in front of the right rear shock; disconnect the hydraulic line that connects the right shock to this valve block too.

**3** Remove the lower shock absorber-to-control arm nut and bolt **(see illustration)**.

**4** Remove the upper mounting bolts **(see illustration)** and remove the shock absorber/coil spring assembly.

9.4 To detach the lower control arm from the crossmember, remove this nut and bolt (arrowed) (unbolt and lower the steering gear before you can pull out the pivot bolt)

10.2a On a vehicle equipped with self-levelling rear suspension, the valve block (arrowed) for the left rear shock is located just in front of the shock absorber

10.2b After depressurising the system, attach a bleed hose to the bleed screw on the left valve block, open the bleed and drain any residual fluid into a catch bottle

10.3 To detach the bottom of the shock absorber/coil spring from the control arm, remove this nut and bolt, then pull out the bolt

10.4 To detach the top of the shock absorber/coil spring from the body, remove these bolts (arrowed) - not all bolts are visible here

10.6a Where applicable, unplug the connector to the ride height sensor and fill the connector with silicone . . .

10.6b . . . then disconnect and remove both valve blocks . . .

10.6c . . . and remove all associated plumbing, including the metal line (arrow) to the valve block in the engine compartment

5 The shock/coil spring assemblies must be dismantled, and the coil springs installed on the new shocks. Although the shock/coil spring assembly is similar in appearance to the a MacPherson strut/coil spring assembly, the spring on this unit is much stiffer. Therefore, DO NOT attempt to take apart this unit yourself with a strut spring compressor tool. Instead, take the unit to a Jaguar dealer service department or to a Jaguar specialist workshop and have the springs installed on the new shocks by professionals.

6 If you are retrofitting conventional shocks - rather than refitting the same or another pair of self-levelling shocks - unplug the electrical connector at the ride height sensor, and fill the connector with silicone (see illustration) to prevent it from shorting out and causing electrical problems. Then disconnect and remove all hydraulic lines (see illustrations).
7 Refitting is the reverse of removal. Be sure to tighten all fasteners to the torque values listed in this Chapter's Specifications.
8 Remove the jack supporting the control

arm, refit the rear wheels and lower the vehicle.
9 Tighten the rear wheel nuts to the torque listed in the Chapter 1 Specifications.
10 If you retrofitted conventional shocks to a vehicle formerly equipped with the self-levelling rear suspension system, disconnect the forward end of the hydraulic line from the valve block and refit the plug included in the kit (see illustrations). Then finish removing the forward section of hydraulic line and the brackets for the line (see illustration).

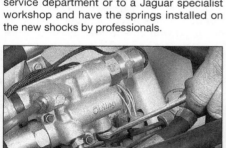

10.10a After the vehicle has been lowered, disconnect the forward end of the hydraulic line from the valve block . . .

10.10b . . . refit the plug included in the retrofit kit . . .

10.10c . . . then remove these bracket screws (arrowed), the brackets and the forward section of hydraulic line

**11.4  Before detaching the hub carrier from the rear control arm, remove the ABS sensor (left arrow), detach the ABS harness clip (right arrow) and cut the cable tie securing the harness**

**11.5  To detach the hub carrier from the rear control arm, remove the carrier-to-control arm nut and bolt**

**11** If you installed another pair of self-levelling shocks, or removed and installed the same pair of self-levelling shocks, be sure to top up the power hydraulic system reservoir (see Chapter 1).

## 11  Hub carrier (rear) - removal and refitting

**1** Loosen the wheel nuts, raise the rear of the vehicle and support it securely on axle stands. Remove the wheel.
**2** Remove the rear caliper and brake pads, the caliper bracket, the brake disc, the handbrake cable and the handbrake shoe assembly (see Chapter 9).
**3** Disconnect the outer end of the propshaft from the hub carrier (see Chapter 8).
**4** Remove the ABS sensor, the ABS harness clip and cut off the cable tie which secures the ABS harness to the carrier **(see illustration)**.
**5** Remove the nut and bolt which attach the carrier to the control arm **(see illustration)**.
**6** Remove the hub carrier assembly.
**7** Refitting is the reverse of removal. Be sure to tighten all fasteners to the torque values listed in this Chapter's Specifications.

## 12  Hub and bearing (rear) - renewal

If you want to renew the rear hub and bearing assembly (or the ABS trigger wheel), remove the hub carrier (see Section 11), then take the carrier to a Jaguar dealer service department or to an automotive machine workshop. These parts require a hydraulic press and special fixtures to dismantle and reassemble.

## 13  Control arm (rear) - removal and refitting

**1** Loosen the wheel nuts, raise the rear of the vehicle and support it securely on axle stands. Remove the wheel.
**2** Remove the rear caliper and brake pads, the caliper bracket, the brake disc, the handbrake cable and the handbrake shoe assembly (see Chapter 9).
**3** Disconnect the outer end of the propshaft from the hub carrier (see Chapter 8).
**4** Disconnect the lower end of the shock absorber/coil spring assembly from the control arm (see Section 10).
**5** Remove the hub carrier (see Section 11).
**6** Remove the control arm pivot bolt nut **(see illustration)**.
**7** Support the differential/crossmember assembly with a trolley jack. Place a block of wood between the jack head and the differential to protect the differential. Disconnect the lower end of the differential tie-bar **(see illustration)** and carefully lower the differential crossmember just enough to

allow the control arm pivot bolt to be pulled out to the rear without hitting the boot well.
**8** Remove the control arm.
**9** Inspect the control arm pivot bolt bushings. If they're cracked, dried out or torn, take the arm to an automotive machine workshop and have them replaced.
**10** Refitting is the reverse of removal. Tighten all suspension fasteners to the torque listed in this Chapter's Specifications. Tighten all brake fasteners to the torque listed in the Chapter 9 Specifications.

## 14  Steering wheel - removal and refitting

⚠️ *Warning: If your car is equipped with an airbag, do not attempt this procedure. Have it done by a dealer service department or other qualified repair workshop.*
**1** Disconnect the negative battery cable.
*Caution: If the radio in your vehicle is equipped with an anti-theft system, make*

**13.6  Hold the pivot bolt and unscrew the nut**

**13.7  Remove this nut (arrowed) and bolt from the lower end of each tie-bar (right above the control arm pivot)**

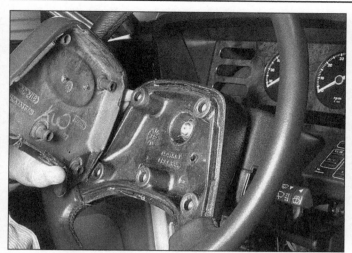

14.2  To remove the centre pad from the steering wheel, simply pry it off

14.3  After removing the steering wheel nut, make a pair of alignment marks on the steering wheel and steering shaft to ensure proper reassembly

*sure you have the correct activation code before disconnecting the battery.*

2  Pry off the centre pad **(see illustration)**.
3  Remove the steering wheel nut and mark the relationship of the steering wheel hub to the shaft **(see illustration)**.
4  Slide the steering wheel off the steering shaft **(see illustration)**.
5  Refitting is the reverse of removal. Make sure you align the match marks you made on the steering wheel and the shaft. Tighten the steering wheel nut to the torque listed in this Chapter's Specifications.

## 15  Tie-rod ends - removal and refitting

1  Loosen the wheel nuts, raise the front of the vehicle and support it securely on axle stands. Remove the front wheel.
2  Back off the locknut that locks the tie-rod end to the tie-rod, then paint an alignment mark on the threads to ensure the new tie-rod end is installed in the same position **(see illustration)**.
3  Loosen the nut on the tie-rod ball stud, then fit a small puller and pop the ball stud loose **(see illustration)**. Remove the nut and separate the ball stud from the steering knuckle. Unscrew the tie-rod end from the tie-rod.
4  Refitting is the reverse of removal. Make sure you thread the tie-rod end all the way up to the mark on the threads, but no further. Tighten the ball stud nut to the torque listed in this Chapter's Specifications. Tighten the locknut securely.
5  Have the toe-in checked and, if necessary, adjusted at a dealer service department or alignment workshop.

## 16  Steering gear boots - renewal

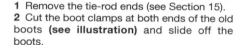

1  Remove the tie-rod ends (see Section 15).
2  Cut the boot clamps at both ends of the old boots **(see illustration)** and slide off the boots.

3  While the boots are removed, inspect the seals in the end of the steering gear. If they're leaking, have them replaced by a dealer service department or other qualified repair workshop, or replace the steering gear with a new or rebuilt unit (see Section 17).
4  Slide the new boots into place and refit new boot clamps.
5  Refit the tie-rod ends (see Section 15).

14.4  To remove the steering wheel, simply pull it straight off

15.2  Back off this locknut and mark the threads to ensure that the new tie-rod end is installed properly

15.3  Loosen the ball stud nut, fit a small puller and pop the ball stud loose from the steering knuckle

16.2  Cut off the boot clamps (arrowed) and slide the boot off the steering gear

17.3 Mark the relationship of the steering shaft U-joint to the steering gear pinion shaft, then unscrew the pressure and return line fittings (arrowed) - plug the lines to prevent contamination from entering the system

17.6 To detach the steering gear from the vehicle, remove these nuts and bolts (arrowed) from the mounting brackets (right bracket shown, left bracket similar)

## 17 Steering gear -
### removal and refitting

**Warning: On models with an airbag, do not apply excessive force or severe shock to the steering column shaft, or accidental deployment of the airbag could occur.**

1 Using a large syringe or hand pump, empty the power steering fluid reservoir.

2 Loosen the wheel nuts, raise the vehicle and support it securely on axle stands. Remove the wheels.

3 Mark the relationship of the steering shaft U-joint to the steering gear pinion shaft **(see illustration)** to ensure proper alignment when they're reassembled. Remove the nut and bolt that clamp the U-joint to the pinion shaft.

4 Disconnect the power steering pressure and return lines from the steering gear. Place a container under the lines to catch spilled fluid. Plug the lines to prevent excessive fluid loss and contamination. Discard the sealing washers (new ones should be used when reassembling).

5 Disconnect the tie-rod ends from the steering knuckle arms (see Section 17).

6 Remove the nuts and bolts from the steering gear mounting brackets **(see illustration)**.

7 Remove the steering gear assembly, detaching the U-joint as you lower it. Don't damage the steering gear dust boots.

8 Refitting is the reverse of removal. Ensure the marks you made on the U-joint and the pinion shaft are aligned before you tighten the U-joint clamp bolt and nut. Tighten the mounting bolts, the tie-rod end nuts and the U-joint shaft clamping bolts to the specified torque.

9 After lowering the vehicle, fill the reservoir with the recommended fluid (see Chapter 1).

10 Bleed the power steering system (see Section 19).

11 Have the front wheels aligned by a dealer service department or alignment workshop after reassembly.

## 18 Power steering pump -
### removal and refitting

1 Raise the vehicle and support it securely on axle stands. Remove the engine under-cover.

2 Loosen the hose clamp and disconnect the fluid return hose from the top of the pump **(see illustration)** and drain the power steering fluid from the reservoir into a clean container. Unscrew the pressure line fitting from the back of the pump. Plug the return hose and the pressure line to prevent fluid from leaking and to protect the power steering system from contamination.

3 Remove the bolts **(see illustration)** that attach the power steering pump adapter to the auxiliary shaft housing.

4 Remove the power steering pump and adapter.

5 Take the power steering pump and adapter to a Jaguar dealer service department and have the adapter removed from the old pump

18.2 Disconnect the steering fluid return hose from the upper pipe (arrowed) and disconnect the pressure line from the back of the pump

18.3 To detach the pump adapter from the auxiliary shaft housing, remove these bolts

**18.6a  This driven coupling is the reason you can't remove the adapter from the pump at home; this requires special tools, and the coupling must be installed on the shaft of the new or rebuilt pump at a very precise height - if you try to pry off the coupling, you will damage it**

**18.6b  The coupling disc fits onto the driven coupling on the pump side . . .**

**18.6c  . . . and on the drive coupling on the auxiliary shaft side; note that the two lugs on each drive coupling fit into their corresponding slots in the coupling disc, 180° apart - all four lugs must be properly engaged or you won't be able to bolt the adapter to the auxiliary shaft housing**

and installed on a new or rebuilt pump. (This procedure requires special tools, and the height of the driven coupling on the shaft must be set with a depth gauge.)

6  Refitting is the reverse of removal. Study the accompanying photos carefully before reattaching the adapter to the auxiliary shaft housing **(see illustrations)**. Be sure to tighten the fasteners securely.

7  Top up the fluid level in the reservoir (see "*Weekly checks*" for vehicles with a separate power steering system, or Chapter 1 for vehicles with a power hydraulic system) and bleed the system (Section 19).

### 19  Power steering system - bleeding

1  To bleed the power steering system, begin by checking the power steering fluid level and adding fluid if necessary (see "*Weekly checks*" or Chapter 1, dependent on system fitted).

2  Raise and support the front of the vehicle on axle stands.

3  Turn the steering wheel from lock-to-lock several times and recheck the fluid level.

4  Start the engine. Turn the steering wheel from lock-to-lock again (three or four times) and recheck the fluid level one more time.

5  Lower the car to the ground. Run the engine and again turn the wheels from lock-to-lock several more times. Set the wheels straight ahead and recheck the fluid level.

### 20  Wheels and tyres - general information

1  All vehicles covered by this manual are equipped with steel belted radial tyres. Use of

other size or type of tyres may affect the ride and handling of the vehicle. Don't mix different types of tyres, such as radials and bias belted, on the same vehicle as handling may be seriously affected. It's recommended that tyres be replaced in pairs on the same axle, but if only one tyre is being replaced, be sure it's the same size, structure and tread design as the other.

2  Because tyre pressure has a substantial effect on handling and wear, the pressure on all tyres should be checked at least once a month or before any extended trips (see Chapter 1).

3  Wheels must be replaced if they are bent, dented, leak air, have elongated bolt holes, are heavily rusted, out of vertical symmetry or if the wheel nuts won't stay tight. Wheel repairs that use welding or peening are not recommended.

4  Tyre and wheel balance is important in the overall handling, braking and performance of the vehicle. Unbalanced wheels can adversely affect handling and ride characteristics as well as tyre life. Whenever a tyre is installed on a wheel, the tyre and wheel should be balanced by a workshop with the proper equipment.

### 21  Wheel alignment - general information

A wheel alignment refers to the adjustments made to the wheels so they are in proper angular relationship to the suspension and the ground. Wheels that are out of proper alignment not only affect vehicle control, but also increase tyre wear. The alignment angles normally measured are camber, caster and toe-in **(see illustration)**. Front-wheel toe-in and caster are adjustable; camber is not adjustable.

**21.1  Front end alignment details**

*A minus B = C (degrees camber)*
*E minus F = toe-in (measured in inches)*
*G - toe-in (expressed in degrees)*

None of these three angles are adjustable on the rear wheels. Even the non-adjustable angles should be checked to determine if any of the suspension components are bent.

Getting the proper wheel alignment is a very exacting process, one in which complicated and expensive machines are necessary to perform the job properly. Because of this, you should have a technician with the proper equipment perform these tasks. We will, however, use this space to give you a basic idea of what is involved with a wheel alignment so you can better understand the process and deal intelligently with the workshop that does the work.

Toe-in is the turning in of the wheels. The purpose of a toe specification is to ensure parallel rolling of the wheels. In a vehicle with zero toe-in, the distance between the front edges of the wheels will be the same as the distance between the rear edges of the wheels. The actual amount of toe-in is normally only a fraction of an inch. Toe-in is controlled by the tie-rod end position on the tie-rod. Incorrect toe-in will cause the tyres to wear improperly by making them scrub against the road surface.

Camber is the tilting of the wheels from vertical when viewed from one end of the vehicle. When the wheels tilt out at the top, the camber is said to be positive (+). When the wheels tilt in at the top the camber is negative (-). The amount of tilt is measured in degrees from vertical and this measurement is called the camber angle. This angle affects the amount of tyre tread which contacts the road and compensates for changes in the suspension geometry when the vehicle is cornering or travelling over an undulating surface.

Caster is the tilting of the front steering axis from the vertical. A tilt toward the rear is positive caster and a tilt toward the front is negative caster. Caster is adjusted by moving shims from one side of the upper control arm balljoint to the other.

# Chapter 11
# Bodywork and fittings

## Contents

## Degrees of difficulty

| | | | | |
|---|---|---|---|---|
| **Easy,** suitable for novice with little experience  | **Fairly easy,** suitable for beginner with some experience  | **Fairly difficult,** suitable for competent DIY mechanic  | **Difficult,** suitable for experienced DIY mechanic  | **Very difficult,** suitable for expert DIY or professional |

## 1 General information

These models feature a "unibody" construction, using a floor pan with front and rear frame side rails which support the body components, front and rear suspension systems and other mechanical components. Certain components are particularly vulnerable to accident damage and can be unbolted and repaired or replaced. Among these parts are the body mouldings, bumpers, front wings, bonnet and boot lids and all glass.

Only general body maintenance practices and body panel repair procedures within the scope of the do-it-yourselfer are included in this Chapter.

## 2 Body - maintenance

1 The condition of your vehicle's body is very important, because the resale value depends a great deal on it. It's much more difficult to repair a neglected or damaged body than it is to repair mechanical components. The hidden areas of the body, such as the wheel wells, the frame and the engine compartment, are equally important, although they don't require as frequent attention as the rest of the body.

2 Once a year, or every 12,000 miles, it's a good idea to have the underside of the body steam cleaned. All traces of dirt and oil will be removed and the area can then be inspected carefully for rust, damaged brake lines, frayed electrical wires, damaged cables and other problems. The front suspension components should be greased after completion of this job.

3 At the same time, clean the engine and the engine compartment with a steam cleaner or water soluble degreaser.

4 The wheel wells should be given close attention, since undercoating can peel away and stones and dirt thrown up by the tyres can cause the paint to chip and flake, allowing rust to set in. If rust is found, clean down to the bare metal and apply an anti-rust paint.

5 The body should be washed about once a week. Wet the vehicle thoroughly to soften the dirt, then wash it down with a soft sponge and plenty of clean soapy water. If the surplus dirt is not washed off very carefully, it can wear down the paint.

6 Spots of tar or asphalt thrown up from the road should be removed with a cloth soaked in solvent.

7 Once every six months, wax the body and chrome trim. If a chrome cleaner is used to remove rust from any of the vehicle's plated parts, remember that the cleaner also removes part of the chrome, so use it sparingly.

## 3 Vinyl trim - maintenance

Don't clean vinyl trim with detergents, caustic soap or petroleum-based cleaners. Plain soap and water works just fine, with a soft brush to clean dirt that may be ingrained. Wash the vinyl as frequently as the rest of the vehicle.

After cleaning, application of a high quality rubber and vinyl protectant will help prevent oxidation and cracks. The protectant can also be applied to weather-stripping, vacuum lines and rubber hoses (which often fail as a result of chemical degradation) and to the tyres.

## 4 Upholstery and carpets - maintenance

1 Every three months remove the carpets or mats and clean the interior of the vehicle (more frequently if necessary). Vacuum the upholstery and carpets to remove loose dirt and dust.

2 Leather upholstery requires special care. Stains should be removed with warm water and a very mild soap solution. Use a clean, damp cloth to remove the soap, then wipe

again with a dry cloth. Never use alcohol, petrol, nail polish remover or thinner to clean leather upholstery.

**3** After cleaning, regularly treat leather upholstery with a leather wax. Never use car wax on leather upholstery.

**4** In areas where the interior of the vehicle is subject to bright sunlight, cover leather seats with a sheet if the vehicle is to be left out for any length of time.

## 5 Body repair - minor damage

### *Repair of minor scratches*

**1** If the scratch is superficial and does not penetrate to the metal of the body, repair is very simple. Lightly rub the scratched area with a fine rubbing compound to remove loose paint and built-up wax. Rinse the area with clean water.

**2** Apply touch-up paint to the scratch, using a small brush. Continue to apply thin layers of paint until the surface of the paint in the scratch is level with the surrounding paint. Allow the new paint at least two weeks to harden, then blend it into the surrounding paint by rubbing with a very fine rubbing compound. Finally, apply a coat of wax to the scratch area.

**3** If the scratch has penetrated the paint and exposed the metal of the body, causing the metal to rust, a different repair technique is required. Remove all loose rust from the bottom of the scratch with a pocket knife, then apply rust inhibiting paint to prevent the formation of rust in the future. Using a rubber or nylon applicator, coat the scratched area with glaze-type filler. If required, the filler can be mixed with thinner to provide a very thin paste, which is ideal for filling narrow scratches. Before the glaze filler in the scratch hardens, wrap a piece of smooth cotton cloth around the tip of a finger. Dip the cloth in thinner and then quickly wipe it along the surface of the scratch. This will ensure that the surface of the filler is slightly hollow. The scratch can now be painted over as described earlier in this section.

### *Repair of dents*

**4** When repairing dents, the first job is to pull the dent out until the affected area is as close as possible to its original shape. There is no point in trying to restore the original shape completely as the metal in the damaged area will have stretched on impact and cannot be restored to its original contours. It is better to bring the level of the dent up to a point which is about 1/8-inch below the level of the surrounding metal. In cases where the dent is very shallow, it is not worth trying to pull it out at all.

**5** If the back side of the dent is accessible, it can be hammered out gently from behind using a soft-face hammer. While doing this, hold a block of wood firmly against the opposite side of the metal to absorb the hammer blows and prevent the metal from being stretched.

**6** If the dent is in a section of the body which has double layers, or some other factor makes it inaccessible from behind, a different technique is required. Drill several small holes through the metal inside the damaged area, particularly in the deeper sections. Screw long, self-tapping screws into the holes just enough for them to get a good grip in the metal. Now the dent can be pulled out by pulling on the protruding heads of the screws with locking pliers.

**7** The next stage of repair is the removal of paint from the damaged area and from an inch or so of the surrounding metal. This is done with a wire brush or sanding disc in a drill motor, although it can be done just as effectively by hand with sandpaper. To complete the preparation for filling, score the surface of the bare metal with a screwdriver or the tang of a file, or drill small holes in the affected area. This will provide a good grip for the filler material. To complete the repair, see the subsection on filling and painting later in this Section.

### *Repair of rust holes or gashes*

**8** Remove all paint from the affected area and from an inch or so of the surrounding metal using a sanding disc or wire brush mounted in a drill motor. If these are not available, a few sheets of sandpaper will do the job just as effectively.

**9** With the paint removed, you will be able to determine the severity of the corrosion and decide whether to replace the whole panel, if possible, or repair the affected area. New body panels are not as expensive as most people think and it is often quicker to refit a new panel than to repair large areas of rust.

**10** Remove all trim pieces from the affected area except those which will act as a guide to the original shape of the damaged body, such as headlight shells, etc. Using metal snips or a hacksaw blade, remove all loose metal and any other metal that is badly affected by rust. Hammer the edges of the hole in to create a slight depression for the filler material.

**11** Wire brush the affected area to remove the powdery rust from the surface of the metal. If the back of the rusted area is accessible, treat it with rust inhibiting paint.

**12** Before filling is done, block the hole in some way. This can be done with sheet metal riveted or screwed into place, or by stuffing the hole with wire mesh.

**13** Once the hole is blocked off, the affected area can be filled and painted. See the following subsection on filling and painting.

### *Filling and painting*

**14** Many types of body fillers are available, but generally speaking, body repair kits which contain filler paste and a tube of resin hardener are best for this type of repair work. A wide, flexible plastic or nylon applicator will be necessary for imparting a smooth and contoured finish to the surface of the filler material. Mix up a small amount of filler on a clean piece of wood or cardboard (use the hardener sparingly). Follow the manufacturer's instructions on the package, otherwise the filler will set incorrectly.

**15** Using the applicator, apply the filler paste to the prepared area. Draw the applicator across the surface of the filler to achieve the desired contour and to level the filler surface. As soon as a contour that approximates the original one is achieved, stop working the paste. If you continue, the paste will begin to stick to the applicator. Continue to add thin layers of paste at 20-minute intervals until the level of the filler is just above the surrounding metal.

**16** Once the filler has hardened, the excess can be removed with a body file. From then on, progressively finer grades of sandpaper should be used, starting with a 180-grit paper and finishing with 600-grit wet-or-dry paper. Always wrap the sandpaper around a flat rubber or wooden block, otherwise the surface of the filler will not be completely flat. During the sanding of the filler surface, the wet-or-dry paper should be periodically rinsed in water. This will ensure that a very smooth finish is produced in the final stage.

**17** At this point, the repair area should be surrounded by a ring of bare metal, which in turn should be encircled by the finely feathered edge of good paint. Rinse the repair area with clean water until all of the dust produced by the sanding operation is gone.

**18** Spray the entire area with a light coat of primer. This will reveal any imperfections in the surface of the filler. Repair the imperfections with fresh filler paste or glaze filler and once more smooth the surface with sandpaper. Repeat this spray-and-repair procedure until you are satisfied that the surface of the filler and the feathered edge of the paint are perfect. Rinse the area with clean water and allow it to dry completely.

**19** The repair area is now ready for painting. Spray painting must be carried out in a warm, dry, windless and dust free atmosphere. These conditions can be created if you have access to a large indoor work area, but if you are forced to work in the open, you will have to pick the day very carefully. If you are working indoors, dousing the floor in the work area with water will help settle the dust which would otherwise be in the air. If the repair area is confined to one body panel, mask off the surrounding panels. This will help minimise the effects of a slight mismatch in paint colour. Trim pieces such as chrome strips, door handles, etc., will also need to be masked off or removed. Use masking tape and several thickness of newspaper for the masking operations.

**20** Before spraying, shake the paint can thoroughly, then spray a test area until the

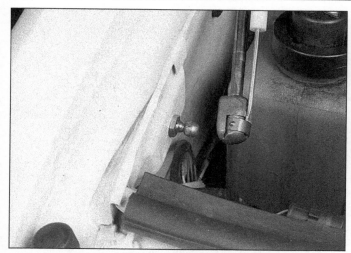

9.2a Use a small screwdriver to prise the clip out of its locking groove, then detach the end of the strut from the mounting stud

9.2b The boot lid support strut requires prising out a locking pin to detach it from the locating stud

spray painting technique is mastered. Cover the repair area with a thick coat of primer. The thickness should be built up using several thin layers of primer rather than one thick one. Using 600-grit wet-or-dry sandpaper, rub down the surface of the primer until it is very smooth. While doing this, the work area should be thoroughly rinsed with water and the wet-or-dry sandpaper periodically rinsed as well. Allow the primer to dry before spraying additional coats.

21 Spray on the top coat, again building up the thickness by using several thin layers of paint. Begin spraying at the top of the repair area and then, using a side-to-side motion, work down until the whole repair area and about two inches of the surrounding original paint is covered. Remove all masking material 10 to 15 minutes after spraying on the final coat of paint. Allow the new paint at least two weeks to harden, then use a very fine rubbing compound to blend the edges of the new paint into the existing paint. Finally, apply a coat of wax.

### 6 Body repair - major damage

1 Major damage must be repaired by an auto body workshop specifically equipped to perform unibody repairs. These workshops have the specialised equipment required to do the job properly.
2 If the damage is extensive, the body must be checked for proper alignment or the vehicle's handling characteristics may be adversely affected and other components may wear at an accelerated rate.
3 Due to the fact that most of the major body components (bonnet, front wings, etc.) are separate and replaceable units, any seriously damaged components should be replaced rather than repaired. Sometimes the

components can be found in a scrapyard that specialises in used vehicle components, often at considerable savings over the cost of new parts.

### 7 Hinges and locks - maintenance

Once every 3000 miles, or every three months, the hinges and latch assemblies on the doors, bonnet and boot should be given a few drops of light oil or lock lubricant. The door latch strikers should also be lubricated with a thin coat of grease to reduce wear and ensure free movement. Lubricate the door and boot locks with spray-on graphite lubricant.

### 8 Windscreen and fixed glass - replacement

Replacement of the windscreen and fixed glass requires the use of special fast-setting adhesive/caulk materials and some specialised tools. It is recommended that these operations be left to a dealer or a workshop specialising in glass work.

### 9 Bonnet and boot lid support struts - removal and refitting

1 Open the bonnet or boot lid and support it securely.
2 Using a small screwdriver, detach the retaining clips at both ends of the support strut. Then pry or pull sharply to detach it from the vehicle (see illustrations).
3 Refitting is the reverse of removal.

### 10 Bonnet - removal, refitting and adjustment

**Note:** *The bonnet is heavy and somewhat awkward to remove and refit - at least two people should perform this procedure.*

#### Removal and refitting

1 Use blankets or pads to cover the wings and the area in front of the bonnet. This will protect the body and paint as the bonnet is lifted off.
2 Make marks or scribe a line around the bonnet hinge to ensure proper alignment during refitting.
3 Disconnect any cables or wires that will interfere with removal.
4 Have an assistant support the bonnet. Remove the hinge-to-bonnet screws or bolts (see illustration).
5 Lift off the bonnet.
6 Refitting is the reverse of removal.

#### Adjustment

7 Before the bonnet can be adjusted properly, both bonnet striker assemblies

10.4 With the help of an assistant to hold the bonnet, remove the retaining bolts (arrowed) from each hinge plate, then lift off the bonnet

10.11 Adjust the position of the bonnet striker by loosening the locknut (A), then adjust the height of the bonnet striker (B) by turning it in or out with a screwdriver

10.12 Remove the rubber bumper then loosen the locknut (A) - adjust the bonnet bumper bolt (B) in or out so the bonnet is flush with the wings in the closed position

11.1 Remove the cable retaining bolt(s) (arrowed) then disengage the cable from the latch assembly

11.2 Bonnet latch retaining bolts (arrowed) are located on both sides of the engine compartment

which are located on the inside of the bonnet must first be loosened to allow correct alignment of the bonnet.

8 Fore-and-aft and side-to-side adjustment of the bonnet is done by moving the bonnet in relation to the hinge plates after loosening the bolts.

9 Scribe or trace a line around the entire hinge plate to judge the amount of movement.

10 Loosen the nuts or bolts and move the bonnet into correct alignment. Move it only a little at a time. Tighten the hinge bolts or nuts and carefully lower the bonnet to check the alignment.

11 After the bonnet has been aligned properly with the cowl and front wings, the height and position of the bonnet striker assembly should be adjusted to provide positive engagement with the latch assembly (see illustration).

12 Adjust the bonnet bumpers on the wings so the bonnet is flush with the wings when closed (see illustration).

13 The bonnet latch assembly, as well as the hinges, should be lubricated with white lithium-base grease to prevent sticking and wear.

## 11 Bonnet release latch and cable - removal and refitting

### *Latch*

1 Disconnect the bonnet release cables by removing the cable retaining bolts and disengaging the cable from the latch assembly.(see illustration).

2 Scribe a line around the latches to aid alignment when refitting, then detach the retaining bolts from the inner footwell (see illustration) and remove the latch.

3 Refitting is the reverse of removal.

### *Cable*

4 Disconnect the bonnet release cable as described in (Section 11).

5 Detach all cable retaining clips located in the engine compartment.

6 Working in the passenger compartment, remove the driver's side kick panel surrounding the bonnet release lever. Pull the release lever forward and detach the release cables from the handle and bracket assembly (see illustration).

11.6 Remove the driver's side kick panel to access the bonnet release cables from the passenger compartment

7 Attach a piece of thin wire or string to the end of the cables to help aid the refitting process.

8 Working in the engine compartment, pull the cables and grommet out of the bulkhead until you can see the wire or string. Ensure that the new cable has a grommet attached then remove the old cable from the wire or string and replace it with the new cable.

9 Working from passenger compartment pull the wire or string back through the bulkhead.

10 Refitting is the reverse of removal. **Note:** *Push on the grommet with your fingers from the engine compartment to seat the grommet in the bulkhead.*

## 12 Radiator grille - removal and refitting

1 Using a Phillips screwdriver, detach the right and left hand grille inserts from the grille assembly **(see illustration)**. **Note:** *The grille can be removed without removing the inserts, but reaching the mounting screws from above is quite difficult.*

2 Working through the grille insert openings, remove the retaining screws securing both ends of the grille frame **(see illustration)**.

3 Pull the grille frame forward and remove it from the vehicle.

4 Refitting is the reverse of removal.

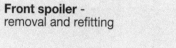

**12.1 Removing one side at a time, remove the grille insert retaining screws (arrowed) - tilt the top edge of the grille insert forward, then lift up and out to remove it**

## 13 Front spoiler - removal and refitting

1 Working on the left side of the vehicle, remove the front spoiler lower cover **(see illustration)**.

2 Remove the screws securing the front air dam panels in the left and right wheel openings **(see illustration)**, then detach the air dam panels from the vehicle. **Note:** *It will probably be necessary to turn the wheels to the right and left for access to the screws.*

3 Detach the retaining bolts securing the sides of the spoiler **(see illustration)**.

4 Working through the grille area of the

**12.2 Working through the grille insert openings, remove the retaining screws from each edge of the grille frame**

spoiler, detach the retaining screws securing the front of the spoiler **(see illustration)**.

5 Pull the spoiler forward and detach it from the vehicle.

6 Refitting is the reverse of removal.

## 14 Bumpers - removal and refitting

1 Detach the direction indicator and side marker light assemblies from the bumper(s) **(see illustrations)**.

2 Disconnect all wire harness connectors attached to the bumper or light assemblies that would interfere with removal.

**13.1 Working underneath the vehicle, remove the screws (arrowed) securing the front spoiler lower cover**

**13.2 Working in the front wheel openings, remove the screws (arrowed) securing the front air dam panels**

**13.3 The retaining bolts (arrowed) securing the sides of the front spoiler are located behind the bumper**

**13.4 Working through the grille area of the spoiler, remove the screws (arrowed) retaining the front of the spoiler**

**14.1a Depress the retaining clips on each side of the side marker lamp assemblies, then gently prise forward to remove it . . .**

**14.1b . . . then detach the direction indicator assemblies from the bumper in the same manner**

**14.3 Remove the two retaining bolts from the bottom of the bumper, then remove the bumper from the vehicle**

**15.4 Remove the bolts (arrowed) securing the inner wing splash shield**

**15.7a Detach the wing retaining bolts (arrowed) at the front of the wing**

**15.7b Remove the wing-to-radiator support bolt (arrowed)**

**15.7c Working in the wheel opening, remove the wing-to-rocker panel bolt (arrowed)**

## 16 Boot lid - removal, refitting and adjustment

**Note:** *The boot lid is heavy and somewhat awkward to remove and refit - at least two people should perform this procedure.*

### Removal and refitting

**1** Open the boot lid and cover the edges of the boot compartment with pads or cloths to protect the painted surfaces when the lid is removed.
**2** Disconnect any cables or wire harness connectors attached to the boot lid that would interfere with removal.
**3** Make alignment marks around the hinge mounting bolts with a marking pen.
**4** While an assistant supports the boot lid, remove the lid-to-hinge bolts on both sides and lift it off **(see illustration)**.
**5** Refitting is the reverse of removal. **Note:** *When refitting the boot lid, align the lid-to-hinge bolts with the marks made during removal.*

### Adjustment

**6** Fore-and-aft and side-to-side adjustment of the boot lid is done by moving the bonnet in relation to the hinge plate after loosening the bolts or nuts.
**7** Scribe a line around the entire hinge plate as described earlier in this section so you can judge the amount of movement.

**15.7d Remove the wing-to-door pillar bolt (arrow; lower bolt not visible)**

**15.7e Detach the bolts along the top of the wing**

**3** Remove two bumper retaining bolts located on the bottom side of the bumper **(see illustration)**. Pull the bumper assembly out and away from the vehicle to remove it.
**4** Refitting is the reverse of removal.

## 15 Front wing - removal and refitting

**1** Loosen the front wheel nuts. Raise the vehicle, support it securely on axle stands and remove the front wheel.
**2** Remove the front bumper assembly (see Section 14).
**3** Remove the front spoiler (see Section 13).

**4** Detach the inner wing splash shield **(see illustration)**.
**5** On 1988 and 1989 models, remove the coolant overflow reservoir located behind the splash shield (see Chapter 3).
**6** On models with round headlights, remove the headlight bezel. On models with composite headlights (1992 Vanden Plas, all 1993 and later models), remove the headlight (see Chapter 12).
**7** Remove the wing mounting bolts and nuts **(see illustrations)**.
**8** Detach the wing. It's a good idea to have an assistant support the wing while it's being moved away from the vehicle to prevent damage to the surrounding body panels.
**9** Refitting is the reverse of removal.

**16.4 With the help of an assistant to hold the boot lid, remove the retaining bolts and lift off the boot lid**

**16.9 Loosen the bolts and move the striker assembly as necessary to adjust the boot lid flush with the quarter panels in the closed position**

**16.10 Turn the bump stops in or out so the boot lid is flush with the rear wings when in the closed position**

**17.2 Remove the retaining screws (arrowed), then unclip the lock rod and disconnect any electrical connections**

**8** Loosen the bolts or nuts and move the boot lid into correct alignment. Move it only a little at a time. Tighten the hinge bolts or nuts and carefully lower the boot lid to check the alignment.
**9** If necessary after refitting, the entire boot lid striker assembly can be adjusted up and down as well as from side to side on the boot lid so the lid closes securely and is flush with the rear quarter panels. To do this, scribe a line around the boot lid striker assembly to provide a reference point. Then loosen the bolts and reposition the striker as necessary **(see illustration)**. Following adjustment, retighten the mounting bolts.
**10** Adjust the bump stops on the boot lid so the boot lid is flush with the rear wings when closed **(see illustration)**.
**11** The boot lid latch assembly, as well as the hinges, should be periodically lubricated with white lithium-base grease to prevent sticking and wear.

**17.6 Detach the clips securing the boot lamp finish panel**

**17.7 Disengage the lock rod (A), then remove the lock cylinder retaining bolts (B)**

## 17 Boot lid latch and lock cylinder - removal and refitting

### Boot lid latch

**1** Open the boot and scribe a line around the boot lid latch assembly for a reference point to help aid the refitting procedure.

**2** The boot lid latch is retained by three Phillips-head screws **(see illustration)**. For adjustment procedures, see Section 16.
**3** Disengage the lock rod from the latch.
**4** Disconnect all electrical connectors and remove the latch.
**5** Refitting is the reverse of removal.

### Boot lock cylinder

**6** Remove the plastic clips securing the boot light finish panel **(see illustration)**.
**7** Looking upward through the boot lid access hole, remove the lock rod and lock cylinder retaining bolts **(see illustration)**.
**8** Disconnect all electrical connections and remove the lock cylinder assembly.
**9** Refitting is the reverse of removal.

## 18 Door trim panel - removal and refitting

**1** Disconnect the negative cable from the battery.
*Caution: If the stereo in your vehicle is equipped with an anti-theft system, make sure you have the correct activation code before disconnecting the battery*
**2** On front door trim panels, remove the retaining screw located under the air duct door seal **(see illustration)**.
**3** Remove the inside handle trim bezel **(see illustrations)**.

**18.2 Lift the air duct-to-body seal to access the trim panel retaining screw (arrowed)**

**18.3a Remove the trim cover . . .**

**18.3b . . . then detach the inside handle retaining screw and bezel**

**18.4 Gently prise out the clips securing the wood finish panel**

**18.5 Detach the screws located behind the wood finisher panel, then remove the upper portion of the door trim panel**

**4** Detach the wood finishing panel **(see illustration)**.

**5** Unscrew the inside lock knob, then remove the remaining screws securing the upper half of the door trim panel and detach it from the vehicle **(see illustration)**.

**6** Detach the screw from the top edge of the lower door trim panel **(see illustration)**.

**7** Pry out the courtesy lamp lens, then detach the retaining screw from inside the lamp housing **(see illustrations)**.

**8** Remove the armrest trim cover, then detach the retaining screws from behind the cover **(see illustrations)**.

**9** Insert a wide putty knife, a screwdriver or a special trim panel removal tool between the trim panel and the head of the retaining clips to disengage the retaining clips along the outer edges of the door panel **(see illustration)**. Pry only at the clip locations or the panel could be damaged.

**10** Once all of the clips are disengaged, detach the trim panel, unplug any electrical connectors and remove the trim panel from the door by gently pulling it up and out.

**11** For access to the inner door, peel back the watershield, taking care not to tear it. To refit the trim panel, first press the watershield back into place. If necessary, add more sealant to hold it in place.

**12** Refitting is the reverse of removal.

## 19 Door - removal, refitting and adjustment

**Note:** *The door is heavy and somewhat awkward to remove and refit - at least two people should perform this procedure.*

### Removal and refitting

**1** Raise the window completely in the door, then disconnect the battery negative cable.
*Caution: If the stereo in your vehicle is equipped with an anti-theft system, make sure you have the correct activation code before disconnecting the battery.*

**18.6 Detach the screws along the top edge of the lower trim panel**

**18.7a Prise out the courtesy lamp lens**

**18.7b Remove the retaining screw from inside the lamp housing**

**18.8a Push up on the bottom to detach the armrest/pull handle trim cover**

**18.8b Remove the screws behind the armrest/pull handle trim cover**

**18.9 Disengage the retaining clips along the outer edge of the door trim panel**

**19.7a Work through the door access hole (arrowed) to remove the hinge-to-door retaining nuts from inside the door**

**19.7b Open the front door to access the rear door hinge-to-body bolts (arrowed)**

**2** Open the door all the way and support it on jacks or blocks covered with rags to prevent damaging the paint.

**3** Remove the door trim panel and water deflector as described in Section 18.

**4** Unplug all electrical connections, ground wires and harness retaining clips from the door. **Note:** *It is a good idea to label all connections to aid the reassembly process.*

**5** From the door side, detach the rubber conduit between the body and the door, then carefully pull the wiring harness through the conduit hole and remove it from the door.

**6** Mark around the door hinges with a pen or a scribe to ease alignment during reassembly.

**7** On front doors, work through the door access hole to remove the hinge-to-door nuts. On rear doors the hinge-to-body bolts are more accessible and can be removed by simply opening the front door and removing the bolts **(see illustrations)**.

**8** Have an assistant hold the door, remove the bolts or nuts and lift the door off.

**9** Refitting is the reverse of removal.

### Adjustment

**10** Having proper door to body alignment is a critical part of a well functioning door

assembly. First check the door hinge pins for excessive play. **Note:** *If the door can be lifted (1/16-inch or more) without the car body moving, the hinges should be replaced.*

**11** Door-to-body alignment adjustments are made by loosening the hinge-to-body or hinge-to-door bolts and moving the door. Proper body alignment is achieved when the top of doors are parallel with the roof section, the front door is flush with the wing, the rear door is flush with the rear quarter panel and the bottom of the doors are aligned with the lower rocker panel. If these goals can't be reached by adjusting the hinge-to-body or hinge-to-door bolts, body alignment shims may have to be purchased and inserted behind the hinges to achieve correct alignment.

**12** To adjust the door closed position, scribe a line or mark around the striker plate to provide a reference point. Check that the door latch is contacting the centre of the latch striker. If not, adjust the up-and-down position first.

**13** Finally, adjust the latch striker position, so the door skin is flush with the rear door (front) or rear quarter panel (rear) and provides positive engagement with the latch mechanism **(see illustration)**.

**20 Door latch, lock cylinder and handles** - removal and refitting

### Door latch

**1** Raise the window, then remove the door trim panel and watershield as described in Section 18.

**2** Working through the large access hole, disengage the outside door handle-to-latch rod and the inside handle-to-latch cable **(see illustration)**.

**3** All door locking rods are attached by plastic clips. The plastic clips can be removed by unsnapping the portion engaging the connecting rod and then by pulling the rod out of its locating hole.

**4** Remove the screws securing the latch to the door **(see illustration)**, then remove the latch assembly from the door.

**5** Refitting is the reverse of removal.

### Outside handle and door lock cylinder

**6** To remove the outside handle and lock cylinder assembly, raise the window then

**19.13 Adjust the door lock striker by loosening the hex nut and gently tapping the striker in the desired direction**

**20.2 Detach the outside handle-to-latch rod (A), then remove the inside handle-to-latch cable (B)**

**20.4 Remove the latch screws (arrowed) from the end of the door, and pull the latch assembly through the access hole.**

20.7 The outside handle retaining nuts (arrowed) can be reached through the access hole in the door

20.8 Detach the plastic clip securing the lock rod

remove the door trim panel and watershield as described in Section 18.

**7** Working through the access hole, detach the outside handle retaining nuts **(see illustration),** then pull the handle away from the door.

**8** Disengage the plastic clip that secures the outside handle-to-latch rod **(see illustration).**

**9** Remove the handle and lock cylinder assembly from the vehicle.

**10** Refitting is the reverse of removal.

### Inside handle and cable

**11** Remove the door trim panel as described in Section 18 and peel away the watershield.

**12** Detach the inside handle-to-latch cable **(see illustration 20.2).**

**13** Remove the inside handle retaining bolts **(see illustration).**

**14** Pull the handle and cable assembly free and remove them from the door.

**15** Refitting is the reverse of removal.

## 21 Door window glass regulator - removal and refitting

**1** To remove the window regulator assembly, raise the window to its full upright position, then remove the door trim panel and watershield as described in Section 18.

**2** Tape the window to the door glass frame to secure the window in the full upright position.

**3** Remove the regulator and motor mounting bolts **(see illustration).**

**4** Disconnect the electrical connector from the window regulator motor.

**5** Slide the equaliser arms out of the window glass channel and remove the regulator and motor assembly through the service hole in the door frame.

**HAYNES HINT** *If the motor or regulator needs replacing, it will be necessary to lock the sector gear to the regulator backplate. This can be done by fastening the sector gear to the backplate with a bolt inserted through one of the holes in the backplate and sector gear and secured with a nut. If none of the holes line up, drill a hole through the backplate and sector gear.*

⚠ *Warning: The regulator arms are under pressure and can cause serious injury if the motor is removed without locking the sector gear. The motor and regulator can now safely be separated.*

**6** Refitting is the reverse of removal.

20.13 After removing the cable from the latch assembly, detach the handle retaining bolts, then pull the handle and cable assembly free from the vehicle

21.3 Detach the window regulator bolts (arrowed)

**22.4a Front door window frame screws**

**22.4b Rear door window frame screws**

**22.5 After removing the window frame retaining screws, pull the window and frame assembly up and out to remove it**

**23.2 Remove the trim cover retaining screws**

**23.4 Disconnect the electrical connector, then detach the three mirror retaining screws and remove the mirror from the vehicle**

## 22 Door window glass -
### removal and refitting

**1** Raise the window to its full upright position, then remove the door trim panel and watershield as described in Section 18.
**2** Tape the window to the door glass frame to secure the window in the full upright position.
**3** Detach the regulator assembly (Section 21) and lower it to the bottom of the door.
**4** Remove the window frame retaining bolts **(see illustrations)**.
**5** Remove the window frame and glass assembly by pulling it up and out **(see illustration)**.
**6** Refitting is the reverse of removal.

## 23 Outside mirrors -
### removal and refitting

**1** Raise the window to the fully closed position and remove the upper half of the door trim panel (see Section 18).
**2** Detach the trim cover retaining screws **(see illustration)**.

**3** Disconnect the wiring plug from the mirror.
**4** Remove the three mirror retaining screws and detach the mirror from the vehicle **(see illustration)**.
**5** Refitting is the reverse of removal.

## 24 Centre console -
### removal and refitting

### Floor console

**1** Disconnect the negative battery cable.

**24.2 Carefully prise out the gear selector trim bezel**

*Caution: If the stereo in your vehicle is equipped with an anti-theft system, make sure you have the correct activation code before disconnecting the battery.*
**2** Pry out the gear selector trim bezel **(see illustration)**.
**3** Open the console compartment and remove the screws securing the ash tray. Pull the ash tray back towards the compartment to remove it **(see illustrations)**.
**4** Working through the ash tray opening, detach the plastic wingnuts securing the rear edge of the radio trim bezel **(see illustration)**.
**5** Apply the handbrake, then move the gear

**24.3a Open the console compartment to access the ash tray screws (arrowed)**

24.3b Pull the ash tray towards the rear of the vehicle to remove it - don't pull it straight up

24.4 Working through the ash tray opening, remove the radio trim bezel wingnuts (arrowed) located under the trim bezel

24.7 After removing the centre trim panel, detach the air conditioning duct

24.8 Remove the retaining screws in the air conditioning duct opening

24.9 Remove the plastic screws (arrowed) from each side of the console

24.13 Remove the plastic screw, then pull the overhead console down and unplug the electrical connectors

selector towards the rear of the vehicle. Pull up on the rear half of the radio trim bezel while gently detaching the clips securing the front, then remove the bezel from the vehicle.

**6** Remove the radio and heater control assembly (see Chapter 12).

**7** Remove the dashboard centre trim panel (see Section 26), then remove the centre air conditioning duct from the vehicle **(see illustration)**.

**8** Remove the retaining screws located in the air conditioning duct opening **(see illustration)**.

**9** Remove the plastic screws securing the lower front section of the console **(see illustration)**.

**10** Unplug any electrical connectors that will interfere with the removal of the console.

**11** Pull the console towards the rear of the vehicle, then lift the console up over the shift lever and remove it from the vehicle.

**12** Refitting is the reverse of removal.

### *Overhead console*

**13** Remove the plastic screw securing the overhead console, then carefully pull the console out of the headliner **(see illustration)**.

**14** Disconnect the electrical connectors from the lights.

**15** Refitting is the reverse of removal.

## 25 Instrument cluster housing - removal and refitting

> ⚠ **Warning: Later models are equipped with airbags. To prevent the accidental deployment of the airbag, which could cause personal injury or damage to the airbag system, DO NOT work in the vicinity of the steering column or instrument panel. The manufacturer recommends that, on airbag equipped models, the following procedure should be left to a dealer service department or other repair workshop because of the special tools and techniques required to disable the airbag system.**

**1** Disconnect the negative battery cable.

*Caution: If the stereo in your vehicle is equipped with an anti-theft system, make sure you have the correct activation code before disconnecting the battery.*

**2** Remove the drivers side knee bolster (see Section 26).

**3** Place the steering wheel in the full rearward position. If the vehicle is equipped with a tilt column, place the steering wheel in the lowest position.

**4** Remove the instrument cluster housing screws **(see illustration)**.

**5** Pull the instrument cluster housing outward to access the electrical connections on the backside **(see illustration)**.

**6** Disconnect all electrical connections from the backside of the cluster housing and remove the housing from the vehicle.

**7** Refitting is the reverse of removal.

25.4 Working in the knee bolster opening, remove two retaining screws from each end of the instrument cluster housing

25.5 Pull outward on the instrument cluster housing and unplug the electrical connectors from the backside

**26.2 Remove the retaining screws along the outer edge of the knee bolster, then remove it from the vehicle**

**26.5 Grasp the centre trim panel with both hands, then unsnap the retaining clips (arrowed) from the dashboard assembly**

## 26 Dashboard trim panels - removal and refitting

⚠ *Warning: Later models are equipped with airbags. To prevent the accidental deployment of the airbag, which could cause personal injury or damage to the airbag system, DO NOT work in the vicinity of the steering column or instrument panel. The manufacturer recommends that, on airbag equipped models, the following procedure should be left to a dealer service department or other repair workshop because of the special tools and techniques required to disable the airbag system.*
*Caution: If the stereo in your vehicle is equipped with an anti-theft system, make sure you have the correct activation code before disconnecting the battery*

### Knee bolster

1 Knee bolsters are located on the lower half of the instrument panel on the driver and passenger sides of the vehicle. The removal of these covers will allow access to a variety of electrical, heating and air conditioning components.
2 Detach the retaining screws along the edges of the knee bolster **(see illustration)**.
3 Pull outward on the lower edge of the knee bolster and detach it from the vehicle.
4 Refitting is the reverse of removal.

### Centre trim panel

5 Carefully pull outward to detach the centre trim panel from the instrument panel **(see illustration)**.
6 Refitting is the reverse of removal.

### Glove box

7 Detach the passenger side knee bolster as described in Steps 2 and 3.

8 Remove the glove box door hinge bolts **(see illustration)**.
9 Open the glove box door, then detach it from the vehicle.
10 Detach the heater duct and the relay mounting panel from the bottom of the glove box.
11 Detach the remaining screws securing the upper edge of the glove box **(see illustration)**.
12 Disconnect the lamp from the glove box and remove the assembly from the vehicle.
13 Refitting is the reverse of removal.

## 27 Steering column cover - removal and refitting

⚠ *Warning: Later models are equipped with airbags. To prevent the accidental deployment of the airbag, which could cause*

**26.8 With the passenger side knee bolster removed, unscrew the glove box door hinge bolts**

**26.11 Remove the screws along the top edge (arrowed), pull the glove box out and remove the lamp assembly**

27.2 Pull off the knob from the instrument panel light rheostat

27.3 Remove the lower steering column cover screws

*personal injury or damage to the airbag system, DO NOT work in the vicinity of the steering column or instrument panel. The manufacturer recommends that, on airbag equipped models, the following procedure should be left to a dealer service department or other repair workshop because of the special tools and techniques required to disable the airbag system.*

**1** Remove the steering wheel (Chapter 10)
**2** Remove the knob from the rheostat (dimmer) for the instrument panel lights **(see illustration)**.
**3** Remove the lower steering column cover screws **(see illustration)**, then detach the lower cover.
**4** Working through the lower cover opening, remove the four screws securing the upper half of the cover, then pull the cover forward and out to remove it **(see illustration)**.
**5** Refitting is the reverse of removal.

## 28 Cowl cover - 
removal and refitting

**1** Remove the windscreen wiper arms (see Chapter 12).

**2** Remove the retaining screws located along the top of the cowl cover **(see illustration)**.
**3** Lift the cowl cover up slightly, then detach the electrical connectors and the spray nozzle hoses from the backside of the cowl cover.
**4** Detach the cowl cover from the vehicle.
**5** Refitting is the reverse of removal.

## 29 Seats - removal and refitting

### Front seat

**1** Position the seat all the way forward or all the way to the rear to access the front seat retaining bolts.
**2** Detach any bolt trim covers and remove the retaining bolts **(see illustration)**.
**3** Tilt the seat upward to access the underneath, then unplug any electrical connectors and lift the seat from the vehicle.
**4** Refitting is the reverse of removal.

### Rear seat

**5** Remove retaining screws at the lower edge of the seat cushion **(see illustration)**. Then lift up on the front edge and remove the cushion from the vehicle.
**6** Detach the retaining bolts at the lower edge of the seat back.
**7** Lift up on the lower edge of the seat back to release the clips securing the top. Then remove it from the vehicle.
**8** Refitting is the reverse of removal.

27.4 Remove the four screws securing the upper half of the steering column cover

28.2 Remove the screws (arrowed) located along the top of the cowl cover

29.2 Use a Torx bit to remove the front seat retaining bolts (arrowed)

29.5 Detach the screws (arrowed) along the lower edge of the seat cove

# Chapter 12
# Body electrical system

## Contents

## Degrees of difficulty

| Easy, suitable for novice with little experience |  | Fairly easy, suitable for beginner with some experience |  | Fairly difficult, suitable for competent DIY mechanic | | Difficult, suitable for experienced DIY mechanic | | Very difficult, suitable for expert DIY or professional |  |
|---|---|---|---|---|---|---|---|---|---|

## 1 General information

The electrical system is a 12-volt, negative earth type. Power for the lights and all electrical accessories is supplied by a lead/acid-type battery which is charged by the alternator.

This Chapter covers repair and service procedures for the various electrical components not associated with the engine. Information on the battery, alternator, distributor and starter motor will be found in Chapter 5.

It should be noted that when portions of the electrical system are serviced, the cable should be disconnected from the negative battery terminal to prevent electrical shorts and/or fires.

## 2 Electrical fault finding - general information

A typical electrical circuit consists of an electrical component, any switches, relays, motors, fuses, fusible links, in-line fuses or circuit breakers related to that component and the wiring and electrical connectors that link the component to both the battery and the chassis. To help you pinpoint an electrical circuit problem, wiring diagrams are included at the end of this Chapter.

Before tackling any troublesome electrical circuit, first study the appropriate wiring diagrams to get a complete understanding of what makes up that individual circuit. Trouble spots, for instance, can often be narrowed down by noting if other components related to the circuit are operating properly. If several components or circuits fail at one time, chances are the problem is in a fuse or earth connection, because several circuits are often routed through the same fuse and earth connections.

Electrical problems usually stem from simple causes, such as loose or corroded connections, a blown fuse, a melted fusible link or a bad relay. Visually inspect the condition of all fuses, wires and connections in a problem circuit before diagnosing it.

If testing instruments are going to be utilised, use the diagrams to plan ahead of time where you will make the necessary connections in order to accurately pinpoint the trouble spot.

The basic tools needed for electrical fault finding include a circuit tester or voltmeter (a 12-volt bulb with a set of test leads can also be used), a continuity tester, which includes a bulb, battery and set of test leads, and a jumper wire, preferably with a circuit breaker incorporated, which can be used to bypass electrical components. Before attempting to locate a problem with test instruments, use the wiring diagram(s) to decide where to make the connections.

### Voltage checks

Voltage checks should be performed if a circuit is not functioning properly. Connect one lead of a circuit tester to either the negative battery terminal or a known good earth. Connect the other lead to a electrical connector in the circuit being tested, preferably nearest to the battery or fuse. If the bulb of the tester lights, voltage is present, which means that the part of the circuit between the electrical connector and the battery is problem free. Continue checking the rest of the circuit in the same fashion. When you reach a point at which no voltage is present, the problem lies between that point and the last test point with voltage. Most of the time the problem can be traced to a loose connection. **Note:** *Keep in mind that some circuits receive voltage only when the ignition key is in the Accessory or Run position.*

### Finding a short

One method of finding shorts in a circuit is to remove the fuse and connect a test light or voltmeter in its place. There should be no voltage present in the circuit. Move the wiring harness from side to side while watching the test light. If the bulb goes on, there is a short

3.1a The left side fusebox is located in the passenger's side kick panel, behind the fuse panel cover

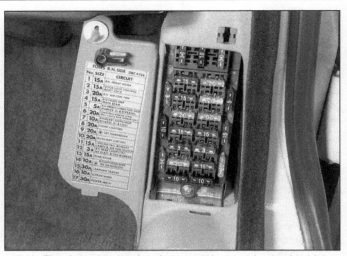

3.1b The right side fusebox is located in the driver's side kick panel, behind the fuse panel cover

to earth somewhere in that area, probably where the insulation has rubbed through. The same test can be performed on each component in the circuit, even a switch.

### Earth check

Perform an earth test to check whether a component is properly earthed. Disconnect the battery and connect one lead of a self-powered test light, known as a continuity tester, to a known good earth. Connect the other lead to the wire or earth connection being tested. If the bulb goes on, the earth is good. If the bulb does not go on, the earth is not good.

### Continuity check

A continuity check is done to determine if there are any breaks in a circuit - if it is passing electricity properly. With the circuit off (no power in the circuit), a self-powered continuity tester can be used to check the circuit. Connect the test leads to both ends of the circuit (or to the "power" end and a good earth), and if the test light comes on the circuit is passing current properly. If the light doesn't come on, there is a break somewhere in the circuit. The same procedure can be used to test a switch, by connecting the continuity tester to the power in and power out sides of the switch. With the switch turned On, the test light should come on.

### Finding an open circuit

When diagnosing for possible open circuits, it is often difficult to locate them by sight because oxidation or terminal misalignment are hidden by the electrical connectors. Merely wiggling an electrical connector on a sensor or in the wiring harness may correct the open circuit condition. Remember this when an open circuit is indicated when diagnosing a circuit. Intermittent problems may also be caused by oxidised or loose connections.

Electrical fault finding is simple if you keep in mind that all electrical circuits are basically electricity running from the battery, through the wires, switches, relays, fuses and fusible links to each electrical component (light bulb, motor, etc.) and to earth, from which it is passed back to the battery. Any electrical problem is an interruption in the flow of electricity to and from the battery.

### 3 Fuses - general information

The electrical circuits of the vehicle are protected by a combination of fuses, circuit breakers and In-line fuses. The fuse blocks are located in the left and right side kick panels and in the centre console glove box (see illustrations).

Each of the fuses is designed to protect a specific circuit, and the various circuits are identified on the fuse panel cover.

Miniaturised fuses are employed in the fuse blocks. These compact fuses, with blade terminal design, allow fingertip removal and renewal. If an electrical component fails, always check the fuse first. The best way to

check the fuses is with a test light. Check for power at the exposed terminal tips of each fuse. If power is present on one side of the fuse but not the other, the fuse is blown. A blown fuse can be confirmed by visual inspection (see illustration).

Be sure to renew blown fuses with the correct type. Fuses of different ratings are physically interchangeable, but only fuses of the proper rating should be used. Replacing a fuse with one of a higher or lower value than specified is not recommended. Each electrical circuit needs a specific amount of protection. The amperage value of each fuse is moulded into the fuse body.

If the renewal fuse immediately fails, don't renew it again until the cause of the problem is isolated and corrected. In most cases, this will be a short circuit in the wiring caused by a broken or deteriorated wire.

### 4 In-line fuses - general information

Some circuits are protected by in-line fuses. In-line fuses are used in such circuits as the windscreen wiper system, headlight

3.1c A third fusebox is located in the centre console glove box

3.3 When a fuse blows, the metal element between the terminals melts - the fuse on the left is blown, the one on the right is ok

**1988 to 1989 relay location details**

wash system, radio memory and the ABS main feed and pump circuits.

In-line fuses are located through out the vehicle depending on the year, make and model. Consult the wiring diagrams at the end of this Chapter for further information.

In-line fuses also have a blade terminal design, which allow fingertip removal and renewal. If an electrical component fails, always check the fuse first. A blown fuse is easily identified through the clear plastic body. Inspect the element for evidence of damage (see illustration 3.3).

Be sure to renew blown fuses with the correct type. Fuses are usually colour-coded to indicate their rating. Fuses of different ratings are physically interchangeable, but only fuses of the proper rating should be used. Replacing a fuse with one of a different value than specified is not recommended. Each electrical circuit needs a specific amount of protection. The amperage value of each fuse is moulded into the fuse body.

If the renewal fuse immediately fails, don't renew it again until the cause of the problem is isolated and corrected. Don't substitute anything else for the fuse. In most cases, this will be a short circuit in the wiring caused by a broken or deteriorated wire.

## 5  Circuit breakers - general information

Circuit breakers generally protect components such as electric windows, central locking and headlights. On some models the circuit breaker resets itself automatically, so an electrical overload in the circuit will cause it to fail momentarily, then come back on. If the circuit doesn't come back on, check it immediately. Once the condition is corrected, the circuit breaker will resume its normal function. Some circuit breakers have a button on top and must be reset manually.

To test a circuit breaker, use an ohmmeter to check continuity between the terminals. A reading of zero to 1.0 ohms indicates a good circuit breaker. An open circuit reading on the meter indicates a bad circuit breaker.

## 6  Relays - general information and testing

### General information

Several electrical accessories in the vehicle, such as the fuel injection system, electric windows, central locking, etc, use relays to transmit the electrical signal to the component. Relays use a low-current circuit (the control circuit) to open and close a high-current circuit (the power circuit). If the relay is defective, that component will not operate properly. The relays are mounted throughout the vehicle (see illustrations). If a faulty relay is suspected, it

**1990 to 1992 relay location details**

can be removed and tested using the procedure below or by a dealer service department or a repair workshop. Defective relays must be replaced as a unit.

### Testing

**1** It's best to refer to the wiring diagram for the circuit to determine the proper connections for the relay you're testing. However, if you're not able to determine the correct connection from the wiring diagrams, you may be able to determine the test connections from the information that follows.
**2** On most relays, two of the terminals are the relay's control circuit (they connect to the relay coil which, when energised, closes the large contacts to complete the circuit). The other terminals are the power circuit (they are connected together within the relay when the control-circuit coil is energised).
**3** Relays are sometimes marked as an aid to help you determine which terminals are the control circuit and which are the power

circuit **(see illustration)**. As a general rule, the two thicker wires connected to the relay are the power circuit; the thinner wires are the control circuit.
**4** Remove the relay from the vehicle and check for continuity between the relay power circuit terminals. There should be no continuity.

**6.3 Most relays are marked on the outside to easily identify the control circuit and power circuits**

**5** Connect a fused jumper wire between one of the two control circuit terminals and the positive battery terminal. Connect another jumper wire between the other control circuit terminal and earth. When the connections are made, the relay should click. On some relays, polarity may be critical, so, if the relay doesn't click, try swapping the jumper wires on the control circuit terminals.
**6** With the jumper wires connected, check for continuity between the power circuit terminals. Now, there should be continuity.
**8** If the relay fails any of the above tests, renew it.

### 7 Direction indicator/hazard flasher - general information

 *Warning: Later model vehicles are equipped with airbags. To prevent accidental deployment*

**1993 to 1994 relay location details**

*of the airbag, which could cause personal injury or damage to the airbag system, DO NOT work in the vicinity of the steering column or instrument panel. The manufacturer recommends that, on airbag equipped models, the following procedure be performed at a dealer service department or other properly equipped repair facility because of the special tools and techniques required to disable the airbag system.*

The direction indicator and hazard flasher systems are governed by the central processing unit. The central processing unit requires special testers and diagnostic procedures which are beyond the scope of this manual.

If the direction indicator/hazard flasher system fails and the indicator bulbs are in working condition take the vehicle to a dealer service department or an automotive electrical specialist for further diagnosis and repair.

## 8  Steering column switches - removal and refitting

⚠️ *Warning: Later models are equipped with airbags. To prevent accidental deployment of the airbag, which could cause personal injury or damage to the airbag system, DO NOT work in the vicinity of the steering column or instrument panel. The manufacturer recommends that, on airbag equipped models, the following procedure be performed at a dealer service department or other properly equipped repair facility because of the special tools and techniques required to disable the airbag system.*
*Caution: If the stereo in your vehicle is equipped with an anti-theft system, make sure you have the correct activation code before disconnecting the battery.*

1 Disconnect the negative battery cable.
2 Remove the steering wheel (Chapter 10).
3 Remove the lower steering column cover (see Chapter 11).
4 Remove the switch retaining screw(s) **(see illustration)**.

**8.4  Remove the switch retaining screws, disconnect the electrical connectors and pull the switches outward (arrowed)**

9.4  Remove the switch mounting plate screws (arrowed). Lower the mounting plate and switch assembly to access the ignition switch/key lock cylinder

9.5  To remove the ignition switch/lock cylinder assembly, drill out the centre of the two retaining bolts (arrowed) and remove them with a screw extractor

5  Disconnect the electrical connectors from underneath the steering column and remove the switch or switches from the vehicle.
6  Refitting is the reverse of removal.

## 9  Ignition switch and key lock cylinder - removal and refitting

**Warning: Later models are equipped with airbags. To prevent accidental deployment of the airbag, which could cause personal injury or damage to the airbag system, DO NOT work in the vicinity of the steering column or instrument panel. The manufacturer recommends that, on airbag equipped models, the following procedure be performed at a dealer service department or other properly equipped repair facility because of the special tools and techniques required to disable the airbag system.**
**Caution: If the stereo in your vehicle is equipped with an anti-theft system, make sure you have the correct activation code before disconnecting the battery.**

1  Disconnect the negative battery cable.
2  Remove the steering wheel (Chapter 10).
3  Remove the steering column trim covers (see Chapter 11).
4  Remove the steering column switch mounting plate screws **(see illustration)**.
5  Remove the shear-head bolts retaining the ignition switch/lock cylinder assembly and separate the bracket halves from the steering column. This can be accomplished by drilling out the centre of the screws and using a screw extractor to remove them **(see illustration)**.
6  Place the new switch assembly in position, refit the new shear-head bolts and tighten them until the heads snap off.
7  The remainder of the refitting is the reverse of removal.

## 10  Instrument panel switches - removal and refitting

**Warning: Later models are equipped with airbags. To prevent accidental deployment of the airbag, which could cause personal injury or damage to the airbag**

**system, DO NOT work in the vicinity of the steering column or instrument panel. The manufacturer recommends that, on airbag equipped models, the following procedure be performed at a dealer service department or other properly equipped repair facility because of the special tools and techniques required to disable the airbag system.**
**Caution: If the stereo in your vehicle is equipped with an anti-theft system, make sure you have the correct activation code before disconnecting the battery.**

1  Remove the lower trim cover(s) **(see illustration)**.
2  To remove the vehicle condition monitor (VCM) switch assembly, simply depress the switch retaining clip and lower the switch assembly from the instrument panel **(see illustration)**.
3  To remove the headlight switch assembly, detach the switch knob and remove the hex nut securing the switch to the instrument panel **(see illustration)**. Depress the retaining clip securing the switch, disconnect the electrical connectors and remove the switch assembly from the instrument panel.
4  Refitting is the reverse of removal.

10.1  Remove the lower trim cover(s) from the instrument panel switch assembly

10.2  Depress the clip on the front, lower the switch assembly from the instrument panel and unplug the connectors

10.3  Detach the headlight switch knob, then remove the hex nut securing the switch to the instrument panel (arrowed)

**12.3 Remove the instrument cluster retaining screws (arrowed) then separate the instrument cluster from the cluster housing**

**13.3 Remove the retaining screws (arrowed) and pull the radio/control panel out enough to unplug the connectors**

## 11 Fuel, oil and temperature gauges - check

⚠ *Warning: Later models are equipped with airbags. To prevent accidental deployment of the airbag, which could cause personal injury or damage to the airbag system, DO NOT work in the vicinity of the steering column or instrument panel. The manufacturer recommends that, on airbag equipped models, the following procedure be performed at a dealer service department or other properly equipped repair facility because of the special tools and techniques required to disable the airbag system.*

1 All tests below require the ignition switch to be turned to ON position when testing.
2 Check the fuse if the gauge pointer does not move from the empty, low or cold positions. If the fuse is OK, locate the particular sender unit for the circuit you're working on (see Chapter 4 for fuel sender unit location, Chapter 2 for oil sender unit location, or Chapter 3 for temperature sender unit location). Connect the sender unit connector to earth If the pointer goes to the full, high or hot position renew the sender unit. If the pointer stays in same position use a jumper wire to earth the terminal on the back of the gauge. If the pointer moves with the back of the gauge earthed the problem lies in the wire between the gauge and the sender unit. If the pointer does not moves with the back of the gauge earthed check for voltage at the other terminal of the gauge. If voltage is present renew the gauge.

## 12 Instrument cluster - removal and refitting

⚠ *Warning: Later models are equipped with airbags. To prevent accidental deployment of the airbag, which could cause personal injury or damage to the airbag system, DO NOT work in the vicinity of the steering column or instrument panel. The manufacturer recommends that, on airbag equipped models, the following procedure be performed at a dealer service department or other properly equipped repair facility because of the special tools and techniques required to disable the airbag system.*
*Caution: If the stereo in your vehicle is equipped with an anti-theft system, make sure you have the correct activation code before disconnecting the battery.*

1 Disconnect the negative battery cable.
2 Remove the instrument cluster housing (see Chapter 11).
3 Remove the instrument cluster mounting screws **(see illustration)**. Separate the instrument cluster from the cluster housing.
4 Refitting is the reverse of removal.

## 13 Radio and speakers - removal and refitting

⚠ *Warning: Later models are equipped with airbags. To prevent accidental deployment of the airbag, which could cause personal injury or damage to the airbag system, DO NOT work in the vicinity of the steering column or instrument panel. The manufacturer recommends that, on airbag*

equipped models, the following procedure be performed at a dealer service department or other properly equipped repair facility because of the special tools and techniques required to disable the airbag system.
*Caution: If the stereo in your vehicle is equipped with an anti-theft system, make sure you have the correct activation code before disconnecting the battery.*

1 Disconnect the negative battery cable.

### Radio

2 Remove the radio trim bezel (Chapter 11).
3 Remove the retaining screws **(see illustration)**, pull the radio/control panel outward to access the backside and disconnect the electrical connectors and aerial lead. Detach the retaining clips and separate the radio from the control panel.
4 Refitting is the reverse of removal.

### Speakers

5 Remove the door trim panel (Chapter 11).
6 Remove the nuts from the speaker mounting studs **(see illustration)**. Disconnect the electrical connector and remove the speaker from the vehicle.
7 Refitting is the reverse of removal.

**13.6 Remove the nuts from the retaining studs (arrowed) to remove the speaker**

**14.1 The aerial mast retaining nut can be removed with an open end spanner**

**14.3 Remove the retaining bolts (arrowed), pull the aerial assembly out and unplug the electrical connectors and aerial lead**

**14.6 With the ignition key and the radio in the ON position, guide the aerial mast out of the motor assembly - note the direction of the "teeth" on the aerial cable**

**15.1 Lift up the wiper arm nut cover, remove the nut and pull the wiper arm straight off the shaft**

**15.3 Use a spanner or socket to remove the drive spindle retaining nut**

**15.4 Remove the bolts (A) along the top edge of the housing and detach the clips (B) along the bottom edge**

## 14 Electric aerial - removal and refitting

### Aerial motor assembly

1 Remove the aerial mast retaining nut **(see illustration)**.
2 Working in the boot, pry out the plastic clips securing the driver's side boot finishing panels to allow access to the aerial motor assembly.
3 Detach the motor assembly retaining bolts **(see illustration)**. Disconnect the electrical connector and earth strap then remove the aerial motor assembly from the vehicle.
4 Refitting is the reverse of removal.

### Aerial mast

5 Remove the aerial mast retaining nut **(see illustration 14.1)**.
6 With an assistant controlling the ignition switch, turn the ignition key and the radio to the ON position. Guide the aerial mast out of the body as the cable unwinds from the motor assembly **(see illustration)**. Note the direction the "teeth" on the aerial cable are facing for refitting purposes.
7 To refit the aerial mast, insert the aerial cable into the motor assembly with the cable teeth facing the direction as noted above. Have your assistant turn the ignition key and the radio to the ON position. Guide the cable

and aerial mast through the opening as the cable winds back into the motor assembly.
8 Refit the aerial mast retaining nut.

## 15 Windscreen wiper motor - removal and refitting

1 Pull the wiper arm nut cover back to access the wiper arm nuts. Remove the nuts and pull the wiper arm straight off the shaft **(see illustration)**.
2 Remove the screws and detach the cowl cover (see Chapter 11).
3 Remove the drive spindle nut **(see illustration)**.
4 Remove the retaining bolts located along the top edge of the wiper motor housing and detach three retaining clips along the bottom edge of the wiper motor housing **(see illustration)**.
5 Disconnect the electrical connector and remove the motor assembly from the vehicle.
6 Refitting is the reverse of removal.

## 16 Heated rear window - check and repair

1 The heated rear window consists of a number of horizontal elements baked onto the glass surface.

2 Small breaks in the element can be repaired without removing the rear window.

### Check

3 Turn the ignition switch and heated rear window switches to the ON position.
4 When measuring voltage during the next two tests, wrap a piece of aluminium foil around the tip of the voltmeter negative probe and press the foil against the heating element with your finger **(see illustration)**. Place the voltmeter positive lead against the heated window positive terminal.
5 Check the voltage at the centre of each heating element **(see illustration)**.

**16.4 When measuring the voltage at the heated rear window grid, wrap a piece of aluminium foil around the negative probe of the voltmeter and press the foil against the element with your finger**

16.5 To determine if a heating element has broken, check the voltage at the centre of each element. If the voltage is 6-volts, the element is unbroken; if the voltage is 12-volts, the element is broken between the centre and the positive end. If there is no voltage, the element is broken between the centre and earth

16.7 To find the break, place the voltmeter positive lead against the heated window positive terminal, place the voltmeter negative lead with the foil strip against the heating element at the positive terminal end and slide it toward the negative terminal end - the point at which the voltmeter reading changes abruptly is the point at which the element is broken

6 If the voltage is 6 volts, the element is okay (there is no break). If the voltage is 12 volts, the element is broken between the centre of the element and the positive end. If the voltage is 0 volts the element is broken between the centre of the element and earth.

7 To find the break, place the voltmeter positive lead against the defogger positive terminal. Place the voltmeter negative lead with the foil strip against the heating element at the positive terminal end and slide it toward the negative terminal end. The point at which the voltmeter deflects from zero to several volts is the point at which the heating element is broken (see illustration).

### Repair

8 Repair the break in the element using a repair kit specifically recommended for this purpose.

9 Prior to repairing a break, turn off the system and allow it to cool off for a few minutes.

10 Lightly buff the element area with fine steel wool, then clean it thoroughly with rubbing alcohol.

11 Use masking tape to mask off the area being repaired.

12 Thoroughly mix the epoxy, following the instructions provided with the repair kit.

13 Apply the epoxy material to the slit in the masking tape, overlapping the undamaged area about 3/4-inch on either end (see illustration).

14 Allow the repair to cure for 24 hours before removing the tape and using the system.

### 17 Headlights - renewal

⚠ *Warning: Later models are equipped with halogen gas-filled headlight bulbs which are under*

*pressure and may shatter if the surface is damaged or the bulb is dropped. Wear eye protection and handle the bulbs carefully, grasping only the base whenever possible. Do not touch the surface of the bulb with your fingers because the oil from your skin could cause it to overheat and fail prematurely. If you do touch the bulb surface, clean it with rubbing alcohol.*

16.13 Apply masking tape to the inside of the window at the damaged area, then brush on the special conductive coating

17.3a Remove the two retaining screws at the top and the one in the grille opening (arrowed)

### Sealed beam units

1 Remove the radiator grille (see Chapter 11).
2 Detach the headlight bezel trim cover (see illustration).
3 Remove the headlight bezel (see illustrations).
4 Remove the screws which secure the retaining ring and withdraw the ring. Support the light as this is done (see illustration).

17.2 Remove the screws (arrowed) and detach the headlight bezel trim cover

17.3b The retaining screw at the outside lower corner can be accessed from under the bumper

**17.4 Loosen the retaining ring screws (arrowed) a few turns - rotate the retaining ring anti-clockwise to remove it**

**17.9 Disconnect the electrical connector and rotate the bulb assembly 1/4-turn anti-clockwise**

**18.2 The headlight horizontal adjustment knob (A) is located at the top of the headlight and the vertical adjustment knob (B) is below the headlight**

**5** Pull the headlight out slightly and disconnect the electrical connector from the rear of the light, then remove the light from the vehicle.

**6** To refit, position the new unit close enough to connect the electrical connector. Make sure that the numbers moulded into the lens are at the top.

**7** Refit and tighten the retaining ring. Test the headlight operation.

**8** The remainder of the refitting is the reverse of removal.

### Halogen gas-filled bulbs

**9** Disconnect the electrical connector from the bulb assembly. Rotate the headlight bulb connector 1/4-turn anti-clockwise (viewed from the rear) **(see illustration)**.

**10** Withdraw the bulb assembly from the headlight housing.

**11** Without touching the glass with your bare fingers (see the **Warning** at the start of the Section), insert the new bulb assembly into the headlight housing and rotate the bulb socket 1/4-turn clockwise to refit it.

**12** Plug in the electrical connector and test headlight operation.

---

**18 Headlights** - adjustment

---

**Note:** *The following procedure is intended for emergency use only, and we strongly recommend that the headlight aim is only checked using optical beam-setting equipment. It is important that the headlights are aimed correctly. If adjusted incorrectly they could blind the driver of an oncoming vehicle and cause a serious accident or seriously reduce your ability to see the road. The headlights should be checked for proper aim every 12 months and any time a new headlight is installed or front end body work is performed.*

**1** Adjustment should be made with the vehicle sitting level, the petrol tank half-full and no unusually heavy load in the vehicle.

**2** Early models with sealed beam headlights have four adjusting knobs protruding through the backside of the radiator support. The vertical (up and down) adjustment knobs are located above the headlight and the horizontal (left to right) adjusting knobs are located below the headlight **(see illustration)**.

**3** On later models with halogen bulbs, adjustments are made in the same manner as described in the previous step, except there are only two adjusting knobs which tilt the headlight housing to the desired angle.

**4** If the headlight housing has been replaced or the vehicle has suffered front-end damage, refer to following procedure.

**5** This method requires a blank wall, masking tape and a level floor.

**6** Position masking tape vertically on the wall in reference to the vehicle centreline and the centrelines of both headlights **(see illustration)**.

**7** Position a horizontal tape line in reference to the centreline of all the headlights. **Note:** *It may be easier to position the tape on the wall with the vehicle parked only a few inches away.*

**18.6 Headlight adjustment details**

**19.2 Remove the headlight housing retaining nuts (arrowed) from the backside of the radiator support**

**20.3 Check for power at the horn terminal with the horn button depressed**

8 Adjustment should be made with the vehicle parked 25 feet from the wall, sitting level, the petrol tank half-full and no unusually heavy load in the vehicle.

9 Starting with the low beam adjustment, position the high intensity zone so it is two inches below the horizontal line and two inches to the right of the headlight vertical line. Adjustments are made by turning the knobs located behind the headlight housings **(see illustration 18.2)**.

10 With the high beams on, the high intensity zone should be vertically centred with the exact centre just below the horizontal line. **Note:** *It may not be possible to position the headlight aim exactly for both high and low beams. If a compromise must be made, keep in mind that the low beams are the most used and have the greatest effect on safety.*

11 Have the headlights adjusted by a dealer service department or service station at the earliest opportunity.

### 19 Headlight housing (1992 to 1994 models) - removal and refitting

 *Warning: These vehicles are equipped with halogen gas-filled headlight bulbs which are under pressure and may shatter if the surface is damaged or the bulb is dropped. Wear eye protection and handle the bulbs carefully, grasping only the base whenever possible. Do not touch the surface of the bulb with your fingers because the oil from your skin could cause it to overheat and fail prematurely. If you do touch the bulb surface, clean it with rubbing alcohol.*

1 Remove the headlight bulb (Section 17).

2 Remove the retaining nuts, detach the housing and withdraw it from the vehicle **(see illustration)**.

3 Refitting is the reverse of removal.

### 20 Horn - check and renewal

#### Check

**Note:** *Check the fuses before beginning electrical diagnosis.*

1 Disconnect the electrical connector from the horn.

2 To test the horn, connect battery voltage to the two terminals with a pair of jumper wires. If the horn doesn't sound, renew it.

3 If the horn does sound, check for voltage at the terminal when the horn button is depressed **(see illustration)**. If there's voltage at the terminal, check for a bad earth at the horn.

4 If there's no voltage at the horn, check the relay (see Section 6). Note that most horn relays are either the four-terminal or externally earthed three-terminal type.

5 If the relay is OK, check for voltage to the relay power and control circuits. If either of the circuits are not receiving voltage, inspect the wiring between the relay and the fuse panel.

6 If both relay circuits are receiving voltage, depress the horn button and check the circuit from the relay to the horn button for continuity

to earth. If there's no continuity, check the circuit for an open. If the circuit is good, renew the horn button.

7 If there's continuity to earth through the horn button, check for an open or short in the circuit from the relay to the horn.

#### Renewal

8 Remove the radiator grille inserts (see Chapter 11).

9 Disconnect the electrical connector and remove the retaining nuts securing the horn brackets **(see illustration)**.

10 Refitting is the reverse of removal.

### 21 Bulb renewal

#### Front direction indicator/rear parking and side marker lights

1 Remove the lens retaining screws and the lens **(see illustration)**.

2 Push inward and rotate the bulb anti-clockwise to remove it from the holder.

3 Renew the bulb, refit the lamp lens and test the bulb operation.

**20.9 Disconnect the electrical connector, remove the retaining nuts (arrowed) - then detach the horn(s)**

**21.1 The front direction indicator/rear parking and side marker light bulbs are accessible after removing the lens screws**

**21.4 The Rear direction indicator, brake, tail and reversing light bulbs are accessible from the boot compartment after removing the plastic knobs (arrowed) securing the bulb housing covers**

**21.5 Remove the bulb cluster from the tail light housing - The bulb is removed by pushing in and turning the bulb anti-clockwise**

**21.6 Detach the lens retaining screws (arrowed) and the lens to access the number plate light bulbs**

**21.9 The interior light bulbs can be accessed after lowering the overhead console**

**21.10 To remove an instrument cluster bulb, depress the bulbholder and rotate it anti-clockwise**

### Rear direction indicator, brake, tail and reversing lights

**4** Open the boot and remove the plastic knobs securing the tail light housing trim cover **(see illustration)**.

**5** Remove two more plastic knobs and detach the tail light bulb cluster from the rear tail light housing. The defective bulb can then be pulled out of the socket and replaced **(see illustration)**.

### Number plate light

**6** Remove the lens retaining screws **(see illustration)**.

**7** Detach the lens and renew the defective bulb.

### High-mounted brake light

**8** The brake light cover is retained by screws. Remove the cover and renew the bulb.

### Interior lights

**9** Remove the overhead console (Chapter 11). Detach the bulb from the retaining clips and renew the bulb **(see illustration)**.

### Instrument cluster illumination

**10** To gain access to the instrument cluster illumination lights, the instrument cluster housing will have to be removed (Chapter 11). The bulbs can then be removed and replaced from the rear of the cluster **(see illustration)**.

### 22 Inertia switch - description and check

**1** The inertia switch is a safety mechanism which governs various electrical circuits such as the central locking, electric window and ignition circuits. In the event of a crash, the inertia switch will automatically unlock the doors, shut off power to all ignition circuits, and lock the boot lid and the fuel filler cap.

**2** To test the inertia switch, turn the ignition key to the ON position, then lock the driver and passenger side doors and unlock the boot lid. Then simply pull upward on the trip/reset button located on top of the inertia

switch. All ignition circuits should shut off, the doors should unlock and the boot lid should lock. To reset the inertia switch, simply push downward on the trip/reset button **(see illustration)**.

**22.2 The inertia switch is located behind the passengers side kick panel - pull upward on the button to trip the switch - push downward on the button to reset the switch**

## 23 Cruise control system - description and check

1 The cruise control system maintains vehicle speed with an independently operated vacuum motor located on the passenger's side inner wing in the engine compartment. When the cruise control switch is turned on, a vacuum actuator (connected the throttle linkage) is activated by vacuum from the vacuum motor. The system consists of the vacuum motor, vacuum actuator, brake switch, control switches, a relay and associated vacuum hoses. Some features of the system require special testers and diagnostic procedures which are beyond the scope of this manual. Listed below are some general procedures that may be used to locate common problems.

2 Locate and check the fuse (see Section 3).

3 Have an assistant operate the brake lights while you check their operation (voltage from the brake light switch deactivates the cruise control).

4 If the brake lights don't come on or don't shut off, correct the problem and re-test the cruise control.

5 Visually inspect the vacuum hose connected to the vacuum motor and vacuum actuator. Check the freeplay between the vacuum actuator stop and the throttle link slot (see illustration).

6 Test drive the vehicle to determine if the cruise control is now working. If it isn't, take it to a dealer service department or an automotive electrical specialist for further diagnosis and repair.

## 24 Electric window system - description and check

1 The electric window system operates electric motors, mounted in the doors, which lower and raise the windows. The system consists of the control switches, relays, the motors, regulators, glass mechanisms and associated wiring.

2 The electric windows can be lowered and raised from the master control switch by the driver or by remote switches located at the individual windows. Each window has a separate motor which is reversible. The position of the control switch determines the polarity and therefore the direction of operation.

3 The circuit is protected by a fuse. Each motor is also equipped with an internal circuit breaker, this prevents one stuck window from disabling the whole system.

4 The electric window system will only operate when the ignition switch is ON. In addition, many models have a window lockout switch at the master control switch which, when activated, disables the switches at the rear windows and, sometimes, the switch at the passenger's window also. Always check these items before diagnosing a window problem.

5 These procedures are general in nature, so if you can't find the problem using them, take the vehicle to a dealer service department or other properly equipped repair facility.

6 If the electric windows won't operate, always check the fuse first.

7 If only the rear windows are inoperative, or if the windows only operate from the master control switch, check the rear window lockout switch for continuity in the unlocked position. Renew it if it doesn't have continuity.

8 Check the wiring between the switches and

fuse panel for continuity. Repair the wiring, if necessary.

9 If only one window is inoperative from the master control switch, try the other control switch at the window. **Note:** *This doesn't apply to the driver's door window.*

10 If the same window works from one switch, but not the other, check the switch for continuity.

11 If the switch tests OK, check for a short or open in the circuit between the affected switch and the window motor.

12 If one window is inoperative from both switches, remove the trim panel from the affected door and check for voltage at the switch and at the motor while the switch is operated (see illustration).

13 If voltage is reaching the motor, disconnect the glass from the regulator (see Chapter 11). Move the window up and down by hand while checking for binding and damage. Also check for binding and damage to the regulator. If the regulator is not damaged and the window moves up and down smoothly, renew the motor. If there's binding or damage, lubricate, repair or renew parts, as necessary.

14 If voltage isn't reaching the motor, check the wiring in the circuit for continuity between the switches and motors. You'll need to consult the wiring diagram for the vehicle. If the circuit is equipped with a relay, check that the relay is earthed properly and receiving voltage.

15 Test the windows after you are done to confirm proper repairs.

## 25 Central locking system - description and check

The central locking system operates the door lock actuators mounted in each door. The system consists of the switches, relays,

**23.5 Check the cruise control throttle linkage for binding**

**24.12 If no voltage is present at the motor with the switch depressed, check for voltage at the switch**

actuators, a control unit and associated wiring. Diagnosis can usually be limited to simple checks of the wiring connections and actuators for minor faults which can be easily repaired. Since this system uses an electronic control unit, in-depth diagnosis should be left to a dealership service department.

Central locking systems are operated by bi-directional solenoids located in the doors. The lock switches have two operating positions; Lock and Unlock. When activated, the switch sends a signal to the door lock control unit to lock or unlock the doors. Depending on which way the switch is activated, the control unit reverses polarity to the solenoids, allowing the two sides of the circuit to be used alternately as the feed (positive) and earth side.

Some vehicles may have an anti-theft system incorporated into the locks. If you are unable to locate the trouble using the following general paragraphs, consult a dealer service department or other properly equipped repair facility.

**1** Always check the circuit protection first. Some vehicles use a combination of circuit breakers and fuses.

**2** Operate the door lock switches in both directions (Lock and Unlock) with the engine off. Listen for the click of the solenoids operating.

**3** Test the switches for continuity. Renew the switch if there's not continuity in both switch positions.

**4** Check the wiring between the switches, control unit and solenoids for continuity. Repair the wiring if there's no continuity.

**5** Check for a bad earth at the switches or the control unit.

**6** If all but one lock solenoid operates, remove the trim panel from the affected door (see Chapter 11) and check for voltage at the solenoid while the lock switch is operated **(see illustration)**. One of the wires should have voltage in the Lock position; the other should have voltage in the Unlock position.

**7** If the inoperative solenoid is receiving voltage, renew the solenoid.

**8** If the inoperative solenoid isn't receiving voltage, check for an open or short in the wire between the lock solenoid and the control unit. **Note:** *It's common for wires to break in the portion of the harness between the body and door (opening and closing the door fatigues and eventually breaks the wires).*

**25.6  Check for voltage at the lock solenoid while the lock switch is operated**

## 26 Electric mirrors - description and check

**1** Most electric mirrors use two motors to move the glass; one for up and down adjustments and one for left-right adjustments.

**2** The control switch has a selector portion which sends voltage to the left or right side mirror. With the ignition ON but the engine OFF, roll down the windows and operate the mirror control switch through all functions (left-right and up-down) for both the left and right side mirrors.

**3** Listen carefully for the sound of the electric motors running in the mirrors.

**4** If the motors can be heard but the mirror glass doesn't move, there's probably a problem with the drive mechanism inside the mirror. Remove and dismantle the mirror to locate the problem.

**5** If the mirrors don't operate and no sound comes from the mirrors, check the fuse (see Chapter 1).

**6** If the fuse is OK, remove the mirror control switch from its mounting without disconnecting the wires attached to it. Turn the ignition ON and check for voltage at the switch. There should be voltage at one terminal. If there's no voltage at the switch, check for an open or short in the circuit between the fuse panel and the switch.

**7** If there's voltage at the switch, disconnect it. Check the switch for continuity in all its operating positions. If the switch does not have continuity, renew it.

**8** Re-connect the switch. Locate the wire going from the switch to earth. Leaving the switch connected, connect a jumper wire between this wire and earth. If the mirror works normally with this wire in place, repair the faulty earth connection.

**9** If the mirror still doesn't work, remove the mirror and check the wires at the mirror for voltage. Check with ignition ON and the mirror selector switch on the appropriate side. Operate the mirror switch in all its positions. There should be voltage at one of the switch-to-mirror wires in each switch position (except the neutral "off" position).

**10** If there's not voltage in each switch position, check the circuit between the mirror and control switch for opens and shorts.

**11** If there's voltage, remove the mirror and test it off the vehicle with jumper wires. Renew the mirror if it fails this test.

## 27 Electric sunroof - description and check

**1** The electric sunroof is powered by a single motor in the roof behind the overhead console. The power circuit is protected by a fuse.

**2** The control switches (tilt and slide) send an earth signal to the sunroof motor when the

switches are pressed. Power is supplied to the motor from the relay. With the ignition ON but the engine OFF, operate the sunroof control switch through the tilt and slide functions.

**3** Listen carefully for the sound of the sunroof motor running in the roof.

**4** If the motors can be heard but the sunroof glass doesn't move, there's probably a problem with the drive mechanism or drive cables.

**5** If the sunroof does not operate and no sound comes from the motor, check the fuse (see Chapter 1).

**6** If the fuse is OK, remove the control switches (see Chapter 11). Disconnect the wires attached to it. Turn the ignition ON and check for voltage at the switch. If there's no voltage at the switch, check for power and earth at the motor. If power and earth exist at the motor and there's still no voltage at the switch renew the motor. If there's no voltage at the motor, check the relay or an open or short in the wiring between the relay and the motor.

**7** If there's voltage at the switch, disconnect it. Check the switch for continuity in all its operating positions. If the switch does not have continuity, renew it.

**8** If the switch has continuity re-connect the switch. Locate the wire going from the switch to earth. Leaving the switch connected, connect a jumper wire between this wire and earth. If the motor works normally with this wire in place, repair the faulty earth connection.

**9** The sunroof can be closed manually by inserting the T-handle spanner which is located inside the overhead console. Insert the spanner into the motor drive shaft and rotate the shaft clockwise **(see illustration)**.

## 28 Airbag system - general information

*Warning: Failure to follow these precautions could result in accidental deployment of the airbag and personal injury.*

**27.9  To close the sunroof manually, insert the T-handle spanner in the motor shaft and rotate it clockwise**

Later models are equipped with a Supplemental Restraint System (SRS), more commonly known as an airbag. This system is designed to protect the driver, and on 1994 models, the passenger from serious injury in the event of a head-on or frontal collision. It consists of an airbag module in the centre of the steering wheel and a passenger airbag module on the right side of the dash above the glove box on 1994 models.

The airbag modules contain an inflater and a sensor assembly which activates from impact energy that is transmitted through the body and steering column upon impact or collision.

DO NOT try to dismantle or remove any component in the vicinity of the steering column or instrument panel on models equipped with air bags. Serious personal injury or damage may result. The manufacturer recommends that, on airbag equipped models, service which requires removal of any component in the vicinity of the instrument panel or steering column should be left to a dealer service department or other properly equipped repair facility because of the special tools and techniques required to disable the air bag system.

## 29 Wiring diagrams - general information

Since it isn't possible to include a complete wiring diagram for every year covered by this manual, the following diagrams are those that are typical and most commonly needed.

Prior to diagnosing any circuits, check the fuse and circuit breakers (if equipped) to make sure they are in good condition. Make sure the battery is properly charged and has clean, tight cable connections (see Chapter 1).

When checking the wiring system, make sure that all electrical connectors are clean, with no broken or loose pins. When unplugging an electrical connector, do not pull on the wires, only on the connector housings themselves.

**Wiring diagrams commence overleaf**

**Typical 1993 and 1994 starting and charging system**

**Typical 1988 to 1992 starting and charging system**

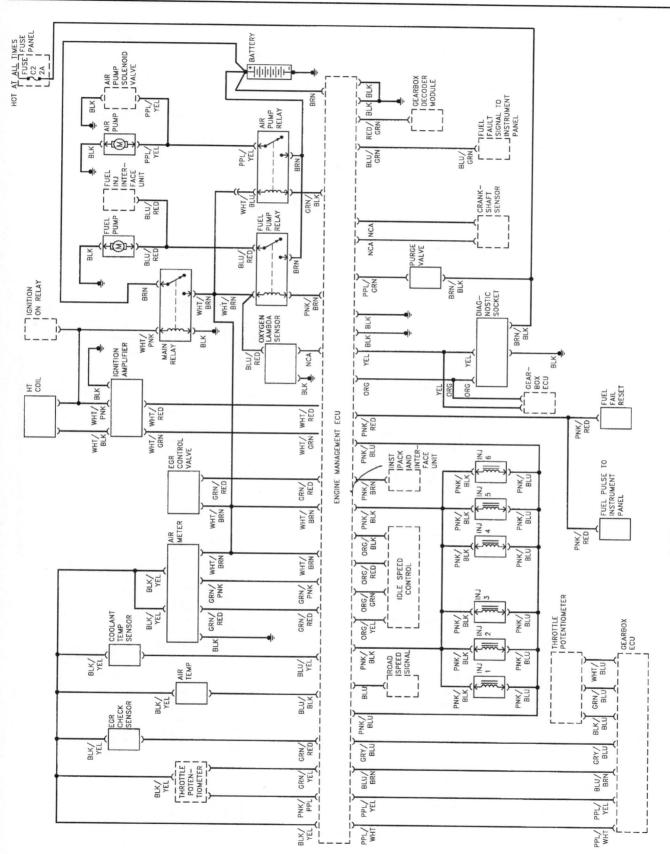

**Typical 1988 to 1992 engine management system**

**Typical 1993 and 1994 engine management system**

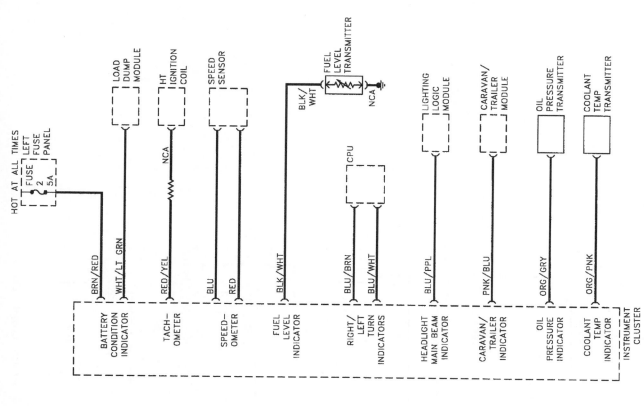

Typical 1988 instrument warning light system

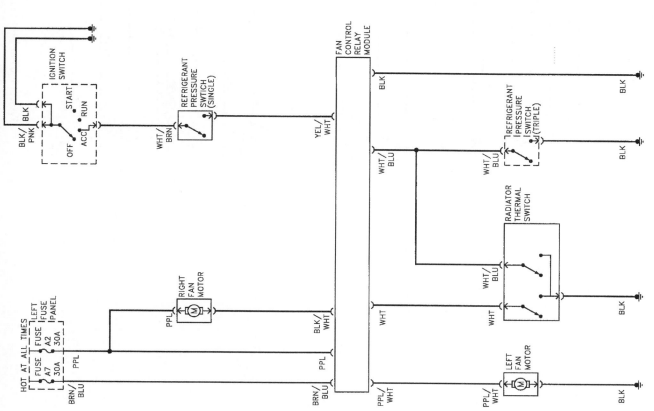

Typical engine cooling fan system

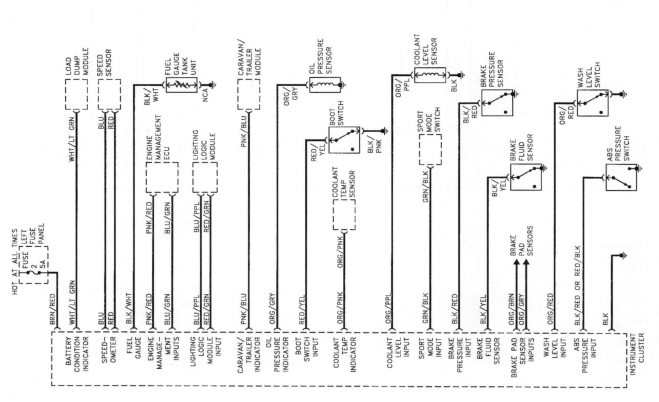

**Typical 1989 to 1994 instrument warning light system**

**Typical headlight system**

**Typical side marker and tail light system**

Typical hazard/turn signal and stop light system

Typical interior lighting system

**Typical instrument cluster lighting system**

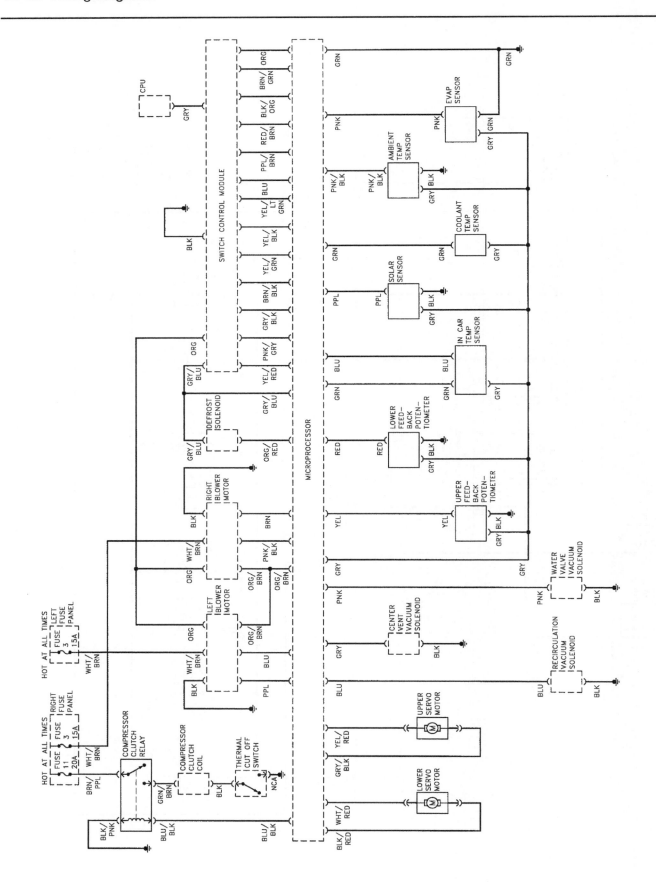

**Typical 1988 heater and air conditioning system**

Typical 1989 to 1992 heater and air conditioning system

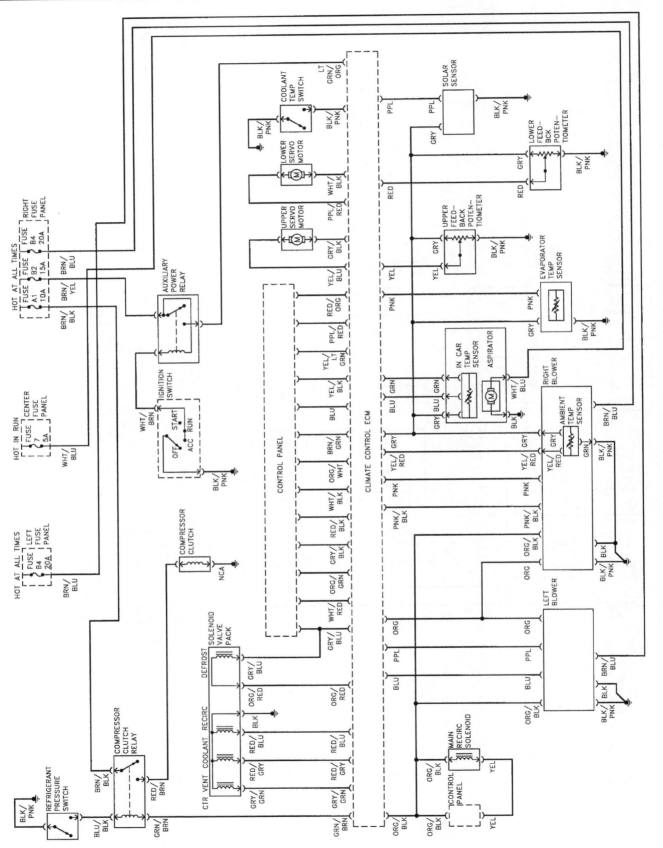

Typical 1993 and 1994 heater and air conditioning system

**Typical 1991 and 1992 cruise control system**

**Typical 1988 to 1990 cruise control system**

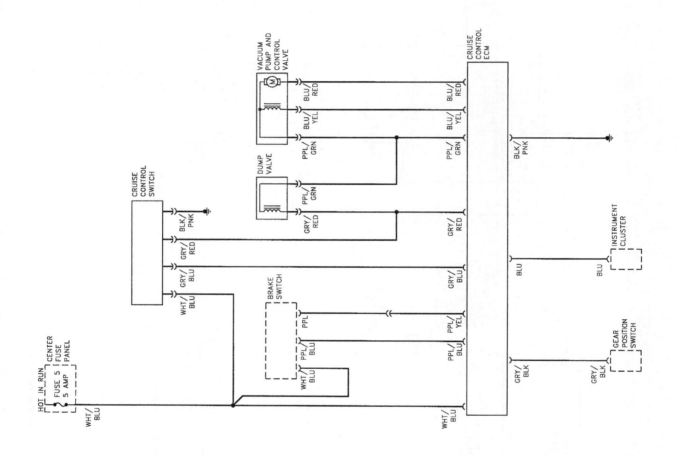

**Typical 1993 and 1994 cruise control system**

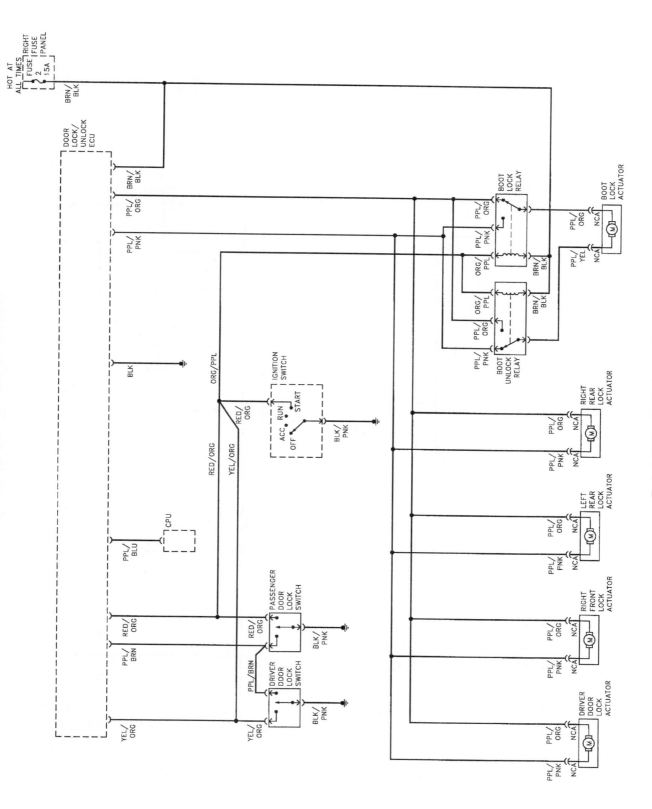

**Typical 1988 central locking system**

**Typical 1989 and 1990 central locking system**

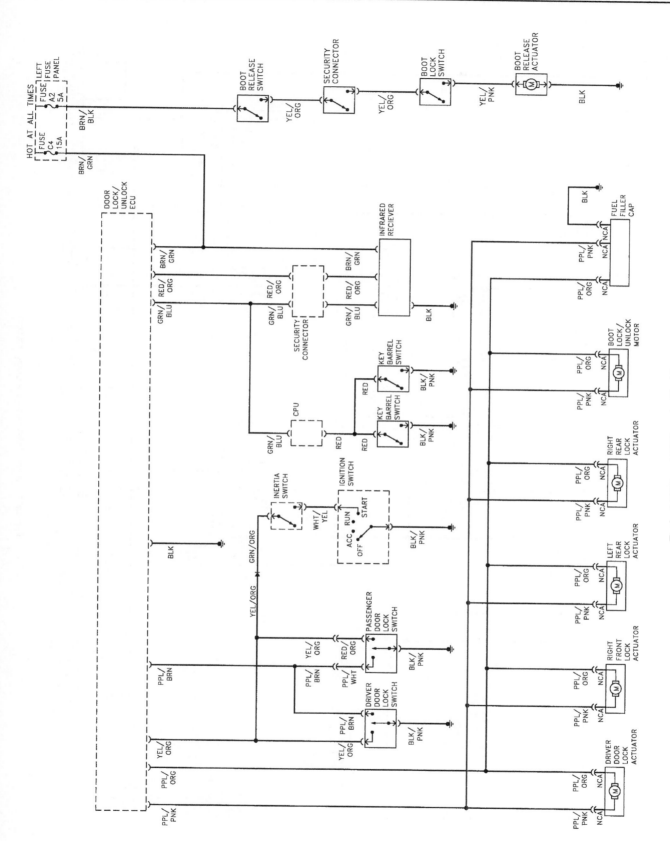

Typical 1991 and 1992 central locking system

Typical 1993 and 1994 central locking system

**Typical 1988 to 1992 electric windows**

Typical 1993 and 1994 electric windows

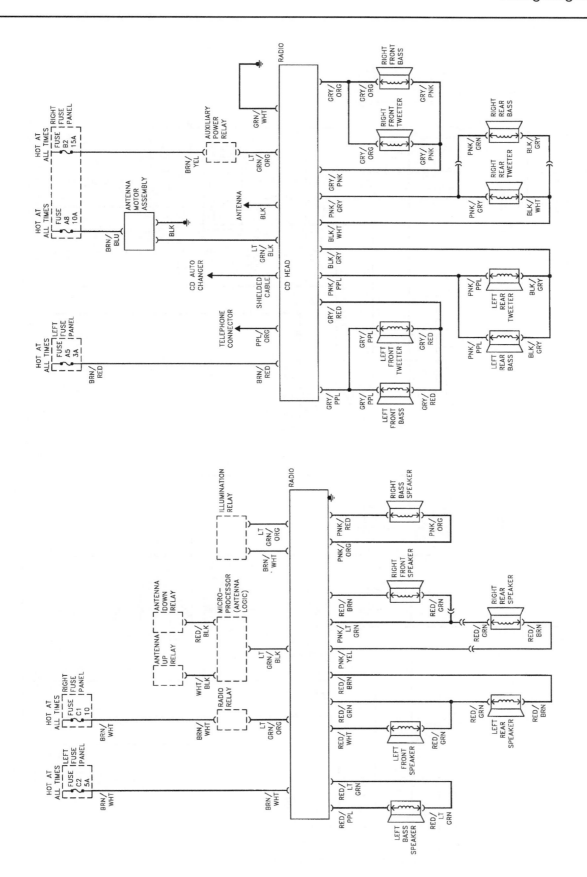

**Typical 1993 and 1994 audio system**

**Typical 1988 to 1992 audio system**

Typical 1991 and 1992 windscreen washer and wiper system

Typical 1988 to 1990 windscreen washer and wiper system

Typical 1993 and 1994 windscreen washer and wiper system

# Notes

# Dimensions and weights

**Note:** *All figures are approximate, and may vary according to model.  Refer to manufacturer's data for exact figures.*

## Dimensions

Overall length . . . . . . . . . . . . . . . . . . . . . . . . . . . . . . . . . . 4988 mm
Overall width (including mirrors) . . . . . . . . . . . . . . . . . . . . . . . . . . . . . 2015 mm
Overall height (unladen) . . . . . . . . . . . . . . . . . . . . . . . . . . . . . . . 1358 mm
Wheelbase . . . . . . . . . . . . . . . . . . . . . . . . . . . . . . . . . . . 2870 mm

## Weights

Kerb weight . . . . . . . . . . . . . . . . . . . . . . . . . . . . . . . . . . . 1770 kg
Maximum gross vehicle weight . . . . . . . . . . . . . . . . . . . . . . . . . . . . 2190 kg
Maximum towing weight:
  Braked trailer . . . . . . . . . . . . . . . . . . . . . . . . . . . . . . . . . . . 1500 kg
  Unbraked trailer . . . . . . . . . . . . . . . . . . . . . . . . . . . . . . . . . 750 kg
Maximum axle load:
  Front axle . . . . . . . . . . . . . . . . . . . . . . . . . . . . . . . . . . 1050 kg
  Rear axle . . . . . . . . . . . . . . . . . . . . . . . . . . . . . . . . . . . . 1170 kg
Maximum roof rack load . . . . . . . . . . . . . . . . . . . . . . . . . . . . . 100 kg

# Jacking and vehicle support

The jack supplied with the vehicle tool kit should only be used for changing the roadwheels - see *"Wheel changing"* at the front of this manual. When carrying out any other kind of work, raise the vehicle using a hydraulic (or "trolley") jack, and always supplement the jack with axle stands positioned under the vehicle jacking points.

To raise the front of the vehicle, place a block of wood on the jack head and position the jack underneath the centre of the front crossmember. Lift the vehicle to the required height and support it on axle stands positioned underneath the vehicle jacking points on the sills.

To raise the rear of the vehicle, place a block of wood on the jack head and position the jack underneath the centre of the rear crossmember. Lift the vehicle to the required height and support it on axle stands positioned underneath the vehicle jacking points on the sills.

The jack supplied with the vehicle locates in the jacking points on the sills. Ensure that the jack head is correctly engaged before attempting to raise the vehicle.

**Never** work under, around, or near a raised vehicle, unless it is adequately supported in at least two places.

# Radio/cassette unit anti-theft system - precaution

Some models are equipped with an audio system which includes an anti-theft feature, to deter thieves. If the power source to the unit is cut, the anti-theft system will activate. Even if the power source is immediately reconnected, the radio/cassette unit will not function until the correct security code has been entered. Therefore if you do not know the correct security code for the unit, **do not** disconnect the battery negative lead, or remove the radio/cassette unit from the vehicle.

The procedure for reprogramming a unit that has been disconnected from its power supply varies from model to model - consult the handbook supplied with the unit for specific details or refer to your Jaguar dealer.

## Length (distance)

| | | | | |
|---|---|---|---|---|
| Inches (in) | x 25.4 | = Millimetres (mm) | x 0.0394 = | Inches (in) |
| Feet (ft) | x 0.305 | = Metres (m) | x 3.281 = | Feet (ft) |
| Miles | x 1.609 | = Kilometres (km) | x 0.621 = | Miles |

## Volume (capacity)

| | | | | |
|---|---|---|---|---|
| Cubic inches (cu in; in$^3$) | x 16.387 | = Cubic centimetres (cc; cm$^3$) | x 0.061 = | Cubic inches (cu in; in$^3$) |
| Imperial pints (Imp pt) | x 0.568 | = Litres (l) | x 1.76 = | Imperial pints (Imp pt) |
| Imperial quarts (Imp qt) | x 1.137 | = Litres (l) | x 0.88 = | Imperial quarts (Imp qt) |
| Imperial quarts (Imp qt) | x 1.201 | = US quarts (US qt) | x 0.833 = | Imperial quarts (Imp qt) |
| US quarts (US qt) | x 0.946 | = Litres (l) | x 1.057 = | US quarts (US qt) |
| Imperial gallons (Imp gal) | x 4.546 | = Litres (l) | x 0.22 = | Imperial gallons (Imp gal) |
| Imperial gallons (Imp gal) | x 1.201 | = US gallons (US gal) | x 0.833 = | Imperial gallons (Imp gal) |
| US gallons (US gal) | x 3.785 | = Litres (l) | x 0.264 = | US gallons (US gal) |

## Mass (weight)

| | | | | |
|---|---|---|---|---|
| Ounces (oz) | x 28.35 | = Grams (g) | x 0.035 = | Ounces (oz) |
| Pounds (lb) | x 0.454 | = Kilograms (kg) | x 2.205 = | Pounds (lb) |

## Force

| | | | | |
|---|---|---|---|---|
| Ounces-force (ozf; oz) | x 0.278 | = Newtons (N) | x 3.6 = | Ounces-force (ozf; oz) |
| Pounds-force (lbf; lb) | x 4.448 | = Newtons (N) | x 0.225 = | Pounds-force (lbf; lb) |
| Newtons (N) | x 0.1 | = Kilograms-force (kgf; kg) | x 9.81 = | Newtons (N) |

## Pressure

| | | | | |
|---|---|---|---|---|
| Pounds-force per square inch (psi; lbf/in$^2$; lb/in$^2$) | x 0.070 | = Kilograms-force per square centimetre (kgf/cm$^2$; kg/cm$^2$) | x 14.223 = | Pounds-force per square inch (psi; lbf/in$^2$; lb/in$^2$) |
| Pounds-force per square inch (psi; lbf/in$^2$; lb/in$^2$) | x 0.068 | = Atmospheres (atm) | x 14.696 = | Pounds-force per square inch (psi; lbf/in$^2$; lb/in$^2$) |
| Pounds-force per square inch (psi; lbf/in$^2$; lb/in$^2$) | x 0.069 | = Bars | x 14.5 = | Pounds-force per square inch (psi; lbf/in$^2$; lb/in$^2$) |
| Pounds-force per square inch (psi; lbf/in$^2$; lb/in$^2$) | x 6.895 | = Kilopascals (kPa) | x 0.145 = | Pounds-force per square inch (psi; lbf/in$^2$; lb/in$^2$) |
| Kilopascals (kPa) | x 0.01 | = Kilograms-force per square centimetre (kgf/cm$^2$; kg/cm$^2$) | x 98.1 = | Kilopascals (kPa) |
| Millibar (mbar) | x 100 | = Pascals (Pa) | x 0.01 = | Millibar (mbar) |
| Millibar (mbar) | x 0.0145 | = Pounds-force per square inch (psi; lbf/in$^2$; lb/in$^2$) | x 68.947 = | Millibar (mbar) |
| Millibar (mbar) | x 0.75 | = Millimetres of mercury (mmHg) | x 1.333 = | Millibar (mbar) |
| Millibar (mbar) | x 0.401 | = Inches of water (inH$_2$O) | x 2.491 = | Millibar (mbar) |
| Millimetres of mercury (mmHg) | x 0.535 | = Inches of water (inH$_2$O) | x 1.868 = | Millimetres of mercury (mmHg) |
| Inches of water (inH$_2$O) | x 0.036 | = Pounds-force per square inch (psi; lbf/in$^2$; lb/in$^2$) | x 27.68 = | Inches of water (inH$_2$O) |

## Torque (moment of force)

| | | | | |
|---|---|---|---|---|
| Pounds-force inches (lbf in; lb in) | x 1.152 | = Kilograms-force centimetre (kgf cm; kg cm) | x 0.868 = | Pounds-force inches (lbf in; lb in) |
| Pounds-force inches (lbf in; lb in) | x 0.113 | = Newton metres (Nm) | x 8.85 = | Pounds-force inches (lbf in; lb in) |
| Pounds-force inches (lbf in; lb in) | x 0.083 | = Pounds-force feet (lbf ft; lb ft) | x 12 = | Pounds-force inches (lbf in; lb in) |
| Pounds-force feet (lbf ft; lb ft) | x 0.138 | = Kilograms-force metres (kgf m; kg m) | x 7.233 = | Pounds-force feet (lbf ft; lb ft) |
| Pounds-force feet (lbf ft; lb ft) | x 1.356 | = Newton metres (Nm) | x 0.738 = | Pounds-force feet (lbf ft; lb ft) |
| Newton metres (Nm) | x 0.102 | = Kilograms-force metres (kgf m; kg m) | x 9.804 = | Newton metres (Nm) |

## Power

| | | | | |
|---|---|---|---|---|
| Horsepower (hp) | x 745.7 | = Watts (W) | x 0.0013 = | Horsepower (hp) |

## Velocity (speed)

| | | | | |
|---|---|---|---|---|
| Miles per hour (miles/hr; mph) | x 1.609 | = Kilometres per hour (km/hr; kph) | x 0.621 = | Miles per hour (miles/hr; mph) |

## Fuel consumption*

| | | | | |
|---|---|---|---|---|
| Miles per gallon (mpg) | x 0.354 | = Kilometres per litre (km/l) | x 2.825 = | Miles per gallon (mpg) |

## Temperature

Degrees Fahrenheit = (°C x 1.8) + 32          Degrees Celsius (Degrees Centigrade; °C) = (°F - 32) x 0.56

*It is common practice to convert from miles per gallon (mpg) to litres/100 kilometres (l/100km), where mpg x l/100 km = 282*

*As the main part of this book has been written in the US, it uses the appropriate US component names, phrases, and spelling. Some of these differ from those used in the UK. Normally, these cause no difficulty, but to make sure, a glossary is printed below. When ordering spare parts, remember the parts list may use some of these words:*

| AMERICAN | ENGLISH | AMERICAN | ENGLISH |
|---|---|---|---|
| Aluminum | Aluminium | Muffler | Silencer |
| Antenna | Aerial | Odor | Odour |
| Authorized | Authorised | Oil pan | Sump |
| Auto parts stores | Motor factors | Open flame | Naked flame |
| Axleshaft | Halfshaft | Panel wagon/van | Van |
| Back-up | Reverse | Parking brake | Handbrake |
| Barrel | Choke/venturi | Parking light | Sidelight |
| Block | Chock | Pinging | Pinking |
| Box-end wrench | Ring spanner | Piston pin or wrist pin | Gudgeon pin |
| Bushing | Bush | Piston pin or wrist pin | Small end, little end |
| Carburetor | Carburettor | Pitman arm | Drop arm |
| Center | Centre | Power brake booster | Servo unit |
| Coast | Freewheel | Primary shoe (of brake) | Leading shoe (of brake) |
| Color | Colour | Prussian blue | Engineer's blue |
| Convertible | Drop head coupe | Pry | Prise (force apart) |
| Cotter pin | Split pin | Prybar | Lever |
| Counterclockwise | Anti-clockwise | Prying | Levering |
| Countershaft (of gearbox) | Layshaft | Quarter window | Quarterlight |
| Dashboard | Facia | Recap | Retread |
| Denatured alcohol | Methylated spirit | Release cylinder | Slave cylinder |
| Dome lamp | Interior light | Repair shop | Garage |
| Driveaxle | Driveshaft | Replacement | Renewal |
| Driveshaft | Propeller shaft | Ring gear (of differential) | Crownwheel |
| Fender | Wing/mudguard | Rocker panel (beneath doors) | Sill panel (beneath doors) |
| Firewall | Bulkhead | Rod bearing | Big-end bearing |
| Flashlight | Torch | Rotor/disk | Disc (brake) |
| Float bowl | Float chamber | Secondary shoe (of brake) | Trailing shoe (of brake) |
| Floor jack | Trolley jack | Sedan | Saloon |
| Freeway, turnpike etc | Motorway | Setscrew, Allen screw | Grub screw |
| Freeze plug | Core plug | Shock absorber, shock | Damper |
| Frozen | Seized | Snap-ring | Circlip |
| Gas tank | Petrol tank | Soft top | Hood |
| Gasoline (gas) | Petrol | Spacer | Distance piece |
| Gearshift | Gearchange | Spare tire | Spare wheel |
| Generator (DC) | Dynamo | Spark plug wires | HT leads |
| Ground (electrical) | Earth | Spindle arm | Steering arm |
| Header | Exhaust manifold | Stabilizer or sway bar | Anti-roll bar |
| Heat riser | Hot spot | Station wagon | Estate car |
| High | Top gear | Stumbles | Hesitates |
| Hood (engine cover) | Bonnet | Tang or lock | Tab washer |
| Installation | Refitting | Throw-out bearing | Thrust bearing |
| Intake | Inlet | Tie-rod or connecting rod (of steering) | Trackrod |
| Jackstands | Axle stands | Tire | Tyre |
| Jumper cable | Jump lead | Transmission | Gearbox |
| Keeper | Collet | Troubleshooting | Fault finding/diagnosis |
| Kerosene | Paraffin | Trunk | Boot (luggage compartment) |
| Knock pin | Roll pin | Turn signal | Indicator |
| Lash | Clearance | TV (throttle valve) cable | Kickdown cable |
| Lash | Free-play | Unpublicized | Unpublicised |
| Latch | Catch | Valve cover | Rocker cover |
| Latches | Locks | Valve lifter | Tappet |
| License plate | Number plate | Valve lifter or tappet | Cam follower or tappet |
| Light | Lamp | Vapor | Vapour |
| Lock (for valve spring retainer) | Split cotter (for valve spring cap) | Vise | Vice |
| Lopes | Hunts | Wheel cover | Roadwheel trim |
| Lug nut/bolt | Wheel nut/bolt | Whole drive line | Transmission |
| Metal chips or debris | Swarf | Windshield | Windscreen |
| Misses | Misfires | Wrench | Spanner |

Spare parts are available from many sources, including maker's appointed garages, accessory shops, and motor factors. To be sure of obtaining the correct parts, it will sometimes be necessary to quote the vehicle identification number. If possible, it can also be useful to take the old parts along for positive identification. Items such as starter motors and alternators may be available under a service exchange scheme - any parts returned should be clean.

Our advice regarding spare parts is as follows.

### Officially appointed garages

This is the best source of parts which are peculiar to your car, and which are not otherwise generally available (eg, badges, interior trim, certain body panels, etc). It is also the only place at which you should buy parts if the vehicle is still under warranty.

### Accessory shops

These are very good places to buy materials and components needed for the maintenance of your car (oil, air and fuel filters, light bulbs, drivebelts, greases, brake pads, touch-up paint, etc). Components of this nature sold by a reputable shop are usually of the same standard as those used by the car manufacturer.

Besides components, these shops also sell tools and general accessories, usually have convenient opening hours, charge lower prices, and can often be found close to home. Some accessory shops have parts counters where components needed for almost any repair job can be purchased or ordered.

### Motor factors

Good factors will stock all the more important components which wear out comparatively quickly, and can sometimes supply individual components needed for the overhaul of a larger assembly (eg, brake seals and hydraulic parts, bearing shells, pistons, valves). They may also handle work such as cylinder block reboring, crankshaft regrinding, etc.

### Tyre and exhaust specialists

These outlets may be independent, or members of a local or national chain. They frequently offer competitive prices when compared with a main dealer or local garage, but it will pay to obtain several quotes before making a decision. When researching prices, also ask what "extras" may be added - for instance fitting a new valve and balancing the wheel are both commonly charged on top of the price of a new tyre.

### Other sources

Beware of parts or materials obtained from market stalls, car boot sales or similar outlets. Such items are not invariably sub-standard, but there is little chance of compensation if they do prove unsatisfactory. In the case of safety-critical components such as brake pads, there is the risk of financial loss, and also of an accident causing injury or death.

Second-hand parts or assemblies obtained from a car breaker can be a good buy in some circumstances, but this sort of purchase is best made by the experienced DIY mechanic.

# Vehicle identification

Modifications are a continuing and unpublicised process in vehicle manufacture, quite apart from major model changes. Spare parts manuals and lists are compiled upon a numerical basis, the individual vehicle identification numbers being essential to correct identification of the part concerned.

When ordering spare parts, always give as much information as possible. Quote the car model, year of manufacture and registration, chassis and engine numbers as appropriate.

The *Vehicle Identification Number (VIN)* plate is attached to the base of the driver's door pillar left-hand wing valance and is visible once the bonnet has been opened. The vehicle identification (chassis) number is also stamped onto a plate located inside the windscreen and may also be stamped onto the right-hand inner wing panel in the engine compartment **(see illustrations)**.

The *trim code and paint code* are also stamped onto the VIN plate.

The *engine number* is stamped onto the right-hand side of the cylinder block, next to the distributor **(see illustration)**.

The *automatic transmission number* is stamped onto a metal label attached to the left-hand side of the transmission housing, just above the sump **(see illustration)**.

**The VIN is stamped on the right inner wing panel of the engine compartment**

**The VIN is also present on the left side of the dashboard**

**The engine identification number is stamped on the right side of the engine block just behind the distributor**

**The transmission identification number is located on the left side of the transmission housing just above the sump**

Whenever servicing, repair or overhaul work is carried out on the car or its components, observe the following procedures and instructions. This will assist in carrying out the operation efficiently and to a professional standard of workmanship.

## Joint mating faces and gaskets

When separating components at their mating faces, never insert screwdrivers or similar implements into the joint between the faces in order to prise them apart. This can cause severe damage which results in oil leaks, coolant leaks, etc upon reassembly. Separation is usually achieved by tapping along the joint with a soft-faced hammer in order to break the seal. However, note that this method may not be suitable where dowels are used for component location.

Where a gasket is used between the mating faces of two components, a new one must be fitted on reassembly; fit it dry unless otherwise stated in the repair procedure. Make sure that the mating faces are clean and dry, with all traces of old gasket removed. When cleaning a joint face, use a tool which is unlikely to score or damage the face, and remove any burrs or nicks with an oilstone or fine file.

Make sure that tapped holes are cleaned with a pipe cleaner, and keep them free of jointing compound, if this is being used, unless specifically instructed otherwise.

Ensure that all orifices, channels or pipes are clear, and blow through them, preferably using compressed air.

## Oil seals

Oil seals can be removed by levering them out with a wide flat-bladed screwdriver or similar implement. Alternatively, a number of self-tapping screws may be screwed into the seal, and these used as a purchase for pliers or some similar device in order to pull the seal free.

Whenever an oil seal is removed from its working location, either individually or as part of an assembly, it should be renewed.

The very fine sealing lip of the seal is easily damaged, and will not seal if the surface it contacts is not completely clean and free from scratches, nicks or grooves. If the original sealing surface of the component cannot be restored, and the manufacturer has not made provision for slight relocation of the seal relative to the sealing surface, the component should be renewed.

Protect the lips of the seal from any surface which may damage them in the course of fitting. Use tape or a conical sleeve where possible. Lubricate the seal lips with oil before fitting and, on dual-lipped seals, fill the space between the lips with grease.

Unless otherwise stated, oil seals must be fitted with their sealing lips toward the lubricant to be sealed.

Use a tubular drift or block of wood of the appropriate size to install the seal and, if the seal housing is shouldered, drive the seal down to the shoulder. If the seal housing is unshouldered, the seal should be fitted with its face flush with the housing top face (unless otherwise instructed).

## Screw threads and fastenings

Seized nuts, bolts and screws are quite a common occurrence where corrosion has set in, and the use of penetrating oil or releasing fluid will often overcome this problem if the offending item is soaked for a while before attempting to release it. The use of an impact driver may also provide a means of releasing such stubborn fastening devices, when used in conjunction with the appropriate screwdriver bit or socket. If none of these methods works, it may be necessary to resort to the careful application of heat, or the use of a hacksaw or nut splitter device.

Studs are usually removed by locking two nuts together on the threaded part, and then using a spanner on the lower nut to unscrew the stud. Studs or bolts which have broken off below the surface of the component in which they are mounted can sometimes be removed using a stud extractor. Always ensure that a blind tapped hole is completely free from oil, grease, water or other fluid before installing the bolt or stud. Failure to do this could cause the housing to crack due to the hydraulic action of the bolt or stud as it is screwed in.

When tightening a castellated nut to accept a split pin, tighten the nut to the specified torque, where applicable, and then tighten further to the next split pin hole. Never slacken the nut to align the split pin hole, unless stated in the repair procedure.

When checking or retightening a nut or bolt to a specified torque setting, slacken the nut or bolt by a quarter of a turn, and then retighten to the specified setting. However, this should not be attempted where angular tightening has been used.

For some screw fastenings, notably cylinder head bolts or nuts, torque wrench settings are no longer specified for the latter stages of tightening, "angle-tightening" being called up instead. Typically, a fairly low torque wrench setting will be applied to the bolts/nuts in the correct sequence, followed by one or more stages of tightening through specified angles.

## Locknuts, locktabs and washers

Any fastening which will rotate against a component or housing during tightening should always have a washer between it and the relevant component or housing.

Spring or split washers should always be renewed when they are used to lock a critical component such as a big-end bearing retaining bolt or nut. Locktabs which are folded over to retain a nut or bolt should always be renewed.

Self-locking nuts can be re-used in non-critical areas, providing resistance can be felt when the locking portion passes over the bolt or stud thread. However, it should be noted that self-locking stiffnuts tend to lose their effectiveness after long periods of use, and should then be renewed as a matter of course.

Split pins must always be replaced with new ones of the correct size for the hole.

When thread-locking compound is found on the threads of a fastener which is to be re-used, it should be cleaned off with a wire brush and solvent, and fresh compound applied on reassembly.

## Special tools

Some repair procedures in this manual entail the use of special tools such as a press, two or three-legged pullers, spring compressors, etc. Wherever possible, suitable readily-available alternatives to the manufacturer's special tools are described, and are shown in use. In some instances, where no alternative is possible, it has been necessary to resort to the use of a manufacturer's tool, and this has been done for reasons of safety as well as the efficient completion of the repair operation. Unless you are highly-skilled and have a thorough understanding of the procedures described, never attempt to bypass the use of any special tool when the procedure described specifies its use. Not only is there a very great risk of personal injury, but expensive damage could be caused to the components involved.

## Environmental considerations

When disposing of used engine oil, brake fluid, antifreeze, etc, give due consideration to any detrimental environmental effects. Do not, for instance, pour any of the above liquids down drains into the general sewage system, or onto the ground to soak away. Many local council refuse tips provide a facility for waste oil disposal, as do some garages. If none of these facilities are available, consult your local Environmental Health Department, or the National Rivers Authority, for further advice.

With the universal tightening-up of legislation regarding the emission of environmentally-harmful substances from motor vehicles, most vehicles have tamperproof devices fitted to the main adjustment points of the fuel system. These devices are primarily designed to prevent unqualified persons from adjusting the fuel/air mixture, with the chance of a consequent increase in toxic emissions. If such devices are found during servicing or overhaul, they should, wherever possible, be renewed or refitted in accordance with the manufacturer's requirements or current legislation.

**Note: It is antisocial and illegal to dump oil down the drain. To find the location of your local oil recycling bank, call this number free.**

## Introduction

A selection of good tools is a fundamental requirement for anyone contemplating the maintenance and repair of a motor vehicle. For the owner who does not possess any, their purchase will prove a considerable expense, offsetting some of the savings made by doing-it-yourself. However, provided that the tools purchased meet the relevant national safety standards and are of good quality, they will last for many years and prove an extremely worthwhile investment.

To help the average owner to decide which tools are needed to carry out the various tasks detailed in this manual, we have compiled three lists of tools under the following headings: *Maintenance and minor repair, Repair and overhaul*, and *Special*. Newcomers to practical mechanics should start off with the *Maintenance and minor repair* tool kit, and confine themselves to the simpler jobs around the vehicle. Then, as confidence and experience grow, more difficult tasks can be undertaken, with extra tools being purchased as, and when, they are needed. In this way, a *Maintenance and minor repair* tool kit can be built up into a *Repair and overhaul* tool kit over a considerable period of time, without any major cash outlays. The experienced do-it-yourselfer will have a tool kit good enough for most repair and overhaul procedures, and will add tools from the *Special* category when it is felt that the expense is justified by the amount of use to which these tools will be put.

## Maintenance and minor repair tool kit

The tools given in this list should be considered as a minimum requirement if routine maintenance, servicing and minor repair operations are to be undertaken. We recommend the purchase of combination spanners (ring one end, open-ended the other); although more expensive than open-ended ones, they do give the advantages of both types of spanner.

- ☐ *Combination spanners:*
  *Metric - 8 to 19 mm inclusive*
- ☐ *Adjustable spanner - 35 mm jaw (approx.)*
- ☐ *Spark plug spanner (with rubber insert) - petrol models*
- ☐ *Spark plug gap adjustment tool - petrol models*
- ☐ *Set of feeler gauges*
- ☐ *Brake bleed nipple spanner*
- ☐ *Screwdrivers:*
  *Flat blade - 100 mm long x 6 mm dia*
  *Cross blade - 100 mm long x 6 mm dia*
  *Torx - various sizes (not all vehicles)*
- ☐ *Combination pliers*
- ☐ *Hacksaw (junior)*
- ☐ *Tyre pump*
- ☐ *Tyre pressure gauge*
- ☐ *Oil can*
- ☐ *Oil filter removal tool*
- ☐ *Fine emery cloth*
- ☐ *Wire brush (small)*
- ☐ *Funnel (medium size)*
- ☐ *Sump drain plug key (not all vehicles)*

## Repair and overhaul tool kit

These tools are virtually essential for anyone undertaking any major repairs to a motor vehicle, and are additional to those given in the *Maintenance and minor repair* list. Included in this list is a comprehensive set of sockets. Although these are expensive, they will be found invaluable as they are so versatile - particularly if various drives are included in the set. We recommend the half-inch square-drive type, as this can be used with most proprietary torque wrenches.

The tools in this list will sometimes need to be supplemented by tools from the *Special* list:

- ☐ *Sockets (or box spanners) to cover range in previous list (including Torx sockets)*
- ☐ *Reversible ratchet drive (for use with sockets)*
- ☐ *Extension piece, 250 mm (for use with sockets)*
- ☐ *Universal joint (for use with sockets)*
- ☐ *Flexible handle or sliding T "breaker bar" (for use with sockets)*
- ☐ *Torque wrench (for use with sockets)*
- ☐ *Self-locking grips*
- ☐ *Ball pein hammer*
- ☐ *Soft-faced mallet (plastic or rubber)*
- ☐ *Screwdrivers:*
  *Flat blade - long & sturdy, short (chubby), and narrow (electrician's) types*
  *Cross blade – long & sturdy, and short (chubby) types*
- ☐ *Pliers:*
  *Long-nosed*
  *Side cutters (electrician's)*
  *Circlip (internal and external)*
- ☐ *Cold chisel - 25 mm*
- ☐ *Scriber*
- ☐ *Scraper*
- ☐ *Centre-punch*
- ☐ *Pin punch*
- ☐ *Hacksaw*
- ☐ *Brake hose clamp*
- ☐ *Brake/clutch bleeding kit*
- ☐ *Selection of twist drills*
- ☐ *Steel rule/straight-edge*
- ☐ *Allen keys (inc. splined/Torx type)*
- ☐ *Selection of files*
- ☐ *Wire brush*
- ☐ *Axle stands*
- ☐ *Jack (strong trolley or hydraulic type)*
- ☐ *Light with extension lead*
- ☐ *Universal electrical multi-meter*

**Sockets and reversible ratchet drive**

**Brake bleeding kit**

**Torx key, socket and bit**

**Hose clamp**

**Angular-tightening gauge**

## Special tools

The tools in this list are those which are not used regularly, are expensive to buy, or which need to be used in accordance with their manufacturers' instructions. Unless relatively difficult mechanical jobs are undertaken frequently, it will not be economic to buy many of these tools. Where this is the case, you could consider clubbing together with friends (or joining a motorists' club) to make a joint purchase, or borrowing the tools against a deposit from a local garage or tool hire specialist. It is worth noting that many of the larger DIY superstores now carry a large range of special tools for hire at modest rates.

The following list contains only those tools and instruments freely available to the public, and not those special tools produced by the vehicle manufacturer specifically for its dealer network. You will find occasional references to these manufacturers' special tools in the text of this manual. Generally, an alternative method of doing the job without the vehicle manufacturers' special tool is given. However, sometimes there is no alternative to using them. Where this is the case and the relevant tool cannot be bought or borrowed, you will have to entrust the work to a dealer.

- ☐ Angular-tightening gauge
- ☐ Valve spring compressor
- ☐ Valve grinding tool
- ☐ Piston ring compressor
- ☐ Piston ring removal/installation tool
- ☐ Cylinder bore hone
- ☐ Balljoint separator
- ☐ Coil spring compressors (where applicable)
- ☐ Two/three-legged hub and bearing puller
- ☐ Impact screwdriver
- ☐ Micrometer and/or vernier calipers
- ☐ Dial gauge
- ☐ Stroboscopic timing light
- ☐ Dwell angle meter/tachometer
- ☐ Fault code reader
- ☐ Cylinder compression gauge
- ☐ Hand-operated vacuum pump and gauge
- ☐ Clutch plate alignment set
- ☐ Brake shoe steady spring cup removal tool
- ☐ Bush and bearing removal/installation set
- ☐ Stud extractors
- ☐ Tap and die set
- ☐ Lifting tackle
- ☐ Trolley jack

## Buying tools

Reputable motor accessory shops and superstores often offer excellent quality tools at discount prices, so it pays to shop around.

Remember, you don't have to buy the most expensive items on the shelf, but it is always advisable to steer clear of the very cheap tools. Beware of 'bargains' offered on market stalls or at car boot sales. There are plenty of good tools around at reasonable prices, but always aim to purchase items which meet the relevant national safety standards. If in doubt, ask the proprietor or manager of the shop for advice before making a purchase.

## Care and maintenance of tools

Having purchased a reasonable tool kit, it is necessary to keep the tools in a clean and serviceable condition. After use, always wipe off any dirt, grease and metal particles using a clean, dry cloth, before putting the tools away. Never leave them lying around after they have been used. A simple tool rack on the garage or workshop wall for items such as screwdrivers and pliers is a good idea. Store all normal spanners and sockets in a metal box. Any measuring instruments, gauges, meters, etc, must be carefully stored where they cannot be damaged or become rusty.

Take a little care when tools are used. Hammer heads inevitably become marked, and screwdrivers lose the keen edge on their blades from time to time. A little timely attention with emery cloth or a file will soon restore items like this to a good finish.

## Working facilities

Not to be forgotten when discussing tools is the workshop itself. If anything more than routine maintenance is to be carried out, a suitable working area becomes essential.

It is appreciated that many an owner-mechanic is forced by circumstances to remove an engine or similar item without the benefit of a garage or workshop. Having done this, any repairs should always be done under the cover of a roof.

Wherever possible, any dismantling should be done on a clean, flat workbench or table at a suitable working height.

Any workbench needs a vice; one with a jaw opening of 100 mm is suitable for most jobs. As mentioned previously, some clean dry storage space is also required for tools, as well as for any lubricants, cleaning fluids, touch-up paints etc, which become necessary.

Another item which may be required, and which has a much more general usage, is an electric drill with a chuck capacity of at least 8 mm. This, together with a good range of twist drills, is virtually essential for fitting accessories.

Last, but not least, always keep a supply of old newspapers and clean, lint-free rags available, and try to keep any working area as clean as possible.

**Micrometers**

**Dial test indicator ("dial gauge")**

**Strap wrench**

**Compression tester**

**Fault code reader**

This is a guide to getting your vehicle through the MOT test. Obviously it will not be possible to examine the vehicle to the same standard as the professional MOT tester. However, working through the following checks will enable you to identify any problem areas before submitting the vehicle for the test.

Where a testable component is in borderline condition, the tester has discretion in deciding whether to pass or fail it. The basis of such discretion is whether the tester would be happy for a close relative or friend to use the vehicle with the component in that condition. If the vehicle presented is clean and evidently well cared for, the tester may be more inclined to pass a borderline component than if the vehicle is scruffy and apparently neglected.

It has only been possible to summarise the test requirements here, based on the regulations in force at the time of printing. Test standards are becoming increasingly stringent, although there are some exemptions for older vehicles.

An assistant will be needed to help carry out some of these checks.

*The checks have been sub-divided into four categories, as follows:*

**1** Checks carried out **FROM THE DRIVER'S SEAT**

**2** Checks carried out **WITH THE VEHICLE ON THE GROUND**

**3** Checks carried out **WITH THE VEHICLE RAISED AND THE WHEELS FREE TO TURN**

**4** Checks carried out on **YOUR VEHICLE'S EXHAUST EMISSION SYSTEM**

**1** Checks carried out **FROM THE DRIVER'S SEAT**

### Handbrake

☐ Test the operation of the handbrake. Excessive travel (too many clicks) indicates incorrect brake or cable adjustment.

☐ Check that the handbrake cannot be released by tapping the lever sideways. Check the security of the lever mountings.

### Footbrake

☐ Depress the brake pedal and check that it does not creep down to the floor, indicating a master cylinder fault. Release the pedal, wait a few seconds, then depress it again. If the pedal travels nearly to the floor before firm resistance is felt, brake adjustment or repair is necessary. If the pedal feels spongy, there is air in the hydraulic system which must be removed by bleeding.

☐ Check that the brake pedal is secure and in good condition. Check also for signs of fluid leaks on the pedal, floor or carpets, which would indicate failed seals in the brake master cylinder.

☐ Check the servo unit (when applicable) by operating the brake pedal several times, then keeping the pedal depressed and starting the engine. As the engine starts, the pedal will move down slightly. If not, the vacuum hose or the servo itself may be faulty.

### Steering wheel and column

☐ Examine the steering wheel for fractures or looseness of the hub, spokes or rim.

☐ Move the steering wheel from side to side and then up and down. Check that the steering wheel is not loose on the column, indicating wear or a loose retaining nut. Continue moving the steering wheel as before, but also turn it slightly from left to right.

☐ Check that the steering wheel is not loose on the column, and that there is no abnormal

movement of the steering wheel, indicating wear in the column support bearings or couplings.

### Windscreen, mirrors and sunvisor

☐ The windscreen must be free of cracks or other significant damage within the driver's field of view. (Small stone chips are acceptable.) Rear view mirrors must be secure, intact, and capable of being adjusted.

290mm

☐ The driver's sunvisor must be capable of being stored in the "up" position.

## Seat belts and seats

**Note:** *The following checks are applicable to all seat belts, front and rear.*

☐ Examine the webbing of all the belts (including rear belts if fitted) for cuts, serious fraying or deterioration. Fasten and unfasten each belt to check the buckles. If applicable, check the retracting mechanism. Check the security of all seat belt mountings accessible from inside the vehicle.

☐ Seat belts with pre-tensioners, once activated, have a "flag" or similar showing on the seat belt stalk. This, in itself, is not a reason for test failure.

☐ The front seats themselves must be securely attached and the backrests must lock in the upright position.

## Doors

☐ Both front doors must be able to be opened and closed from outside and inside, and must latch securely when closed.

## 2 Checks carried out WITH THE VEHICLE ON THE GROUND

## Vehicle identification

☐ Number plates must be in good condition, secure and legible, with letters and numbers correctly spaced – spacing at (A) should be at least twice that at (B).

☐ The VIN plate and/or homologation plate must be legible.

## Electrical equipment

☐ Switch on the ignition and check the operation of the horn.

☐ Check the windscreen washers and wipers, examining the wiper blades; renew damaged or perished blades. Also check the operation of the stop-lights.

☐ Check the operation of the sidelights and number plate lights. The lenses and reflectors must be secure, clean and undamaged.

☐ Check the operation and alignment of the headlights. The headlight reflectors must not be tarnished and the lenses must be undamaged.

☐ Switch on the ignition and check the operation of the direction indicators (including the instrument panel tell-tale) and the hazard warning lights. Operation of the sidelights and stop-lights must not affect the indicators - if it does, the cause is usually a bad earth at the rear light cluster.

☐ Check the operation of the rear foglight(s), including the warning light on the instrument panel or in the switch.

☐ The ABS warning light must illuminate in accordance with the manufacturers' design. For most vehicles, the ABS warning light should illuminate when the ignition is switched on, and (if the system is operating properly) extinguish after a few seconds. Refer to the owner's handbook.

## Footbrake

☐ Examine the master cylinder, brake pipes and servo unit for leaks, loose mountings, corrosion or other damage.

☐ The fluid reservoir must be secure and the fluid level must be between the upper (A) and lower (B) markings.

☐ Inspect both front brake flexible hoses for cracks or deterioration of the rubber. Turn the steering from lock to lock, and ensure that the hoses do not contact the wheel, tyre, or any part of the steering or suspension mechanism. With the brake pedal firmly depressed, check the hoses for bulges or leaks under pressure.

## Steering and suspension

☐ Have your assistant turn the steering wheel from side to side slightly, up to the point where the steering gear just begins to transmit this movement to the roadwheels. Check for excessive free play between the steering wheel and the steering gear, indicating wear or insecurity of the steering column joints, the column-to-steering gear coupling, or the steering gear itself.

☐ Have your assistant turn the steering wheel more vigorously in each direction, so that the roadwheels just begin to turn. As this is done, examine all the steering joints, linkages, fittings and attachments. Renew any component that shows signs of wear or damage. On vehicles with power steering, check the security and condition of the steering pump, drivebelt and hoses.

☐ Check that the vehicle is standing level, and at approximately the correct ride height.

## Shock absorbers

☐ Depress each corner of the vehicle in turn, then release it. The vehicle should rise and then settle in its normal position. If the vehicle continues to rise and fall, the shock absorber is defective. A shock absorber which has seized will also cause the vehicle to fail.

## Exhaust system

☐ Start the engine. With your assistant holding a rag over the tailpipe, check the entire system for leaks. Repair or renew leaking sections.

**3** Checks carried out **WITH THE VEHICLE RAISED AND THE WHEELS FREE TO TURN**

*Jack up the front and rear of the vehicle, and securely support it on axle stands. Position the stands clear of the suspension assemblies. Ensure that the wheels are clear of the ground and that the steering can be turned from lock to lock.*

## Steering mechanism

☐ Have your assistant turn the steering from lock to lock. Check that the steering turns smoothly, and that no part of the steering mechanism, including a wheel or tyre, fouls any brake hose or pipe or any part of the body structure.

☐ Examine the steering rack rubber gaiters for damage or insecurity of the retaining clips. If power steering is fitted, check for signs of damage or leakage of the fluid hoses, pipes or connections. Also check for excessive stiffness or binding of the steering, a missing split pin or locking device, or severe corrosion of the body structure within 30 cm of any steering component attachment point.

## Front and rear suspension and wheel bearings

☐ Starting at the front right-hand side, grasp the roadwheel at the 3 o'clock and 9 o'clock positions and rock gently but firmly. Check for free play or insecurity at the wheel bearings, suspension balljoints, or suspension mountings, pivots and attachments.

☐ Now grasp the wheel at the 12 o'clock and 6 o'clock positions and repeat the previous inspection. Spin the wheel, and check for roughness or tightness of the front wheel bearing.

☐ If excess free play is suspected at a component pivot point, this can be confirmed by using a large screwdriver or similar tool and levering between the mounting and the component attachment. This will confirm whether the wear is in the pivot bush, its retaining bolt, or in the mounting itself (the bolt holes can often become elongated).

☐ Carry out all the above checks at the other front wheel, and then at both rear wheels.

## Springs and shock absorbers

☐ Examine the suspension struts (when applicable) for serious fluid leakage, corrosion, or damage to the casing. Also check the security of the mounting points.

☐ If coil springs are fitted, check that the spring ends locate in their seats, and that the spring is not corroded, cracked or broken.

☐ If leaf springs are fitted, check that all leaves are intact, that the axle is securely attached to each spring, and that there is no deterioration of the spring eye mountings, bushes, and shackles.

☐ The same general checks apply to vehicles fitted with other suspension types, such as torsion bars, hydraulic displacer units, etc. Ensure that all mountings and attachments are secure, that there are no signs of excessive wear, corrosion or damage, and (on hydraulic types) that there are no fluid leaks or damaged pipes.

☐ Inspect the shock absorbers for signs of serious fluid leakage. Check for wear of the mounting bushes or attachments, or damage to the body of the unit.

## Driveshafts (fwd vehicles only)

☐ Rotate each front wheel in turn and inspect the constant velocity joint gaiters for splits or damage. Also check that each driveshaft is straight and undamaged.

## Braking system

☐ If possible without dismantling, check brake pad wear and disc condition. Ensure that the friction lining material has not worn excessively, (A) and that the discs are not fractured, pitted, scored or badly worn (B).

☐ Examine all the rigid brake pipes underneath the vehicle, and the flexible hose(s) at the rear. Look for corrosion, chafing or insecurity of the pipes, and for signs of bulging under pressure, chafing, splits or deterioration of the flexible hoses.

☐ Look for signs of fluid leaks at the brake calipers or on the brake backplates. Repair or renew leaking components.

☐ Slowly spin each wheel, while your assistant depresses and releases the footbrake. Ensure that each brake is operating and does not bind when the pedal is released.

☐ Examine the handbrake mechanism, checking for frayed or broken cables, excessive corrosion, or wear or insecurity of the linkage. Check that the mechanism works on each relevant wheel, and releases fully, without binding.

☐ It is not possible to test brake efficiency without special equipment, but a road test can be carried out later to check that the vehicle pulls up in a straight line.

## Fuel and exhaust systems

☐ Inspect the fuel tank (including the filler cap), fuel pipes, hoses and unions. All components must be secure and free from leaks.

☐ Examine the exhaust system over its entire length, checking for any damaged, broken or missing mountings, security of the retaining clamps and rust or corrosion.

## Wheels and tyres

☐ Examine the sidewalls and tread area of each tyre in turn. Check for cuts, tears, lumps, bulges, separation of the tread, and exposure of the ply or cord due to wear or damage. Check that the tyre bead is correctly seated on the wheel rim, that the valve is sound and properly seated, and that the wheel is not distorted or damaged.

☐ Check that the tyres are of the correct size for the vehicle, that they are of the same size and type on each axle, and that the pressures are correct.

☐ Check the tyre tread depth. The legal minimum at the time of writing is 1.6 mm over at least three-quarters of the tread width. Abnormal tread wear may indicate incorrect front wheel alignment.

## Body corrosion

☐ Check the condition of the entire vehicle structure for signs of corrosion in load-bearing areas. (These include chassis box sections, side sills, cross-members, pillars, and all suspension, steering, braking system and seat belt mountings and anchorages.) Any corrosion which has seriously reduced the thickness of a load-bearing area is likely to cause the vehicle to fail. In this case professional repairs are likely to be needed.

☐ Damage or corrosion which causes sharp or otherwise dangerous edges to be exposed will also cause the vehicle to fail.

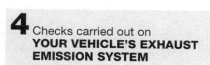

**4** Checks carried out on **YOUR VEHICLE'S EXHAUST EMISSION SYSTEM**

## Petrol models

☐ Have the engine at normal operating temperature, and make sure that it is in good tune (ignition system in good order, air filter element clean, etc).

☐ Before any measurements are carried out, raise the engine speed to around 2500 rpm, and hold it at this speed for 20 seconds. Allow the engine speed to return to idle, and watch for smoke emissions from the exhaust tailpipe. If the idle speed is obviously much too high, or if dense blue or clearly-visible black smoke comes from the tailpipe for more than 5 seconds, the vehicle will fail. As a rule of thumb, blue smoke signifies oil being burnt (engine wear) while black smoke signifies unburnt fuel (dirty air cleaner element, or other carburettor or fuel system fault).

☐ An exhaust gas analyser capable of measuring carbon monoxide (CO) and hydrocarbons (HC) is now needed. If such an instrument cannot be hired or borrowed, a local garage may agree to perform the check for a small fee.

## CO emissions (mixture)

☐ At the time of writing, for vehicles first used between 1st August 1975 and 31st July 1986 (P to C registration), the CO level must not exceed 4.5% by volume. For vehicles first used between 1st August 1986 and 31st July 1992 (D to J registration), the CO level must not exceed 3.5% by volume. Vehicles first used after 1st August 1992 (K registration) must conform to the manufacturer's specification. The MOT tester has access to a DOT database or emissions handbook, which lists the CO and HC limits for each make and model of vehicle. The CO level is measured with the engine at idle speed, and at "fast idle". The following limits are given as a general guide:

*At idle speed -*
    CO level no more than 0.5%
*At "fast idle" (2500 to 3000 rpm) -*
    CO level no more than 0.3%
    (Minimum oil temperature 60°C)

☐ If the CO level cannot be reduced far enough to pass the test (and the fuel and ignition systems are otherwise in good condition) then the carburettor is badly worn, or there is some problem in the fuel injection system or catalytic converter (as applicable).

## HC emissions

☐ With the CO within limits, HC emissions for vehicles first used between 1st August 1975 and 31st July 1992 (P to J registration) must not exceed 1200 ppm. Vehicles first used after 1st August 1992 (K registration) must conform to the manufacturer's specification. The MOT tester has access to a DOT database or emissions handbook, which lists the CO and HC limits for each make and model of vehicle. The HC level is measured with the engine at "fast idle". The following is given as a general guide:

*At "fast idle" (2500 to 3000 rpm) -*
    HC level no more than 200 ppm
    (Minimum oil temperature 60°C)

☐ Excessive HC emissions are caused by incomplete combustion, the causes of which can include oil being burnt, mechanical wear and ignition/fuel system malfunction.

## Diesel models

☐ The only emission test applicable to Diesel engines is the measuring of exhaust smoke density. The test involves accelerating the engine several times to its maximum unloaded speed.

**Note:** *It is of the utmost importance that the engine timing belt is in good condition before the test is carried out.*

☐ The limits for Diesel engine exhaust smoke, introduced in September 1995 are:
*Vehicles first used before 1st August 1979:*
    Exempt from metered smoke testing, but must not emit "dense blue or clearly visible black smoke for a period of more than 5 seconds at idle" or "dense blue or clearly visible black smoke during acceleration which would obscure the view of other road users".
*Non-turbocharged vehicles first used after 1st August 1979:* 2.5m-1
*Turbocharged vehicles first used after 1st August 1979:* 3.0m-1

☐ Excessive smoke can be caused by a dirty air cleaner element. Otherwise, professional advice may be needed to find the cause.

# Engine . . . . . . . . . . . . . . . . . . . . . . . . . . . . . .1

- ☐ Engine backfires
- ☐ Engine diesels (continues to run) after switching off
- ☐ Engine hard to start when cold
- ☐ Engine hard to start when hot
- ☐ Engine lacks power
- ☐ Engine lopes while idling or idles erratically
- ☐ Engine misses at idle speed
- ☐ Engine misses throughout driving speed range
- ☐ Engine rattles at start-up
- ☐ Engine rotates but will not start
- ☐ Engine runs with oil pressure light on
- ☐ Engine stalls
- ☐ Engine starts but stops immediately
- ☐ Engine stumbles on acceleration
- ☐ Engine surges while holding accelerator steady
- ☐ Engine will not rotate when attempting to start1
- ☐ Oil puddle under engine
- ☐ Pinking or knocking engine sounds during acceleration or uphill
- ☐ Starter motor noisy or excessively rough in engagement

# Fuel system . . . . . . . . . . . . . . . . . . . . . .2

- ☐ Excessive fuel consumption
- ☐ Fuel leakage and/or fuel odour

# Cooling system . . . . . . . . . . . . . . . . . . . .3

- ☐ Coolant loss
- ☐ External coolant leakage
- ☐ Internal coolant leakage
- ☐ Overcooling
- ☐ Overheating
- ☐ Poor coolant circulation

# Automatic transmission . . . . . . . . . . . . . .4

- ☐ Engine will start in gears other than Park or Neutral
- ☐ Fluid leakage
- ☐ Shift cable problems
- ☐ Transmission fluid brown or has a burned smell
- ☐ Transmission slips, shifts roughly, is noisy or has no drive
- ☐ in forward or reverse gears
- ☐ Transmission will not downshift with accelerator pedal pressed to the floor

# Brakes . . . . . . . . . . . . . . . . . . . . . . . . . . . . .5

- ☐ Brake pedal feels spongy when depressed
- ☐ Brake pedal travels to the floor with little resistance
- ☐ Brake roughness or chatter (pedal pulsates)
- ☐ Dragging brakes
- ☐ Excessive brake pedal travel
- ☐ Excessive pedal effort required to stop vehicle
- ☐ Grabbing or uneven braking action
- ☐ Noise (high-pitched squeal when the brakes are applied)
- ☐ Handbrake does not hold
- ☐ Vehicle pulls to one side during braking

# Suspension and steering systems . . . . . . .6

- ☐ Abnormal noise at the front end
- ☐ Abnormal or excessive tyre wear
- ☐ Cupped tyres
- ☐ Erratic steering when braking
- ☐ Excessive pitching and/or rolling around corners or during braking
- ☐ Excessive play or looseness in steering system
- ☐ Excessive tyre wear on inside edge
- ☐ Excessive tyre wear on outside edge
- ☐ Hard steering
- ☐ Poor returnability of steering to centre
- ☐ Rattling or clicking noise in rack-and-pinion
- ☐ Shimmy, shake or vibration
- ☐ Suspension bottoms
- ☐ Tyre tread worn in one place
- ☐ Vehicle pulls to one side
- ☐ Wander or poor steering stability
- ☐ Wheel makes a "thumping" noise

# Electrical system . . . . . . . . . . . . . . . . . . . .7

Battery will not hold a charge
Discharge warning light fails to come on when key is turned on
Discharge warning light fails to go out

# Introduction

This Section provides an easy reference guide to the more common problems which may occur during the operation of your vehicle. These problems and their possible causes are grouped under headings denoting various components or systems, such as Engine, Cooling system, etc. They also refer you to the Chapter and/or Section which deals with the problem.

Remember that successful troubleshooting is not a mysterious "black art" practised only by professional mechanics. It is simply the result of the right knowledge combined with an intelligent, systematic approach to the problem. Always work by a process of elimination, starting with the simplest solution and working through to the most complex - and never overlook the obvious. Anyone can run the petrol tank dry or leave the lights on overnight, so don't assume that you are exempt from such oversights.

Finally, always establish a clear idea of why a problem has occurred and take steps to ensure that it doesn't happen again. If the electrical system fails because of a poor connection, check all other connections in the system to make sure that they don't fail as well. If a particular fuse continues to blow, find out why - don't just replace one fuse after another. Remember, failure of a small component can often be indicative of potential failure or incorrect functioning of a more important component or system.

# 1 Engine

### Engine will not rotate when attempting to start

- ☐ Battery terminal connections loose or corroded (Chapter 1).
- ☐ Battery discharged or faulty (Chapter 1).
- ☐ Damaged left rear window harness shorting against glass rail inside door, causing battery to drain (Chapter 12).
- ☐ Automatic transmission not completely engaged in Park (Chapter 7).
- ☐ Broken, loose or disconnected wiring in the starting circuit (Chapters 5 and 12).
- ☐ Starter motor pinion jammed in flywheel ring gear (Chapter 5).
- ☐ Starter solenoid faulty (Chapter 5).
- ☐ Starter motor faulty (Chapter 5).
- ☐ Ignition switch faulty (Chapter 12).
- ☐ Starter pinion or flywheel teeth worn or broken (Chapter 5).
- ☐ Internal engine problem (Chapter 2B).
- ☐ Inertia switch activated (Chapter 12).
- ☐ Starter relay defective (Chapter 5).

### Engine rotates but will not start

- ☐ Fuel tank empty.
- ☐ Battery discharged (engine rotates slowly) (Chapter 5).
- ☐ Battery terminal connections loose or corroded (Chapter 1).
- ☐ Leaking fuel injector(s), faulty fuel pump, pressure regulator, etc. (Chapter 4).
- ☐ Fuel not reaching fuel injection system (Chapter 4).
- ☐ Ignition components damp or damaged (Chapter 5).
- ☐ Fuel injector stuck open (Chapter 4).
- ☐ Worn, faulty or incorrectly gapped spark plugs (Chapter 1).
- ☐ Broken, loose or disconnected wiring in the starting circuit (Chapter 5).
- ☐ Loose distributor is changing ignition timing (Chapter 1).
- ☐ Broken, loose or disconnected wires at the ignition coil or faulty coil (Chapter 5).
- ☐ 1988 and 1989 models may have electrical connector damage between the fuel pump relay and the fuel pump (Chapter 12).
- ☐ Coolant temperature sensor shorting on bonnet liner (Chapter 11).
- ☐ Defective Mass Airflow (MAF) sensor (Chapter 6).

### Engine hard to start when cold

- ☐ Battery discharged or low (Chapter 1).
- ☐ Fuel system malfunctioning (Chapter 4).
- ☐ Injector(s) leaking (Chapter 4).
- ☐ Distributor rotor carbon tracked (Chapter 5).
- ☐ Water enters the air cleaner housing near the left front wheel arch (Chapter 4).

### Engine hard to start when hot

- ☐ Air filter clogged (Chapter 1).
- ☐ Fuel not reaching the fuel injection system (Chapter 4).
- ☐ Corroded battery connections, especially ground (Chapter 1).
- ☐ Fuel vaporises at fuel pump inlet. Refit dual fuel pumps (Chapter 4).
- ☐ Fuel vapours from charcoal canister enter intake during idle and cause idling, stalling and starting problems (Chapter 6).

### Starter motor noisy or excessively rough in engagement

- ☐ Pinion or flywheel gear teeth worn or broken (Chapter 5).
- ☐ Starter motor mounting bolts loose or missing (Chapter 5).

### Engine starts but stops immediately

- ☐ Loose or faulty electrical connections at distributor, coil or alternator (Chapter 5).
- ☐ Insufficient fuel reaching the fuel injector(s) (Chapters 1 and 4).
- ☐ Damaged fuel injection system speed sensors (Chapter 5).
- ☐ Faulty fuel injection relays (Chapter 5).
- ☐ Leaking threaded adapter on the EGR valve - where fitted (Chapter 6)

### Oil puddle under engine

- ☐ Sump gasket and/or sump drain bolt seal leaking (Chapter 2).
- ☐ Oil pressure sending unit leaking (Chapter 2).
- ☐ Valve cover gaskets leaking (Chapter 2).
- ☐ Engine oil seals leaking (Chapter 2).
- ☐ Cylinder head rear plate gasket leaking (Chapter 2).
- ☐ Alternator mounting bolt threads leaking oil (Chapter 5).
- ☐ Oil cooler or oil cooler lines leaking (Chapter 3).

### Engine misses while idling or idles erratically

- ☐ Vacuum leakage (Chapter 2).
- ☐ Air filter clogged (Chapter 1).
- ☐ Fuel pump not delivering sufficient fuel to the fuel injection system (Chapter 4).
- ☐ Leaking head gasket (Chapter 2).
- ☐ Timing belt/chain and/or sprockets worn (Chapter 2).
- ☐ Camshaft lobes worn (Chapter 2).
- ☐ EGR valve stuck open - where fitted (Chapter 6).

### Engine misses at idle speed

- ☐ Spark plugs worn or not gapped properly (Chapter 1).
- ☐ Faulty spark plug leads (Chapter 1).
- ☐ Vacuum leaks (Chapter 1).
- ☐ Incorrect ignition timing (Chapter 5).
- ☐ Uneven or low compression (Chapter 2).
- ☐ Restricted EGR vacuum hose - where fitted (Chapter 6).

### Engine misses throughout driving speed range

- ☐ Fuel filter clogged and/or impurities in the fuel system (Chapter 1).
- ☐ Low fuel output at the injectors (Chapter 4).
- ☐ Faulty or incorrectly gapped spark plugs (Chapter 1).
- ☐ Incorrect ignition timing (Chapter 5).
- ☐ Cracked distributor cap, disconnected distributor wires or damaged distributor components (Chapter 1).
- ☐ Leaking spark plug leads (Chapter 1).
- ☐ Faulty emission system components (Chapter 6).
- ☐ Low or uneven cylinder compression pressures (Chapter 2).
- ☐ Weak or faulty ignition system (Chapter 5).
- ☐ Vacuum leak in fuel injection system, intake manifold or vacuum hoses (Chapter 4).
- ☐ Crankshaft sensor teeth damaged or missing (see Chapter 12).
- ☐ Distributor installed incorrectly (see Chapter 5)

### Engine stumbles on acceleration

- ☐ Spark plugs fouled (Chapter 1).
- ☐ Fuel injection system malfunctioning (Chapter 4).
- ☐ Fuel filter clogged (Chapters 1 and 4).
- ☐ Incorrect ignition timing (Chapter 5).
- ☐ Intake manifold air leak (Chapter 4).
- ☐ Collapsed or damaged fuel tank caused by blocked EVAP system - where fitted (see Chapter 6).

# 1 Engine (continued)

### Engine surges while holding accelerator steady

☐ Intake air leak (Chapter 4).
☐ Fuel pump faulty (Chapter 4).
☐ Loose fuel injector harness connections (Chapters 4 and 6).
☐ Defective ECU (Chapter 6).

### Pinking or knocking engine sounds during acceleration or uphill

☐ Incorrect grade of fuel.
☐ Distributor installed incorrectly (Chapter 5).
☐ Fuel injection system in need of adjustment (Chapter 4).
☐ Improper or damaged spark plugs or wires (Chapter 1).
☐ Worn or damaged distributor components (Chapter 5).
☐ Faulty emission system (Chapter 6).
☐ Vacuum leak (Chapter 4).
☐ Fuel rail feed (inlet) hose has hardened, resulting in knocking noise near dash (see Chapter 4).

### Engine lacks power

☐ Incorrect ignition timing (Chapter 5).
☐ Excessive play in distributor shaft (Chapter 5).
☐ Worn rotor, distributor cap or wires (Chapters 1 and 5).
☐ Faulty or incorrectly gapped spark plugs (Chapter 1).
☐ Fuel injection system malfunctioning (Chapter 4).
☐ Faulty coil (Chapter 5).
☐ Brakes binding (Chapter 1).
☐ Automatic transmission fluid level incorrect (Chapter 1).
☐ Fuel filter clogged and/or impurities in the fuel system (Chapter 1).
☐ Emission control system not functioning properly (Chapter 6).
☐ Low or uneven cylinder compression pressures (Chapter 2).

### Engine rattles at start-up

☐ Failure of upper timing chain tensioner (Chapter 2).

### Engine backfires

☐ Emissions system not functioning properly (Chapter 6).
☐ Ignition timing incorrect (Chapter 1).
☐ Faulty secondary ignition system (cracked spark plug insulator, faulty plug leads, distributor cap and/or rotor) (Chapters 1 and 5).
☐ Fuel injection system malfunctioning (Chapter 4).
☐ Vacuum leak at fuel injector(s), intake manifold or vacuum hoses (Chapter 4).

### Engine stalls

☐ Idle speed incorrect (Chapter 1).
☐ Fuel filter clogged and/or water and impurities in the fuel system (Chapter 1).
☐ Distributor components damp or damaged (Chapter 5).
☐ Faulty emissions system components (Chapter 6).
☐ Faulty or incorrectly gapped spark plugs (Chapter 1).
☐ Faulty spark plug leads (Chapter 1).
☐ Vacuum leak in the fuel injection system, intake manifold or vacuum hoses (Chapter 4).

### Engine runs with oil pressure light on

☐ Low oil level (Chapter 1).
☐ Idle rpm too low (Chapter 1).
☐ Short in wiring circuit (Chapter 12).
☐ Faulty oil pressure sending unit (Chapter 2).
☐ Worn engine bearings and/or oil pump (Chapter 2).

### Engine diesels (continues to run) after switching off

☐ Idle speed too high (Chapter 4).
☐ Excessive engine operating temperature (Chapter 3).
☐ Incorrect fuel octane grade.

# 2 Fuel system

### Excessive fuel consumption

☐ Dirty or clogged air filter element (Chapter 1).
☐ Incorrectly set ignition timing (Chapter 5).
☐ Emissions system not functioning properly (Chapter 6).
☐ Fuel injection internal parts worn or damaged (Chapter 4).
☐ Low tyre pressure or incorrect tyre size (Chapter 1).

### Fuel leakage and/or fuel odour

☐ Leak in a fuel feed or vent line (Chapter 4).
☐ Tank overfilled.
☐ Fuel injector internal parts excessively worn (Chapter 4).

# 3 Cooling system

### Overheating

☐ Insufficient coolant in system (Chapter 1).
☐ Water pump drivebelt defective or out of adjustment (Chapter 1).
☐ Radiator core blocked or grille restricted (Chapter 3).
☐ Thermostat faulty (Chapter 3).
☐ Radiator cap not maintaining proper pressure (Chapter 3).
☐ Ignition timing incorrect (Chapter 5).

### Overcooling

☐ Faulty thermostat (Chapter 3).

### External coolant leakage

☐ Deteriorated/damaged hoses; loose clamps (Chapters 1 and 3).
☐ Water pump seal defective (Chapters 1 and 3).
☐ Leakage from radiator core or manifold tank (Chapter 3).
☐ Engine drain or water jacket core plugs leaking (Chapter 2).
☐ Hoses behind water pump leaking (Chapter 3).

### Internal coolant leakage

☐ Leaking cylinder head gasket (Chapter 2).
☐ Cracked cylinder bore or cylinder head (Chapter 2).

### Coolant loss

☐ Too much coolant in system (Chapter 1).
☐ Coolant boiling away because of overheating (Chapter 3).
☐ Internal or external leakage (Chapter 3).
☐ Faulty radiator cap (Chapter 3).

### Poor coolant circulation

☐ Inoperative water pump (Chapter 3).
☐ Restriction in cooling system (Chapters 1 and 3).
☐ Water pump drivebelt defective/out of adjustment (Chapter 1).
☐ Thermostat sticking (Chapter 3).

# 4 Automatic transmission

**Note:** *Due to the complexity of the automatic transmission, it is difficult for the home mechanic to properly diagnose and service this component. For problems other than the following, the vehicle should be taken to a dealer or transmission workshop.*

## Fluid leakage

☐ Automatic transmission fluid is a deep red colour. Fluid leaks should not be confused with engine oil, which can easily be blown by air flow to the transmission.

☐ To pinpoint a leak, first remove all built-up dirt and grime from the transmission housing with degreasing agents and/or steam cleaning. Then drive the vehicle at low speeds so air flow will not blow the leak far from its source. Raise the vehicle and determine where the leak is coming from. Common areas of leakage are:

a) Sump pan (Chapters 1 and 7)
b) Dipstick/filler tube (see below)
c) Transmission fluid cooler lines (Chapter 7)
d) Speedometer sensor (Chapter 7)

☐ Make sure the dipstick is a tight fit inside the filler tube. If the seal at the top of the dipstick is worn or damaged, replace the seal or the dipstick. If fluid continues to leak from the top of the dipstick tube, inspect the breather, which is a plastic cap secured by a clip to the top of the extension housing. This breather can be plugged by the noise-deadening foam installed in the transmission tunnel, causing transmission fluid to leak from the top of the dipstick tube.

## Transmission fluid brown or has a burned smell

☐ Transmission fluid burned (Chapter 1).

## Shift cable problems

☐ Chapter 7 deals with adjusting the shift cable. Common problems which may be attributed to a poorly adjusted shift cable are:

a) Engine starting in gears other than Park or Neutral.
b) Indicator on shift lever pointing to a gear other than the one actually being used.
c) Vehicle moves when in Park.

☐ Refer to Chapter 7 for the shift cable adjustment procedure.

## Transmission will not downshift with accelerator pedal pressed to the floor

☐ Kickdown cable out of adjustment (Chapter 7).

## Engine will start in gears other than Park or Neutral

☐ Neutral start/reversing light switch malfunctioning (Chapter 7).
☐ Shift cable out of adjustment (Chapter 7).

## Transmission slips, shifts roughly, is noisy, or has no drive in forward or reverse gears

☐ There are many probable causes for the above problems, but the home mechanic should be concerned with only one possibility - fluid level. Before taking the vehicle to a dealer service department or transmission repair workshop, check the level and condition of the fluid as described in Chapter 1. Correct the fluid level as necessary or change the fluid if needed. If the problem persists, have a professional diagnose the probable cause.

# 5 Brakes

**Note:** *Before assuming that a brake problem exists, make sure that:*
a) The tyres are in good condition and properly inflated (Chapter 1).
b) The front end alignment is correct (Chapter 10).
c) The vehicle is not loaded with weight in an unequal manner.

## Vehicle pulls to one side during braking

☐ Incorrect tyre pressures (Chapter 1).
☐ Front end out of line (have the front end aligned).
☐ Unmatched tyres on same axle.
☐ Restricted brake lines or hoses (Chapter 9).
☐ Malfunctioning caliper assembly (Chapter 9).
☐ Loose suspension parts (Chapter 10).
☐ Loose calipers (Chapter 9).
☐ Brake pads contaminated with oil or grease (Chapter 9).

## Noise (high-pitched squeal when the brakes are applied)

☐ Front and/or rear disc brake pads worn out. The noise comes from the wear sensor rubbing against the disc. Replace pads with new ones immediately (Chapter 9).

## Brake roughness or chatter (pedal pulsates)

☐ Excessive lateral disc runout (Chapter 9).
☐ Parallelism not within specifications (Chapter 9).
☐ Uneven pad wear caused by caliper not sliding due to improper clearance or dirt (Chapter 9).
☐ Defective disc (Chapter 9).

## Excessive pedal effort required to stop vehicle

☐ Malfunctioning power brake servo (Chapter 9).
☐ Partial system failure (Chapter 9).
☐ Excessively worn pads (Chapter 9).
☐ Piston in caliper stuck or sluggish (Chapter 9).
☐ Brake pads contaminated with oil or grease (Chapter 9).
☐ New pads installed and not yet seated. It will take a while for the new material to seat against the disc.
☐ Accumulator in power hydraulic system defective (see a Jaguar dealer).

## Excessive brake pedal travel

☐ Partial brake system failure (Chapter 9).
☐ Insufficient fluid in master cylinder (Chapters 1 and 9).
☐ Air trapped in system (Chapters 1 and 9).

## Dragging brakes

☐ Master cylinder pistons not returning correctly (Chapter 9).
☐ Restricted brakes lines or hoses (Chapters 1 and 9).
☐ Incorrect handbrake adjustment (Chapter 9).

## Grabbing or uneven braking action

☐ Malfunction of power brake servo unit (Chapter 9).
☐ Binding brake pedal mechanism (Chapter 9).
☐ Brake pads contaminated with oil or grease (Chapter 9).

# 5 Braking system (continued)

### Brake pedal feels spongy when depressed

☐ Air in hydraulic lines (Chapter 9).
☐ Master cylinder mounting bolts loose (Chapter 9).
☐ Master cylinder defective (Chapter 9).

### Brake pedal travels to the floor - no resistance

☐ Little or no fluid in the master cylinder reservoir caused by leaking caliper piston(s), damaged or disconnected brake lines (Chapter 9).

### Handbrake does not hold

☐ Handbrake cable or handbrake shoes improperly adjusted (Chapter 9).
☐ Handbrake shoes need replacement (Chapter 9).

# 6 Suspension and steering systems

**Note:** *Before attempting to diagnose the suspension and steering systems, perform the following preliminary checks:*
  *a) Tyres for wrong pressure and uneven wear.*
  *b) Steering universal joints from the column to the steering gear for loose connectors or wear.*
  *c) Front and rear suspension and the rack and pinion assembly for loose or damaged parts.*
  *d) Out-of-round or out-of-balance tyres, bent rims and loose and/or rough wheel bearings.*

### Vehicle pulls to one side

☐ Mismatched or uneven tyres (Chapter 10).
☐ Broken or sagging springs (Chapter 10).
☐ Wheel alignment out of specifications (Chapter 10).
☐ Front brakes dragging (Chapter 9).

### Abnormal or excessive tyre wear

☐ Wheel alignment out of specifications (Chapter 10).
☐ Sagging or broken springs (Chapter 10).
☐ Tyre out-of-balance (Chapter 10).
☐ Worn shock absorber (Chapter 10).
☐ Overloaded vehicle.
☐ Tyres not rotated regularly.

### Wheel makes a "thumping" noise

☐ Blister or bump on tyre (Chapter 10).
☐ Improper shock absorber action (Chapter 10).

### Shimmy, shake or vibration

☐ Tyre or wheel out-of-balance or out-of-round (Chapter 10).
☐ Loose, worn or out-of-adjustment wheel bearings (Chapter 1).
☐ Worn tie-rod ends (Chapter 10).
☐ Worn balljoints (Chapter 10).
☐ Excessive wheel runout (Chapter 10).
☐ Blister or bump on tyre (Chapter 10).

### Hard steering

☐ Lack of lubrication at balljoints, tie-rod ends and rack-and-pinion assembly (Chapter 1).
☐ Front wheel alignment (Chapter 10).
☐ Low tyre pressure(s) (Chapter 1).

### Poor returnability of steering to centre

☐ Lack of lubrication at balljoints and tie-rod ends (Chapter 1).
☐ Binding in balljoints (Chapter 10).
☐ Binding in steering column (Chapter 10).
☐ Lack of lubricant in rack-and-pinion assembly (Chapter 10).
☐ Front wheel alignment (Chapter 10).

### Abnormal noise at the front end

☐ Lack of lubrication at balljoints and tie-rod ends (Chapter 1).
☐ Damaged shock absorber mounting (Chapter 10).

☐ Worn control arm bushings or tie-rod ends (Chapter 10).
☐ Loose stabiliser bar (Chapter 10).
☐ Loose wheel nuts (Chapter).
☐ Loose suspension bolts (Chapter 10).

### Wander or poor steering stability

☐ Mismatched or uneven tyres (Chapter 10).
☐ Lack of lubrication at balljoints and tie-rod ends (Chapter 1).
☐ Worn shock absorbers (Chapter 10).
☐ Loose stabiliser bar (Chapter 10).
☐ Broken or sagging springs (Chapter 10).
☐ Front or rear wheel alignment (Chapter 10).

### Erratic steering when braking

☐ Wheel bearings worn (Chapter 1).
☐ Broken or sagging springs (Chapter 10).
☐ Leaking wheel cylinder or caliper (Chapter 9).
☐ Warped discs (Chapter 9).

### Excessive pitching and/or rolling around corners or during braking

☐ Loose stabiliser bar (Chapter 10).
☐ Worn shock absorbers or mounts (Chapter 10).
☐ Broken or sagging springs (Chapter 10).
☐ Overloaded vehicle.

### Suspension bottoms

☐ Overloaded vehicle.
☐ Worn shock absorbers (Chapter 10).
☐ Incorrect, broken or sagging springs (Chapter 10).
☐ Defective power hydraulic system or leaking rear shock absorbers (Chapter 10).

### Cupped tyres (wear on both edges)

☐ Front wheel or rear wheel alignment (Chapter 10).
☐ Worn shock absorbers (Chapter 10).
☐ Wheel bearings worn (Chapter 10).
☐ Excessive tyre or wheel runout (Chapter 10).
☐ Worn balljoints (Chapter 10).

### Excessive tyre wear on outside edge

☐ Inflation pressures incorrect (Chapter 1).
☐ Excessive speed in turns.
☐ Front end alignment incorrect (excessive toe-in). Have professionally aligned.
☐ Suspension arm bent or twisted (Chapter 10).

### Excessive tyre wear on inside edge

☐ Inflation pressures incorrect (Chapter 1).
☐ Front end alignment incorrect (toe-out). Have professionally aligned.
☐ Loose or damaged steering components (Chapter 10).

# 6 Suspension and steering systems (continued)

### Tyre tread worn in one place

☐ Tyres out-of-balance.
☐ Damaged or buckled wheel. Inspect and replace if necessary.
☐ Defective tyre (Chapter 1).

### Excessive play or looseness in steering system

☐ Wheel bearing(s) worn (Chapter 10.

☐ Tie-rod end loose or worn (Chapter 10).
☐ Steering gear loose or worn (Chapter 10).

### Rattling or clicking noise in rack-and-pinion

☐ Insufficient or improper power steering fluid in steering system (Chapter 10).
☐ Steering gear mounts loose (Chapter 10).

# 7 Electrical system

### Battery will not hold a charge

☐ Alternator drivebelt defective or not adjusted properly (Chapter 1).
☐ Electrolyte level low (Chapter 1).
☐ Battery terminals loose or corroded (Chapter 1).
☐ Alternator not charging properly (Chapter 5).
☐ Loose, broken or faulty wiring in the charging circuit (Chapter 5).
☐ Short in vehicle wiring (Chapters 5 and 12).
☐ Internally defective battery (Chapters 1 and 5).
☐ Damaged left rear window harness shorting against glass rail inside door, causing battery to drain (Chapter 12).

### Charge warning light fails to go out

☐ Faulty alternator or charging circuit (Chapter 5).
☐ Alternator drivebelt defective or out of adjustment (Chapter 1).
☐ Alternator voltage regulator inoperative (Chapter 5).

### Charge warning light fails to come on when key is turned on

☐ Warning light bulb defective (Chapter 12).
☐ Fault in the printed circuit, dash wiring or bulb holder (Chapter 12).

# A

**ABS (Anti-lock brake system)** A system, usually electronically controlled, that senses incipient wheel lockup during braking and relieves hydraulic pressure at wheels that are about to skid.

**Air bag** An inflatable bag hidden in the steering wheel (driver's side) or the dash or glovebox (passenger side). In a head-on collision, the bags inflate, preventing the driver and front passenger from being thrown forward into the steering wheel or windscreen.

**Air cleaner** A metal or plastic housing, containing a filter element, which removes dust and dirt from the air being drawn into the engine.

**Air filter element** The actual filter in an air cleaner system, usually manufactured from pleated paper and requiring renewal at regular intervals.

*Air filter*

**Allen key** A hexagonal wrench which fits into a recessed hexagonal hole.

**Alligator clip** A long-nosed spring-loaded metal clip with meshing teeth. Used to make temporary electrical connections.

**Alternator** A component in the electrical system which converts mechanical energy from a drivebelt into electrical energy to charge the battery and to operate the starting system, ignition system and electrical accessories.

**Ampere (amp)** A unit of measurement for the flow of electric current. One amp is the amount of current produced by one volt acting through a resistance of one ohm.

**Anaerobic sealer** A substance used to prevent bolts and screws from loosening. Anaerobic means that it does not require oxygen for activation. The Loctite brand is widely used.

**Antifreeze** A substance (usually ethylene glycol) mixed with water, and added to a vehicle's cooling system, to prevent freezing of the coolant in winter. Antifreeze also contains chemicals to inhibit corrosion and the formation of rust and other deposits that would tend to clog the radiator and coolant passages and reduce cooling efficiency.

**Anti-seize compound** A coating that reduces the risk of seizing on fasteners that are subjected to high temperatures, such as exhaust manifold bolts and nuts.

**Asbestos** A natural fibrous mineral with great heat resistance, commonly used in the composition of brake friction materials.

Asbestos is a health hazard and the dust created by brake systems should never be inhaled or ingested.

**Axle** A shaft on which a wheel revolves, or which revolves with a wheel. Also, a solid beam that connects the two wheels at one end of the vehicle. An axle which also transmits power to the wheels is known as a live axle.

**Axleshaft** A single rotating shaft, on either side of the differential, which delivers power from the final drive assembly to the drive wheels. Also called a driveshaft or a halfshaft.

# B

**Ball bearing** An anti-friction bearing consisting of a hardened inner and outer race with hardened steel balls between two races.

**Bearing** The curved surface on a shaft or in a bore, or the part assembled into either, that permits relative motion between them with minimum wear and friction.

*Bearing*

**Big-end bearing** The bearing in the end of the connecting rod that's attached to the crankshaft.

**Bleed nipple** A valve on a brake wheel cylinder, caliper or other hydraulic component that is opened to purge the hydraulic system of air. Also called a bleed screw.

**Brake bleeding** Procedure for removing air from lines of a hydraulic brake system.

*Brake bleeding*

**Brake disc** The component of a disc brake that rotates with the wheels.

**Brake drum** The component of a drum brake that rotates with the wheels.

**Brake linings** The friction material which contacts the brake disc or drum to retard the vehicle's speed. The linings are bonded or riveted to the brake pads or shoes.

**Brake pads** The replaceable friction pads that pinch the brake disc when the brakes are applied. Brake pads consist of a friction material bonded or riveted to a rigid backing plate.

**Brake shoe** The crescent-shaped carrier to which the brake linings are mounted and which forces the lining against the rotating drum during braking.

**Braking systems** For more information on braking systems, consult the *Haynes Automotive Brake Manual*.

**Breaker bar** A long socket wrench handle providing greater leverage.

**Bulkhead** The insulated partition between the engine and the passenger compartment.

# C

**Caliper** The non-rotating part of a disc-brake assembly that straddles the disc and carries the brake pads. The caliper also contains the hydraulic components that cause the pads to pinch the disc when the brakes are applied. A caliper is also a measuring tool that can be set to measure inside or outside dimensions of an object.

**Camshaft** A rotating shaft on which a series of cam lobes operate the valve mechanisms. The camshaft may be driven by gears, by sprockets and chain or by sprockets and a belt.

**Canister** A container in an evaporative emission control system; contains activated charcoal granules to trap vapours from the fuel system.

*Canister*

**Carburettor** A device which mixes fuel with air in the proper proportions to provide a desired power output from a spark ignition internal combustion engine.

**Castellated** Resembling the parapets along the top of a castle wall. For example, a castellated balljoint stud nut.

**Castor** In wheel alignment, the backward or forward tilt of the steering axis. Castor is positive when the steering axis is inclined rearward at the top.

**Catalytic converter** A silencer-like device in the exhaust system which converts certain pollutants in the exhaust gases into less harmful substances.

*Catalytic converter*

**Circlip** A ring-shaped clip used to prevent endwise movement of cylindrical parts and shafts. An internal circlip is installed in a groove in a housing; an external circlip fits into a groove on the outside of a cylindrical piece such as a shaft.

**Clearance** The amount of space between two parts. For example, between a piston and a cylinder, between a bearing and a journal, etc.

**Coil spring** A spiral of elastic steel found in various sizes throughout a vehicle, for example as a springing medium in the suspension and in the valve train.

**Compression** Reduction in volume, and increase in pressure and temperature, of a gas, caused by squeezing it into a smaller space.

**Compression ratio** The relationship between cylinder volume when the piston is at top dead centre and cylinder volume when the piston is at bottom dead centre.

**Constant velocity (CV) joint** A type of universal joint that cancels out vibrations caused by driving power being transmitted through an angle.

**Core plug** A disc or cup-shaped metal device inserted in a hole in a casting through which core was removed when the casting was formed. Also known as a freeze plug or expansion plug.

**Crankcase** The lower part of the engine block in which the crankshaft rotates.

**Crankshaft** The main rotating member, or shaft, running the length of the crankcase, with offset "throws" to which the connecting rods are attached.

*Crankshaft assembly*

**Crocodile clip** See Alligator clip

## D

**Diagnostic code** Code numbers obtained by accessing the diagnostic mode of an engine management computer. This code can be used to determine the area in the system where a malfunction may be located.

**Disc brake** A brake design incorporating a rotating disc onto which brake pads are squeezed. The resulting friction converts the energy of a moving vehicle into heat.

**Double-overhead cam (DOHC)** An engine that uses two overhead camshafts, usually one for the intake valves and one for the exhaust valves.

**Drivebelt(s)** The belt(s) used to drive accessories such as the alternator, water pump, power steering pump, air conditioning compressor, etc. off the crankshaft pulley.

*Accessory drivebelts*

**Driveshaft** Any shaft used to transmit motion. Commonly used when referring to the axleshafts on a front wheel drive vehicle.

**Drum brake** A type of brake using a drum-shaped metal cylinder attached to the inner surface of the wheel. When the brake pedal is pressed, curved brake shoes with friction linings press against the inside of the drum to slow or stop the vehicle.

## E

**EGR valve** A valve used to introduce exhaust gases into the intake air stream.

**Electronic control unit (ECU)** A computer which controls (for instance) ignition and fuel injection systems, or an anti-lock braking system. For more information refer to the *Haynes Automotive Electrical and Electronic Systems Manual*.

**Electronic Fuel Injection (EFI)** A computer controlled fuel system that distributes fuel through an injector located in each intake port of the engine.

**Emergency brake** A braking system, independent of the main hydraulic system, that can be used to slow or stop the vehicle if the primary brakes fail, or to hold the vehicle stationary even though the brake pedal isn't depressed. It usually consists of a hand lever that actuates either front or rear brakes mechanically through a series of cables and linkages. Also known as a handbrake or parking brake.

**Endfloat** The amount of lengthwise movement between two parts. As applied to a crankshaft, the distance that the crankshaft can move forward and back in the cylinder block.

**Engine management system (EMS)** A computer controlled system which manages the fuel injection and the ignition systems in an integrated fashion.

**Exhaust manifold** A part with several passages through which exhaust gases leave the engine combustion chambers and enter the exhaust pipe.

## F

**Fan clutch** A viscous (fluid) drive coupling device which permits variable engine fan speeds in relation to engine speeds.

**Feeler blade** A thin strip or blade of hardened steel, ground to an exact thickness, used to check or measure clearances between parts.

*Feeler blade*

**Firing order** The order in which the engine cylinders fire, or deliver their power strokes, beginning with the number one cylinder.

**Flywheel** A heavy spinning wheel in which energy is absorbed and stored by means of momentum. On cars, the flywheel is attached to the crankshaft to smooth out firing impulses.

**Free play** The amount of travel before any action takes place. The "looseness" in a linkage, or an assembly of parts, between the initial application of force and actual movement. For example, the distance the brake pedal moves before the pistons in the master cylinder are actuated.

**Fuse** An electrical device which protects a circuit against accidental overload. The typical fuse contains a soft piece of metal which is calibrated to melt at a predetermined current flow (expressed as amps) and break the circuit.

**Fusible link** A circuit protection device consisting of a conductor surrounded by heat-resistant insulation. The conductor is smaller than the wire it protects, so it acts as the weakest link in the circuit. Unlike a blown fuse, a failed fusible link must frequently be cut from the wire for replacement.

## G

**Gap**  The distance the spark must travel in jumping from the centre electrode to the side electrode in a spark plug. Also refers to the spacing between the points in a contact breaker assembly in a conventional points-type ignition, or to the distance between the reluctor or rotor and the pickup coil in an electronic ignition.

*Adjusting spark plug gap*

**Gasket**  Any thin, soft material - usually cork, cardboard, asbestos or soft metal - installed between two metal surfaces to ensure a good seal. For instance, the cylinder head gasket seals the joint between the block and the cylinder head.

*Gasket*

**Gauge**  An instrument panel display used to monitor engine conditions. A gauge with a movable pointer on a dial or a fixed scale is an analogue gauge. A gauge with a numerical readout is called a digital gauge.

## H

**Halfshaft**  A rotating shaft that transmits power from the final drive unit to a drive wheel, usually when referring to a live rear axle.

**Harmonic balancer**  A device designed to reduce torsion or twisting vibration in the crankshaft. May be incorporated in the crankshaft pulley. Also known as a vibration damper.

**Hone**  An abrasive tool for correcting small irregularities or differences in diameter in an engine cylinder, brake cylinder, etc.

**Hydraulic tappet**  A tappet that utilises hydraulic pressure from the engine's lubrication system to maintain zero clearance (constant contact with both camshaft and valve stem). Automatically adjusts to variation in valve stem length. Hydraulic tappets also reduce valve noise.

## I

**Ignition timing**  The moment at which the spark plug fires, usually expressed in the number of crankshaft degrees before the piston reaches the top of its stroke.

**Inlet manifold**  A tube or housing with passages through which flows the air-fuel mixture (carburettor vehicles and vehicles with throttle body injection) or air only (port fuel-injected vehicles) to the port openings in the cylinder head.

## J

**Jump start**  Starting the engine of a vehicle with a discharged or weak battery by attaching jump leads from the weak battery to a charged or helper battery.

## L

**Load Sensing Proportioning Valve (LSPV)** A brake hydraulic system control valve that works like a proportioning valve, but also takes into consideration the amount of weight carried by the rear axle.

**Locknut**  A nut used to lock an adjustment nut, or other threaded component, in place. For example, a locknut is employed to keep the adjusting nut on the rocker arm in position.

**Lockwasher**  A form of washer designed to prevent an attaching nut from working loose.

## M

**MacPherson strut**  A type of front suspension system devised by Earle MacPherson at Ford of England. In its original form, a simple lateral link with the anti-roll bar creates the lower control arm. A long strut - an integral coil spring and shock absorber - is mounted between the body and the steering knuckle. Many modern so-called MacPherson strut systems use a conventional lower A-arm and don't rely on the anti-roll bar for location.

**Multimeter**  An electrical test instrument with the capability to measure voltage, current and resistance.

## N

**NOx**  Oxides of Nitrogen. A common toxic pollutant emitted by petrol and diesel engines at higher temperatures.

## O

**Ohm**  The unit of electrical resistance. One volt applied to a resistance of one ohm will produce a current of one amp.

**Ohmmeter**  An instrument for measuring electrical resistance.

**O-ring**  A type of sealing ring made of a special rubber-like material; in use, the O-ring is compressed into a groove to provide the sealing action.

**Overhead cam (ohc) engine**  An engine with the camshaft(s) located on top of the cylinder head(s).

**Overhead valve (ohv) engine**  An engine with the valves located in the cylinder head, but with the camshaft located in the engine block.

**Oxygen sensor**  A device installed in the engine exhaust manifold, which senses the oxygen content in the exhaust and converts this information into an electric current. Also called a Lambda sensor.

## P

**Phillips screw**  A type of screw head having a cross instead of a slot for a corresponding type of screwdriver.

**Plastigage**  A thin strip of plastic thread, available in different sizes, used for measuring clearances. For example, a strip of Plastigage is laid across a bearing journal. The parts are assembled and dismantled; the width of the crushed strip indicates the clearance between journal and bearing.

*Plastigage*

**Propeller shaft**  The long hollow tube with universal joints at both ends that carries power from the transmission to the differential on front-engined rear wheel drive vehicles.

**Proportioning valve**  A hydraulic control valve which limits the amount of pressure to the rear brakes during panic stops to prevent wheel lock-up.

## R

**Rack-and-pinion steering**  A steering system with a pinion gear on the end of the steering shaft that mates with a rack (think of a geared wheel opened up and laid flat). When the steering wheel is turned, the pinion turns, moving the rack to the left or right. This movement is transmitted through the track rods to the steering arms at the wheels.

**Radiator**  A liquid-to-air heat transfer device designed to reduce the temperature of the coolant in an internal combustion engine cooling system.

**Refrigerant**  Any substance used as a heat transfer agent in an air-conditioning system. R-12 has been the principle refrigerant for many years; recently, however, manufacturers have begun using R-134a, a non-CFC substance that is considered less harmful to the ozone in the upper atmosphere.

**Rocker arm**  A lever arm that rocks on a shaft or pivots on a stud. In an overhead valve engine, the rocker arm converts the upward movement of the pushrod into a downward movement to open a valve.

**Rotor** In a distributor, the rotating device inside the cap that connects the centre electrode and the outer terminals as it turns, distributing the high voltage from the coil secondary winding to the proper spark plug. Also, that part of an alternator which rotates inside the stator. Also, the rotating assembly of a turbocharger, including the compressor wheel, shaft and turbine wheel.

**Runout** The amount of wobble (in-and-out movement) of a gear or wheel as it's rotated. The amount a shaft rotates "out-of-true." The out-of-round condition of a rotating part.

## S

**Sealant** A liquid or paste used to prevent leakage at a joint. Sometimes used in conjunction with a gasket.

**Sealed beam lamp** An older headlight design which integrates the reflector, lens and filaments into a hermetically-sealed one-piece unit. When a filament burns out or the lens cracks, the entire unit is simply replaced.

**Serpentine drivebelt** A single, long, wide accessory drivebelt that's used on some newer vehicles to drive all the accessories, instead of a series of smaller, shorter belts. Serpentine drivebelts are usually tensioned by an automatic tensioner.

*Serpentine drivebelt*

**Shim** Thin spacer, commonly used to adjust the clearance or relative positions between two parts. For example, shims inserted into or under bucket tappets control valve clearances. Clearance is adjusted by changing the thickness of the shim.

**Slide hammer** A special puller that screws into or hooks onto a component such as a shaft or bearing; a heavy sliding handle on the shaft bottoms against the end of the shaft to knock the component free.

**Sprocket** A tooth or projection on the periphery of a wheel, shaped to engage with a chain or drivebelt. Commonly used to refer to the sprocket wheel itself.

**Starter inhibitor switch** On vehicles with an automatic transmission, a switch that prevents starting if the vehicle is not in Neutral or Park.

**Strut** See MacPherson strut.

## T

**Tappet** A cylindrical component which transmits motion from the cam to the valve stem, either directly or via a pushrod and rocker arm. Also called a cam follower.

**Thermostat** A heat-controlled valve that regulates the flow of coolant between the cylinder block and the radiator, so maintaining optimum engine operating temperature. A thermostat is also used in some air cleaners in which the temperature is regulated.

**Thrust bearing** The bearing in the clutch assembly that is moved in to the release levers by clutch pedal action to disengage the clutch. Also referred to as a release bearing.

**Timing belt** A toothed belt which drives the camshaft. Serious engine damage may result if it breaks in service.

**Timing chain** A chain which drives the camshaft.

**Toe-in** The amount the front wheels are closer together at the front than at the rear. On rear wheel drive vehicles, a slight amount of toe-in is usually specified to keep the front wheels running parallel on the road by offsetting other forces that tend to spread the wheels apart.

**Toe-out** The amount the front wheels are closer together at the rear than at the front. On front wheel drive vehicles, a slight amount of toe-out is usually specified.

**Tools** For full information on choosing and using tools, refer to the *Haynes Automotive Tools Manual*.

**Tracer** A stripe of a second colour applied to a wire insulator to distinguish that wire from another one with the same colour insulator.

**Tune-up** A process of accurate and careful adjustments and parts replacement to obtain the best possible engine performance.

**Turbocharger** A centrifugal device, driven by exhaust gases, that pressurises the intake air. Normally used to increase the power output from a given engine displacement, but can also be used primarily to reduce exhaust emissions (as on VW's "Umwelt" Diesel engine).

## U

**Universal joint or U-joint** A double-pivoted connection for transmitting power from a driving to a driven shaft through an angle. A U-joint consists of two Y-shaped yokes and a cross-shaped member called the spider.

## V

**Valve** A device through which the flow of liquid, gas, vacuum, or loose material in bulk may be started, stopped, or regulated by a movable part that opens, shuts, or partially obstructs one or more ports or passageways. A valve is also the movable part of such a device.

**Valve clearance** The clearance between the valve tip (the end of the valve stem) and the rocker arm or tappet. The valve clearance is measured when the valve is closed.

**Vernier caliper** A precision measuring instrument that measures inside and outside dimensions. Not quite as accurate as a micrometer, but more convenient.

**Viscosity** The thickness of a liquid or its resistance to flow.

**Volt** A unit for expressing electrical "pressure" in a circuit. One volt that will produce a current of one ampere through a resistance of one ohm.

## W

**Welding** Various processes used to join metal items by heating the areas to be joined to a molten state and fusing them together. For more information refer to the *Haynes Automotive Welding Manual*.

**Wiring diagram** A drawing portraying the components and wires in a vehicle's electrical system, using standardised symbols. For more information refer to the *Haynes Automotive Electrical and Electronic Systems Manual*.

**Note:** *References throughout this index are in the form - "Chapter number" • "page number"*

# W

# Haynes Manuals – The Complete **UK Car** List

| Title | Book No. |
|---|---|
| **ALFA ROMEO** Alfasud/Sprint (74 - 88) up to F * | 0292 |
| Alfa Romeo Alfetta (73 – 87) up to E * | 0531 |
| **AUDI** 80, 90 & Coupe Petrol (79 – Nov 88) up to F | 0605 |
| Audi 80, 90 & Coupe Petrol (Oct 86 – 90) D to H | 1491 |
| Audi 100 & A6 Petrol & Diesel (May 91 – May 97) H to P | 3504 |
| Audi A3 Petrol & Diesel (96 – May 03) P to 03 | 4253 |
| Audi A3 Petrol & Diesel (June 03 – Mar 08) 03 to 08 | 4884 |
| Audi A4 Petrol & Diesel (95 – 00) M to X | 3575 |
| Audi A4 Petrol & Diesel (01 – 04) X to 54 | 4609 |
| Audi A4 Petrol & Diesel (Jan 05 – Feb 08) 54 to 57 | 4885 |
| **AUSTIN** A35 & A40 (56 – 67) up to F * | 0118 |
| Mini (59 – 69) up to H * | 0527 |
| Mini (69 – 01) up to X | 0646 |
| Austin Healey 100/6 & 3000 (56 – 68) up to G * | 0049 |
| **BEDFORD**/Vauxhall Rascal & Suzuki Supercarry (86 – Oct 94) C to M | 3015 |
| **BMW** 1-Series 4-cyl Petrol & Diesel (04 – Aug 11) 54 to 11 | 4918 |
| BMW 316, 320 & 320i (4-cyl)(75 – Feb 83) up to Y * | 0276 |
| BMW 3- & 5- Series Petrol (81 – 91) up to J | 1948 |
| BMW 3-Series Petrol (Apr 91 – 99) H to V | 3210 |
| BMW 3-Series Petrol (Sept 98 – 06) S to 56 | 4067 |
| BMW 3-Series Petrol & Diesel (05 – Sept 08) 54 to 58 | 4782 |
| BMW 5-Series 6-cyl Petrol (April 96 – Aug 03) N to 03 | 4151 |
| BMW 5-Series Diesel (Sept 03 – 10 ) 53 to 10 | 4901 |
| BMW 1500, 1502, 1600, 1602, 2000 & 2002 (59 – 77) up to S * | 0240 |
| **CHRYSLER** PT Cruiser Petrol (00-09) W to 09 | 4058 |
| **CITROEN** 2CV, Ami & Dyane (67 – 90) up to H | 0196 |
| Citroen AX Petrol & Diesel (87- 97) D to P | 3014 |
| Citroen Berlingo & Peugeot Partner Petrol & Diesel (96 – 10) P to 60 | 4281 |
| Citroen C1 Petrol (05 – 11) 05 to 11 | 4922 |
| Citroen C2 Petrol & Diesel (03 – 10) 53 to 60 | 5635 |
| Citroen C3 Petrol & Diesel (02 – 09) 51 to 59 | 4890 |
| Citroen C4 Petrol & Diesel (04 – 10) 54 to 60 | 5576 |
| Citroen C5 Petrol & Diesel (01 – 08) Y to 08 | 4745 |
| Citroen C15 Van Petrol & Diesel (89 – Oct 98) F to S | 3509 |
| Citroen CX Petrol (75 – 88) up to F | 0528 |
| Citroen Saxo Petrol & Diesel (96 – 04) N to 54 | 3506 |
| Citroen Xantia Petrol & Diesel (93 – 01) K to Y | 3082 |
| Citroen XM Petrol & Diesel (89 – 00) G to X | 3451 |
| Citroen Xsara Petrol & Diesel (97 – Sept 00) R to W | 3751 |
| Citroen Xsara Picasso Petrol & Diesel (00 – 02) W to 52 | 3944 |
| Citroen Xsara Picasso (Mar 04 – 08) 04 to 58 | 4784 |
| Citroen ZX Diesel (91 – 98) J to S | 1922 |
| Citroen ZX Petrol (91 – 98) H to S | 1881 |
| **FIAT** 126 (73 – 87) up to E * | 0305 |
| Fiat 500 (57 – 73) up to M * | 0090 |
| Fiat 500 & Panda (04 – 12) 53 to 61 | 5558 |
| Fiat Bravo & Brava Petrol (95 – 00) N to W | 3572 |
| Fiat Cinquecento (93 – 98) K to R | 3501 |
| Fiat Grande Punto, Punto Evo & Punto Petrol (06 – 15) 55 to 15 | 5956 |
| Fiat Panda (81 – 95) up to M | 0793 |
| Fiat Punto Petrol & Diesel (94 – Oct 99) L to V | 3251 |
| Fiat Punto Petrol (Oct 99 – July 03) V to 03 | 4066 |
| Fiat Punto Petrol (03 – 07) 03 to 07 | 4746 |

| Title | Book No. |
|---|---|
| Fiat Punto Petrol (Oct 99 – 07) V to 07 | 5634 |
| Fiat X1/9 (74 – 89) up to G * | 0273 |
| **FORD** Anglia (59 – 68) up to G * | 0001 |
| Ford Capri II (& III) 1.6 & 2.0 (74 – 87) up to E * | 0283 |
| Ford Capri II (& III) 2.8 & 3.0 V6 (74 – 87) up to E | 1309 |
| Ford C-Max Petrol & Diesel (03 – 10) 53 to 60 | 4900 |
| Ford Escort Mk I 1100 & 1300 (68 – 74) up to N * | 0171 |
| Ford Escort Mk I Mexico, RS 1600 & RS 2000 (70 – 74) up to N * | 0139 |
| Ford Escort Mk II Mexico, RS 1800 & RS 2000 (75 – 80) up to W * | 0735 |
| Ford Escort (75 – Aug 80) up to V * | 0280 |
| Ford Escort Petrol (Sept 80 – Sept 90) up to H | 0686 |
| Ford Escort & Orion Petrol (Sept 90 – 00) H to X | 1737 |
| Ford Escort & Orion Diesel (Sept 90 – 00) H to X | 4081 |
| Ford Fiesta Petrol (Feb 89 – Oct 95) F to N | 1595 |
| Ford Fiesta Petrol & Diesel (Oct 95 – Mar 02) N to 02 | 3397 |
| Ford Fiesta Petrol & Diesel (Apr 02 – 08) 02 to 58 | 4170 |
| Ford Fiesta Petrol & Diesel (08 – 11) 58 to 11 | 4907 |
| Ford Focus Petrol & Diesel (98 – 01) S to Y | 3759 |
| Ford Focus Petrol & Diesel (Oct 01 – 05) 51 to 05 | 4167 |
| Ford Focus Petrol (05 – 11) 54 to 61 | 4785 |
| Ford Focus Diesel (05 – 11) 54 to 61 | 4807 |
| Ford Focus Petrol & Diesel (11 – 14) 60 to 14 | 5632 |
| Ford Fusion Petrol & Diesel (02 – 11) 02 to 61 | 5566 |
| Ford Galaxy Petrol & Diesel (95 – Aug 00) M to W | 3984 |
| Ford Galaxy Petrol & Diesel (00 – 06) X to 06 | 5556 |
| Ford Granada Petrol (Sept 77 – Feb 85) up to B * | 0481 |
| Ford Ka (96 – 08) P to 58 | 5567 |
| Ford Ka Petrol (09 – 14) 58 to 14 | 5637 |
| Ford Mondeo Petrol (93 – Sept 00) K to X | 1923 |
| Ford Mondeo Petrol & Diesel (Oct 00 – Jul 03) X to 03 | 3990 |
| Ford Mondeo Petrol & Diesel (July 03 – 07) 03 to 56 | 4619 |
| Ford Mondeo Petrol & Diesel (Apr 07 – 12) 07 to 61 | 5548 |
| Ford Mondeo Diesel (93 – Sept 00) L to X | 3465 |
| Ford Transit Connect Diesel (02 – 11) 02 to 11 | 4903 |
| Ford Transit Diesel (Feb 86 – 99) C to T | 3019 |
| Ford Transit Diesel (00 – Oct 06) X to 56 | 4775 |
| Ford Transit Diesel (Nov 06 – 13) 56 to 63 | 5629 |
| Ford 1.6 & 1.8 litre Diesel Engine (84 – 96) A to N | 1172 |
| **HILLMAN** Imp (63 – 76) up to R * | 0022 |
| **HONDA** Civic (Feb 84 – Oct 87) A to E | 1226 |
| Honda Civic (Nov 91 – 96) J to N | 3199 |
| Honda Civic Petrol (Mar 95 – 00) M to X | 4050 |
| Honda Civic Petrol & Diesel (01 – 05) X to 55 | 4611 |
| Honda CR-V Petrol & Diesel (02 – 06) 51 to 56 | 4747 |
| Honda Jazz (02 to 08) 51 to 58 | 4735 |
| **JAGUAR** E-Type (61 – 72) up to L * | 0140 |
| Jaguar Mk I & II, 240 & 340 (55 – 69) up to H * | 0098 |
| Jaguar XJ6, XJ & Sovereign, Daimler Sovereign (68 – Oct 86) up to D | 0242 |
| Jaguar XJ6 & Sovereign (Oct 86 – Sept 94) D to M | 3261 |
| Jaguar XJ12, XJS & Sovereign, Daimler Double Six (72 – 88) up to F | 0478 |
| Jaguar X Type Petrol & Diesel (01 – 10) V to 60 | 5631 |
| **JEEP** Cherokee Petrol (93 – 96) K to N | 1943 |
| **LAND ROVER** 90, 110 & Defender Diesel (83 – 07) up to 56 | 3017 |

| Title | Book No. |
|---|---|
| Land Rover Discovery Petrol & Diesel (89 – 98) G to S | 3016 |
| Land Rover Discovery Diesel (Nov 98 – Jul 04) S to 04 | 4606 |
| Land Rover Discovery Diesel (Aug 04 – Apr 09) 04 to 09 | 5562 |
| Land Rover Freelander Petrol & Diesel (97 – Sept 03) R to 53 | 3929 |
| Land Rover Freelander (97 – Oct 06) R to 56 | 5571 |
| Land Rover Freelander Diesel (Nov 06 – 14) 56 to 64 | 5636 |
| Land Rover Series II, IIA & III 4-cyl Petrol (58 – 85) up to C | 0314 |
| Land Rover Series II, IIA & III Petrol & Diesel (58 – 85) up to C | 5568 |
| **MAZDA** 323 (Mar 81 – Oct 89) up to G | 1608 |
| Mazda 323 (Oct 89 – 98) G to R | 3455 |
| Mazda B1600, B1800 & B2000 Pick-up Petrol (72 – 88) up to F | 0267 |
| Mazda MX-5 (89 – 05) G to 05 | 5565 |
| Mazda RX-7 (79 – 85) up to C * | 0460 |
| **MERCEDES-BENZ** 190, 190E & 190D Petrol & Diesel (83 – 93) A to L | 3450 |
| Mercedes-Benz 200D, 240D, 240TD, 300D & 300TD 123 Series Diesel (Oct 76 – 85) up to C | 1114 |
| Mercedes-Benz 250 & 280 (68 – 72) up to L * | 0346 |
| Mercedes-Benz 250 & 280 123 Series Petrol (Oct 76 – 84) up to B * | 0677 |
| Mercedes-Benz 124 Series Petrol & Diesel (85 – Aug 93) C to K | 3253 |
| Mercedes-Benz A-Class Petrol & Diesel (98 – 04) S to 54 | 4748 |
| Mercedes-Benz C-Class Petrol & Diesel (93 – Aug 00) L to W | 3511 |
| Mercedes-Benz C-Class (00 – 07) X to 07 | 4780 |
| Mercedes-Benz E-Class Diesel (Jun 02 – Feb 10) 02 to 59 | 5710 |
| Mercedes-Benz Sprinter Diesel (95 – Apr 06) M to 06 | 4902 |
| **MGA** (55 – 62) | 0475 |
| MGB (62 – 80) up to W | 0111 |
| MGB 1962 to 1980 (special edition) * | 4894 |
| MG Midget & Austin-Healey Sprite (58 – 80) up to W * | 0265 |
| **MINI** Petrol (July 01 – 06) Y to 56 | 4273 |
| MINI Petrol & Diesel (Nov 06 – 13) 56 to 13 | 4904 |
| **MITSUBISHI** Shogun & L200 Pick-ups Petrol (83 – 94) up to M | 1944 |
| **MORRIS** Minor 1000 (56 – 71) up to K | 0024 |
| **NISSAN** Almera Petrol (95 – Feb 00) N to V | 4053 |
| Nissan Almera & Tino Petrol (Feb 00 – 07) V to 56 | 4612 |
| Nissan Micra (83 – Jan 93) up to K | 0931 |
| Nissan Micra (93 – 02) K to 52 | 3254 |
| Nissan Micra Petrol (03 – Oct 10) 52 to 60 | 4734 |
| Nissan Primera Petrol (90 - Aug 99) H to T | 1851 |
| Nissan Qashqai Petrol & Diesel (07 – 12) 56 to 62 | 5610 |
| **OPEL** Ascona & Manta (B-Series) (Sept 75 – 88) up to F * | 0316 |
| Opel Ascona Petrol (81 – 88) | 3215 |
| Opel Ascona Petrol (Oct 91 – Feb 98) | 3156 |
| Opel Corsa Petrol (83 – Mar 93) | 3160 |
| Opel Corsa Petrol (Mar 93 – 97) | 3159 |
| Opel Kadett Petrol (Oct 84 – Oct 91) | 3196 |
| Opel Omega & Senator Petrol (Nov 86 – 94) | 3157 |
| Opel Vectra Petrol (Oct 88 – Oct 95) | 3158 |
| **PEUGEOT** 106 Petrol & Diesel (91 – 04) J to 53) | 1882 |
| Peugeot 107 Petrol (05 – 11) 05 to 11 | 4923 |
| Peugeot 205 Petrol (83 – 97) A to P | 0932 |

* Classic reprint

| Title | Book No. |
|---|---|
| Peugeot 206 Petrol & Diesel (98 – 01) S to X | 3757 |
| Peugeot 206 Petrol & Diesel (02 – 09) 51 to 59 | 4613 |
| Peugeot 207 Petrol & Diesel (06 – July 09) 06 to 09 | 4787 |
| Peugeot 306 Petrol & Diesel (93 – 02) K to 02 | 3073 |
| Peugeot 307 Petrol & Diesel (01 – 08) Y to 58 | 4147 |
| Peugeot 308 Petrol & Diesel (07 – 12) 07 to 12 | 5561 |
| Peugeot 405 Diesel (88 – 97) E to P | 3198 |
| Peugeot 406 Petrol & Diesel (96 – Mar 99) N to T | 3394 |
| Peugeot 406 Petrol & Diesel (Mar 99 – 02) T to 52 | 3982 |
| Peugeot 407 Diesel (04 -11) 53 to 11 | 5550 |
| **PORSCHE** 911 (65 – 85) up to C | 0264 |
| Porsche 924 & 924 Turbo (76 – 85) up to C | 0397 |
| **RANGE ROVER** V8 Petrol (70 – Oct 92) up to K | 0606 |
| **RELIANT** Robin & Kitten (73 – 83) up to A * | 0436 |
| **RENAULT** 4 (61 – 86) up to D * | 0072 |
| Renault 5 Petrol (Feb 85 – 96) B to N | 1219 |
| Renault 19 Petrol (89 – 96) F to N | 1646 |
| Renault Clio Petrol (91 – May 98) H to R | 1853 |
| Renault Clio Petrol & Diesel (May 98 – May 01) R to Y | 3906 |
| Renault Clio Petrol & Diesel (June 01 – 05) Y to 55 | 4168 |
| Renault Clio Petrol & Diesel (Oct 05 – May 09) 55 to 09 | 4788 |
| Renault Espace Petrol & Diesel (85 – 96) C to N | 3197 |
| Renault Laguna Petrol & Diesel (94 – 00) L to W | 3252 |
| Renault Laguna Petrol & Diesel (Feb 01 – May 07) X to 07 | 4283 |
| Renault Megane & Scenic Petrol & Diesel (96 – 99) N to T | 3395 |
| Renault Megane & Scenic Petrol & Diesel (Apr 99 – 02) T to 52 | 3916 |
| Renault Megane Petrol & Diesel (Oct 02 – 08) 52 to 58 | 4284 |
| Renault Megane Petrol & Diesel (Oct 08 – 14) 58 to 64 | 5955 |
| Renault Scenic Petrol & Diesel (Sept 03 – 06) 53 to 06 | 4297 |
| Renault Trafic Diesel (01 – 11) Y to 11 | 5551 |
| **ROVER** 216 & 416 Petrol (89 – 96) G to N | 1830 |
| Rover 211, 214, 216, 218 & 220 Petrol & Diesel (Dec 95 – 99) N to V | 3399 |
| Rover 25 & MG ZR Petrol & Diesel (Oct 99 – 06) V to 06 | 4145 |
| Rover 414, 416 & 420 Petrol & Diesel (May 95 – 99) M to V | 3453 |
| Rover 45 / MG ZS Petrol & Diesel (99 – 05) V to 55 | 4384 |
| Rover 618, 620 & 623 Petrol (93 – 97) K to P | 3257 |
| Rover 75 / MG ZT Petrol & Diesel (99 – 06) S to 06 | 4292 |
| Rover 820, 825 & 827 Petrol (86 – 95) D to N | 1380 |
| Rover 3500 (76 – 87) up to E * | 0365 |
| **SAAB** 95 & 96 (66 – 76) up to R * | 0198 |
| Saab 90, 99 & 900 (79 – Oct 93) up to L | 0765 |
| Saab 900 (Oct 93 – 98) L to R | 3512 |
| Saab 9000 4-cyl (85 – 98) C to S | 1686 |
| Saab 9-3 Petrol & Diesel (98 – Aug 02) R to 02 | 4614 |
| Saab 9-3 Petrol & Diesel (92 – 07) 52 to 57 | 4749 |
| Saab 9-3 Petrol & Diesel (07-on) 57 on | 5569 |
| Saab 9-5 4-cyl Petrol (97 – 05) R to 55 | 4156 |
| Saab 9-5 (Sep 05 – Jun 10) 55 to 10 | 4891 |
| **SEAT** Ibiza & Cordoba Petrol & Diesel (Oct 93 – Oct 99) L to V | 3571 |
| Seat Ibiza & Malaga Petrol (85 – 92) B to K | 1609 |
| Seat Ibiza Petrol & Diesel (May 02 – Apr 08) 02 to 08 | 4889 |
| **SKODA** Fabia Petrol & Diesel (00 – 06) W to 06 | 4376 |
| Skoda Felicia Petrol & Diesel (95 – 01) M to X | 3505 |
| Skoda Octavia Petrol (98 – April 04) R to 04 | 4285 |
| Skoda Octavia Diesel (May 04 – 12) 04 to 61 | 5549 |
| **SUBARU** 1600 & 1800 (Nov 79 – 90) up to H * | 0995 |
| **SUNBEAM** Alpine, Rapier & H120 (68 – 74) up to N * | 0051 |
| **SUZUKI** SJ Series, Samurai & Vitara 4-cyl Petrol (82 – 97) up to P | 1942 |
| Suzuki Supercarry & Bedford/Vauxhall Rascal (86 – Oct 94) C to M | 3015 |
| **TOYOTA** Avensis Petrol (98 – Jan 03) R to 52 | 4264 |
| Toyota Aygo Petrol (05 – 11) 05 to 11 | 4921 |
| Toyota Carina E Petrol (May 92 – 97) J to P | 3256 |
| Toyota Corolla (Sept 83 – Sept 87) A to E | 1024 |
| Toyota Corolla (Sept 87 – Aug 92) E to K | 1683 |
| Toyota Corolla Petrol (Aug 92 – 97) K to P | 3259 |
| Toyota Corolla Petrol (July 97 0 Feb 02) P to 51 | 4286 |
| Toyota Corolla Petrol & Diesel (02 – Jan 07) 51 to 56 | 4791 |
| Toyota Hi-Ace & Hi-Lux Petrol (69 – Oct 83) up to A | 0304 |
| Toyota RAV4 Petrol & Diesel (94 – 06) L to 55 | 4750 |
| Toyota Yaris Petrol (99 – 05) T to 05 | 4265 |
| **TRIUMPH** GT6 & Vitesse (62 0 74) up to N * | 0112 |
| Triumph Herald (59 – 71) up to K * | 0010 |
| Triumph Spitfire (62 – 81) up to X | 0113 |
| Triumph Stag (70 – 78) up to T * | 0441 |
| Triumph TR2, TR3, TR3A, TR4 & TR4A (52 – 67) up to F * | 0028 |
| Triumph TR5 & TR6 (67 – 75) up to P * | 0031 |
| Triumph TR7 (75 – 82) up to Y * | 0322 |
| **VAUXHALL** Astra Petrol (Oct 91 – Feb 98) J to R | 1832 |
| Vauxhall/Opel Astra & Zafira Petrol (Feb 98 – Apr 04) R to 04 | 3758 |
| Vauxhall/Opel Astra & Zafira Diesel (Feb 98 – Apr 04) R to 04 | 3797 |
| Vauxhall/Opel Astra Petrol (04 – 08) | 4732 |
| Vauxhall/Opel Astra Diesel (04 – 08) | 4733 |
| Vauxhall/Opel Astra Petrol & Diesel (Dec 09 – 13) 59 to 13 | 5578 |
| Vauxhall/Opel Calibra (90 – 98) G to S | 3502 |
| Vauxhall Cavalier Petrol (Oct 88 0 95) F to N | 1570 |
| Vauxhall/Opel Corsa Diesel (Mar 93 – Oct 00) K to X | 4087 |
| Vauxhall Corsa Petrol (Mar 93 – 97) K to R | 1985 |
| Vauxhall/Opel Corsa Petrol (Apr 97 – Oct 00) P to X | 3921 |
| Vauxhall/Opel Corsa Petrol & Diesel (Oct 03 – Aug 06) 53 to 06 | 4617 |
| Vauxhall/Opel Corsa Petrol & Diesel (Sept 06 – 10) 56 to 10 | 4886 |
| Vauxhall/Opel Corsa Petrol & Diesel (00 – Aug 06) X to 06 | 5577 |
| Vauxhall/Opel Frontera Petrol & Diesel (91 – Sept 98) J to S | 3454 |
| Vauxhall/Opel Insignia Petrol & Diesel (08 – 12) 08 to 61 | 5563 |
| Vauxhall/Opel Meriva Petrol & Diesel (03 – May 10) 03 to 10 | 4893 |
| Vauxhall/Opel Omega Petrol (94 – 99) L to T | 3510 |
| Vauxhall/Opel Vectra Petrol & Diesel (95 – Feb 99) N to S | 3396 |
| Vauxhall/Opel Vectra Petrol & Diesel (Mar 99 – May 02) T to 02 | 3930 |
| Vauxhall/Opel Vectra Petrol & Diesel (June 02 – Sept 05) 02 to 55 | 4618 |
| Vauxhall/Opel Vectra Petrol & Diesel (Oct 05 – Oct 08) 55 to 58 | 4887 |
| Vauxhall/Opel Vivaro Diesel (01 – 11) Y to 11 | 5552 |
| Vauxhall/Opel Zafira Petrol & Diesel (05 -09) 05 to 09 | 4792 |
| Vauxhall/Opel 1.5, 1.6 & 1.7 litre Diesel Engine (82 – 96) up to N | 1222 |
| **VW** Beetle 1200 (54 – 77) up to S | 0036 |
| VW Beetle 1300 & 1500 (65 – 75) up to P | 0039 |
| VW 1302 & 1302S (70 – 72) up to L * | 0110 |
| VW Beetle 1303, 1303S & GT (72 – 75) up to P | 0159 |
| VW Beetle Petrol & Diesel (Apr 99 – 07) T to 57 | 3798 |
| VW Golf & Jetta Mk 1 Petrol 1.1 & 1.3 (74 – 84) up to A | 0716 |
| VW Golf, Jetta & Scirocco Mk 1 Petrol 1.5, 1.6 & 1.8 (74 – 84) up to A | 0726 |
| VW Golf & Jetta Mk 1 Diesel (78 – 84) up to A | 0451 |
| VW Golf & Jetta Mk 2 Petrol (Mar 84 – Feb 92) A to J | 1081 |
| VW Golf & Vento Petrol & Diesel (Feb 92 – Mar 98) J to R | 3097 |
| VW Golf & Bora Petrol & Diesel (Apr 98 – 00) R to X | 3727 |
| VW Golf & Bora 4-cyl Petrol & Diesel (01 – 03) X to 53 | 4169 |
| VW Golf & Jetta Petrol & Diesel (04 – 09) 53 to 09 | 4610 |
| VW Golf Petrol & Diesel (09 – 12) 58 to 62 | 5633 |
| VW LT Petrol Vans & Light Trucks (76 – 87) up to E | 0637 |
| VW Passat 4-cyl Petrol & Diesel (May 88 – 96) E to P | 3498 |
| VW Passat 4-cyl Petrol & Diesel (Dec 96 – Nov 00) P to X | 3917 |
| VW Passat Petrol & Diesel (Dec 00 – May 05) X to 05 | 4279 |
| VW Passat Diesel (June 05 – 10) 05 to 60 | 4888 |
| VW Polo Petrol (Nov 90 – Aug 94) H to L | 3245 |
| VW Polo Hatchback Petrol & Diesel (94 – 99) M to S | 3500 |
| VW Polo Hatchback Petrol (00 – Jan 02) V to 51 | 4150 |
| VW Polo Petrol & Diesel (02 – Sep 09) 51 to 59 | 4608 |
| VW Polo Petrol & Diesel (Oct 09 – Jul 14 (59 to 14) | 5638 |
| VW Transporter 1600 (68 – 79) up to V | 0082 |
| VW Transporter 1700, 1800 & 2000 (72 – 79) up to V * | 0226 |
| VW Transporter (air cooled) Petrol (79 – 82) up to Y * | 0638 |
| VW Transporter (water cooled) Petrol (82 – 90) up to H | 3452 |
| VW T4 Transporter Diesel (90 – 03) H to 03 | 5711 |
| VW T5 Transporter Diesel (July 03 – 14) 03 to 64 | 5743 |
| VW Type 3 (63 – 73) up to M * | 0084 |
| **VOLVO** 120 & 130 Series (& P1800) (61 – 73) up to M * | 0203 |
| Volvo 142, 144 & 145 (66 – 74) up to N * | 0129 |
| Volvo 240 Series Petrol (74 – 93) up to K | 0270 |
| Volvo 440, 460 & 480 Petrol (87 – 97) D to P | 1691 |
| Volvo 740 & 760 Petrol (82 – 91) up to J | 1258 |
| Volvo 850 Petrol (92 – 96) J to P | 3260 |
| Volvo 940 Petrol (90 – 98) H to R | 3249 |
| Volvo S40 & V40 Petrol (96 – Mar 04) N to 04 | 3569 |
| Volvo S40 & V50 Petrol & Diesel (Mar 04 – Jun 07) 04 to 07 | 4731 |
| Volvo S40 & V50 Diesel (July 07 - 13) 07 to 13 | 5684 |
| Volvo S60 Petrol & Diesel (01 – 08) X to 09 | 4793 |
| Volvo S70, V70 & C70 Petrol (96 – 99) P to V | 3573 |
| Volvo V70 / S80 Petrol & Diesel (98 – 07) S to 07 | 4263 |
| Volvo V70 Diesel (June 07 – 12) 07 to 61 | 5557 |
| Volvo XC60 / 90 Diesel (03 – 12) 52 to 62 | 5630 |

* Classic reprint

CL 07.05.15

# Preserving Our Motoring Heritage

<
*The Model J Duesenberg Derham Tourster. Only eight of these magnificent cars were ever built – this is the only example to be found outside the United States of America*

Almost every car you've ever loved, loathed or desired is gathered under one roof at the Haynes Motor Museum. Over 300 immaculately presented cars and motorbikes represent every aspect of our motoring heritage, from elegant reminders of bygone days, such as the superb Model J Duesenberg to curiosities like the bug-eyed BMW Isetta. There are also many old friends and flames. Perhaps you remember the 1959 Ford Popular that you did your courting in? The magnificent 'Red Collection' is a spectacle of classic sports cars including AC, Alfa Romeo, Austin Healey, Ferrari, Lamborghini, Maserati, MG, Riley, Porsche and Triumph.

## A Perfect Day Out

Each and every vehicle at the Haynes Motor Museum has played its part in the history and culture of Motoring. Today, they make a wonderful spectacle and a great day out for all the family. Bring the kids, bring Mum and Dad, but above all bring your camera to capture those golden memories for ever. You will also find an impressive array of motoring memorabilia, a comfortable 70 seat video cinema and one of the most extensive transport book shops in Britain. The Pit Stop Cafe serves everything from a cup of tea to wholesome, home-made meals or, if you prefer, you can enjoy the large picnic area nestled in the beautiful rural surroundings of Somerset.

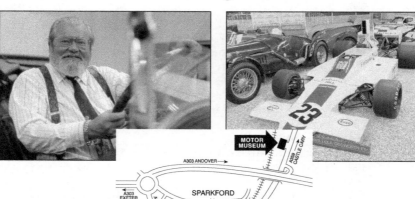

>
*John Haynes O.B.E., Founder and Chairman of the museum at the wheel of a Haynes Light 12.*

<
*Graham Hill's Lola Cosworth Formula 1 car next to a 1934 Riley Sports.*

The Museum is situated on the A359 Yeovil to Frome road at Sparkford, just off the A303 in Somerset. It is about 40 miles south of Bristol, and 25 minutes drive from the M5 intersection at Taunton.
Open 9.30am - 5.30pm (10.00am - 4.00pm Winter) 7 days a week, *except Christmas Day, Boxing Day and New Years Day*
Special rates available for schools, coach parties and outings  Charitable Trust No. 292048